STUDIES IN
EARLY
CHRISTIANITY

A Collection of Scholarly Essays

edited by
Everett Ferguson
ABILENE CHRISTIAN UNIVERSITY

with
David M. Scholer
NORTH PARK COLLEGE AND THEOLOGICAL SEMINARY

and
Paul Corby Finney
CENTER OF THEOLOGICAL INQUIRY

A Garland Series

CONTENTS OF SERIES

VOLUME XIV

Women
in Early Christianity

edited with an introduction by
David M. Scholer

Garland Publishing, Inc.
New York & London
1993

Library of Congress Cataloging-in-Publication Data

Women in early Christianity / edited with an introduction by David M.
Scholer.
    p.   cm. — (Studies in early Christianity ; v. 14)
    Includes bibliographical references.
    ISBN 0–8153–1074–9 (alk. paper)
    1. Women in Christianity—History—Early Church, ca. 30–600.
I. Scholer, David M. II. Series.
BR195.W6W65   1993
270.1'082—dc20
                                         93–2813
                                           CIP

Printed on acid-free, 250-year-life paper
Manufactured in the United States of America

Contents

Series Introduction

Christianity has been the formative influence on Western civilization and has maintained a significant presence as well in the Near East and, through its missions, in Africa and Asia. No one can understand Western civilization and the world today, much less religious history, without an understanding of the early history of Christianity.

The first six hundred years after the birth of Jesus were the formative period of Christian history. The theology, liturgy, and organization of the church assumed their definitive shape during this period. Since biblical studies form a separate, distinctive discipline, this series confines itself to sources outside the biblical canon, except as these sources were concerned with the interpretation and use of the biblical books. During the period covered in this series the distinctive characteristics of the Roman Catholic and Eastern Orthodox Churches emerged.

The study of early Christian literature, traditionally known as Patristics (for the church fathers), has experienced a resurgence in the late twentieth century. Evidences of this are the flourishing of a new professional society, the North American Patristics Society, a little over twenty years old; the growing number of teachers and course offerings at major universities and seminaries; the number of graduate students studying and choosing to write their dissertations in this area; the volume of books published in the field; and attendance at the quadrennial International Conferences on Patristic Studies at Oxford as well as at many smaller specialized conferences. This collection of articles reflects this recent growing interest and is intended to encourage further study. The papers at the International Conferences on Patristic Studies from the first conference in 1951 to the present have been published in the series *Studia Patristica*, and interested readers are referred to these volumes for more extensive treatment of the topics considered in this series of reprints and many other matters as well.

The volumes in this series are arranged topically to cover biography, literature, doctrines, practices, institutions, worship, missions, and daily life. Archaeology and art as well as writings are drawn on in order to give reality to the Christian movement in its early centuries. Ample attention is also given to the relation of Christianity to pagan thought and life, to the Roman state, to Judaism, and to doctrines and practices that came to be judged as heretical or schismatic. Introductions to each volume will attempt to tie the articles together so that an integrated understanding of the history will result.

The aim of the collection is to give balanced and comprehensive coverage. Early on I had to give up the idealism and admit the arrogance of attempting to select the "best" article on each topic. Criteria applied in the selection included the following: original and excellent research and writing, subject matter of use to teachers and students, groundbreaking importance for the history of research, foundational information for introducing issues and options. Preference was given to articles in English where available. Occasional French and German titles are included as a reminder of the international nature of scholarship.

The *Encyclopedia of Early Christianity* (New York: Garland, 1990) provides a comprehensive survey of the field written in a manner accessible to the average reader, yet containing information useful to the specialist. This series of reprints of Studies in Early Christianity is designed to supplement the encyclopedia and to be used with it.

The articles were chosen with the needs of teachers and students of early church history in mind with the hope that teachers will send students to these volumes to acquaint them with issues and scholarship in early Christian history. The volumes will fill the need of many libraries that do not have all the journals in the field or do not have complete holdings of those to which they subscribe. The series will provide an overview of the issues in the study of early Christianity and the resources for that study.

Understanding the development of early Christianity and its impact on Western history and thought provides indispensable insight into the modern world and the present situation of Christianity. It also provides perspective on comparable developments in other periods of history and insight into human nature in its religious dimension. Christians of all denominations may continue to learn from the preaching, writing, thinking, and working of the early church.

Introduction

Although the study of women in early Christianity has become a major topic of scholarly and ecclesiastical concern in the past thirty years, the subject is not new. Issues concerning women in the early church are evident in the New Testament (e.g., 1 Corinthians 7; 11:2–16; 14:34–35; Galatians 3:28; Romans 16:1–16; 1 Timothy 2:8–15 et al.) and in much early Christian literature. An outstanding collection of primary sources in English translation is provided by Elizabeth A. Clark, *Women in the Early Church* (Message of the Fathers of the Church 13; Wilmington: Michael Glazier, 1983).

Current discussion and debate about the perceptions, place, and activities of women in the early church continue unabated. This volume collects sixteen important articles in English on women in early Christianity, half of them written by women, half by men. Three articles were written before 1960; the other articles were originally published between 1974 and 1988. Discussing women from the second to the fourth century, these articles attempt to understand women in early Christianity from the perspective of both women and men of that time. The topics addressed in these studies include the Virgin Mary, ordination and authority, sexuality, asceticism and celibacy, martyrdom and social status. These articles discuss the place of women in the so-called Great Church ("orthodoxy") as well as in the movements known as Gnosticism and Montanism.

One of the emerging features of the current study of women in early Christianity is a renewed interest, especially within feminist studies, in the Virgin Mary. This is represented in the article by McNamara. Also included here are three older (pre-1960) studies of the Virgin Mary by Benko, Milburn, and Ramsay, all of which provide some historical perspectives on the present discussions.

One of the very important, but too often neglected, aspects of women's involvement in early Christianity is the place of women as significant martyrs of the early church. The martyrdom of women shows not only their importance within the community, but also their exercise of authority. Broad consideration is given to these concerns in the articles of

Cardman and Klawiter. The significance of the martyrs Blandina (died A.D. 177) and Perpetua (died A.D. 203) is discussed in the article of Frend. [An English translation (with the original Greek or Latin texts) of the ancient martyr accounts is most conveniently found in Herbert Musurillo, *The Acts of the Christian Martyrs: Introduction, Texts and Translations* (Oxford: Clarendon, 1972).]

According to the literature from the early church, some women were strongly attracted to asceticism and celibacy. Since this involved the denial of a woman's sexuality, some feminists have argued that this data is but one more attestation of the patriarchal and misogynist oppression of women in the early church. However, many other feminists and early church historians understand, undoubtedly correctly, that this aspect of life for women should be understood in its own cultural context as "liberation" and empowerment for women, even though it is surrounded by various oppressive patriarchal features. These issues are explored well for the early period in the articles of Corrington, Kraemer, and Ruether and for the later period in the article of Simpson.

The church fathers, as suggested in the previous paragraph, generally had a very negative view of women (see the book of primary sources collected by E. A. Clark mentioned in the opening paragraph). The article of Ruether in particular discusses these issues in a powerful way. Coyle's article sheds additional light on the complex of issues related to the fathers' attitudes toward women and women's participation in the church (see also the article of J. G. Davies, "Deacons, Deaconesses and the Minor Orders in the Patristic Period," in Volume XIII in this series, *The Early Church and Its Ministry and Organization*). Two fathers in particular, Tertullian (active around A.D. 200) and John Chrysostom (ca. A.D. 347–407), who had very negative views of women and their place in the leadership of the church, are discussed in the articles of Church (for Tertullian) and Clark (for John Chrysostom).

The social reality for women in the early church is often difficult to identify (see the general collection of primary source selections in Ross S. Kraemer, *Maenads, Martyrs, Matrons, Monastics: A Sourcebook on Women's Religions in the Greco-Roman World* [Philadelphia: Fortress, 1988]). The articles already noted on the subjects of martyrdom, asceticism, and celibacy explore these questions in significant ways. The article by Yarbrough gives attention to some of these concerns in the later period of early Christianity.

A particular arena for pursuing these issues has been the study of Montanism and Gnosticism. Both of these movements within the early church appear rather clearly to have involved women in leadership more than in the so-called Great Church ("orthodoxy"). Yet, there are genuinely difficult and complex historical and sociological questions to be faced in attempting to assess the evidence. Klawiter's article specifically discusses the role of women in Montanism (an ecstatic prophetic movement founded by Montanus, probably about A.D. 170).

Assessing the place and roles of women in Gnosticism is even more difficult, due primarily to the nature of the surviving sources (on Gnosticism see Volume V in this series, *Gnosticism in the Early Church*). Gnosticism was a movement in early Christianity, generally considered a "heresy" by the church fathers, which emphasized salvation through a secret, revealed knowledge (*gnosis* = knowledge) in the context of an anti-cosmic, anti-material worldview. The article by Goehring is an exploration of these difficult questions. One should also consult for this concern the articles in Volume V of this series, *Gnosticism in the Early Church*, by E. H. Pagels ("What Became of God the Mother? Conflicting Images of God in Early Christianity",) P. Perkins ("Sophia and the Mother-Father? The Gnostic Goddess") and especially that of F. Wisse ("Flee Femininity: Antifemininity in Gnostic Texts and the Question of Social Milieu").

For New Testament scholars, early church historians, Roman historians, and scholars in feminist studies, this volume provides a collection of important essays from a wide range of sources that enable one to understand clearly the issues in the study of women in early Christianity and the contemporary debates within scholarship over these issues.

Women
in Early Christianity

Second Century References to the Mother of Jesus

STEPHEN BENKO

BOTH THE PAPAL DOCUMENTS which proclaimed the recent Marian dogmas claim the support of the second-century Fathers. The bull, *Ineffabilis Deus*, announcing the Roman Catholic doctrine of the Immaculate Conception, says:

> . . . to demonstrate the original innocence and sanctity of the Mother of God, not only did they frequently compare her to Eve while yet a virgin, while yet innocent, while yet incorrupt, while not yet deceived by the deadly snares of the most treacherous Serpent; but they have also exalted her above Eve with a wonderful variety of expressions. Eve listened to the Serpent with lamentable consequences; she fell from original innocence and became his slave. The most blessed Virgin, on the contrary, ever increased her original gift, and not only never lent an ear to the Serpent, but by divinely given power she utterly destroyed the force and dominion of the Evil One.[1]

Similarly the bull, *Munificentissimus Deus*, announcing the doctrine of the Assumption of Mary, refers to this idea of the Fathers with the following words:

> We must remember especially that, since the Second Century, the Virgin Mary has been designated by the holy Fathers as the new Eve, who, although subject to the New Adam, is most intimately associated with Him in that struggle against the infernal foe, which, as foretold in the protevangelium, finally resulted in that most complete victory over sin and death, which are always associated in the writings of the Apostle of the Gentiles. . . .[2]

These references in themselves are substantially right, but they might be misleading if we fail to realize that the reference of the Fathers to the mother of Jesus is not exhausted with this parallel between the Virgin Eve and the Virgin Mary. Generally speaking, there is a sort of confusion concerning this problem in both Protestant and Roman Catholic opinion.

---

[1] Doheny, W. J., and Kelly, J. P., *Papal Documents on Mary*, The Bruce Publishing Company, Milwaukee, 1954, p. 20.

[2] *Ibid.*, p. 237.

STEPHEN BENKO, B.D., Th.D., is Pastor of Bethany Presbyterian Church, Chester, Pennsylvania. In this article he analyzes the teachings of the Church Fathers concerning the Virgin Mary, and finds that these do not coincide with modern Catholic dogma, but also do not justify Protestant indifference.

2

On the one hand, Protestants like to think that the mariological development has nothing to do with the life of the early Christian Church; on the
other hand, Roman Catholics like to emphasize this parallelism as if it were
the most characteristic element of the mind of the Fathers concerning Mary.
Both opinions are exaggerated and false. It is the purpose of this study
to show that references to the mother of Jesus in the second century were
more numerous than many Protestants would admit, and to show at the
same time that these references have quite another character from that
which the papal documents imply.

I

1. To start with, we know that the famous parallelism occurs first in
Justin Martyr's *Dialogue With Trypho* (written after A.D. 155), Chapter
100:

> He became man by the Virgin, in order that the disobedience which proceeded
> from the serpent might receive its destruction in the same manner in which it derived
> its origin. For Eve, who was a virgin and undefiled, having conceived the word of
> the serpent, brought forth disobedience and death. But the Virgin Mary received faith
> and joy, when the angel Gabriel announced the good tidings to her. . . .[3]

The very first word of this sentence shows that the point in the idea is not
the person of Mary, but the Incarnation of Jesus Christ. *"He became
man"*—this is the truth which is in the center of Justin's theology. Everything else is only a means to prove this truth against the Jew, Trypho, or
is a consequence which follows from this truth. The addition that "He
became man *by the Virgin*" is a necessity and is easily understandable, when
we keep in mind the fact that Justin is engaged here in a discussion with
the Jewish opinion that Isaiah 7:14 rightly translated means "young
woman" and not "virgin," and that the Messiah should be born in a natural
way—"a man born of men." It is a theological a priori for Justin that the
starting point of the human existence of Jesus is the person of the Virgin
Mary, and it seems to me that it is only for the sake of the emphasis of this
"new start" for the world that Justin offers the comparison between the
beginning of "disobedience and death" and its "destruction." But in any
case, it cannot be overlooked that in the mind of Justin it is Jesus Christ
alone who destroys disobedience and death.

We face similar problems in Irenaeus. The most quoted passage is
in *Adversus Haereses* III, 22, 4: "And even as (Eve) . . . having become

---

[3] *The Ante-Nicene Fathers*, I, 249.

disobedient, was made the cause of death . . . so also did Mary . . . by yielding obedience, become the cause of salvation. . . ." [4] If we see only this sentence alone, disregarding the general conception of the entire *Adversus Haereses,* we will have a completely false impression of the mind of Irenaeus. What we have to do is to put this passage in the light of his theory of recapitulation. From this point of view we will understand that the theory requires Irenaeus to find a counterpart for everything connected with the entering of sin into the world, so that in his recapitulation the balance might be restored. Actually we find that it is not only the obedience of the Virgin Mary which counterbalances the disobedience of the virgin Eve, but also the tree in the garden of Eden has its counterpart in the cross, the first-created man in the First-begotten, and the serpent in the dove.[5]

It is only in the light of this conception that we understand how Irenaeus can speak of Mary as the "cause of salvation." She is that insofar as everything can be called a "cause of salvation" which counterbalances in any way the original sin. The term could be applied to the *obedience* of Mary, the cross of Jesus, or the angel Gabriel, depending on what one would take as the cause of original sin. And in this point Irenaeus is by no means consistent. He can designate Eve as such,[6] but he also can speak of Adam as the one by whose disobedience sin entered.[7] In this latter case the natural counterpart is Jesus Christ. Actually, before he sets up the parallelism, "Eve—Mary," Irenaeus many times characterizes the recapitulation in terms of the parallelism, "Adam—Jesus."

For as by the disobedience of the one man who was originally moulded from virgin soil, the many were made sinners, and forfeited life; so was it necessary that, by the obedience of one man, who was originally born from a virgin, many should be justified and receive salvation.

There can be absolutely no doubt that in the mind of Irenaeus Jesus Christ himself is the real cause of salvation. He expresses this belief many times. And when he speaks about the protevangelium he also says that it is the "seed" (and not Mary) which treads down the head of the serpent.[8]

2. In addition to the parallelism, "Eve—Mary," there are innumer-

---

[4] *Ibid.,* I, 455.
[5] *Adv. Haer.* V, 19, 1.
[6] *Ibid.,* III, 22, 4.
[7] *Ibid.,* III, 18, 7; III, 21, 10.
[8] *Ibid.,* III, 23, 7.

4

able references to the virginity of Mary in the writings of the Fathers. There is absolutely no doubt in their writings concerning the fact that Mary was a virgin when the supernatural conception of Jesus took place and that she remained a virgin after conception. But let there be no mistake about it, the Fathers speak only of her virginity before the birth of Jesus ("*virginitas ante partum*"). They make no reference to an extended virginity of Mary after the birth. References of this sort are limited to the very early apocryphal writings. But the *virginitas ante partum* is considered to be a basic truth in the Christian faith, and this truth is proved and defended against heathen, Jews, and Gnostics. Both the *First Apology* of Justin and his *Dialogue With Trypho* are filled with arguments in favor of this thesis. So it is also with the *Adversus Haereses* of Irenaeus.

The locus classicus upon which the theory of the virgin birth is built is the prophecy in Isaiah 7:14: "Therefore the Lord himself will give you a sign. Behold, a virgin shall conceive and bear a son and shall call his name Immanuel." Both Justin and Irenaeus consider the birth of Jesus Christ as the fulfillment of this prophecy; but they very peculiarly do not conceive of the virginity of Mary as something which has value in itself, or is an essential necessity in the Incarnation. The value of virginity is only that it is *the sign* of the coming of the Messiah, the external token of the divinity of Jesus Christ.

This is the reason Justin cannot accept the suggestion of Trypho that he could more easily believe in Jesus as Messiah if he had been born in a natural way. "For if He also were to be begotten of sexual intercourse, like all other first-born sons, why did God say that He would give *a sign* which is not common to all the first-born sons?" [9] In the same manner Justin rejects the idea that Isaiah has "young woman" and not "virgin." There is nothing exceptional when a young woman begets from sexual intercourse, there is no *sign* in that. The *sign* of the Incarnation of the Messiah is that a *virgin* conceives and bears.

Essentially the same argumentation can be found in Irenaeus:

For what great thing or *what sign* should have been in this, that a young woman conceiving by a man should bring forth—a thing which happens to all women that produce offspring? But since an unlooked-for salvation was to be provided for men through the help of God, so also was the unlooked-for birth from a virgin accomplished; God giving *this sign*, but man not working it out.[10]
. . . the Lord Himself gave us a *sign*, . . . which man did not ask for, because

---

[9] *Dial.,* 84. ANF, I, 241.
[10] *Adv. Haer.* III, 21. 6. ANF. I, 453.

5

he never expected that a virgin could conceive, or that it was possible that one remaining a virgin could bring forth a son. . . .[11]

God, then, was made man, and the Lord did Himself save us, giving us *the token* of the Virgin.[12]

It is worthy of our special attention that Origen, too, in his *Homily XVII* on the Gospel of Luke designates the virgin motherhood of Mary as such a sign given by God: "Virgo mater est, *signum est*, cui contradicitur."

It is obvious that in the mind of the Fathers the Incarnation is the significant event. Everything around it has peripheral importance only. The person of Mary is important only so far as she is that "human womb" [13] through which the Incarnation took place. The virginity of Mary is important only so far as it is the *sign* of the Messiahship of Jesus.

3. But the virginity of Mary is not the only thing the Fathers emphasize, and the parallelism, "Virgin Eve—Virgin Mary," is not the sole allegory the Fathers use concerning Mary. There is another equally important allegory which we should not forget. This allegory arises in connection with that in the messianic work of Jesus which brings something entirely "new" into his day, and which stands over against the "old." It is the contrast of "old law" and "new law," synagogue and church, Judaism and Christianity. In this contrast Mary is considered as belonging to that part which is described as the "old" in comparison to the "new." This is an entirely neglected aspect of the early Christian mariology, and it cannot be disposed of with the remark that it is found in Tertullian and that he was not a Catholic. Tertullian's idea appears again in Hilarius. And if modern exegetes are right, this idea is hidden in many passages of the Fourth Gospel.

Tertullian voices this opinion when he comes to speak about the events recorded in Mark 3:31-35 and parallels. This is the account of the incident when Jesus was teaching in a house and his mother and his brothers came and wished to talk with him. He pointed to those who sat around him and listened to him, and said that these were his real mother and brothers. The allegorical meaning of this text, according to Tertullian, is this: Mary, the abjured mother, is a symbol of the synagogue, and the brethren represent the Jews. They remained outside, but the new disciples who were with Christ within represent the Church, which Christ prefers to any carnal relationship. Tertullian also suggests that we should understand Luke 11:

---

[11] *Ibid.*, III, 19, 3. ANF. I, 449.
[12] *Ibid.*, III, 21, 1. ANF. I, 451.
[13] Justin, *Dial.*, 83.

27-28 in this same sense.[14] Hilarius in his *Commentary on Matthew*, XII, 24, says the same thing. Mary represents the synagogue and the brethren of Jesus the Israelites.

This symbolism coincides with what we have been lately so emphatically reminded of, by K. L. Schmidt, Cullmann, Bauer, Bultmann, etc.: namely, that a symbolic exegesis of the Cana miracle, and John's account of the words of Jesus from the cross to his mother and to the disciple, puts Mary to that side of the parallel which is supposed to represent in the first instance the "old" opinion, and in the second that of Judaism. I do not know of any Christian author from the first three centuries who would exegete these passages from the Gospel of John in this fashion; but the coincidence with these assertions of Tertullian and Hilarius shows that such a conception of Mary might not have been strange to the Fathers.

Already from these facts it is evident that it is entirely insufficient to refer only to the parallelism, "Virgin Eve—Virgin Mary," when the attempt is made to present the "mind of the Fathers" concerning Mary.

II

From the point of view of modern mariology our presentation is negative. Indeed, the first two centuries contribute only negatively to modern mariology, and it is well known that none of the Mary doctrines of the Roman Catholic Church can be documented from this early period. Nevertheless, the writings of the Fathers are full of references to Mary and her virginity. The expression, "Virgin Mary," is familiar as early as Ignatius. But this points up a contradiction: if Mary played only a secondary role in the theology of the Fathers, why do they still refer to her so very many times? If she were so unimportant, she would not occupy as prominent a place in their writings as she actually does. Why did the Fathers start to write so exhaustively about the mother of Jesus? The answer to this question rests in the answer to the earlier problem concerning the origins of mariology.

1. The first references to Mary seem to be strongly connected with the refutation of the early heresy of *docetism*. To fight this view, to prove that Jesus had a real human existence, the church referred to the historical character of the birth of Jesus and emphasized the fact that he did have a real mother. Let us listen to Ignatius and see in what connection he mentions the mother of Jesus.

---

[14] *De Carne Christi* 7: *Corpus Scriptorum Ecclesiasticorum Latinorum.* 70, 212.

7

Be deaf, then, to any talk that ignores Jesus Christ, of David's lineage, of Mary; *who was really born,* ate and drank; who was really persecuted under Pontius Pilate. . . .[15]

Son of God according to God's will and power, *actually born of a virgin.*[16]

Rather do I urge you to be thoroughly *convinced of the birth,* passion and resurrection, which occurred while Pontius Pilate was governor. Yes, all that was actually and assuredly done by Jesus Christ.[17]

Basically the same assertions are to be found in *Ign. Eph.* 7:1-2 and 18:2. With these the references of Ignatius to Mary are just about complete. There is absolutely no other connection in which Ignatius mentions Mary except when he proves the reality of the body of Jesus against docetistic views. In exactly the same manner he refers to Pontius Pilate to underline the historical character of the death and resurrection of Jesus. As far as Ignatius is concerned, he mentions Mary only as a proof of the real humanity of Jesus Christ.

2. Searching the writings of Justin Martyr, we will find that he refers to Mary in the *First Apology* in connection with the proof of the divine origin of Jesus through his generation by the power of the Spirit. In order to make this point clear to the pagan Roman emperor Antoninus Pius he comes to the prophecy in Isaiah 7:14, the fulfillment of which he finds in the wonderful conception and birth of Jesus. Mary appears here as a proof of the Incarnation.

In the *Dialogue With Trypho,* Mary plays about the same role as she had in the theology of Ignatius. There she was a means to combat docetism, and here she is referred to in order to refute the *Judaism* represented by Trypho. What are the main arguments of Trypho? He says that the Jewish expectation was that the Messiah would be a man born of men, and that thus the supernatural generation of Jesus is a contradiction to the Jewish hope.[18] To this Justin answers that the birth of Jesus is the fulfillment of Isaiah 7:14. Then Trypho says that the prophecy was given respecting Hezekiah, and also fulfilled in him. Justin denies that, and proves that no one since Abraham was born from a virgin except Jesus.[19] The third main argument of Trypho is that the text does not say "virgin" but "young woman." To this Justin answers with an explanation of the "sign" referred to above. It is evident that the real concern of Justin is the Incarnation of Jesus Christ and the proof of his messiahship. Every-

---

[15] *Trall.* 9. *Library of Christian Classics,* I, 100.
[16] *Smyrn.* 1:1-2. LCC. I, 113.
[17] *Magn.* 11. LCC. I, 97.
[18] *Dial.* 47, 49.
[19] *Ibid.,* 66, 67.

thing in the *First Apology* and the *Dialogue* said directly or indirectly about Mary serves this one purpose, and Justin says not one word more about the Virgin than is necessary for this purpose.

We can see that Mary is mentioned by the Fathers only in those cases in which there is special reason to mention her. These might be heretical views concerning Jesus Christ which had to be refuted, e.g. docetism or Judaism; or they might be basic Christian truths which had to be proved, e.g. the Incarnation or the conception by the Holy Spirit. But if there is no such reason, Mary is not mentioned. Such is the case in I Clement. This letter has no reference to Mary at all, not even in Chapter 55 where it sets some women (Judith and Esther) as examples before the congregation. This would have been impossible if Mary had been either a prominent figure in the life of the early church or of theological importance. Polycarp, Barnabas, Didache, and II Clement say nothing about her.

3. In the second century it was *Gnosticism,* a systematic denial of the humanity of Christ, which provoked Irenaeus to prove the Christian belief in the human reality of Christ through his birth from a human mother. Gnostic ideas concerning Jesus Christ varied, as Irenaeus himself testifies in the *Adversus Haereses.* There were some who maintained that Christ was produced by the Demiurge, that when he was born he passed through Mary just as water flows through a tube, and that the Savior, who belonged to the Pleroma, descended upon him at his baptism. Others held that Jesus was the natural son of Mary and Joseph, and that the Christ was a different person. Again, others said that the Savior was without body, without birth, and without figure. Such were the ideas of the Gnostics. We can see at a glance that they are rooted in a principle common to them all, namely, the denial of the Christian belief that Jesus was the Christ and that he was a human being who was at the same time the Son of God.

Irenaeus' main effort was therefore to prove the humanity of Jesus Christ, and this he did with constant references to Mary, a human being, as really the mother of Jesus Christ, the one from whom he took flesh and all that was human in his existence. ". . . why did he come down into her if he were to take nothing of her?" Examples follow, showing the humanity of Jesus: he was hungry, wearied, sorrowful, etc. "For all these are tokens of the flesh which had been derived from the earth, which He had recapitulated in Himself, bearing salvation to His own handiwork." [20] "And why did He acknowledge Himself to be the Son of man, if He had not gone

---

[20] *Adv. Haer.* III, 22, 2. ANF. I, 455.

through that birth which belongs to a human being?"[21] Now, he who was
born of Mary was Christ himself, says Irenaeus.[22] Neither the Gospel nor
the apostles knew any other Son of man, only him, who was of Mary.[23] To
separate Jesus from Christ would be the same as if one were to try to separate
the Apostle Paul as the person who had been born from the womb from
that person who preached the gospel. This is impossible![24]

The two different qualities in the person of Jesus Christ were bound
together in one person, namely, in that one which was born of Mary. But
his deity and his humanity were two counterpoles in Jesus Christ. His
deity was the consequence of his generation by the Holy Spirit, and his
humanity was a consequence of his conception in and birth from Mary. This
was the perfect union of God and man[25] which was necessary in order that
Jesus Christ might be able to recapitulate in himself the ancient formation
of Adam and to accomplish the redemption of mankind. Mary was in this
process clearly the means of the Incarnation—in the words of Justin, that
"human womb" through which Jesus received his humanity. Irenaeus
emphasized this humanity so much that he even called the Gospel according
to St. Matthew "the Gospel of the humanity" of Jesus Christ.[26] And this
is the point, I think, which makes evident the real importance of Mary in
the theology of Irenaeus—she communicated to Jesus his human nature.

Mary's function in this communication is passive. The Son of God was
made the Son of man[27] through her. The interest of the Fathers in Mary
is restricted to this fact, and even when they refer to her in their struggle
against docetism, Judaism, and Gnosticism, this is what they see in her and
what they know her to be—the mother of Jesus, not less and not more.

The mariological development was furthered in the Church's later
struggle against Manicheism and Nestorianism. Accompanying these
struggles were other contributing elements not present in the first two centuries. These "other" elements were the influx of pagans who entered the
Church, bringing with them the primitive desire for their goddesses; the
growing popularity of the apocryphal writings the origins of which were
mostly Gnostic; and the influence of a quite natural and human mother-
complex, strongly represented in the polytheistic and syncretistic religions

---

[21] *Ibid.*, IV, 33, 2. ANF. I, 507. Cf. also III, 18, 3; 19, 1; 20, 3; 21, 4, etc.
[22] *Ibid.*, III, 16, 4.
[23] *Ibid.*, III, 12, 7; III, 16, 4-5.
[24] *Ibid.*, V, 12, 4-5.
[25] *Ibid.*, V, 1, 2.
[26] *Ibid.*, III, 11, 8.
[27] *Ibid.*, III, 16, 3.

and also in Christian circles in the Gnostic systems (*Achamoth*). The reason, however, for the first references to Mary was the fight against these alien religious systems and their influence in the Christian Church.

III

As indicated, an adequate understanding of the mind of the Fathers concerning the mother of Jesus must bear in mind *all* these elements at the same time. And in the light of this understanding one comes to the following double conclusion:

1. The roots of the interest in the mother of Jesus go deeper into the history of Christian doctrine than the average Protestant minister or layman would admit. The fact that Justin Martyr in A.D. 155, and, even before him, Ignatius about A.D. 110, could refer to Mary in the most natural manner shows us that she was commonly known in Christian congregations. If it is true that Mary and her part in the Incarnation were already well known in A.D. 110, then it is quite logical to think that the beginning of the interest in her was even earlier. And if it was only fifteen or twenty years earlier, we are not merely close to, but in the Apostolic Age, in the time when the books of the New Testament were written. It is not impossible that in Galatians 4:4 we have the first use of and pattern for the way of argumentation Ignatius used so enthusiastically and Irenaeus brought to such a perfection, in proving the humanity of Jesus.

It is necessary also to make sure just what was the object of this early interest in Mary. My answer to this is, that the Fathers were interested in her merely as the mother of Jesus. And there is absolutely no reason to think that general public opinion at the time thought about her differently. Because Jesus Christ was bound together with the human race through his birth by the Virgin Mary, she is therefore the source of his humanity. Though a passive part in the Incarnation, she is still a part. All of this has nothing to do with the new Roman Catholic doctrines, and nothing whatever to do with primitive, superstitious mariolatry. The mistake many Protestants make is that, in their entirely right and just fight against an unbiblical mariology and mariolatry, they completely forget that according to the predestined plans of God, Jesus Christ had to have a mother. Incarnation means to take on flesh, and Jesus Christ took flesh through the Virgin Mary. Perhaps not more, but at least this much does belong to the theology of the Fathers, and it should have a place in the expression of our faith today.

2. Further it is clear that the reference of the two papal bulls to the

parallelism, "Virgin Eve—Virgin Mary," is wholly insufficient if such reference is supposed to represent the opinion of the Fathers concerning Mary. Just to call to mind that the Fathers compared Mary with Eve before she committed sin is not enough, because it is misleading. It creates the impression that the synthesis of the teaching of the Fathers is what the *Ineffabilis Deus* says: "that she approaches as near to God Himself as is possible for a created being." But as has been indicated, this is positively not in the parallelism either of Justin or of Irenaeus. The thought of the Fathers cannot be fully expressed with the observation that they compared Mary to Eve and in so doing implied that she too was pure, innocent, and sinless in a "just created" way, because this alone is not the whole truth.

The suggestion in the *Ineffabilis Deus* that "The most blessed Virgin, on the contrary [to Eve], *ever increased her original gift . . .*" is not in the teachings of Justin and Irenaeus. The fact of the matter is that there is no idea like that included, meant, or suggested in their parallelism of Mary and Eve. Likewise it is wrong when the bull goes on: ". . . and not only *never lent an ear to the Serpent,* but by divinely given power *she utterly destroyed the force and dominion of the Evil One.*" Justin and Irenaeus at no time even approached this notion of whether or not Mary "lent an ear to the Serpent," and it is wrong to suggest that they did.

It is, further, contrary to the teaching of the Fathers to indicate that the serpent of the protevangelium was destroyed by Mary. Both Justin and Irenaeus say clearly, and it cannot be misunderstood, that the destruction of the serpent was the work of Jesus Christ. This is what Justin says after the comparison of Mary to Eve:[28]

And by her has He been born . . . *by whom God destroys* both the serpent and those angels and men who are like him; but works deliverance from death to those who repent of their wickedness and believe upon Him.

Similarly Irenaeus:[29]

For this end did He put enmity between the serpent and the woman and her seed, they keeping it up mutually: He, the sole of whose foot should be bitten, having power also to tread upon the enemy's head; but the other biting, killing and impeding the steps of man, *until the seed did come appointed to tread down his head,*—which was born of Mary, of whom the prophet speaks. . . .

The bull *Munificentissimus Deus* is more cautious. Instead of saying that Mary "destroyed the force and the dominion of the Evil One," it says that Mary was "most intimately associated" with Jesus Christ "*in that*

---

[28] *Dial.* 100. ANF. I, 249.
[29] *Adv. Haer.* III, 23, 7. ANF. I, 457.

struggle against the infernal foe." But this also is not said by the Fathers. They do not suggest that Jesus *and* Mary destroyed the serpent; they hold strictly to the biblical truth that Jesus Christ destroyed him. In spite, however, of the more moderate phrase, "most intimate association," the conclusions drawn from it are far from moderate. "Consequently, just as the glorious Resurrection of Christ was an essential part and the final sign of this victory, similarly that struggle which was common to the Blessed Virgin and her divine Son should be brought to a close by the glorification of her virginal body . . ."[30] This not only is not included, meant, or suggested in the writings of the Fathers; it is something which Irenaeus certainly would call "a system which they falsely dream into existence, and thus inflict injury on the Scriptures, while they build up their own hypothesis."[31]

IV

What I have set as my aim in the introduction of this study seems to be sufficiently proven. Now I shall sum up my conclusions briefly.

In contrast to the common Protestant belief, Mary as mother of Jesus does have an important role in the early Christian theology. Jesus received his human form out of her. Thus she represents the *human* element at the birth of the Savior. In consequence of this belief, in the thinking of the early Fathers Mary is connected always with the *physical* side of Jesus' life. The Fathers referred to her only in those passages which, in some form or other, dealt with the problem of the human side of Jesus.

All references to Mary were made only in connection with Jesus. She had no characteristics or qualities that would be of any value in themselves. This is particularly true of her conception in a virginal state, which is the *signum incarnationis*, and of her motherhood, which constitutes simply the "human womb," the physical means of the Incarnation.

In the writings of the early Fathers there is absolutely no clue that would indicate the presence of any knowledge of the Roman Catholic doctrines of "Immaculate Conception" and "Assumption." The papal bulls are misleading in suggesting such. Rather we have reason to assume that, in the mind of the Fathers, Mary represented an "old law" attitude to which Jesus was openly opposed.

---

[30] Doheny and Kelly, *op. cit.*, p. 237.
[31] *Adv. Haer.* I, 9, 3. ANF. I, 330.
Since this article was published, Prof. Benko has published the following books:
Protestants, Catholics and Mary (Judson Press, 1968)
Virgin Goddess (E.J. Brill, 1993)

V

THE WORSHIP OF THE VIRGIN MARY AT EPHESUS

I. THE HOUSE OF THE VIRGIN

THE recent discovery of the so-called House of the Virgin at Ephesus, where the mother of the Saviour spent the latter part of her life, and where she died and was buried, forms a curious and interesting episode in the history of religion—not indeed the history of the Christian religion, for it hardly touches even the fringe thereof, but certainly the history of Anatolian religion or religiosity. Briefly put, the story is that an uneducated woman in a German convent saw in a vision the place in the hills south of Ephesus where the Virgin Mary had lived, and described it in detail, immediately after she had the vision; that her vision was printed and published in Germany; that after the lapse of fifty years the book came in 1890 into the hands of some Roman Catholics in Smyrna, by whom the trustworthiness of the vision was keenly discussed; that a priest in Smyrna, who took a leading part in controverting the authority of the vision, made a journey into the mountains in order to prove by actual exploration that no such House existed; that on the third day of continuous search in the rugged unknown mountains, on Wednesday, 29th July, 1891 (the Feast of St. Martha), he found the House exactly as it was described

(125)

15

in the published account of the vision, some miles south of Ephesus, amid surroundings which were also accurately described therein ; and that he returned to Smyrna convinced of the truth against his previous judgment. A Roman Catholic festival has since the discovery been arranged and celebrated annually at the holy spot. Though the justifiability of this festival is warmly disputed by other Catholics outside of the neighbourhood of Smyrna and Ephesus, it may perhaps gradually make its way to general recognition and ultimately receive official authorisation.

What seems to be the most real point of interest in this story is that through this strange and roundabout method the permanence of Anatolian religion has asserted itself. Those Catholics who maintain that this is the House of the Virgin have really restored the sanctity of a locality where the Virgin Mother was worshipped thousands of years before the Christian era, and have worked out in perfection a chapter in the localisation of Anatolian religion. We do not mean by this that there has been any deception in the gradual evolution of the "discovery". When the story was first told to the present writer at Smyrna in 1901, the highest character was attributed by quite trustworthy and unprejudiced informants to the Catholic priest who finally made the discovery of the House. He was described as an engineer, a man of science and education, who had entered the priesthood in mature years after a life of activity and experience, and also as a man of honour and unimpeachable veracity; and his original attitude of scepticism and strong disapproval in face of the statements narrated in the vision, at the time when the book first became known in Smyrna, was said to have been a public and well-authenticated fact. There seems to be no reason

16

(apart from the fixed resolve to disbelieve) for doubting his good faith and his change of opinion when he went and saw for himself.

Equally improbable is it to suppose that there can be any bad faith or deception in the earliest stages of the evolution of this modern legend. The earliest publication of the visions of the German nun, Anne Catharine Emmerich, is not accessible to the present writer, and Professor A. Souter finds that it is not in the Bodleian Library; but a translation in English was published long before the actual discovery took place; and any person may with a little trouble satisfy himself of the existence of the printed record of this and other visions in the first half of the nineteenth century.[1]

Nor is it a reasonable supposition that Anne Catharine Emmerich had access to any careful description of the localities south of Ephesus. Those hills have been unexplored and unknown. Although the sacred place is not far from the site of the ancient city, yet the scanty population of the modern village Ayassoluk (Hagios Theológos, St. John) have no interest or knowledge in such matters; and western explorers had never penetrated into the hill

[1] The fundamental authority seems to be the publication of C. Brentano on the *Life of the Blessed Virgin founded on the Visions of A. C. Emmerich* (Cotta, Stuttgart, 1841). See also the *Life of A. C. E.* by Helen Ram (London, Burns & Oates, 1874); and also various works published after the "discovery," *Panaghia-Capouli, ou Maison de la Sainte Vierge près d'Éphèse* (Oudin, Paris and Poitiers, 1896); *Éphèse ou Jerusalem Tombeau de la Sainte Vierge* (id., ib., 1897); *The Death of the Blessed Virgin Mary and her Assumption into Heaven*, from the Meditations of A. C. E.: translated from the French by Geo. Richardson (Duffy & Co., Dublin, 1897). I have seen only the third and fourth of these five books; also a Greek counterblast by Archdeacon Chrysostomos, printed at Athens and published at Smyrna in 1896, under the title of Καπουλῆ-Παναγία. I have visited Ephesus with a French translation of the first in my hands.

country, which was extremely dangerous as a resort of
brigands until a quite recent date. Moreover, the nun is
described as having had little education: she was the
daughter of poor peasants of Westphalia, who is said to
have had an aversion to reading, and rarely to have
touched a book. Her visions, so far as we know them,
confirm this account. They are the imaginings of a simple
mind, trained in the popular Roman Catholic ideas and
traditions about the Saints, Anna, Joachim, and the rest,
and weaving slightly elaborated forms of the ordinary tales.
There are also some evident traces of information gained
from reading or hearing descriptions of Ephesus (as distinguished from the hills south of Ephesus), and this information is not always accurately worked up in the details.

One who was bent on finding deception in the incidents
would seize on the circumstances in which the visions
were committed to writing. The nun's fame came to the
knowledge of the world when there appeared marks on her
body like those on the body of the Saviour; and medical
and ecclesiastical examination vindicated her personal
character. Count Stolberg's letter to a friend, describing
his visit to her, was printed, and attracted the attention
of the poet Brentano. The latter went to see her for the
first time on 24th September, 1818; and in subsequent
visits he wrote down her visions, which he afterwards
published. Probably the literary power of the amanuensis
improved the literary quality of the visions; but we may
justifiably refuse to think that Brentano invented anything,
or made pure additions to the words of Anne. It is, however, true that a considerable interval elapsed between his
hearing the visions from Anne and his publication of them.
Anne died in 1824, and Brentano's book appeared only in

1841. But even those who would maintain that the visions are the highly idealised memory or the invention of Brentano, and not the imaginings of Anne, only put the difficulty one step away. They explain nothing. There is no reason to think that Brentano could have had access to any peculiar source of knowledge of Ephesian localities and mountains, from which he could learn anything important about the history of that nook among the hills during the Middle Ages.

The remarkable fact, quite inexplicable by the hypothesis of fraud or deliberate invention, remains that there is a sacred place where the House was discovered: it has been a sacred place, to which the Orthodox Greek peasants went on pilgrimage, throughout later Christian times: in the present article an attempt will be made to prove that it was a sacred place in the remote pre-Christian times. It seems a more credible thing that the vision of a secluded and imaginative maiden should have suggested the search and the discovery of this obscure locality than that the fanciful invention of a German poet should do so.

But it is really an unimportant detail whether the nun saw in her ecstatic meditation the House among the Ephesian hills (as it seems to us most probable that she did), or the poet invented the·description by reconstructing into a poetic picture with happy power the elements which he had gained from reading and study. Either of these theories is almost equally remote from the one practical fact, *viz.*, the process whereby the unity of Ephesian religion worked itself out, turning to its own purposes certain Christian names and forms, and trampling under foot all the spirit of Christianity.

The brief reference to this subject in the present writer's

9

Letters to the Seven Churches of Asia, p. 218, has caused some inquiries, and this episode in the history of religion seems worthy of more careful and detailed study.

II. The Survival of Pagan Cults

The fundamental fact, *viz.*, the continuity of religious history in Asia Minor, is one which there is no need to prove. Yet it forms so remarkable a chapter in the history of religious ideas, that we may profitably give a sketch of the prominent facts.

The introduction of Christianity into the country broke the continuity for the moment. But the old religious feeling was not extirpated: it soon revived, and took up the struggle once more against its new rival. Step by step it conquered, and gradually destroyed the real quality of Christianity. The old local cults took on new and outwardly Christianised forms; names were changed, and outward appearance; a show of Christian character was assumed. The Iconoclasts resisted the revival for a time, but the new paganism was too strong for them. The deep-seated passion for art and beauty was entirely on the side of that Christianised paganism, into which the so-called Ortho-dox Church had degenerated ; and architecture together with the painting of images (though not sculpture) was its chosen servant. Whereas the rhetorician Aristides in the second century had invoked in his sickness the guidance and healing power of Asklepios of Smyrna, the emperor John Vatatzes, in the thirteenth century, when he was afflicted by disease, went to invoke the Christ of Smyrna.[1]

[1] Ὅπως τῷ ἐκεῖσε προσκυνήσῃ Χριστῷ, *Acrop.*, p. 91. See *Histor. Geogr. of Asia Minor*, p. 116, *Church in R. Emp.*, p. 466. I know no other case in which the person of Christ is degraded into a mere local deity. As a general

The old Greek sailors and Roman merchants, when voyaging or about to voyage in the changeable weather of the Black Sea (where dangerous and sudden storms might occur at almost any season of the year and where there was no sure season of fair weather, such as could be calculated on with confidence in the Aegean or the Mediterranean), had appealed to Achilles Pontarches, the Lord of the Sea (Pontus), to protect and guide them. The sailors of the Christian period appealed to St. Phocas of Sinope for aid. Similarly the sailors of the Levant, who had formerly prayed to the Poseidon of Myra, afterwards invoked St. Nicholas of Myra.[1] There is little essential difference in religious feeling between the older practice and the new : paganism is only slightly disguised in these outwardly Christianised cults.

Examples might be multiplied. They occur in all parts of the country, as exploration enables us to gather some idea of the religious history of the different districts. Local variety is inevitably hostile to the Christian spirit, because Christianity is unity, and its essence lies in the common brotherly feeling of the scattered parts of a great single whole. In the centre of Cappadocia one of the greatest sanctuaries of the land was that of Zeus of Venasa (where the name Zeus is the Hellenisation of a native

rule, some saint takes the place of the old local impersonation of Divine power, and the figure of the Saviour stands apart on a higher plane ; but here (and perhaps in other cases unobserved by me) the analogy of Asklepios the Saviour has been seductive. Zeus the Saviour would also be a tempting analogy.

[1] *St. Paul the Traveller* (1895), p. 298. Add to the remarks there given a reference to *Mélanges Perrot* (1902), p. 25, where M. Bourguet remarks that the existence of a Church of St. Nicholas at Castri, the ancient Delphi, would alone have been a sufficient proof that Poseidon had a worship there in old time, but that now epigraphic proof has been discovered of the existence of a shrine of Poseidon called Poteidanion.

21

Cappadocian divine idea); his annual progress through his own country was one of the greatest festivals of the year; and it may be taken for granted that in the usual Anatolian style the chief priest wore the dress and even bore the name of the god. In the fourth century, when we find that a Christian deacon at Venasa takes the leading part in a festival of somewhat orgiastic character accompanied by a dancing chorus of women celebrants, and that this leader does not appear in his own character, but wears the dress and plays the part of the Patriarch, we recognise the old pagan elements in a slightly varied garb. This particular manifestation of the reviving paganism was put down by the strict puritan spirit of Basil the Great; but it was rare that such tendencies, which broke out broadcast over the land, found a champion of Christian purity to resist them. The feeling of the mass of the Cappadocian Christians seems rather to have been against Basil in this case, though his energy and intense fervour of belief, combined with his authority as supreme bishop of the province, swept away all opposition, and converted lukewarm friends or even opponents into his agents and servants in resisting the new paganism.[1]

On the frontier of Pisidia and Phrygia there is a fine fountain of cold water beside the village of Yassi-Euren. The village is purely Mohammedan; but the Christians once a year come on pilgrimage to it as a sacred fountain, or Ayasma, and this Christian name is applied to it even by the Mohammedan villagers. Finding there a Latin inscription dedicated to Hercules Restitutor, we cannot doubt that Hercules (who is often known as the god of

[1] On the whole episode see *The Church in the Roman Empire*, chap. xviii., p. 443 ff.

medicinal, and especially of hot, springs) was regarded as the Divine power who restored health to the sick by means of this healing spring, Hercules being, of course, merely a Latinised expression for the native Anatolian god of the healing power.   Article VI. gives other cases.

Frequently the same saint is, through some natural and obvious association, selected in widely different localities to be the Christian embodiment of a pagan deity.   The choice of St. Nicholas at Delphi, already quoted, may be a case of transference and imitation.   But the choice of St. Demetrios in place of the goddess Demeter in various parts of Greece was probably suggested separately and independently in several different places; and the cause must have been pure resemblance of name, since the sex differs and there is no other apparent correspondence.   Moreover, in Anatolia, the Great Mother, the Meter, experiences the same transformation, and, beyond all doubt, the same reason caused the selection of this particular Christian substitute; thus, for example, the holy Phrygian city, Metropolis,[1] the city of the Mother goddess, was transformed into the Christian Demetrioupolis.

For a totally different reason the correspondence of the goddess Artemis to the Virgin Mary was equally striking and widely recognised.   In both cases the virgin nature was a fundamental principle in the cult, and yet in both cases motherhood was an equally, if not more, deep-seated element of the worship on its mystic side.   For reasons

---

[1] The proof seems now fairly complete and convincing that the site of this Metropolis was a few miles farther north than I formerly placed it. It was the city centre of the territory in which were the great monuments of early Phrygia, the tombs of Midas and the other kings of the archaic dynasty, the true metropolis of early Phrygia.

that have been fully explained often elsewhere [1] the Virgin Artemis was the divine mother and teacher and guide of her people. It will not be difficult to show that there was a similar thought underlying the worship of the Virgin in Anatolia.

The best authority for the early stage of the worship of the Virgin Mother of God at Ephesus is the Acts of the Council held there in A.D. 431 (on which see below, § iii.). A sermon delivered in A.D. 429 by Proclus, Bishop of Cyzicus, apparently at Constantinople, forms a sort of introduction to the Acts of the Council. The occasion and sacred ceremony at which the sermon was delivered is there formally entitled "The Panegyris of the Virgin" (παρθενικὴ πανήγυρις).

The subject of the sermon is "celebrating the glorification of the race of women"; it is "the glory of the Female,"[2] due to her "who was in due time Mother and Virgin". "Earth and Sea [3] do honour to the Virgin." "Let Nature skip in exultation: women are honoured. Let Humanity dance in chorus: virgins are glorified. The sacred Mother of God, Mary, has brought us here together." She is called, in terms hardly distinguishable from the language of paganism, "the fleece very pure, moist from the rain of heaven, through whose agency the Shepherd put on Him (the form and nature of) the sheep,[4] she who is slave and mother, virgin and heaven, the sole bridge by which God passes to men."

[1] *E.g.*, Hastings' *Dictionary*, art. "Diana," and " Religion of Greece and Asia Minor ".

[2] Τοῦ γένους τῶν γυναικῶν καύχημα τὸ τελούμενον and δόξα τοῦ θήλεος.

[3] Capitals are needed here to express the strong personification, which approximates to the pagan conception of Gaia and Thalassa as deities.

[4] Ὁ τοῦ ἐξ οὐρανῶν ὑετοῦ καθαρώτατος πόκος, ἐξ οὗ ὁ Ποιμὴν τὸ πρόβατον ἐνεδύσατο.

It seems impossible to mistake or to deny the meaning implied in this language. The Anatolian religious feeling desiderated some more clear and definite expression of an idea dear to it, beyond the expression which was otherwise contained in the rites and language of Christianity. That idea was the honour, the influence, the inevitableness in the world, of the female element in its double aspect of purity and motherhood. " Purity is the material,"[1] but purity that is perfected in maternity. The Virgin, the Mother, the purity of motherhood, was to the popular Anatolian religious sentiment the indispensable crown of the religious idea. This beautiful and remarkable senti- ment shows on what a real and strong foundation the worship of the Virgin in Anatolia rested, and how the Iconoclast movement was weakened by its opposition to a deep-seated Anatolian sentiment. Perhaps in the West the worship of the Virgin rests on a different basis. So far as I am aware her character has been regarded in the West rather as a mere adjunct or preparation for the Divine nature of her Son, while in the Anatolian cult (if I am right) it has been looked at and glorified for its own sake and as an end in itself, as the Divine prototype of the nature and duty of womanhood in its most etherealised form.

It would be an interesting and useful task to investigate how far the view which was taken in the West can be traced as guiding the writings of the great writers and theologians who championed the worship of the Virgin in the Eastern Church. There was, certainly, a marked diversity in the East between the popular view and what may be called the sacerdotal view, held by the educated

[1] Ἔχει γὰρ ἁγνείας ὑπόθεσιν.

25

theologians. The former was much more frankly pagan. The latter took on a superficial adaptation to Christian doctrine, and for this purpose the person of Christ had to be made the central, governing thought and the Mother must be regarded only as subsidiary. But this subject lies outside the scope of this article, and beyond the powers and knowledge of the present writer. It may be added, however, that the divergence can probably be traced down to the present day in the cult of the Virgin Mother at Ephesus. The Greek sacerdotal view seems never to have been that the Virgin Mary lived or died at Ephesus, though it recognised the holiness of the sacred place and regarded it as specially devoted to the person of the Virgin and as a special abode of her power. The popular view desired her personal presence there during her life, and maintained in a half-articulate fashion the idea that she came to Ephesus and lived there and died there. The sacerdotal expression seems in some cases to have shrunk from a frank and pointed contradiction of the popular view, while it could not formally declare it in its thoroughgoing form. In the Acts of the Council of Ephesus this intermediate form of expression seems to rule. As we shall see in § iii. there is nothing said there which can be taken as proving that the belief in the real living presence of the Virgin Mary at Ephesus was held. But the champions of Mariolatry relied on the popular support; and, in the Council which was called to judge and condemn the views of Nestorius, the opponent of Mariolatry, they were unwilling to say anything that could be seized on by him and his followers as telling against the worship of Mary, or that might tend to alienate popular feeling.

It is equally impossible to overlook the fact that something approximating to that idea of the sanctity and Divine authority of the maternal and the feminine element was peculiarly characteristic of Anatolian religion and society in all ages and variations of the common general type. The idea was not so beautifully expressed in the older religion; the ritual form was frequently allied to much that was ugly and repulsive; it was often perverted into a mere distortion of its original self. But in many cases these perversions allow the originally beautiful idea to shine through the ugliness that has enveloped it, and we can detect with considerable probability that the ugliness is due, at least in part, to degradation and degeneration. The article "Diana of the Ephesians," in Hastings' *Dictionary of the Bible*, suffers from the failure to distinguish between earlier and later elements in the Anatolian ritual; the writer attained to a clearer conception of the subject in preparing the article in the same work on the "Religion of Greece and Asia Minor," though even there it is not expressed with sufficient precision and definiteness.

Closely connected with this fundamental characteristic in Anatolian religion is the remarkable prominence of the female in the political and social life of the country. Many of the best attested cases of *Mutter-recht* in ancient history belong to Asia Minor. Even under the Roman rule (when Western ideas, springing from war, conquest, and the reign of violence and brute strength were dominant), the large number of women mentioned as magistrates and officials, even in the most Hellenised and Romanised cities of the whole country, strikes every student of the ancient monuments as an unusual feature. It can hardly be explained except through the power of that old native belief and respect for the mother and the teacher. The Mother-

Goddess was merely the religious prototype and guarantee and enforcement of the social custom.[1]

An indubitable example of the Virgin Artemis transformed into the Christian Mother of God is found at the northern end of the great double lake, called Limnai in ancient times, and now known by two names for the two parts, Hoiran-Göl and Egerdir-Göl. Near the north-eastern corner of the lakes there is still said to be a sacred place of the Christians, to which they come on pilgrimage from a distance, though there is no Christian settled population nearer than Olu-Borlu (the ancient Apollonia). A large body of inscriptions has been collected from the neighbourhood, showing that there was here a peculiar worship of the goddess Artemis, which preserved the native Anatolian character unimpaired through the Greek and Roman periods, and to which strangers came from great distances.

Our view is that the similar Virgin Artemis of Ephesus, who in the mystic ritual was set before her worshippers as the mother, nurse, governor and leader of her swarming people, the great Queen-Bee, was transformed into the Ephesian Mother of God ; and that the same change was made independently all over the Anatolian land. She is shown in Greek and Anatolian ideals on and facing p. 160.

But the question may be asked whether the view advocated in this article is not prejudiced and one-sided. Are we not advocating too strongly the Anatolian element and neglecting the possibility of development within the bounds

---

[1] A young French scholar, who collected with much diligence from inscriptions examples of the custom surviving in the Roman time, advanced the theory as an explanation that these magistrates were rich women whom the people wanted to wheedle out of their money ; P. Paris *Quatenus feminae in Asia Minore r. p. attigerint.*

of Christianity? The dogmatic side may safely be left to others. There are plenty of able advocates always ready to discuss matters of dogma and systematic theology, and the present writer never has presumed to state an opinion on such lofty matters. But there are some historical points which may be briefly noticed in the following § iii.

As I sit writing these lines and looking out over the site of the Temple of the Ephesian goddess, I have before me a small terra-cotta image which was found in the excavations now going on amid the ruins of that famous Temple. This statuette, which is given below, p. 160, represents the goddess sitting and holding an infant in her arms. This rather rudely formed expression of popular belief was taken at the first moment of discovery by some of those who saw it as a mediæval image of the Madonna and Child, though more careful contemplation showed that it must have been made several centuries before the time of Christ. It is a complete proof, in its startling resemblance to the later Christian representation, of the perfect continuity of Anatolian religious sentiment amid outward differences.

There is, therefore, in this popular tendency a real cause, continuously and effectively operative, in many, doubtless in all, parts of the Anatolian country. It was strenuously opposed by a party in the Church. The conflict between the two opinions lasted for many centuries; but finally the popular opinion was victorious and established itself as the "Orthodox" principle, while the more purely Christian opinion became the "heretical" view and its supporters were proscribed and persecuted; and the division seriously weakened the Christian Empire in its struggle against Mohammedanism.

The view which this paper is intended to support is that

the establishment of the cult of the Virgin Mother of God at Ephesus is a critical, epoch-making date in the development of Byzantine government and religion. The whole process by which it was established is an important page in the history of the Empire. Ephesus, which had long been the champion of a purer faith[1] and the touchstone of error, as both John and Ignatius emphatically declare, was now made the stronghold of an Anatolian development, a recrudescence of the old religion of the Divine Mother.

III. EARLY WORSHIP OF THE MOTHER OF GOD IN EPHESUS[2]

The Ephesian tradition has all the appearance of being a popular growth, frowned on at first by the Church, and never fully and cordially accepted, but only permitted as a concession to popular feeling. The Orthodox Church gained the general support of the populace in the fifth century by tacitly (or even sometimes openly) permitting the reinvigoration of the old paganism under outwardly Christianised forms, freed from the most debasing elements and accretions which were formerly attached to it. The views of the people about the world and the life of man and the constitution of society were dominated by certain ideas and principles, which had been wrought into form by the experience of many generations and thus had sunk deep into, and almost constituted the fabric of, their minds. In the old pagan religion those ideas were envisaged and ex-

---

[1] *Letters to the Seven Churches*, pp. 239-242.

[2] I am indebted to my friend and old pupil, Professor A. Souter of Mansfield College, for much help and all the quotations which are here printed. The article had to be written far from books during the journey, in the course of which I visited Ephesus at the beginning of May, 1905.

pressed to them as gods and guides of their life; and the Christianised people began to long once more for Divine figures which might impersonate to them those ideas. The Divine Mother, the God-Son, were ideas that came close to the popular nature and lay deep in the popular heart, and the purely Christian theology and ethics were too remote and incomprehensible to insufficiently educated minds. The old paganism, amid much that was ugly and hateful, had contained in its hieratic forms much of the gradually elaborated wisdom of the race. The rules of worship and ritual were the rules of useful practical life and conduct in the family and society. The ugliest part was due to degeneration and degradation.[1] The earlier steps in this recrudescence of pagan ideas in the Christian Church of Asia (a growth which was vainly, and not always wisely, resisted by the various Iconoclastic[2] sects) cannot now be traced. In the fifth century the traces become clear and evident: in the fourth century they can be guessed.

The oldest allusion to the worship of the Virgin Mary at Ephesus as already a popular cult (perhaps the earliest[3] in the whole of Anatolia) is contained in the Acts of the Council or Synod which met at Ephesus in A.D. 431.[4] The sermon, which had been preached by Proclus, Bishop of

[1] This is a brief, and therefore too dogmatic and harsh, *résumé* of the thesis which was gradually worked out in the process of writing the article on " Religion of Greece and Asia Minor " in Hastings' *Dictionary*, vol. v.

[2] The term " Iconoclastic " is used here generically.

[3] The allusion in the epitaph of Avircius Marcellus (St. Abercius), *c.* A.D. 192, shows great respect for her, and places her relation to Jesus among the most sacred and fundamental articles of the Christian faith, without the slightest trace of worship; but that stage is already clearly marked in the letters of Ignatius.

[4] Several extracts from the exordium of this sermon have been quoted on page 134 f.; for the complete sermon, see Migne, *P. G.*, lxv., p. 680 ff.

Cyzicus, in 429, is incorporated in the record of the Council ;
and this fact seems to show that the proceedings and the
sermon must be read in the light which each throws on the
other.   The sermon was considered to be a fair statement
of the view which the Council regarded as right ; and thus
we must interpret the formal business of the Synod, which
was really a protest by the "Orthodox" party against the
depreciation of the worship of the Virgin Mother of God by
Nestorius and his followers.   The circumstances in which
the Synod was called are as follows :—

Theodosius II. had summoned Nestorius from Syrian
Antioch to be patriarch of Constantinople; and he brought
with him Anastasius, a presbyter of Antioch.   The latter
in a sermon had declared that the title "Mother of God"
ought not to be applied to Mary, inasmuch as God cannot
be born of woman; Mary was the mother only of the man
Jesus, while the Divine Jesus was the Son of God alone.
Mary, as he said, was only the mother of Christ, not Mother
of God (Christotokos, not Theotokos).   The orthodox majority of the Church rose in horror against this duplication
of the person of Christ, and condemned the authors at the
Council of Ephesus.   Along with this condemnation it was
inevitable that the actual worship of the Virgin Mother of
God (as she was henceforward officially called) received new
strength in the popular mind, as if it had been now formally
sanctioned.

The Council assembled at Ephesus "in the most holy
church which is called Maria".   The very existence of a
church bearing such a name is in itself proof that a strong
idea of the divinity of the Virgin Mother of the Saviour
had already fixed itself in the popular mind at Ephesus.

The name applied to the church called "Maria" was

apparently popular rather than official. The expression used strongly indicates this;[1] and no other origin for the name seems possible. The church was in A.D. 431 not "the church of Maria," or "the church dedicated to Maria"; it was "the church called Maria". Probably the full expression of the meaning of the Greek would be "the most holy church (of God), which bears the name Maria". Popular feeling gave the name, and attached its own character to the worship; but the official or sacerdotal view did not formally approve this, though it went a long way in making concession to it, and in practice apparently gave almost full freedom to it. Where a strong popular feeling is concerned, the Council which condemned the one great opponent of that feeling, and formally authorised, as binding on all Christians, one expression of that feeling (*viz.*, the expression "Mother of God") must be regarded as tacitly permitting those other expressions, public at the time, which it did not condemn. It is of course certain that afterwards the dedication to the Virgin Mary of this and other churches was fully accepted by the priesthood and by most of the Church leaders.

The opinion has been expressed by the present writer in an article on Ephesus (Hastings' *Dictionary of the Bible*, vol. i.) that the "church called Maria" was the double church whose remains must be familiar to all visitors to the ruins, as they form one of the loftiest and most imposing buildings on the site. The recent Austrian excavations have confirmed this opinion. The eastern church in this connected pair, which is the later of the two, has been found to be of the age of Justinian; the older western half was almost certainly in existence before 431, and was dedicated to

[1] ἐν τῇ ἁγιωτάτῃ ἐκκλησίᾳ τῇ καλουμένῃ Μαρίᾳ.

the Virgin, and Mr. Heberdey, the distinguished director of the Austrian enterprise, considers it to be the church in which the Council was held.   It remains uncertain as yet whether the eastern church also was dedicated to her.

It was only during the fourth century that the leaders or the great writers of the Christian Church seem to have begun to interest themselves in the story of the life of the Virgin Mary for her own sake.   Epiphanius about A.D. 375 remarks that the Scriptures say nothing about the death of the Virgin, whether she died or not, whether she was buried or not, and that in the Scriptures there is no authority for the opinion that when John went away into (the Province) Asia, he took her with him.[1]

But from these words of Epiphanius it seems clear and certain that popular tradition had already before his time been busy with her later life.   Starting from the one recorded fact that she remained until her death under the care and keeping of St. John, it had woven into this something in the way of an account of her death, and the circumstances connected with it and with the burial.   Doubtless it had interwoven some marvellous incidents in the story; and it would be possible to guess how these originated and were gradually elaborated.   But the one thing that concerns our purpose is that Epiphanius must have known of the story that the Virgin had gone with St. John to Ephesus; otherwise he would not have taken the trouble to deny that it rested on any Scriptural foundation.

---

[1] Epiph. *adv.   Haer.* III., 1, haer. 78, § 11 (Migne, *P. G.*, xlii., 716ʙ): Ἀλλὰ καὶ εἰ δοκοῦσί τινες ἐσφάλθαι, ζητήσωσι τὰ ἴχνη τῶν γραφῶν, καὶ εὑρωσιν ἂν οὔτε θάνατον Μαρίας, οὔτε εἰ τέθνηκεν, οὔτε εἰ μὴ τέθνηκεν, οὔτε εἰ τέθαπται, οὔτε εἰ μὴ τέθαπται.   Καίτοι γε τοῦ Ἰωάννου περὶ τὴν Ἀσίαν ἐνστειλαμένου τὴν πορείαν, καὶ οὐδαμοῦ λέγει ὅτι ἐπηγάγετο μεθ᾽ ἑαυτοῦ τὴν ἁγίαν παρθένον κ.τ.λ.

The popular tradition in Asia is therefore as old at least as the middle of the fourth century. And, whereas in the fifth century the Church leaders (as we have already seen) in the time of the Council of Ephesus, A.D. 431, refrained from either contradicting or confirming expressly the popular Ephesian belief, Epiphanius in the fourth century points out that this and all other stories about her death and burial were devoid of authoritative foundation. We are in presence of a popular belief, disclaimed and set aside as valueless in the fourth century, but treated with more careful respect, though not confirmed, in the fifth century. The sacerdotal teaching could not admit the popular belief as authoritative, but it tacitly permitted the belief to reign in the popular mind, and to govern popular action and religion, in the same way as it gradually came to acquiesce, without either affirmation or denial, in most of the popular local cults of saints.

This Ephesian tradition has continued in effective operation to the present day. When the Roman Catholic discoverers of the "House" of the Virgin began to inquire into the situation, they found that the Greeks of Kirkindje, a village among the hills south-east of Ephesus, to which the remnants of the Christian population are said to have retired in the middle ages, regarded the place as sacred, called it Panagia Kapulu,[1] "the All Holy (Virgin) of the Door," and held certain annual ceremonies there. Since the Catholics made the discovery, they have bought a large tract of ground round the ruin ; and the Greeks have in some degree lost their devotion to the spot. An English lady, however, who speaks Greek as fluently as she does English, told me that she asked the Greek servant who guided her to the Panagia Kapulu whether the Orthodox

---

[1] Kapulu is a Turkish word, "possessed of or connected with a door".

10

Christians [1] held a Panegyris at this place.   He replied that they had no Panegyris there, but only a Litourgia; and that in case of trouble or sickness it was customary to take a priest to the place and perform service and offer prayers there. The annual ceremony, therefore, seems to have been abandoned, though popular belief still clings to the holy place, and attracts to it those who are in trouble.   But the Greek priests appear not to have held, and certainly now they utterly disclaim, the belief that the Panagia herself ever was there; and they maintain that this House is only a ruined little church dedicated to her.

As to the ruins, the photographs show clearly a small mediæval building, with an apse.   One would unhesitatingly set it down as a mediæval church, for the religious needs of the population of the secluded glen in which it is situated.

By an unfortunate accident at Ephesus I was prevented from visiting the Panagia Kapulu after all arrangements had been made; and, while my son went, I had to rest in the house for two days.   But, as I understand, a friend of trained and practised experience in archæological research considers that part of the building is older than the walls generally, and might date from as early as the first century.

The glen in which the building is situated is divided from the city of Ephesus by a high, jagged ridge of mountain, along the crest of which ran the south wall of the Grecian city, built by Lysimachus about B.C. 280.   This part of the wall is still fairly well preserved: its lofty position and remoteness from the haunts of men have saved it from destruction at the hands of mediæval or modern builders.

[1] In strict Greek expression " Christians " are the Orthodox alone ; other sects are Catholics, Protestants, Armenians, etc., but none of these are in popular phraseology denominated Christians.

IV. THE VISION OF ANNE CATHARINE EMMERICH

Now arises the question how far any value as evidence can be set on the vision of the German nun, Anne Catharine Emmerich. In the first place, I should repeat what was already stated in Section I. of this article, that it seems unjustifiable to throw doubt on the honest intentions both of the seer and of the reporter, the poet Brentano. After fully weighing all the evidence, I do not entertain the smallest doubt that she saw those visions or dreams, and that they have been faithfully reported to us. The visions are exactly what a nun in such surroundings as Anne Catharine's would think, and ought to think. But they lie almost wholly within the narrowest circle of commonplace mediæval pseudo-legend, hardly worthy to be called legendary, because it is all so artificial.

The experience of a foreign friend, whose name (if I were free to mention it) would be a certificate of wide reading and literary power, illustrates the probable bent of Anne Catharine's mind. His family travelled for some time in the company of a lady educated in a convent: her conversation generally showed quite remarkable lack of knowledge or interest, but in picture-galleries she displayed an equally remarkable familiarity with lives of the saints, identifying at a glance every picture relating to them, telling the story connected with each sacred picture in the fullest detail, and explaining numerous little points about the symbolism, which might escape even fairly well-informed observers.

In hurriedly reading over the visions about the life of the Virgin in a French translation, while I was visiting Ephesus in the beginning of May, 1905, I have observed only two points which seem to lie outside of this narrow circle.

One of these is the date of the birth of Christ. It is not fixed at Christmas, but on the 24th November. I do not know how far this divergence may be connected with any stories or legends likely to be within the ordinary circle of knowledge of a German nun, of humble origin and without any special education, at the beginning of the nineteenth century. But it seems not at all impossible or improbable that she may have come in contact with educated persons, or may have learned in other ways so much of the results of historical investigation as to hear that there is no substantial foundation for the common ceremonial practice of celebrating the birth of Christ at the end of December.

The other and by far the most interesting passage in the whole book is the minutely detailed account of the home of the Virgin and the small Christian settlement in the neighbourhood of Ephesus. It is worth quotation in full.

" After the Ascension of our Lord Jesus Christ, Mary lived three years on Sion, three years at Bethany, and nine years at Ephesus, to which place John had conducted her shortly after the Jews had exposed Lazarus and his sisters on the sea.

" Mary did not live exactly at Ephesus, but in the environs, where were settled already many women who were her friends. Her dwelling was situated three leagues and a half from Ephesus, on a mountain which was seen to the left in coming from Jerusalem, and which rapidly descended towards Ephesus—coming from the south-east the city was seen as if altogether at the foot of a mountain, but it is seen to extend all round as you continue to advance. Near Ephesus there are grand avenues of trees, under which the yellow fruits are lying on the ground. A little to the south, narrow paths lead to an eminence covered with wild plants.   There is seen an undulating plain covered with vegetation, which has a circuit of half a league ; it is there that this settlement was made.   It is a solitary country, with many small, agreeable and fertile elevations, and some grottoes hollowed in the rock, in the midst of little sandy places.   The country is rough without being barren ; there are here and there a number of trees of pyramidal form with smooth trunks, whose branches overshadow a large space.

"When St. John conducted to this spot the Blessed Virgin, for whom he had already erected a house, some Christian families and many holy women were already residing in this country.   They were living, some under tents, others in caves, which they had rendered habitable by the aid of carpentry and wainscoting.   They had come here before the persecution had burst forth with full force. As they took advantage of the caves which they found there, and of the facilities which the nature of the places offered, their dwellings were real hermitages, often separated a quarter of a league from each other ; and this kind of colony presented the appearance of a village with its houses scattered at a considerable distance from each other. Mary's house stood by itself, and was constructed of stone. At some distance behind the house the land rises and proceeds across the rocks to the highest point of the mountain, from the top of which, over the small elevations and trees, the city of Ephesus is visible, [and the sea] with its numerous islands.   The place is nearer the sea than Ephesus itself, which lies at some distance.   The country is solitary and little frequented.   In the neighbourhood was a castle, occupied, if I mistake not, by a deposed king.   St. John visited him frequently, and converted him.   This place became, later on, a bishopric. Between this dwelling of the Blessed Virgin and Ephesus a river flowed, winding in and out with innumerable turnings."[1]

What value can be set upon this extremely interesting passage?

It is unnecessary to do more than mention the impossibility of the assumption made in the vision that St. John, going to Ephesus in the sixth year after the Crucifixion, could have found there already a Christian community. This is as absurd as the statement (made at a later point in the book) that before the Virgin's death, less than fifteen years after the Crucifixion, Thomas had already evangelised India and Bactria, Philip Egypt, James Spain, etc. But it might quite fairly and reasonably be argued by any defender of the general trustworthiness of the nun's visions, that, in regard to numbers and estimates of time and distance, her evidence stands on a less satisfactory basis than in other more important respects. Her statements of distance would be regarded by such a champion as only conjectural estimates according to the appearance presented in her vision, and therefore standing, so to say, outside the vision, as her own opinion about what she saw. The lapse of years was expressed as part of the visions: she saw the numbers

[1] *The Death of the Blessed Mary, and Her Assumption into Heaven, containing a Description of Her House at Ephesus, recently discovered. From the Meditations of Anne Catharine Emmerich. Translated from the French.* By George Richardson (Dublin: Duffy & Co., 1897), pp. 1-4. When I read over this extract from the English translation, as it was inserted in the proof sheets by the care of Mr. Souter, I feel that it gives a different impression from the French translation, which I read at Ephesus. I have not the opportunity of comparing the two; but the English (published after the discovery of the House) strikes me as perhaps more in accordance with the localities than the French (published before) seemed to be when I was reading it at Ephesus; but I may be wronging the translator.

of years presented to her eyes in Roman figures,[1] and in relating what she had seen she stated that she saw a V with a I beside it which she understood to mean six, *viz.*, the number of years that the Virgin remained in (or near) Jerusalem after the Crucifixion. Such a defender might point out that the Virgin is described as being in extreme old age, and yet the years of her life are stated as sixty-four; and he might fairly argue that a healthy Jewess of sixty has not the appearance or feebleness of extreme age, and that the numbers must therefore be regarded on a secondary plane, so that St. John's journey to Ephesus with her can be placed at a reasonable and possible date, later than the formation of a Christian Church in Ephesus, and probably even later than the death of St. Paul, when the Virgin Mary was a very old woman, over ninety years of age.

That seems a quite fair method of interpretation; but though it avoids chronological difficulties, it leaves others untouched. The idyllic picture of the Christians living in a little community of their own away from the city, apart from the ways of men, separate from their pagan fellow-townsmen, is the dream that springs from a mind moulded by monastic habits and ideas, but is as unlike as can be to the historic facts. Had Christianity begun by retiring out of the world, it would never have conquered the world. Every inquirer into history knows that the Christians of that first period were involved in the most strenuous and crowded struggle of life. The nun's vision is a picture of

---

[1] The editor of the French translation mentions this in a footnote, and explains the discrepancy between two statements about the time of the Virgin's residence at Jerusalem (which is given as four years in one passage, and six in another) as due to Anne Catharine's unfamiliarity with Roman symbols, which caused her to confuse between iv. and vi.

quiet seclusion and peace.   This alone is sufficient to show
that the vision has a purely subjective origin.

Still more evident is the nature of the vision, when we
consider the localities described.   The minuteness of detail
with which the description is given stands in remarkable
contrast to the rest of the book.   There is a clear conception of the approach from Jerusalem (through the Mæander
valley and) across the mountains, so as to approach Ephesus
from the south-east.   The view of the city, as one comes
near it, is very beautiful; and the description given in the
vision, though rather general in its character, is quite good,
except in three important respects.[1]

In the first place, at a distance of three leagues and a
half no view of the city can possibly be got; the road at
that point is still entirely secluded among the mountains :
only when one comes within about two or three miles of
the south-eastern gate of Ephesus, the Magnesian Gate, does
the city come into view.

In the second place, there is not at any point on the road,
or near it on the left, this complete view of the city as a
whole.   From any such point considerable part of the city
is hidden behind Mount Pion.   This complete view can be
obtained only by approaching from the north, as modern
travellers and tourists do in almost every case.

In the third place, a winding river is described as running between the approaching travellers and the city.   This
winding river is the Cayster, now called the Menderez (*i.e.*,
Mæander).   Its course is quite as circuitous and tortuous as
the vision represents it; but it is hardly visible from the
south-eastern road, or from a point on the left hand of that

[1] The plan of Ephesus in the writer's *Letters to the Seven Churches*
compared with a map of Kapulu Panagia on p. 124.

PLATE I.

FIG. 1.—Ephesus, looking from the Top of the Theatre (in West Side of Mount Pion) looking down the Street to the City Harbour and Hill of St. Paul. On the left is Mount Coressus, behind which lies the Panagia Kapulu (Mr. D. G. Hogarth).

To face p. 152.

road. It is only as one comes from the north that this river and its wanderings form so striking a part of the scene ; and further, one must come over the higher ground in order to get the view perfectly. Moreover, this mæandering river runs on the north side of the city ; so that only to the traveller coming from the north does it flow between him and the city.

In the fourth place there are not at the present day numerous islands [1] visible from the peak above Kapulu Panagia. Samos shuts out the view of those beyond it. But in ancient times there were several islets in the gulf of Ephesus (which is now silted up and converted into solid land or marsh), so that the ancient state of things was less unfavourable to the nun's description than the modern state is. It is however uncertain whether the islets in the gulf would be visible from the peak : this point has never been investigated.

It seemed beyond doubt or question to me, as I sat in the Ephesian plain and read the description, that the whole has taken its origin from a description given by some traveller or tourist of his approach to Ephesus. How this came to Anne Catharine's knowledge is uncertain ; but there seems no difficulty in supposing that some traveller or some reader of a printed description had talked to her (she is said not to have been a reader) ; and the narrative had sunk into her mind and moulded quite unconsciously the vision that she saw. Only the appearance from a rising-ground on the north is inaccurately represented as seen by the traveller coming from the south-east. There is, thus, a curious mixture of accuracy and inaccuracy. St. John approaches, as he would in fact do, from the south-

---

[1] The expression in the French translation, I think. is *innombrables.*

east; but he sees the view that would be presented to a traveller coming from the north, if he diverged a little from the low road to a rising-ground, or if he approached by a short path across the hills.

Again, it is a detail which at first sight seems very impressive that the travellers approaching from the south-east diverged a little from the road towards the left and there found the small Christian community. In such a situation, some miles off to the left of that road, the so-called " House of the Virgin" was found by the Catholic explorers. This House lies among the mountains in a secluded glen, divided by the high ridge of Mount Coressus from the city; and beyond doubt no modern traveller had ever penetrated into those mountains away from the regular paths, until the Catholic explorers went to seek for the House and found it beside the spring.

It is also a striking point that there is a peak over the House, and that this peak is nearer the sea than Ephesus is, just as the vision has it; but from the peak one sees (as I am informed by several visitors) only the site of the temple of Diana outside the city, together with the Magnesian Gate and the walls on the highest ridge of Coressus, while the city as a whole is hidden behind Coressus.

In short, the view of the city which is described in the vision is plainly and certainly the view got from a ledge or shelf on the hills that bound the valley, where they slope down towards the city and the plain, and not from a point shut off from most of the plain by a lofty ridge of mountains. A continuous slope with an uninterrupted view down over the city is described in the vision ; and one could almost look to identify the shelf that is described, were it not that such a feature can be found in almost any similar sloping hillside.

It is needless to touch on the supposed correspondence between the shape and interior arrangements of the "House" and those described in the vision. To the nun it seemed clear that the Virgin must have lived and died in a building of the nature and shape of a church, having an apse : she had acquired sufficient knowledge of the form of the Eastern churches. It is certain that the mind of the person who saw those visions was fixed steadily on those subjects; and I cannot but think that she must have often conversed and asked about Eastern places and things, and that from the little knowledge she thus acquired, combined with her training in the mediæval Western legends of the saints and the Holy Family, the visions gradually took their form without conscious effort on her part. But she had heard two descriptions of Ephesus, one as the city first appears to the tourist (who always approaches it from the north, as Smyrna is the harbour from which Ephesus is easily accessible) beyond a winding river, the other stating its relation to the road that comes from Jerusalem; and these two descriptions have unconsciously welded themselves together in her fancy into a single picture.

V. Conclusion

We have thus arrived at the result, first, that the Ephesian belief as to the residence of the Virgin Mary in their city, though existing at least as early as the fourth century, rests on no recorded authority, but was a purely popular growth, and is therefore possessed of no more credibility than belongs to the numberless popular legends, which everywhere grow up in similar circumstances; and, secondly, that the nun's vision, interesting as it is, furnishes no real evidence.

The Roman Catholic writer[1] of a book already quoted, *Panaghia-Capouli*, p. 90, while fully admitting that the entire body of Greek clerical opinion has been against that Ephesian tradition, argues that a tradition which persists in the popular mind through the centuries, in spite of the contrary teaching of the clergy, is likely to rest on a real foundation.

We can only repeat what has been shown in detail in Section II., that numberless examples can be quoted of the growth of such popular beliefs without any historical foundation. They spring from the nature of the human mind; and they prove only the vitality of the old religious ideas. Take an example which came to my knowledge after the former part of this paper was printed. Three or four miles south of Pisidian Antioch we found in a village cemetery an altar dedicated to the god Hermes. On the top of the altar there is a shallow circular depression, which must probably have been intended to hold liquid offerings poured on the altar, and which was evidently made when the altar was constructed and dedicated. A native of the village, who was standing by as we copied the inscription, told us that the stone was possessed of power, and that if any one who was sick came to it and drank of the water that gathered in the cup, he was cured forthwith of his sickness. This belief has lasted through the centuries; it has withstood the teaching and denunciation of Christians and Mohammedans alike; but it is not therefore possessed of any real foundation. It springs from the superstitious nature of

---

[1] Though it has no bearing on the question of credibility, it is right to guard against the impression that general Roman Catholic opinion is in favour of the Ephesian tradition. The ruling opinion in Roman Catholic circles is against it; but as a rule the Catholics of the Smyrna district avour it.

the popular mind, and the stubborn persistence of the old beliefs.   You may in outward appearance convert a people to a new and higher faith; but if they are not educated up to the level of intellectual and moral power which that higher faith requires, the old ideas will persist in the popular mind, all the stronger in proportion to the ignorance of each individual; and those ideas will seize on and move the people especially in cases of trouble and sickness and the presence or dread of death.

Such is the nature of the Ephesian tradition.   The Virgin Mother in Ephesus had been worshipped from time immemorial; and the people could not permanently give her up.   They required a substitute for her, and the Christian Mother of God took her place, and dwelt beside her in the hearts of the people.   This belief soon created a locality for itself, for the Anatolian religion always found a local home. The home was marked out at Ortygia in the mountains on the south of the Ephesian valley, where the pagan Virgin Artemis was born, and where probably her original home had been, until she as the great Queen-bee led her mourning people to their new home in the valley by the shore of the sea[1] and became the "goddess and mother and queen" of Ephesus.   The Christian worship of the Virgin Mother seems to have originated at so early a period that it could not establish itself directly on the home of the older Virgin Artemis.   It could only seek a neighbouring home in the same hilly country a little farther eastwards.   When this home was found for the new belief, a sacred legend inevit-

---

[1] *Letters to the Seven Churches*, p. 217. On the map there Ortygia, which lies really outside of the limits of the map, is indicated wrongly. It was necessary to put in the name, but the actual locality is a little south-east of the place where the name stands.

ably grew up around it according to the usual process in the popular religion of antiquity. The legend had to be adapted to the Christian history. It could not imitate exactly the pagan legend that the Virgin was born at Ortygia; but the belief that the Mother of God had lived in old age and died there, grew up and could readily be adapted to the record.

It will always remain a question, as to which opinions will differ widely, how far it is right or permissible to make concessions to so deep-seated a feeling as that belief must have been. On the one hand, a concession which takes the form of an unhistorical legend and a ceremonial attached to a false locality will meet with general disapproval. On the other hand, it seems certain that injudicious proselytising combined with wholesale condemnation and uprooting of popular beliefs has often done much harm in the history of Christianity. The growing experience and wisdom of primitive races wrought out certain rules of life, of sanitation, purity, consideration for the community, and many other steps in civilisation; and these rules were placed under the Divine guardianship, because there was no other way of enforcing them on all. Practical household wisdom was expressed in the form of a system of household religious rites. It is true that these rules were often widened by false analogy, and applied in ways that were needless and useless; but there remained in them the residuum of wisdom and usefulness.[1] It has often been an unwise and almost fatal error of Christian missionaries (an error recognised and regretted by many of them in recent time) to treat all these rules as superstitious and try to eradicate them before any

---

[1] See " Religion of Greece and Asia Minor " in Dr. Hastings' *Dictionary of the Bible*, v., 133 and *passim*. The process of degradation constantly came in to make these rules deteriorate, as is shown in that article.

system of habitual good conduct in society and ordinary life had been settled and rooted in the minds of proselytes.

That the belief in the Mother, and especially the Virgin Mother, as the teacher, guide and nourisher of her people, was capable of infinite expansion as a purifying and elevating principle, has been shown in Section I. That it has been of immense influence on Asia Minor is patent in the history of the country; even Turkish Conquest, though it attained its purposes by general massacre, especially of the male population, has not wholly eradicated it. That it is a principle which belongs to a settled and peaceful age and state of society, and that it must be weakened in a state of war and disorder, is evident in itself, and has been shown in detail elsewhere.[1]

The vision of the nun in Westphalia and the rediscovery of the House of the Virgin form simply an episode in the history of that religious principle and a proof of its vitality.

[1] See the article quoted in the preceding footnote.

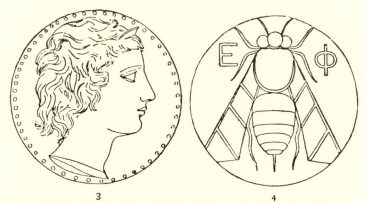

The Hellenic Virgin Goddess of Ephesus and the Anatolian Mother of
Ephesus, the Queen-Bee.

The Anatolian Mother of Ephesus, half anthropomorphized.

PLATE II.

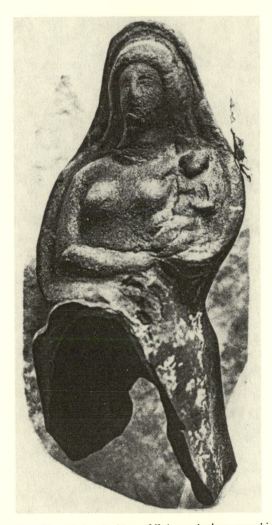

FIG. 2.—The Mother-Goddess of Ephesus Anthropomorphized
(Mr. A. E. Henderson).

To face p. 160.   *See p.* 159.

APPENDIX

THE HISTORICAL BACKGROUND OF THE DOCTRINE OF THE ASSUMPTION

The Biblical record concerning the life of the Virgin is fragmentary and abrupt. It is stated in the Acts of the Apostles (i. 14) that, after the Ascension, 'Mary, the mother of Jesus', together with the women, his brethren and the Twelve, 'continued stedfastly in prayer' at Jerusalem, but at that point historical sources fail, and the natural curiosity of the devout is thereafter appeased by a rich outpouring of apocryphal narrative. Orthodox churchmen appear to have maintained the reserve, or ignorance, of the writers of Scripture. For when, in the latter part of the fourth century, a notable increase in respect and veneration was accorded to Mary, no allusion is made to any exceptional occurrences connected with her death. St. Ambrose, for instance, describes her as the ideal virgin, *imago virginitatis*,[1] who 'gave birth to the Author of salvation',[2] and, reversing the achievements of Eve, 'rains down upon earth the grace of Christ',[3] securing the 'redemption of all'; [4] but no reference to any doctrine of an Assumption crowns his panegyric. He has, indeed, nothing at all to say on the subject of her death beyond noting, in his commentary on St Luke's Gospel,[5] that it is a mistake to interpret the text (ii. 35) 'a sword shall pierce through thine own soul' as a reference to martyrdom: 'neither Scripture nor history teaches that Mary departed this life by suffering a martyr's death' (*corporalis necis passione*).

Uncertainty about the manner of Mary's death is displayed even more notably by Epiphanius, bishop of Salamis (*c*. A.D. 315–403). Epiphanius, a zealous champion of orthodox faith, was for over thirty years head of a monastic community at Eleutheropolis, near Jerusalem, and would thus have been well acquainted with any local traditions on the subject of the Assumption if these had been current in his day. But, though keenly interested in the Virgin and her privileges, his ignorance of the facts makes him refuse to commit himself even on the question whether the Virgin died or was translated to Heaven without experiencing death.

Two passages in Epiphanius' work *Against the Heresies*[6] bear on the matter. He writes as follows: 'Now if any persons think that I am mistaken, let them search through the Scriptures, and they will find there no mention of Mary's death and no indication whether she died or did

---

[1] *De virginibus*, ii. 15.   [2] *De instit. virginis*, 88.   [3] *Ibid.* 81.
[4] *Ep.* xlix. 2.   [5] ed. C. Schenkl in C.S.E.L. xxxii, p. 74.   [6] lxxviii. 11.

not die, whether she was buried or not buried. Moreover, though John accomplished his journey to Asia, yet he nowhere states that he took the holy Virgin along with him, but Scripture is completely silent on this subject because of its marvellous nature so as not to confuse the mind of man. For my part, I venture on no pronouncement, but keep my own counsel and remain silent.' Epiphanius goes on to say that some people have discovered hints about what finally happened to the Virgin in the Lucan reference to a 'sword piercing through thine own soul', and in the picture which the book of Revelation[1] offers of the woman to whom were given 'the two wings of the great eagle, that she might fly into the wilderness . . . from the face of the serpent'. 'But,' continues Epiphanius, 'I make no precise definition as regards this subject. I do not affirm that she remained immortal, neither do I assert that she died. For Scripture surpasses the mind of man and has left the matter an open question, for the sake of that precious and most noble vessel so that no one should connect her with earthly things. The fact is that we do not know whether she died or not.' A little later on in his book Epiphanius again discusses the matter in a mood of reverent agnosticism:[2] 'If indeed the holy Virgin died and was buried, yet her falling asleep was honourable, her death was unsullied and her crown a virgin's crown. If she was slain in accordance with the prophecy that a "sword should pierce through her own heart", she enjoys a martyr's fame and her holy body, by means of which she brought Light into the world, is held in honour. Perhaps indeed she remained alive. For it is quite possible for God to do exactly as he wishes, and nobody knows anything about what happened to her in the end.' Language such as this makes it extremely difficult to imagine that there was any reputable tradition of the Virgin's Assumption current in Palestine towards the end of the fourth century, and it remains to consider how the story arose.

It must be premised that the word Assumption, in its normal present-day usage, signifies the ascent of the Virgin, in body as well as in soul, to the blessedness of Heaven. But, in writings of the patristic age, this is certainly not always the meaning of the word *assumere*, or *assumptio*. Augustine calls the death of the Apostles their *assumptio*,[3] and Gregory of Tours can, in similar fashion, speak of the 'assumption of St. Martin'[4] when he means the entry of a holy person into heaven without any suggestion that his body was exalted along with the soul. To take a later example, Usuard, in the ninth century, notes that August 15th is the day on which the 'Falling-asleep of Mary, the holy mother of God'[5] is

---

[1] xii. 14.   [2] lxxviii. 24. *P.G.* xlii. 737.   [3] *C. Faustum*, xxxiii. 3.
[4] *De miraculis S. Martini*, i. 32.   [5] *P.L.* cxxiv.

162

56

celebrated and he then goes on to say that the resting-place of the Virgin's body is unknown, and that a reverent admission of ignorance on such a subject is preferable to apocryphal fancies. He is therefore in no way committed to a doctrine of the Assumption as this is taught today, yet he can without any feeling of inconsistency describe August 14th as *Vigilia Assumptionis sanctae Mariae.*

But while there may be considerable ambiguity about the use of the term *assumptio*, the manner in which the doctrine of the corporeal departure of the Virgin from earth to heaven developed is fairly clear. During the fifth century, the *cultus* of the Virgin came to be quickened by doctrinal controversy. In their zeal to attribute to the Saviour human experiences and a real victory which was not merely a sham fight, the Nestorians found themselves drawn on to emphasize the manhood rather than the Godhead of Jesus. They tended to interpret the mystery of the Incarnation as an indwelling of God within the human personality, unique in degree but logically comparable with the indwelling of God in the saints, and they recoiled in particular from the use of the word Theotokos to describe the Virgin. 'Has God a mother?' enquires Nestorius. 'In that case we may excuse paganism for giving mothers to its divinities; and in that case Paul was a liar when he testified concerning Christ that he was "without father, without mother, without genealogy". No, my friend, Mary was not the mother of God, for "that which is born of the flesh is flesh, and that which is born of the spirit is spirit".'[1] Remarks of this nature stimulated such replies as the panegyric preached in 429 by Proclus, bishop of Cyzicus and later patriarch of Constantinople, on the 'Virgin Mother of God in whose womb He dwelt whom Heaven could not contain'.[2] The Council of Ephesus, in 431, enthusiastically approved this high estimate of the part played by Mary in the scheme of redemption[3] and, even though the threat of Nestorian speculations was soon removed, devotion to the Virgin continued to grow.

Popular piety was therefore well attuned to accept colourful, if imaginary, stories designed to proclaim her dignity and privileges, and prominent amongst such apocryphal narratives may be ranged the series of texts which tell of Mary's death and assumption into Heaven. This legend is found with many variations in Greek, Latin, Coptic, Syriac, Arabic, Armenian and other languages, and, in its original form, cannot be later than the fifth century, by which time there was a clear need of

[1] Loofs, *Nestoriana*, p. 252.   [2] *P.G.* lxv. 681.
[3] However, the *Encomium in S. Mariam Deiparam*, attributed to Cyril of Alexandria (*P.G.* lxxvii. 1029), is probably not genuine.

dramatic narrative concerning the Virgin's death to match the *passiones* customarily read in Church on the days set apart for the commemoration of martyrs. The significant silences of the writers of Syria and Palestine, and of pilgrims to the holy places, make it unlikely that the story of the Assumption arose in any such part of the world as that, and Egypt is the probable place of origin. At any rate Egypt provides several versions of the story, written both in the Sahidic and in the Bohairic dialect.

The Sahidic narrative which claims to have been composed by 'Cyril, archbishop of Jerusalem,' excludes a corporeal assumption, and treats rather of the Virgin's body as concealed until the Day of Judgement. According to this account, the Jews displayed great animosity and fear: 'And they passed a decree unanimously, saying, "We must not let her be buried in the city, lest mighty deeds be worked at her tomb similar to those which her Son performed, and lest the people believe in her and change our Law". And the high priests and scribes said "Let us go and burn her body with fire, so that no man will ever be able to find it". And the Jews lighted a fire, and they pursued the Apostles with the bier whereon was the body of the Virgin. And when the Apostles had arrived at the valley of Jehoshaphat they looked behind them, and they saw the Jews pursuing them, and they dropped the bier upon the ground, for they were afraid that the godless Jews would kill them. And whilst the Jews were rushing on to overtake them the Apostles betook themselves to flight and escaped. Now the body of the holy Virgin they could not find, and all that they found was the wooden bier, and they lighted a fire and threw the bier into it. And they went into every place, saying "Perhaps her body hath been carried away secretly", but they could not find it. And a very strong sweet smell emanated from the place whereon the body of the Virgin had been laid, and a mighty voice came from heaven, saying unto them, "Let no man give himself the trouble of seeking after the body of the Virgin until the great day of the appearing of the Saviour". And the Jews fled, greatly alarmed.'[1]

However, in the other versions of the story, to which 'Cyril's' narrative is closely akin, the Assumption is included as an integral part. The Bohairic text, which pretends to be an eye-witness account compiled by 'Evodius, the archbishop of the great city Rome, who was second after Peter the Apostle', explains that the Apostles, together with a number of 'ministers' including Evodius, and the Virgin attended by her maidens, were gathered together in a house, hiding from the hostility

[1] E. A. Wallis Budge, *Miscellaneous Coptic Texts* (1915), p. 648.

164

of the Jews. Christ appears in the sight of all and, after announcing that He 'must needs take a great offering' from their midst the next day, departs, leaving them in a state of joyful but questioning expectancy.

With much fulsome repetition the narrative proceeds, in language which again and again echoes passages from Scripture: 'Now it came to pass at the hour of the light on the twenty-first of the month Tobi, which was the morrow, that Christ the true Word came unto us riding on a chariot of cherubim, thousand thousands of angels following Him, the powers of light surrounding Him and singing before Him, and David the holy singer riding on a chariot of light, having his spiritual harp, crying out and saying, "Let us sing unto the Lord, for with glory hath He been glorified". And our Saviour stood in our midst, the doors being shut, and stretched forth his hand towards us all, the multitude of the disciples being gathered together, and said unto us, "Peace be unto you all".'[1]

Christ then informs the Apostles that the time has come to 'receive my virgin mother, who has been to Me a dwelling-place on the earth for nine months, and take her up with Me to the heavenly places of the heavens, and give her as a gift to my good Father'. Both the Apostles and the women in attendance on the Virgin express grief and distress, and Mary herself weeps at the thought of the terrors of death until reassured by Christ's promise of his unfailing succour. The account of her death runs as follows: 'In a moment and in the twinkling of an eye, he appeared whose name is bitter with all men, even Death.   It came to pass when she saw him with her eyes, her soul leaped from her body into the bosom of her beloved Son in the place where He was sitting; for God the Word was sitting with us in the place where we were and He fills heaven and earth. And it came to pass, when He had hold of the soul of his virgin mother—for it was white as snow—He saluted it, and wrapped it in garments of fine linen, and gave it to Michael the holy archangel, who bare it on his wings of light, until He appointed the place for her holy body. All the women that were gathered to her, when they saw that she was dead, wept and groaned.'

Christ then pronounces an elaborate blessing on his mother's body, and the burial is described in these words: 'Now when our good Saviour had said these things over the body of his mother He wept, and we also were all weeping with Him. He arose and took hold of the heavenly garments and shrouded her holy body. And our Saviour spake with the Apostles, saying, "Arise, take up the body of my beloved mother, which was to Me a holy temple, and bear it on your shoulders.

[1] Forbes Robinson, *Coptic Apocryphal Gospels*, p. 52.

12

165

59

... Do thou, my chosen Peter, bear her head on thy shoulder, and let John also carry her feet; for ye are my brethren and my holy members. Let the rest of the Apostles sing before her. Go ye all forth with her from the least to the greatest to the east of Jerusalem, in the field of Jehoshaphat. Ye shall find a new tomb, wherein no man has yet been laid. Lay her holy body there, and keep watching it three and a half days. Be not afraid. I am with you." '

Reference is then made to Psalm xlv. 15 and Psalm cxxxii. 8, and the narrative continues: 'Straightway our Saviour rode upon his chariot of cherubim, all the orders of the heavens following Him and singing his praise, so that the air was filled with the abundance of the sweet savour. Thus did He receive the soul of his mother into his bosom, wrapped in napkins of fine linen, sending forth flashes of light; and went up into the heavens whilst we all looked at Him. Straightway they took up the body of the Virgin. My father Peter was carrying her head, my father John was carrying her feet, and the rest of the Apostles, with censers of incense in their hands, went before us singing, and all the virgins went behind her.' The Jews expressed wonder and penitence: 'But the Apostles bore the body of the Virgin, and put it into the tomb according to the word of our Saviour, and they remained watching it three and a half days'.

The story concludes with the corporeal assumption: 'Now when they had reached mid-day on the fourth day, the Apostles being gathered together with one another, and with virgins also by the tomb wherein was the body of the Virgin singing and making melody, behold! a great voice came from heaven like the sound of a trumpet, saying, "Go ye everyone to his place until the seventh month" ... And it came to pass in the seventh month from the time that the Virgin, the holy God-bearer, Mary, went forth from the body, which is the month Mesore, we arose on the fifteenth of this month, and gathered together to the tomb wherein was the body of the Virgin, the virgins also being with us. We spent all night watching and singing, offering up incense, the virgins having their lamps burning. Now at the hour of the light on this same night, there came unto us in the place where we were dwelling our Lord Jesus Christ in great glory, and said unto us, "Peace be unto you all, my holy Apostles. ... The body of my beloved mother, behold! it is with you, and my angels watch it according to the command of my Father, because it was a temple of his Son, even of Me; but her soul is in the heavenly places of heaven, and the powers of the height sing her praise. And now I have sent for her to be brought, that she may come and manifest to you the honours wherein she dwells, which

166

I promised you in return for those things which you left behind you here." Whilst our Saviour was yet speaking with us, we heard hymns in the height. Straightway we looked, and saw a great chariot of light. It came and stayed in our midst, cherubim drawing it, the holy Virgin Mary sitting upon it, and shining ten thousand times more than the sun and the moon. And we were in fear, and fell on our face, and worshipped her, and she stretched her hand towards us all, and blessed us, and gave us the salutation of peace. . . . And the Lord called into the tomb and raised the body of his virgin mother, and put her soul into her body again; and we saw it living in the body even as it was with us formerly, wearing the flesh. And our Saviour stretched out his hand and set her on the chariot with Him. And our Saviour answered and said to us in his gentle voice, "Behold my beloved mother. This is she whose virgin womb carried Me nine months, and I was three years also receiving suck from her breasts which were sweeter than honey. Behold! you see her face to face, raised by me from the dead, and she has blessed you all." . . . And when our Saviour had said these things, He spent all that day with us and with his virgin mother. Afterwards He gave us the salutation of peace; and went up to the heavens in glory, the angels singing before Him.'

The Greek narrative, which claims John the Evangelist as its author, is similar in general outline. It includes the story of the impious Jew who snatched at the bed, as the Apostles were bearing the body of the Virgin off for burial, and ends up in this way: 'At the departure of her spotless soul, the place was filled with fragrance and a marvellous light, and behold! a voice from heaven was heard saying "Blessed art thou amongst women". And Peter ran and I, John, and Paul and Thomas and we embraced her precious feet so as to be sanctified. And the twelve Apostles placed her precious, holy body on a bed and carried it forth. And behold! as they were carrying it, a certain Hebrew named Jephonias, mighty of body, rushed up and grabbed at the bed, which the Apostles were carrying, and behold! an angel of the Lord with invisible might severed his two hands from his shoulders with a sword of fire, and left them hanging right up in the air near the bed. At this miracle, the whole people of the Jews who saw it cried out: "He who was born of thee, Mary, ever-virgin mother of God, is indeed the true God". And Jephonias himself, at Peter's command, so that the marvellous works of God might be made manifest, stood up behind the bed and cried out, "Holy Mary who didst bear the Divine Christ, have mercy on me". And Peter turned and said to him, "In the name of Him who was born of her, the hands of which you were deprived shall be restored". And straightway at Peter's word, the hands that were hanging near the bed of our lady went back and were restored to Jephonias. And he, moreover, believed and glorified the Divine Christ who had been born of her.

'After this miracle, the Apostles carried the bed on, and laid her precious and holy body in a new tomb at Gethsemane. And behold! a sweet-smelling perfume came out of the holy sepulchre of our Lady the mother of God. And for three days there were heard the voices of invisible angels glorifying Christ our God who was born of her. And when the third day was fulfilled the voices were heard no longer, and thereafter everyone perceived that her spotless, precious body had been translated and was in Paradise.

'And after it was translated, lo! we beheld Elizabeth, mother of the holy John the Baptist, and Anne the mother of our Lady, and Abraham and Isaac and Jacob and David, playing harps and singing Alleluia, and all the choirs of the saints worshipping the precious body of the Lord's mother, and we saw a place filled with a light which nothing can surpass in radiance, and we perceived the great fragrance of that place where her holy and precious body lay, after its translation, in Paradise, and we heard a melody of them that praised Him who had been born of her, a sweet melody which it is granted only to virgins to hear and of which no-one can have a surfeit. So we the Apostles, having all of a sudden witnessed the translation of her holy body, glorified God who had shown us his marvels at the departure of the mother of our Lord Jesus Christ.'

This is the version printed by Tischendorf (1866) from the twelfth-century *codex Monacensis* 276. Other manuscripts, however, record that, along with the Virgin, the Apostles were translated, on twelve clouds of light, into Paradise; and one manuscript[1] ends abruptly without giving any details of the vision of Heaven.

The Latin narrative *de Transitu beatae Mariae* purports to have been composed by Melito, bishop of Sardis, from information furnished by St. John. At the beginning, strictures are passed on 'a certain Leucius' who is alleged to have corrupted the traditions concerning the adventures of the Apostles and death of the Virgin by rewriting the stories in the dualist, or Manichee, interest. 'Melito's' narrative certainly reflects an interest in St. John, and it starts off with a note of his care for the Virgin who had been entrusted to him with the words 'Behold thy mother'. The story then continues with a remodelled Annunciation, in the course of which Mary receives from the angel a palm branch

[1] Ven. Marc. cl. ii, cod. xlii.

168

culled in heaven, and with stress laid on the miraculous calling together
of the Apostles:[1] 'And behold, suddenly, while St. John was preaching
at Ephesus, on the Lord's day, at the third hour of the day, a great
earthquake occurred and a cloud raised him up and took him away
from the sight of all and brought him before the door of the house
where Mary was. And, knocking at the door, he immediately entered.
But when Mary saw him she rejoiced exultantly and said, "I ask thee,
my son John, be mindful of the words of my Lord Jesus Christ, in
which He commended me to thee. For lo! I am about to depart from
my body in three days' time, and I have heard the counsels of the Jews
who say, "Let us wait for the day when she shall die who bore that
deceiver, and let us burn her body with fire". So she called St. John
and brought him into the secret part of the house, and she showed him
her grave-clothes and that palm of light which she had received from
the angel, charging him that he should cause it to be carried before her
bier when she was on the way to her tomb. And St. John said to her
"How shall I alone prepare thy burial unless my brethren, fellow-
apostles of my lord Jesus Christ, come to pay honour to thy body?"
And lo! suddenly, at the command of God, all the Apostles were lifted
up from the places in which they were preaching God's word and swept
away in a cloud and put down before the door of the house where
Mary dwelt. And they greeted each other and marvelled, saying
"What is the reason for which the Lord has gathered us together here?"'
St. John comes out of the house and answers their question, and all
enter to greet the Virgin and watch with her. 'And they took their
places round about her and comforted her. And when they had passed
three days in praising God, lo! on the third day round about the third
hour of the day, sleep fell upon all who were in that house and nobody
at all could keep awake save only the Apostles and three virgins who
were there. And lo! the Lord Jesus Christ appeared suddenly with a
great host of angels, and a great light came down upon that place, and
the angels were singing a hymn and extolling the Lord. Then the
Saviour spoke, saying, "Come, most precious pearl, enter the treasury
of eternal life".'

The Virgin then prays to Jesus, and receives the assurance of his protection: 'And as the Lord spake these words, Mary rose from the ground
and lay down upon her bed, and rendering thanks to God she gave up
the ghost. But the Apostles saw her soul, that it was of such whiteness

---

[1] *Transitus* B text. Tischendorf, *Apocalypses Apocryphae*. M. R. James, *The Apocryphal New Testament*, pp. 194-227, gives translations, summaries and short notes on the Assumption legends.

169

as cannot be worthily described by the tongue of mortal men; for it surpassed the whiteness of snow and all metal and silver that shines with great brilliance of light. Then the Saviour spoke, saying "Arise, Peter, and take up the body of Mary and bear it to the right hand quarter of the city eastwards, and you shall find a new tomb in which ye shall lay her: there wait until I come to you". And, saying this, the Lord handed over the soul of St. Mary to Michael who was set in charge of Paradise and the prince of the people of the Jews; and Gabriel went together with them. And straightway the Saviour was received up into Heaven accompanied by the angels.' The virgins then prepared Mary's body for burial, and found that it shone with bright radiance and gave forth a sweet fragrance. The Apostles, chanting solemnly, bore the body away as they had been instructed. Angelic voices were heard, so that the onlookers were amazed; but a malevolent Jewish priest stirred the people to hostility. He tried to overthrow the body to the earth, whereat his hands withered and clave to the bier, while angels struck the people blind. However, the afflicted Jewish priest, after confessing Jesus to be Son of God, is restored to wholeness; and the people who had been smitten with blindness are cured also, with the exception of those who remain obdurate and refuse to believe, when St. John 'lays the palm upon their eyes': 'But the Apostles carrying Mary came to the place of the valley of Josaphat, which the Lord had shown them, and they placed her in the new tomb, and closed the sepulchre. Now they sat down at the door of the tomb, just as the Lord had bidden them; and lo! suddenly the Lord Jesus Christ appeared with a great host of angels and a flashing radiance of great brightness, and said to the Apostles "Peace be with you". But they replied and said "Let thy mercy, O Lord, be upon us, like as we have hoped in thee".' The Lord asks the Apostles what treatment they would regard as appropriate for the Virgin, and Peter declares that her body should be raised up and taken to the blessedness of Heaven. 'Then said the Saviour "Be it done according to your wish". And He commanded Michael the archangel to bring the soul of the holy Mary. And lo! Michael the archangel rolled back the stone from the door of the tomb, and the Lord said "Rise up, my beloved and my kinswoman: thou who didst not suffer corruption by union of the flesh mayest not suffer destruction of the body in the sepulchre". And straightway Mary arose from the tomb and blessed the Lord and fell at the Lord's feet and worshipped Him. . . . And the Lord kissed her and departed, and entrusted her soul[1] to angels to bear it into

[1] *Tradidit animam eius angelis ut deferrent eam in paradisum.* But no doubt the body is meant along with the soul, as is made perfectly clear in the *Transitus* A text, a later production.

170

Paradise. And He said to the apostles "Come unto me". And when they had come near, He kissed them and said "Peace be with you. As I was even with you, so shall I be even unto the end of the world." And straightway when the Lord had said this He was lifted up in a cloud and received into heaven, and the angels accompanied Him, bearing the blessed Mary into the Paradise of God.'

It is notable that in the Decretal[1] attributed to Pope Gelasius I (A.D. 492–496) the 'book which is called the Passing, that is to say the Assumption, of the Holy Mary' is condemned as being apocryphal and unsuitable for reading by churchmen. Whether this work was precisely the same as the *de Transitu Mariae* of 'Melito' can hardly be determined, but, in any case, the cautious protestations at the beginning of the Latin Transitus-text seem designed to remove the tincture of heresy which stained the story of the Assumption. For the earliest Coptic Christianity was Gnostic rather than orthodox, and the Coptic versions of the Assumption legend bear marks of the dualism which character- izes the treatise *Pistis Sophia* or the *Apocryphon of John*[2] contained in the Berlin papyrus, P. 8502. The general picture displayed in such works points towards a sharp contrast between the Supreme God and the God of the Old Testament who created this beggarly universe, and empha- sizes the struggle between the Powers of Light and the Powers of Dark- ness in which man plays his important part. So, in the version of 'Evodius' (xi), Mary prays 'O my beloved Son, let the tyrannies of death and the powers of darkness flee from me. Let the angels of light draw nigh unto me. Let the accusers of Amenti shut their mouths before me.' The fact that the legend had a Gnostic smack to it may well account in part for its hesitant and comparatively late acceptance in orthodox circles.[3]

The unsubstantial, indeed fanciful, nature of all forms of the Assump- tion legend is obvious enough to any reader of the texts, yet it is clearly on the basis of such narratives that the doctrine of the Virgin's corporeal reception into Heaven found its way into the works of the Church fathers. Gregory of Tours is the first writer in the West precisely to declare the resurrection of the Virgin, followed by her assumption both

[1] It seems probable that the Decretal was, in fact, composed in Gaul or North Italy some few years after Gelasius' death.

[2] Walter C. Till, 'Die Gnosis in Aegypten', *La Parola del Passato*, xii (1949). Cf. H. Idris Bell, *Cults and Creeds in Graeco-Roman Egypt*, 92 ff. A similarly Egyptian and Gnostic tone rings through the prayers and lamentations found in the 'History of Joseph the Carpenter', ed. S. Morenz, *Texte und Untersuchungen*, lvi (Berlin, 1951).

[3] W. H. C. Frend, 'The Gnostic Origins of the Assumption Legend'. *Modern Church- man*, March 1953.

171

in body and soul. In his treatise *de gloria martyrum*, composed about A.D. 590, he puts the matter thus: 'Then after the blessed Mary had fulfilled the course of this life and was being summoned to depart from the world, all the Apostles assembled from various places to her abode. And when they learned that she was about to be taken from the world, they kept watch together with her. And, behold! the Lord Jesus arrived in the company of his angels, and taking her soul, He entrusted it to Michael the Archangel, and departed. But at daybreak the Apostles lifted up her body, along with the bed, and placed it in a sepulchre, and guarded it, waiting for the coming of the Lord. And, behold! the Lord stood beside them a second time, and commanded that the sacred body should be lifted up in a cloud and taken off to Paradise, where now, reunited to the soul, it rejoices together with his elect and enjoys the blessings of eternity which shall never have an ending.'[1]

In this passage there is no hint of theological arguments designed to prove the inevitability of the Assumption. The death and translation of the Virgin are put forward in terms of history, history that is obviously derived from the *de Transitu Mariae* or from some closely similar document. Gregory speaks, in the same treatise, of the Virgin 'who was translated to Paradise amidst choirs of angels, the Lord going on before',[2] and a little later on reference is made to her *festivitas*, celebrated in January. It is not, however, made clear whether this was a general feast of the maternity of Mary or was particularly connected with the Assumption, as is the case with the festival assigned to January 18th in certain of the Gallican calendars, such as that of Corbie.

Be that as it may, while Rome remained silent it was in Gaul that liturgical observance of the Assumption became well established. The *Missale Gothicum*, composed before the end of the seventh century, bears witness to the doctrine in the *contestatio* appointed for the festival, when it declares, with elaborate parallelism: 'It would perchance have been too light a thing if Christ had hallowed thee merely at thy coming in, and had not glorified a mother such as thee at thy departure. Rightly hast thou been taken up in joyous assumption by Him whom thou didst bear in sanctity . . . so that the sepulchre of rock might not retain thee who hadst no awareness of earthly things.'[3] By contrast, the earliest Roman liturgies contain nothing of the kind, and, even when subjected to Gallican influences, they speak in general terms of the 'holy mother of God who underwent temporal death but could not be held captive

---

[1] *P.L.* lxxi. 708.
[2] *Ibid.* 713.
[3] *Missale Gothicum*, ed. H. M. Bannister, Henry Bradshaw Society, p. 32.

172

by the bonds of death'.[1] Indeed the reception accorded to the festival of the Assumption appears to have been unenthusiastic, at any rate in official circles, if one may judge from the fact that Charlemagne, at the beginning of the ninth century, after listing sixteen feasts as worthy of universal observance adds, 'as regards the assumption of holy Mary we have left the matter open for further enquiry'.[2]

In the East, the doctrine of the Assumption gained a more tardy acceptance by orthodox writers. The earliest attestation appears to be a turgid, rhetorical sermon, an 'Encomium on the Falling-asleep of the God-bearer',[3] attributed to Modestus, patriarch of Jerusalem A.D. 633–634. The grammarian Photius took little interest in this work, on the ground that it differs in many respects from Modestus' customary style, and the sermon probably belongs to the end rather than the beginning of the seventh century. 'Modestus' complains of the silence of the Apostles concerning Mary's death, and then goes on to show knowledge of the apocryphal narratives. The Apostles are described as hastening from all over the world, 'guided and assisted by the powerful influence from above', to be present at the Virgin's deathbed. Christ appeared, and 'the blessed Virgin looked towards Him and departed from the holy body, entrusting to his hands her all-blessed, all-holy soul'. The body was placed upon 'a litter that bore a holy burden', and then taken by the Apostles to be buried at Gethsemane; but the reference to the Assumption, though definite, is not very clearly expressed. Certain details of the legend are dismissed as apocryphal, and 'Modestus' merely states: 'She is made alive by Christ, being united with Him bodily ($\sigma\acute{v}\sigma\sigma\omega\mu\sigma\varsigma$) in eternal incorruptibility, since He raised her from the tomb and took her to Himself, in a manner known to Him alone'. About 680, John, bishop of Thessalonica, introduced the observance of the Falling Asleep of the Virgin into his diocese. In his oration he adopts a somewhat apologetic tone and refers to the difficulty caused by heretical falsifications. He transcribed the apocryphal legend but, though he included the death of the Virgin, he omitted the account of the Assumption and passed on to a concluding peroration.[4]

[1] *Gregorian Sacramentary*, ed. H. A. Wilson, H.B.S. p. 97. Cf. *Gelasian Sacramentary*, ed. H. A. Wilson, p. 193.

[2] *Capitula de presbyteris*, xix, *P.L.* xcvii. 326. Nevertheless, the festival is included in the *Regula* of Chrodegang of Metz (*P.L.* lxxxix. 1090) and in the list approved by the Council of Mainz (A.D. 813).

[3] *P.G.* lxxxvi. 3277.

[4] *Patrologia Orientalis*, xix. 375 ff. The ending varies in the different manuscripts. The original form, as shown in *codex Vaticanus* 2072, merely records that the Apostles, when they opened the tomb three days after the burial, found the grave-clothes and nothing else. This account is not inconsistent with the story of the Assumption, but perhaps the author

173

The homilies of Andrew, archbishop of Crete (d. A.D. 720), who had been a monk at Jerusalem, illustrate the tendency to harden and elaborate the stories told about saintly persons. Andrew gives details of the Virgin's childhood, and discusses the life of her parents, Joachim and Anna, just as he delights to recount the miraculous exploits of St. George and St. Nicholas. The Assumption is discussed freely, but in language which implies that its acceptance is something of a novelty. After a reference to Enoch and Elijah, Andrew declares: 'The things accomplished in her of old, but triumphantly proclaimed by us now, might perhaps seem strange and out of accord with the laws of nature, but when considered in relation to the astounding fact of the marvellous Birth would reasonably be held to be suitable in her case. . . . Now it was certainly a novel occurrence and beyond the scope of human reason that a woman who exceeded the nature of the heavens in purity should find her way into the inmost sanctuary of heaven. . . . How did the corpse disappear? How was it that the winding sheets were not in the coffin? Only because the body escaped corruption and the treasure was translated.'[1]

Andrew refers in this connexion to a patristic comment which was to be widely influential. The work 'Concerning the Divine Names' was composed, along with other treatises and letters, by an author who identified himself with Dionysius the Areopagite, mentioned in Acts xvii and held to be a companion of Peter and Paul. These documents are now attributed, with practical certainty, to a period about A.D. 500,[2] but in the eighth century they had come to enjoy high repute as writings of the apostolic age. In the treatise 'Concerning the Divine Names' it is stated, after a concise reference to the Virgin's death: 'When, as you know, both we and Hierotheus and many of our holy brethren had gathered together to behold the life-giving, God-receiving body, there were also present James, the brother of the Lord, and Peter, the most distinguished and aged prince of theologians. Thereupon it seemed good, after that sight, that all the holy prelates, as each one was able, should hymn and extol the nobility of weakness endued by God with infinite power.'[3] No allusion is made to an assumption of any kind, but later theologians, eager to find support for this doctrine, grasped on to this passage and interpreted it as though 'Dionysius' had been an eyewitness of the Virgin's corporeal departure from earth to Heaven.

had in mind a translation to an earthly Paradise, as suggested by a number of Eastern theologians, e.g. the tenth-century John the Geometer.

[1] Sermo in dormitionem Mariae, ii, P.G. xcvii. 1081.
[2] Bardenhewer, Geschichte der altkirchlichen Literatur, iv. 282 ff.   [3] P.G. iii. 681.

174

Germanus, patriarch of Constantinople[1] (d. A.D. 733), wrote in much the same strain as Andrew of Crete; but it is rather the honoured name of John Damascene, the great doctor of the Eastern Church, whose attacks on the Iconoclasts earned him high praise at the second Council of Nicaea, that furthered the rapid spread of the doctrine. Three homilies 'on the Falling-Asleep of the Blessed Virgin Mary' appear amongst his works, the first and third being short and restrained, while the second is a luxuriant composition, in which the preacher imagines himself to be present, along with the Apostles, on that occasion and recounts at length what he would have seen and the thoughts with which he would have been occupied. The Roman Breviary has, since the sixteenth century, drawn on this second homily to provide lections for August 18th, during the octave of the Assumption, but the homily appears, in fact, to be the work of an interpolator rather than of John Damascene himself.[2]

The passage which treats of the Assumption offers several points of difficulty. In the first place it is stated to be a quotation from the 'Euthymian History', a work which is otherwise unknown. In the second place it describes how the emperor Marcian and his wife Pulcheria sent for Juvenal of Jerusalem and other bishops at the time of the Council of Chalcedon (A.D. 451) and declared that they wished to acquire, for the protection of Constantinople, the Virgin's tomb which, as they had heard, was 'in the place which is called Gethsemane'. Juvenal's reply includes a long quotation from the treatise of the pseudo-Dionysius on the 'Divine Names', which, however, was almost certainly not written until fifty years or more after the Council of Chalcedon. For reasons such as these the historical value of the homily is negligible, a fact which did not prevent it from becoming widely influential.

Juvenal's reply to the emperor and empress runs as follows: 'In the holy and divinely-inspired Scriptures nothing is found that bears on the death of Mary, the holy God-bearer. But we have learnt from an ancient and most true tradition that, at the time of her glorious falling-asleep, all the holy Apostles, who were travelling about the world for the salvation of the nations, were in a moment of time borne aloft and brought to Jerusalem. And when they arrived in the presence of Mary, they had a vision of angels and heard the divine harmony of the heavenly Powers. And thus, amidst divine and heavenly glory, she committed her holy soul into the hands of God in an ineffable manner. But her body which had received God was carried away, to the sound of chanting from

[1] *P.G.* xcviii. 340. [2] Bardenhewer, *op. cit.* v. 61.

175

angels and Apostles, and given burial, being placed in a tomb at Geth-semane, where for three days the chanting of the angelic choir continued without ceasing. After the third day, however, the angelic chanting ceased. The Apostles who were present (one of them, namely Thomas, who had been absent arrived after the third day and wished to venerate the body that had borne God) opened the tomb. But they were com-pletely unable to find the body whose praises all men sing, and when they found only the grave-clothes lying there and had taken their fill of an ineffable fragrance proceeding therefrom, they closed the tomb. Then, overcome with wonder at the mystery, they could only conclude that He who had condescended to become incarnate in his own person and be made man of her and be born in the flesh though He was God the Word and Lord of glory, and who had preserved her virginity unharmed after her child-bearing, had Himself pleased to honour her pure, undefiled body with incorruptibility even after her departure from this life by translating her before the general resurrection of all.'[1] John Damascene then quotes the passage from 'Dionysius', in a form somewhat different from the text found in the 'Divine Names', and adds that Marcian and Pulcheria requested that the sarcophagus and shroud should be handed over to them for safe custody in the church of St. Mary at Blachernae.

The silence of all the Fathers of the Church, during the first five cen-turies, on the subject of the Assumption finds its counterpart in the accounts of pilgrimages made to the holy places of Palestine. It is, indeed, certain that in the fourth century no tomb of the Virgin was known at or near Jerusalem.[2] Eusebius, in the Life of Constantine, makes no mention of it amongst the numerous shrines built in Palestine by the empress Helen and her son, shrines which appealed to the curiosity, as well as to the piety, of pilgrims from far and wide. In A.D. 333 these holy places were visited by a pilgrim from Bordeaux, who left a careful record of all that he saw, but has nothing to say concerning the Virgin's tomb. The enterprising and devoted Etheria (Silvia), who gives a full account of her travels to Jerusalem and other sacred sites about A.D. 400, is likewise silent on this subject. So also is Jerome who, after conducting the Roman ladies Paula and Eustochium on a visit to the monks of Egypt, settled with them at Bethlehem and established, along with mon-asteries for men and women, a 'hospice for pilgrims by the high way, remembering that Mary and Joseph had not found a resting-place'.[3]

[1] P.G. xcvi. 748.
[2] The statement of Nicephoros Kallistos (P.G. cxlvi. 113) that Helena set up a church over the Virgin's grave is late and wholly unreliable.　　　　　[3] Ep. cviii. 14.

There was, indeed, a variant tradition, strongly supported by the Turks today, that the resting-place of the Virgin was not Jerusalem at all but Ephesus, whither St. John had led her. The Council of Ephesus (A.D. 431) met in the city ἔνθα ὁ θεολόγος Ἰωάννης καὶ ἡ θεοτόκος παρθένος ἡ ἁγία Μαρία: "where are John the theologian and the God-bearing virgin, holy Mary". The precise meaning of this elliptical phrase is obscure: does it refer to the tomb of the Virgin or merely to her church? There was indeed a famous church of the Virgin at Ephesus, and, at the time of the Council, Cyril of Alexandria preached a vigorously anti-Nestorian sermon in the 'church of Mary, mother of God', into which the holy Trinity 'had gathered us all together';[1] but perhaps the more natural meaning of the words is that the tombs of the Virgin and of John were to be seen at Ephesus, and certainly this was the tradition which came to be fostered locally. The truth may well be that, the Virgin's burial-place being unknown, Jerusalem vied with Ephesus in claiming the distinction of possessing it. This would lead to the construction of rival churches; and August 15th, the date fixed by the emperor Maurice, about A.D. 600, on which the Dormition should be commemorated, was perhaps originally the dedication-day of such a church at or near Jerusalem.[2]

During the sixth century, numerous relics, such as the crown of thorns or the charger on which John the Baptist's head lay, came to be exhibited to the gaze of pilgrims, and, by a similar process, the holy places worthy of a devout visit were notably multiplied. A certain Theodosius, who describes the topography of the Holy Land on the basis of a pilgrimage which he made about A.D. 530, records: 'There is the valley of Josaphat, where Judas betrayed the Lord. There is the church of saint Mary, mother of the Lord',[3] a succinct notice which, though it invited and received embellishment by later hands, gives no hint that the Virgin's tomb was, at that date, regarded as wonderful or even clearly identified.

The pilgrims from Piacenza,[4] when they visited the valley of Gethsemane about A.D. 570, noted that 'in the same valley is a basilica of saint Mary, which they say was her house, where indeed she was taken up out of her body'. This last statement—*in qua et de corpore*

---

[1] *Homily IV*, P.G. lxxvii. 992.

[2] Doubts concerning the burial-place may be compared with doubts about the birth-place of the Virgin, which gradually came to be settled under the influence of the apocryphal *Protevangelium of James*.

[3] Palestine Pilgrims Text Society, ii, p. 11. C.S.E.L. xxxix. 142.

[4] *Of the Holy Places visited by Antoninus Martyr*, P.P.T.S. ii, p. 14. Geyer, *Itinera Hierosolymitana*, C.S.E.L. xxxix. 170. 203.

177

sublatam fuisse—becomes slightly suspect by reason of its omission from the St. Gall manuscript (133), one of the two best authorities for the text. But, whatever may be the value of this reading, it is modified in the interests of precision and developed belief and becomes, in an inferior manuscript tradition, *de qua eam dicunt ad caelos fuisse sublatam*, 'from which they say that she was raised up to Heaven'.[1]

Even by the seventh century those who piously visited the Virgin's tomb were in no way committed to belief in the corporeal Assumption. For instance, Arculf, a bishop of Gaul, undertook a pilgrimage to the Holy Places about A.D. 670 and, on his way home, was driven by contrary winds to the western coast of Britain. He was hospitably entertained by Adamnan, abbot of Iona, who made careful notes of the topographical details supplied by his guest. According to this record, Arculf visited the Virgin's church in the valley of Josaphat which contained 'the empty stone tomb of the holy Mary, in which she rested for some time after her burial. But how or when or by what persons her sacred body was removed from that same tomb, or where it awaits the Resurrection, nobody, so it is said, can know for certain.'[2] Arculf and Adamnan seem ignorant of any doctrine of the Assumption, and they take it that, whatever may have happened to the Virgin's body, it follows the normal human destiny and quietly awaits the day of Resurrection. Similarly, Bede, though the festival of the Assumption had by his day come to be observed by the Anglo-Saxons, records of the church in the valley of Jehoshaphat that, adjoining it, there was an 'empty tomb in which saint Mary, the mother of God, is said to have reposed for a time; but by whom or when the body was taken away nobody knows'.[3]

Another Englishman, St. Willibald, explored the Holy Places about A.D. 725 and an account of his travels was written up many years later, when he was an old man. This *Hodoeporicon*, compiled by a nun of Heidenheim Abbey who was a relation of Willibald, shows knowledge of the legendary accounts of the Virgin's death. Mention is made of the impious Jew whose hands were glued to the bier, and it is recorded that when the eleven had carried Mary to Jerusalem 'then the angels came and took her from the hands of the Apostles and carried her up to Paradise',[4]

---

[1] Cf. Sophronius, *Anacreontica*, xx (about A.D. 625).

$$\text{Γεθσημανῆ τέμενος λαμπρὸν ἀείδω}$$
$$\text{Ἔνθα τέτυκτο τάφος Μητρὶ θεοῖο.}$$

[2] P.P.T.S. iii, p. 17.
[3] *Concerning the Holy Places*, v. *P.L.* xciv. 1183.   [4] P.P.T.S. iii, p. 21.

apparently before any entombment had taken place. The sepulchre in the valley of Josaphat is described as having been erected 'as a memorial of her'.

However, another version of Willibald's travels, composed, with additional matter, by one of his companions, strikes a more agnostic note: 'They came into the valley of Josaphat where the tomb of saint Mary is shown. But whether the Apostles buried her there when she had been released from her body left here below, or whether, while they were intending to bury her after they had dug out the tomb there, she was assumed with her body, or, if after being buried she was hidden there, whether she was taken thence and transferred elsewhere or, having received true immortality, she has risen again, it is better to be in doubt than to define anything apocryphal.'[1]

This sturdy refusal to accept doctrines based on dubious tradition is echoed by several more or less contemporary writers. It may be noted, for instance, in an eighth-century 'Letter to Paula and Eustochium concerning the assumption of the blessed Virgin Mary',[2] which gained spurious repute on the ground that it had been written by Saint Jerome and found its way into various breviaries, including the Roman Breviary until the revision initiated by the Council of Trent. Though he speaks with enthusiasm about the Virgin's departure into Heaven, and the festival commemorating it, the author can hardly intend to preach a corporeal assumption to judge from the note of reverent caution which he strikes: 'If perchance an apocryphal work called *de Transitu Virginis Mariae* has fallen into your hands, you should not take doubtful matter as assured truth. It is a work which many Latins, with their love of piety and zeal for reading, embrace rather too eagerly, particularly since nothing of these matters can be known for certain except that on this day the Virgin whom we honour departed from the body.' Reference is then made to the tomb in the valley of Jehoshaphat 'where she is said by all, as you know, to have been buried; but now the tomb is shown empty to people who go to look at it. I speak thus for the reason that many of our friends are doubtful whether the Virgin was assumed together with the body or whether she left her body behind at her departure. But how or when or by whom that most holy body was taken away from the tomb or where it has been laid or whether it rose again is unknown; though some like to maintain that it has already been received and is clothed by Christ with blessed immortality in heaven.'

The author goes on to say that similar traditions are current about

[1] P.P.T.S. iii, p. 46.   [2] *P.L.* xxx. 123.

179

St. John, in whose tomb only manna is found: 'We are indeed in doubt concerning the precise truth of these matters. Yet we find it better to entrust everything to God, with whom nothing is impossible, than to desire to make any rash definitions on our own authority when we lack proof.' The author alludes to St. Matthew's account of the resurrection of the 'bodies of the saints' at the time of the Crucifixion, and to the view held by some that this represented their final resurrection into Heaven. He closes the debate with the words, 'We do not deny that this happened in the case of the blessed Virgin Mary, though for the sake of caution, and to safeguard the faith, it should be regarded as a pious hope and opinion rather than defined unadvisedly. Ignorance on such a matter does us no harm.' The author thus declares that, while God has the power to effect the assumption of Mary, there is no proof that He, in fact, did so since the only source from which the doctrine is drawn is the unreliable *de Transitu Virginis*.

The ninth-century martyrologists Ado[1] and Usuard[2] speak in the same strain. Usuard puts the matter thus: 'Even though the most holy body of saint Mary, mother of God, is not found on earth, yet pious Mother Church keeps the festival of her revered memory, so as not to doubt that, so far as the flesh is concerned, she has been translated. But where that revered temple of the Holy Spirit has been hidden by the will and counsel of God, the Church with its sound sense has preferred not to know rather than to hold and teach some frivolous, apocryphal story about it.' Such hesitations, however, failed to satisfy the minds of churchmen eager to believe, and this in spite of continued protests such as that voiced in a sermon 'on the Assumption' which is attributed, though falsely, to Ildefonsus, bishop of Toledo: 'We must certainly not omit a story which many, through motives of piety, grasp at most eagerly, namely that the Virgin's body was raised up to the heavenly palaces by her Son, our Lord Jesus Christ. Now this may be a pious belief, yet we should not affirm it lest we seem to be taking doubtful stories as true.'[3] Another sermon, attributed to St. Augustine, but, in fact, a later work and perhaps composed by Ambrosius Aupertus, is expressed more strongly:[4] 'No catholic history records the manner of the Virgin's passing from earth to heaven. And the Church is said not merely to reject apocryphal stories of this sort, but even to remain in ignorance of them.' After comparing the uncertainty that surrounds the departure of the Virgin with the unknown fate of Moses' body, the preacher reminds his hearers that even St. John, who cared for the Virgin

---

[1] *P.L.* cxxiii. 202.   [2] *P.L.* cxxiv. 365.
[3] *P.L.* xcvi. 266.   [4] *Sermo CCVIII, P.L.* xxxix. 2130.

in her old age, has nothing to say on the subject:[1] 'It remains therefore that no man should, in lying fashion, invent as true what God wished to remain hid'.

Such scruples had little chance of prevailing over the general eagerness to enjoy a clear-cut, attractive picture of the Falling-asleep of the Virgin—*advocata nostra*, around whose every action was woven a shimmering web of mystery. Moreover, the enthusiasm of popular devotion gradually hardened into dogmatic definition, so that, by the thirteenth century, such scholastic philosophers as Albertus Magnus could declare: 'It is obvious that the most blessed mother of God was assumed in flesh and spirit; and we believe this to be true in every respect'.[2]

From time to time, however, controversy revived. In the middle of the seventeenth century, for instance, the canons of Paris split into two factions, the subject of vehement dispute being whether the passage from Usuard or some homily rather more positive concerning the mystery of the day should be used on August 15th. Canon Claude Joly, with the support of others, demanded the restoration of the Usuard passage which 'in no way detracts from the honour of the blessed Virgin and is not opposed to her corporeal Assumption but merely refrains from affirming it'.[3] 'We ought not', Joly continued, 'to make rash statements, lest we offend the most holy Virgin, the mother of Him who is the way, the *truth* and the life. For this reason she takes no pleasure in statements made about her which either add to or detract from *truth*.' The rival canons, led by Jacques Gaudin and Nicolas Billiard, protested that they could not 'remain silent, while old-established and seemly devotion to the mother of God and thus of all Christians is torn in pieces'.[4] Pleading the numerous voices raised on behalf of the doctrine and the need for certainty in such matters, Gaudin expressed his horror that, if the tradition of the corporeal assumption had to be attacked, this impious work should be carried out by a canon of Paris. The learned Tillemont, a little later, inclined towards Joly's view, but preferred to remain silent on a subject of widespread and popular belief.

A number of influences, therefore, seem to have operated in favour of the doctrine of the Assumption. First and foremost comes that love of the miraculous which characterizes the 'mediaeval' outlook; secondly there is the impatience felt at the silences of Scripture and the Fathers

---

[1] This presents a contrast with the plea made at the Vatican Council of 1870 that the Assumption should be defined dogmatically because it was an 'apostolic tradition, based on a divine revelation with which the apostle John had, perhaps, been favoured'. Martin, 'Les Travaux du concile du Vatican', quoted in *Dictionnaire de théologie catholique*, i. 2. 2140.

[2] *Opera* (Lyons, 1651), xx, p. 87.   [3] *De verbis Usuardi* (Sens, 1669), p. 154.

[4] J. Gaudin, *Assumptio Mariae Virginis vindicatae* (Paris, 1670), p. 415.

13   181

which would not allow of a neat and clear-cut picture of the Virgin. Then again, love of parallelism drew men on to attribute to the Virgin experiences which reproduced, in a minor key, those of her Son; so that the Assumption provided an appropriate counterpart to the Ascension. To such reasons may perhaps be added ecclesiastical rivalry, whereby Jerusalem and Ephesus were both impelled to claim the empty tomb where the Virgin had lain. There were also genuine misunderstandings of an author's meaning, and such misunderstandings seem to have occurred in the artistic as well as in the literary field.

The conventional manner in which Christian artists represented the human soul was to show it as a diminutive, childish figure wrapped in swaddling bands, and it is as such that the Virgin's soul is depicted in the first illustrations of her Falling-asleep. The earliest examples were destroyed in the course of the Iconoclastic controversy, but the primitive form of the picture was carefully retained for centuries, and spread widely from the East, where it originated, to the West. As displayed, for instance, in the mosaics of Daphni[1] or of the Martorana at Palermo,[2] it shows the Apostles ranged in two groups, at the head and at the feet of the Virgin as she lies on her bed. Christ stands behind the bed, holding the swathed and mummy-like figure of the soul with both hands, while overhead two large angels hover. A striking example of this *motif*, worked out with the vigorous and expressive realism of thirteenth-century Gothic sculpture, occurs in the porch of the south transept of Strasbourg Cathedral. Here the angels are not shown, but, instead, Mary Magdalene is introduced, crouching at the bedside and wringing her hands in dismay, while, on the other side of the couch, Christ raises his right hand in blessing while his left hand supports the figure of a graceful child which represents the Virgin's soul.[3] Sometimes the illustration, while preserving the traditional form, is modified, as on an ivory preserved in the Musée Cluny at Paris, in that two scenes are shown simultaneously. The grouping is exactly the same but one of the two angels has changed his posture and is flying away clasping a soul similar to that which Christ holds. Christ, in fact, is receiving the Virgin's soul at her death, while an angel bears it off to Heaven.[4]

---

[1] C. Diehl, *Manuel d'art byzantin*, ii, pp. 524 ff.

[2] O. Demus, *The Mosaics of Norman Sicily*, pp. 78 ff., pl. 56.

[3] E. H. Gombrich, *The Story of Art*, p. 138.

[4] K. Künstle, *Ikonographie der christlichen Kunst*, i, p. 567. In thirteenth-century glass at Chartres Cathedral, the soul of St. Martin is shown as a figure, naked except for his mitre, ascending to Heaven in an aureole of light. Similarly a relief in the church of S. Gregorio at Rome shows the soul of the monk Justus, depicted as a fully grown man, being raised up to Heaven by angels in response to Gregory's prayers. Künstle, *op. cit.* i, p. 494.

182

In such pictures, the soul is often a close replica, in miniature, of the body of the Virgin. An observer might therefore be excused for interpreting the Virgin's departure to Heaven as a bodily ascension, which, indeed, it clearly becomes when the scene is remodelled by the ingenuity of western artists. The first stage of variation is marked by the removal of Christ from the bedside. He is shown instead as enclosed in a mandorla of light and bearing on his knees a round medallion in which the Virgin is depicted as an *Orans* while an attendant angel hovers at each side.[1] This form of the picture exhibits a natural development when, as in an eleventh-century sacramentary from Augsburg,[2] the Virgin appears alone, full-length in a mandorla of light, being raised up to Heaven by four angels. Here, the Assumption is set forth in a manner closely comparable with that which had earlier been used to depict the Ascension of Christ, for, in the church of S. Clemente at Rome, a wall-painting which dates from the time of Pope Leo IV (A.D. 847–855) shows Christ in a mandorla being borne heavenwards by angels,[3] an art-form of Syrian origin which appears in the Gospels of Rabula[4] (A.D. 586). Similar parallelism is to be noted in the early and unusual example provided by an ivory ascribed to Tutilo of St. Gallen (*c.* A.D. 900) where, under an inscription *Ascensio Sce Marie*, the Virgin is shown as an *Orans* standing with two angels on each side of her in a grouping elsewhere used of Christ's Ascension.[5]

The early illustrations of the death of the Virgin thus display two tendencies of the primitive and mediaeval Church—the desire to assimilate the history of the Virgin to the events recorded of her Son, and, in particular, the pious eagerness to convert metaphor, or reverie, into concrete fact.

Moreover, the doctrine of the Assumption grew up in a world where miraculous translations were an accepted sign of God's especial favour and a mark of pre-eminent holiness. Examples of this belief occur both in the Graeco-Roman and in the Jewish tradition. The story of Heracles, in its later form,[6] records that the hero, tormented by the poison prepared for him by Deianira, climbed up the slopes of Mount Oeta and, under the instructions of Apollo, built his own funeral pyre with the wood of beech and fir trees. He then lay upon the pyre, in full armour,

---

[1] As in a Reichenau manuscript, preserved at Munich. Künstle, *op. cit.* i, p. 568.
[2] British Museum, Harl. 2908.
[3] Wilpert, *Die römischen Mosaiken und Malereien*, ii. 528.
[4] Illustrated in Diehl, *op. cit.* i. 251.   [5] Shown in Künstle, *op. cit.* i, p. 570.
[6] Sophocles, *Trachiniae*; not in the *Odyssey*. Cf. L. R. Farnell, *Greek Hero Cults*, pp. 166 ff., M. P. Nilsson, 'Der Flammentod des Herakles auf dem Oite', in *Archiv für Religionswissenschaft*, 1922, pp. 310 ff.

183

while Poeas, father of Philoctetes, performed the office of kindling the fire. The wood soon blazed up, but a cloud descended and Heracles was taken up into heaven in a four-horse chariot, with an angelic being, Athena or sometimes Nike, as his companion.[1] No trace could ever be found of his bones or his ashes, for which earth could provide no worthy resting-place.

The Igel monument, near Trèves, shows Heracles in his chariot being greeted by Minerva (Athena) who no longer sits by his side but emerges from the clouds to meet him and extends her hand to draw him within the gates of Heaven, a *motif* which is repeated, with a difference, on later Roman medallions of consecration where the hand of God is stretched out to raise the Christian emperor. But the theme of the assumption of the emperor into Heaven is found long before the days of Constantine. It typifies the divinization which could be conferred by senatorial decree and was linked with cremation, the body being, as it were, snatched away from the pyre and transported heavenwards.

The earliest example of the apotheosis of an emperor is provided by an altar set up by Augustus, that stands in the precincts of the Vatican.[2] The divine Julius is borne aloft in the four-horse chariot to be received by Jupiter, shown within the curving folds of the mantle of the Cosmos. The chariot of the sun also appears in the left upper corner of the monument, while Augustus, who, with other members of the imperial household, witnesses the assumption, raises his hand in a last greeting. The theme of apotheosis is treated in a somewhat similar manner on the Antonine column, where Antoninus Pius and Faustina are shown as Jupiter and Juno being borne aloft on the back of a gigantic winged angel, while, down below, Roma raises her hand in salutation. But the thought of bodily departure to the gods is illustrated even more clearly by an ivory at the British Museum.[3] Here the emperor, who may be Constantius Chlorus, is borne aloft by two winged angels (possibly Sleep and Death) to Heaven where five gods are seated, two of whom stretch out their hands to welcome him as one of their number. Underneath is shown the funeral pyre, and the chariot of the sun with two flying eagles preceding it, while still lower down elephants are shown drawing a funeral chariot which contains the image of the now divinized emperor.[4]

[1] Illustrated by a number of vase-paintings. Daremberg-Saglio, *Dictionnaire des antiquités*, fig. 3778. Cf. Roscher, *Griechische und römische Mythologie*, i. 2240, 2250.

[2] Mrs. A. Strong, *Apotheosis and After-life*, pl. vii.

[3] Strong, *op. cit.* pl. xxxi.

[4] Cf. Justin, *Apology*, i. 21. 3. E. Bickermann, 'Die römische Kaiserapotheose', *Archiv für Religionswissenschaft*, 1929.

184

Pictures produced under this inspiration began again in the seventeenth century, when Rubens illustrated the apotheosis of King Henry IV of France. Ingres, in his designs for the painted ceiling of the Hôtel de Ville at Paris, kept even closer to his classical models. For Napoleon is shown as being borne aloft in a four-horse chariot while Nike, his companion, crowns him and an eagle flies overhead. Below, an empty throne takes the place of the funeral pyre, and Paris, represented by a female figure in deep mourning, gazes upwards as she waves her hand in a last salute. A remarkable combination of classical and mediaeval forms is provided by the carving,[1] executed by G. Schadow in 1811, of the apotheosis of Queen Luise. Here, as the queen floats upwards from the globe of earth, she is attended by the Virtues, while the seven stars more commonly associated with the Virgin Mary shine over her head.

The idea that persons of especial sanctity were appropriately delivered by God from the shock of death and the humiliation of the tomb was congenial to Hebrew thought also. The temporary assumption of the prophet Ezekiel whom 'the spirit lifted up between the earth and the heaven'[2] for the purpose of revelation is probably not intended to be understood any more literally than St. Paul's description of himself as being 'caught up into Paradise',[3] but the mind of man has a natural tendency to objectify metaphorical language, and the story of Habakkuk being snatched away to Babylon 'by the hair of his head'[4] is told with naïve realism.

According to some accounts, both Abraham[5] and Isaiah[6] were, during their lifetime, whirled up to the heights of Heaven to enjoy supernatural revelations, and similar stories were told of Mohammed. But this was a case of transient experiences only; and the three classic[7] examples of translation at death were provided by Enoch, Elijah and Moses. According to the book of Genesis,[8] 'Enoch walked with (LXX. 'pleased') God: and he was not: for God took him', words which may

[1] At Paretz. Cf. O. Schmitt, *Reallexicon zur deutschen Kunstgeschichte, s.v.* Apotheose.

[2] Ezek. viii. 3.

[3] II Cor. xii. 4. The newly discovered Coptic *Ascension of Paul* (H. C. Puech in *Coptic Studies presented to W. E. Crum*), however, gives certain details of Paul's ascent and purports to explain the nature of the 'ineffable words'. Cf. Epiphanius, *adv. Haer.*: xxxviii. 2. 5.

[4] *Bel and the Dragon*, 36.

[5] *Apocalypse of Abraham*, ch. xv. ff. (ed. G. H. Box, S.P.C.K. 1919).

[6] *Ascension of Isaiah*, vi-xi, ed. R. H. Charles.

[7] But not the only ones. Others included Ezra (II Esdras viii. 19) and Baruch (*Apocalypse of Baruch*).

[8] v. 24. Cf. Livy's notice about Romulus (i. 16), 'he was not thenceforth on earth'.

185

mean no more than that Enoch died after a life that was, by patriarchal standards, a short one but marked by happy communion with God. This notice was, however, developed along two lines. The *Book of Enoch* consists largely of visions which it was Enoch's high privilege to receive and communicate to men, while the Slavonic *Apocalypse of Enoch* introduces the idea of bodily translation: 'The angels hasted and took Enoch and carried him into the highest heaven, where the Lord received him'. This is in accord with the predominant tradition of the Scriptures. In the Septuagint version of Genesis, it is stated that Enoch 'was not found, for God translated him', while the author of Ecclesiasticus is still more explicit: 'Enoch pleased the Lord and was translated': 'upon the earth was no man created like Enoch; for he was taken up from the earth'.[1] This belief is echoed in the Epistle to the Hebrews:[2] 'By faith Enoch was translated that he should not see death; and was not found, because God had translated him'.

Elijah is similarly favoured. According to the '*Apocalypse of Elijah*', he, too, enjoyed heavenly visions; while the Second Book of Kings[3] relates that Elijah was parted from Elisha by the appearance of a chariot and horses of fire, whereat 'Elijah went up by a whirlwind into heaven'. Later versions of the story make Elijah depart in the chariot of fire itself: he was 'taken up in a whirlwind of fire, and in a chariot of fiery horses'.[4] The exceptional nature of the reward is stressed in the First Book of Maccabees:[5] 'Elijah, for that he was exceeding zealous for the law, was taken up into heaven'.

Later traditions about Moses were no less dramatic, and were based on the Biblical statements, 'Moses went up into the mount and the cloud covered the mount'[6] and 'he was buried . . . in the land of Moab over against Bethpeor; but no man knoweth his sepulchre unto this day'.[7] The former passage was held to justify an apocalypse of visions accorded to Moses, the second forms the basis of the belief that he was taken up bodily into Heaven. Josephus cautiously observes: 'As he was saying goodbye to Eleazar and Joshua and conversing with them still, a cloud suddenly encompassed him and he disappeared in a ravine. The writer in the Holy Scriptures recorded that he died, for fear that, by reason of their very great affection for him, they might venture to say

---

[1] Ecclus. xliv. 16, xlix. 14.

[2] xi. 5. Josephus (*Ant.* i. 3. 4) says of Enoch: 'He lived for 365 years and then departed to Heaven; for which reason they have written up nothing about the end of his life'.

[3] ii. 11.

[4] Ecclus. xlviii. 9. Christian tradition identified Enoch and Elijah with the 'two witnesses' of Rev. xi who 'ascended up to heaven in a cloud'.

[5] ii. 58.   [6] Exod. xxiv. 15.   [7] Deut. xxxiv. 6.

186

that he had departed to heaven.'[1] The first-century *Assumption of Moses*[2] appears to have been far more colourful and definite, though, the text being defective, the details of the narrative have to be gathered from scattered references in the Epistle of Jude,[3] Clement of Alexandria[4] and Origen.[5] The picture that may be drawn from these sources is as follows: Michael receives the commission to bury Moses, but is opposed in this task by Satan who claims the body on the ground that he is the lord of matter. This claim Michael rebuts, with the reply that God created the world and is therefore lord of matter, and he adds the countercharge that it was Satan who malevolently inspired the serpent to tempt Adam and Eve. Opposition being thus overcome, the departure of Moses follows, and Joshua and Caleb observe its twofold aspect. Moses 'living in the spirit' is raised up to Heaven, while Moses 'dead in the body' is buried secretly in the recesses of the mountains.

The influence of such narratives in forming the legend of the Assumption is not hard to trace, and the interpretation of the Falling-asleep of the Virgin in terms of the Falling-asleep of Moses is particularly noticeable in a Syriac poem[6] written by Jacob of Serug, at the end of the fifth century, for a monophysite council assembled at Nisibis. According to this account, a veil of bright cloud descended upon the Mount of Olives, and the Virgin's death occurred in the presence of Christ, his angels and a gathering of souls of Old Testament worthies. Christ thereupon carried the body of his mother to the mountain-top, and the author notes that the burial of Mary on the summit of a mountain of Galilee (identified with the Mount of Olives) resembles that of Moses, in that it was carried out by God. The body is placed by St. John in the tomb, while the soul is borne heavenwards by the hierarchy of angels amidst the jubilations of nature. For Jacob of Serug, the location of the grave of Mary, like that of Moses, was unknown. Even though the monophysite school of thought, to which he belonged, was inclined to press the veneration due to Mary, the general picture as presented by Jacob of Serug is that Mary's body is committed to the silence of the grave while her soul is taken up to Heaven to enjoy fellowship with her son. That this Palestinian form of the story did not entirely yield to the Transitus-texts and the great name of Dionysius the Areopagite is shown by a liturgical poem of some antiquity incorporated by the emperor Theodore Lascaris II into the late Byzantine Great Office of

---

[1] *Antiquities*, iv. 326.　　[2] Ed. R. H. Charles (1897).
[3] Verse 9.　　[4] *Stromateis*, vi. 15. 132.
[5] *De Principiis*, iii. 2. 1. *Hom. in Iosuam*, ii. 1. Charles notes other patristic references, *op. cit.* pp. 108-110.　　[6] Baumstark in *Oriens Christianus*, iv.

intercession addressed to the most-holy Mother of God.[1] In this poem the Virgin entrusts her body to the Apostles for burial while 'her Son and God' is asked to receive her soul. So, in the pictures of the standard Byzantine type, it is with the soul of his mother rather than with her body that Christ concerns Himself.

On the mediaeval view of things the Virgin Mary was not the only New Testament figure who was honoured by a corporeal assumption into Heaven. Of John the Evangelist it had been said, 'If I will that he tarry till I come, what is that to thee?'[2] and this enigmatic saying formed the basis of a tradition that he was spared the humiliation of normal death. St. Ambrose, when commenting on the necessity for all who wish to enter Paradise to be tested by fire, notes concerning St. John: 'Some have had doubts regarding his death, but we can have no doubt that he passed through fire; for he is in Heaven and not separated from Christ'.[3] St. Augustine somewhat hesitantly mentions[4] the tradition that he slumbered beneath the earth, which moved with his breath; but more widely acceptable was the account, based on some versions of the second-century Acts of John[5] and illustrated in the windows of Chartres, Bourges and Rheims cathedrals, of the manner in which he arranged his own burial at Ephesus. Having received the command of Christ: 'Come, my friend to me; for it is time that thou came. Eat and be fed at my table with thy brethren',[6] he ordered a pit to be dug and, bidding his friends farewell, descended into it, whereupon a blinding light flashed all around and, when the people were able to see the grave again, they discovered that it contained nothing but manna. The *Golden Legend* continues: 'Some say and affirm that he died without pain of death, and that he was in that clearness borne into heaven body and soul, whereof God knoweth the certainty'.

A comparable tradition about Mary Magdalene arose later and was less widespread. The *Golden Legend*[7] is content to state that she was 'every day lift up by the hands of angels into the air' and that her dead body exhaled a sweet fragrance for seven days after her death. But, from the fifteenth century onwards, Mary Magdalene, borrowing from the legends of both the Virgin Mary and Mary of Egypt, is shown not infrequently as a naked woman, clad in little save her own hair, being raised up to heaven by a choir of angels. Early examples are provided by

---

[1] Ὡρολόγιον τὸ μέγα (Venice, 1884), p. 457.

Ἀπόστολοι, ἐκ περάτων συναθροισθέντες ἐνθάδε Γεθσημανῇ τῷ χωρίῳ, κηδεύσατέ μου τὸ σῶμα· καὶ σύ, Υἱὲ καὶ Θεέ μου, παράλαβέ μου τὸ πνεῦμα.

[2] John xxi. 22.   [3] *Expositio in Psalmum CXVIII*, P.L. xv. 1487.

[4] *In Ioannem*, 124. 2.   [5] M. R. James, *Apocryphal New Testament*, p. 270.

[6] *Golden Legend* (ed. F. S. Ellis), ii. 173.   [7] *Op. cit.* iv. 84.

188

a stone-screen at Thorn, by a wood-carving in the Marienkirche at Danzig,[1] and by a panel of Swiss glass[2] by Hans Fries, of Fribourg, now preserved in the Victoria and Albert Museum, while remarkable illustrations of the same theme are offered by Riemenschneider and Donatello.

It was, then, natural enough that men should be drawn on to foster legends like that of the Assumption. Apart from other impulses to such a course, there was the strong desire to let the imagination play around the well-loved figure of the Virgin and affectionately to fill in such details of her life as would make her stand out even more distinctly from the mists of time long past. On those engaged in this agreeable task no limits were imposed by any nice scrupulosity concerning historical facts, or, as Coulton put it, 'if the early Christians had known more about the Mother of the Lord, the mediaeval mind would have known far less'.[3]

The longing to entwine the figure of the Virgin with a garland of fantasy is illustrated by the Coptic discourses, probably of fourth- or fifth-century date, that pass under the names of Cyril of Jerusalem, the mythical Demetrius of Antioch, Epiphanius of Salamis and Cyril of Alexandria.[4] 'Cyril of Jerusalem' starts off in a mood of self-conscious rectitude: 'We are wholly unable to follow the fictitious statements which are found in the fabulous lives of the Virgin, and which resemble the writings of the Greek poets, who in their works on theology relate mere myths about their gods; neither will we invent lives of her in order to gratify her'. However, the impulse to tell a satisfying story about her is never very far away, and 'Cyril' declares: 'There is no trouble whatsoever in discussing the queen, who became the mother of the King, and he who listeneth is not wearied by her history. It is like unto one who goeth to draw water from a spring; as soon as he stretcheth forth his hand to draw therefrom, the spring sendeth water in great abundance. And this is my own case when I begin to describe the life of the Virgin, for the fountain of my speech bubbleth up abundantly.'[5] 'Cyril's' is the kind of world wherein lack of miracles implies lack of any exceptional holiness, where, for instance, as the Holy Family go down into Egypt, 'the Child rode upon the light cloud that transporteth those who are without sin. And the mountains and the rocks levelled

[1] Künstle, *Ikonographie der christlichen Kunst*, ii. 432. Cf. Braun, *Tracht und Attribute der Heiligen*, p. 498, where an illustration is given of a carved figure at Tiefenbronn, dated 1525.

[2] About A.D. 1500. B. Rackham, *A Guide to the Collections of Stained Glass*, pl. 53.

[3] Coulton, *Five Centuries of Religion*, I, p. 155.

[4] E. A. Wallis Budge, *Miscellaneous Coptic Texts*, pp. 626 ff.

[5] Budge, *op. cit.* p. 642.

189

themselves before them, and smooth roads whereon they could walk easily made themselves ready for their feet, and they crossed rivers and streams without the help of ship or sailor.' So also with the life of the Virgin: 'She was in the Temple before the gift of the Lord was given unto her, and there was no limit to her beauty, and the Temple was wont to be filled with angels because of her sweet fragrance, and they used to come to visit her for the sake of her conversation'. With this atmosphere of miracle and devotion the remarkable stories which 'Cyril' adds concerning the Virgin's birth on the one hand and her death and assumption on the other are in complete harmony.

Some of the details given in these encomiums of the Virgin are no more than reflective word-painting, as the writer sets before his eyes the scene at Bethlehem or Nazareth. Thus Cyril of Alexandria describes in an attractive manner how 'Mary used to take hold of Jesus' hand and lead Him along the roads, saying "My sweet Son, walk a little way", in the same manner as all other babes are taught to walk. And He, Jesus, the very God, followed after her untroubled, as He clung to her with his little fingers. He stopped from time to time and hung on the skirts of Mary his mother,—He upon whom the whole universe hangs.' But 'Demetrius' and Epiphanius carry their interest in the Virgin's ancestry to the point of concocting spurious genealogical lore, and picturesque marvels are never far away: 'And Mary sat in Joseph's house for three years, and his sons ministered unto her, and the angels were round about her at all times, for they earnestly desired to remain with her because of her purity, and they were in the form of doves or some other kind of holy bird. They flew about her in the place where she used to sit working at her handicraft, and they would alight upon the window of her room, and they longed to hear her holy voice, which was sweet and pretty and holy.'

This type of imaginative novel-writing not seldom took the specialized form of apocalypse, perhaps the most influential of these compositions, though its fourth-century date makes it a fairly late one, being the *Apocalypse of Paul*. Condemned by a decree of Pope Gelasius and viewed askance by the established writers of orthodoxy, its popularity was nevertheless widespread and persistent, and it is echoed even by Dante.[1] The author, who draws freely on the much earlier *Apocalypse of Peter*, tells with considerable gusto of the various punishments which, in St. Paul's sight, were inflicted on the malefactors in Hell. Those who were jealous for the Virgin's honour felt impelled to include her also in the small and distinguished circle of those who had been allowed to wit-

[1] *Inferno*, ii. 28, where there is an allusion to the visit to Hell paid by the 'chosen vessel'.

190

84

ness the torments of the damned; so the *Apocalypse of Paul* was rewritten around the figure of the Virgin, and Mary, no less than certain chosen Apostles, views the varied tribulation of those whose 'worm dieth not' in the 'place of gnashing of teeth'.[1] Still more certainly was it due to Mary's pre-eminent holiness that she should be included with Enoch and Elijah and such other of the patriarchs as had been by God's especial favour taken, body and soul, into Heaven without having to wait for the general Resurrection. Of Moses it was related, by the beginning of the Christian era, that no place upon earth was fit to receive his body. 'And now,' says Joshua, 'what place shall receive thee? Or what shall be the sign that marks thy sepulchre? Or who will dare to move thy body thence as that of a mere man from place to place? For all men when they die have according to their age their sepulchres upon earth; but thy sepulchre is from the rising to the setting sun, and from the south to the confines of the north: all the world is thy sepulchre.'[2] In a similar spirit, but with greater exuberance, Christian writers from the eighth century onwards wrote of the exceptional honours rightly accorded to the 'Queen and lady of all'. Thus Theodore of Studium calls on all the world to celebrate with joy the 'funeral and translation of Mary mother of God. For she passes from this earth and approaches the heavenly mountains, the true mount Zion where it has pleased God to dwell.'[3] After relating the story of the Assumption in terms of the Transitus-texts, Theodore goes on to ask: 'Who ever saw such a translation as that of which the mother of my Lord was found worthy? And rightly so. For no one has ever ranked higher: she is greater than all.' The emperor Leo VI presses the point that bodily incorruption is to be expected as a part of the Virgin's high privilege: 'Those hands, whereby everything is held together, receive your blameless soul, and your pure, spotless body was translated to be in the realms of complete purity. Because thou didst bear God clothed in flesh, thou art borne by the hands of God now that thou hast put off the flesh.'[4] About the same time as Leo's oration, the preacher of a Latin sermon on the Assumption of the Blessed Virgin Mary spoke to similar effect: 'I cannot imagine

---

[1] The (Ethiopic) *Apocalypse of the Virgin*. M. R. James, *op. cit.* 563.

[2] R. H. Charles, *op. cit.* p. 45. This extract is from the writing that usually goes under the name of *Assumption of Moses* but is, in fact, a cognate work, the *Testament of Moses*, with which the *Assumption of Moses* was combined at an early date.

[3] P.G. xcix. 720. Theodore lived A.D. 759–826.

[4] P.G. cvii. 162. χειρῶν μὲν ἐκείνων, αἷς πάντα συνέχεται, τὴν πανάμωμον δεχομένων ψυχήν· τοῦ δὲ καθαροῦ καὶ ἀσπίλου σώματος ἐν καθαρωτάτοις μεθισταμένου χωρίοις. ὅτι ἐβάστασας Θεὸν σάρκα ἠμφιεσμένον, βαστάζῃ Θεοῦ παλάμαις ἀπαμφιασαμένη τὴν σάρκα. Leo VI reigned A.D. 886–912.

191

that most holy body, from which Christ took flesh thus uniting divine with human nature, delivered over as a prey to worms, as also I shrink from saying that it is subject to the common lot of corruption and dust'.[1] By this time, use was being made of new arguments, based not on history or pretended history but on what was deemed appropriate, a principle which was later summed up in the Scholastic maxim '*potuit*; *decuit*; *ergo fecit*'—God has the power, the action was fitting; therefore He must have done it.[2] But reflection on the fallibility of human knowledge and perceptions might well cause the theologian to hesitate before pronouncing what God must have done in an exceptional and mysterious case. And the historian will perhaps display his reverence rather by presenting a record, often imperfect and incomplete, of events that he has collected and arranged to the best of his ability than by allowing fantasy, however pious, to masquerade as fact and thus to weaken the firm foundation of truth.

[1] *P.L.* xl. 1146.

[2] The view that the unique position of the Virgin demands unique honour was stated thus by Cardinal Newman (*Discourses to Mixed Congregations*, xviii.): 'It was becoming that she should be taken up into heaven and not lie in the grave until Christ's second coming, who had passed a life of sanctity and miracle such as hers'. The theological arguments are clearly and concisely summarized by V. Bennett and R. Winch, *The Assumption of Our Lady and Catholic Theology* (S.P.C.K., 1950), where the historical evidence also is reviewed.

192

BLANDINA AND PERPETUA:
TWO EARLY CHRISTIAN HEROINES

BY

WILLIAM H. C. FREND

(Glasgow) (in absentia)

Twenty five years separate the martyrdom of Blandina at Lyon
and Perpetua in the amphitheatre at Carthage, probably on 7 March
203.   To most people living at the time, the actions of both in
defying the authorities and placing themselves in the situation
where torture and condemnation to the beasts awaited them, were
indefensible folly.   At Lyon the crowds, at times prepared to show
a modicum of mercy were finally enraged beyond control by
Blandina's persistence and contempt for her pagan opponents,
while at Carthage Perpetua, having once been respited and allowed
through the Gate of Life from the amphitheatre, was in the end
returned for public execution on the demand of the spectators.
The execration felt by the latter for those who appeared to have
insulted the gods was intense.   The best that people at Lyon could
say for Blandina and her companions was the incredulous, "Where
is their God, and what good was their religion to them, which they
preferred even to their lives?"[1].   Most were happy to see their
corpses dismembered so that their claim to rise from the dead
would be frustrated.   They were relieved that the gods had
triumphed[2].   In Carthage, the confessors were regarded as
perpetrators of black magic who would be able to use their arts to
escape justice[3].   Fear and hatred were the dominant emotions of
the crowds whether at Lyon or Carthage at this time.

---

1. EUSEBIUS, *Hist. Eccl.* V.1.60.   Both *Acta* have been edited and translated into
English by H. Musurillo, *Acts of the Christian Martyrs* (Oxford Early Christian Texts,
ed. H. Chadwick, Oxford 1972).
2. EUSEBIUS, *H.E.*, V.1.63.
3. *Passio Perpetuae* 16.2.

Few doubted that the gods both existed and would be vindicated. The last quarter of the second century AD saw the high watermark in the growth and prosperity of the Greco-Roman cities around the Mediterranean. Population was visibly increasing[1]. There was relative security, an element of social mobility, lip-service at least to marital fidelity[2] and above all, confidence in the justice and permanence of the system represented by the emperor and his officials[3]. The Antonines and their Severan successors had some right to proclaim to their subjects the Happiness of the Times under the providential care of the emperor.

Yet, there was opposition. In Palestine and Syria many Jews still hoped for the coming of the messiah[4], and their risings under Marcus Aurelius[5] and Severus[6] demonstrated their continuing discontent. They were the only group actually to take up arms against the empire, but the Cynics maintained a barrage of criticism against authority, wealth and power, and the Christians, sometimes identified with the Cynics[7], added their own rejection of the religion of Rome and the Roman way of life.

Of these three opposition groups, some observers believed the Christians were potentially the most dangerous. Celsus, circa 178, an educated provincial probably resident in Syria or Palestine, was prepared to concede the right of the Jews to their religion on the grounds of its antiquity[8], but was not prepared to see the Christians tolerated similarly. To him, they were renegades and apostates from Judaism, whose differences with the Jews were so minimal as to amount to no more "than a fight about the shadow of an ass"[9]. They shared the same wrong-headed ideas of God and of man, but they were also subversive attempting all the time to

---

1. TERTULLIAN, *De Anima* 30.   See FREND, *The Donatist Church*, Oxf 1971, p. 42-3.

2. For instance, an inscription from Zriba near Segermes (publ. in *Bull-Arch du Comité* of 1934, p. 322) "... Furio Donato coniux/[in]comparabili benigno adfectu ac mente bona..."

3. Note, for instance, the confident appeal by the *coloni* on the Imperial estate around Henchir Mettich to the emperor Commodus in 183, *CIL* VIII 10570 ("ut beneficio maiestatis tuae rustici tui vernulae et alumni saltum tuorum non ultra a conductoribus agrorum fiscalium in quiete manere...").

4. Celsus, cited by Origen, *Contra Celsum* II.29 (ed. and tr, H. Chadwick, Cambridge 1953).

5. AMMIANUS MARCELLINUS, *Historia* XXII.5.5, "malodorous and rebellious Jews".

6. AELIUS SPARTIANUS, *Severus* 16.7, "Iudaicum triumphum", *Scriptores Hist. Aug.*, ed. Hohl, I, p. 149.

7. See FREND, *Martyrdom and Persecution in the Early Church* (Blackwell, Oxford, 1965), p. 273-6.

8. *Contra Celsum*, V.41.

9. *Ibid.* III.1.

influence the "ignorant and uneducated", and destroy the traditional authority of the pater-familias over his dependants.   It
was in private houses that "they get hold of children in private
and some stupid women with them, and they let out some astounding statements, as for example, that they must not pay any
attention to their father or school teacher but must obey them"[1].
Moreover, what they taught must be accepted without argument.

This is an important passage.   It certainly relates to what may
have happened in Vibia Perpetua's household, and it may concern
Blandina also.   We learn that her mistress (but not her master)
was a Christian and herself a confessor, who feared simply that her
favourite slave, small and delicate in physique as she was, would not
stand up to the ordeals that she might have to face[2].

Of the heroism and dedication of both martyrs there can be no
question.   At Lyon Blandina emerges as the leader and inspiration of the confessors after the death of Bishop Pothinus.   The
survivor of the massacre who wrote the account of events to the
Churches of Asia and Phrygia tells how popular hatred fastened on
her, of her first encounter in the amphitheatre after torture "so
that her entire body was broken and torn"[3].   She was hung on a
post and exposed to the beasts, but she "seemed to hang in the
form of a cross", and none of the beasts would touch her.   There,
she inspired her fellow confessors and won the crown of immortality
for herself[4].   From then on the authorities realized that she was
the leader.   She was kept back until the final day of the games,
and with a youth named Ponticus, faced the full fury of the crowd.
On this occasion also she inspired others "like a noble mother
encouraging her children" and finally went triumphantly to her
death.   Even those who wished her end conceded "that no woman
had suffered so much in their experience"[5].

Vibia Perpetua showed exactly the same qualities.   A member
of the urban upper middle classes, whose family may have held an
estate near Carthage[6] as well as property at Thuburbo some 40 miles

---

1. *Ibid.* III.55.
2. Eusebius, *H.E.*, V.1.18.
3. *Ibid.*, 1, 16 and 18.
4. *Ibid.*, 1.41-2.
5. *Ibid.*, 1.56.
6. See H. Leclercq's discussion of A. L. Delattre's discoveries in the Basilica
Majorum at Carthage (*Dict. d'Arch. chrétienne et de Liturgie (= DACL)*, IV.1, art
"Carthage", col. 2248).   While much must remain speculation, the names "Vibia"
and "Perpetua" occur on early levels on the site.   The inscriptions, left in a disordered
state after the excavation, are now being researched and catalogued by Mme Liliane
Ennabli for the "Institut national d'Archéologie et d'Art de Tunisie".

away, she was also the acknowledged leader of the group of Christians arrested probably early in 203. She knew Greek and much of the material (Chs 3-14) comes from the diary which she kept in prison. This must be an authentic narrative. This is not only a matter of the direct and conversational style suggestive of what an educated Roman-African would write. One can surely catch the ring of actuality in her remark after her arrest and baptism. "A few days later we were lodged in the prison; and I was terrified, as I had never before been in such a dark hole. What an awful time it was. With the crowd the heat was terrible and there was the extortion of the soldiers, and to crown all, I was tortured with worry for my baby there"[1]. It is surely the experience of the stark reality of prison now that the heroics before the procurator and her father were past. She was happy to be transferred to a more salubrious part of the dungeon. She discusses reasonably about the future of her baby with her (pagan?) brother and her mother. She describes her hesitations whether to give it up or not, and perhaps not until she decides to do so does she finally steel herself to become a martyr. Her diary shows a glimpse of her struggle between her duty to her infant and her duty to her faith[2]. There is little doubt that the barest acknowledgment the emperor's genius would have been greeted with sighs of relief. In being required to sacrifice "for the welfare of the emperors" she was asked to do no more than Jews had done willingly in the years before the revolt of 66. Christians were more extreme in their attitude, and this could fairly enough be regarded as a treasonable outlook by the procurator before whom she appeared[3]. To "blaspheme the times and the emperors and speak ill of the idols" was costing a Christian at Corinth her life at the same time[4].

But if Perpetua was embarrased at first, she proceeded to show herself completely divorced from her family and utterly ready for death. "Perpetua", the continuator of the narrative and editor of her diary wrote, "went along (to the amphitheatre) with shining countenance and calm step as the beloved of God, as a wife of Christ, overthrowing the (hostile) stares of all by her intense

1. *Passio Perpetuae*, 3.6.
2. For example *ibid*. 3.6 and 3.8, and Ch 6.8.
3. By the third century treason ("maiestas") as well as belonging to an illegal association had become grounds for prosecuting Christians. See, for instance, TERTULLIAN, *Apol.* X.1, "You Christians do not worship the gods; you do not sacrifice for the emperors" and the Acta Proconsularia relating to Cyprian's condemnation in 258 (ed W. HARTEL, *CSEL* III.3, Vienna, 1871, p. CXII-CXIII).
4. Hippolytus (d 235) cited in Palladius *Lausiac History* 65 (ed W. H. Lowther Clarke, London, 1919, p. 171-2), and see Frend, *Martyrdom and Persecution*, p. 323.

gaze"[1]. She was by now a fanatic, and even after being tossed by a maddened cow found strength to address her other brother (a catechumen as she had been) and catechumens. "You must all stand firm in the faith and love one another, and do not be weakened by what we have gone through"[2]. These could be the words of a modern extremist leader. They are almost incredible in the mouth of a young woman amid the peace and apparent prosperity of the Severan age.

What lay behind this attitude? The first thing that strikes the reader of both *Acta Martyrum* is the strength of conviction that the Last Times were at hand. At Lyon, the Christians regarded the sudden persecution as "the Adversary swooping down with full force", in this way anticipating his final coming which "is sure to come"[3]. He is directly opposed by the Spirit working within the confessors, inspiring their example to would-be backsliders, and their bearing in the arena. The confessors themselves "boil with the Spirit"[4] and "overwhelm the Adversary", and they are rewarded with insensitivity to pain and in Blandina's case, also "converse with the Lord"[5]. What at Q'mran[6] is portrayed as the struggle between the two spirits in each human being was translated by the Christians to the cosmological plane of a combat between the Adversary and his allies, the pagans, informers, backsliders, etc. and the Spirit, represented by the Confessors and none more than Blandina.

In the *Passio Perpetuae* the eschatological theme is even more prominent. In his introduction, the editor reminds his readers with reference to Joel 2[7] that these were the last times, that the Spirit would be poured out on all flesh, that their sons and daughters would prophecy and that these extraordinary graces had been promised for the last stage of time[7]. Perpetua like Blandina believes that she is engaged in a personal combat with the Devil (in the guise of an Egyptian)[8]. There is, however, a more developed theology of the Spirit than is discernible in the Acta of

---

1. *Passio*, 18.2.
2. *Ibid.*, 20.10.
3. Eusebius, *H.E.*, V.1.5.
4. *Ibid.*, 1.9 (Vettius Epagathus of whom the writer ways "Called the Christian's advocate he possessed the Advocate within him, the Spirit that filled Zacharias...").
5. *Ibid.*, 19 and 56.
6. On the rival spirits striving to dominate the world and each individual featuring among the beliefs of the sectaries, see 1Q S3 : 17-23. Cited from F. M. Cross. *The Ancient Library of Q'mran*, London, 1957, p. 156-158.
7. *Passio*, 1.3-5.
8. *Ibid.*, 10.14.

the Lyon martyrs.   The Spirit urges the confessors to martyrdom.
Water-baptism precedes the baptism of blood[1].   Where converse
with Christ *(Homilia)* is merely mentioned with reference to
Blandina, this is transformed in the *Passio Perpetuae* into a vivid
series of visions that the heroine could expect as a matter of course.
"For I knew", she writes, "I could speak with the Lord whose
blessings I had come to experience.   And so I said (addressing her
catechumen brother), I will tell you to-morrow, and this is the vision
that I had"[2].   There follows the vision of the ladder reaching to
heaven guarded by a dragon and her own entry into Paradise.
At the end, the confessors tell the mocking bystanders to remember
their faces so that "they would recognize us on the day"[3].   In the
amphitheatre itself, the male confessors threatened the procurator
Hilarianus.   "You (have condemned) us; but God (will condemn)
you"[4].   The sentiments and ideals are those reflected in Tertullian's panorama of the Day of Judgment in *De Spectaculis* 30.

With conviction that Judgment was approaching, is associated
an interpretation of Christianity that owed little to the synoptic
Gospels and Epistles.   It appears to be based on the Pentateuch
and late-Jewish and Jewish-Christian writings.   Links with the
Montanists of Carthage also must have been close.   Perpetua was
a catechumen at the time of her arrest, and her visions and those
of her companions, provide some insight into how they had been
instructed.   Perpetua's vision of the ladder must surely be a
reminiscence of Jacob's ladder *(Gen* 28[12]) while the Egyptian
wrestler against whom she is pitted (Ch. 10) could be a "Pharaoh"
figure.   The rest of her material would seem to be derived from
late-Jewish and New Testament apocalyptic.   Paradise is imagined as a park in terms of the Book of Enoch (32.3) and perhaps the
Apocalypse of Peter.   While the angels chanting endlessly, "Holy,
holy, holy" come from Rev 4[8], the white garments of the righteous
and the fragrance of Paradise may be from the *Apocalypse of
Peter* describing how the perfume (of the flowers and fruits of
Paradise) "was so great that it was borne thence even to us"[5].
The "aged man with youthful face and white hair" *(Passio* 12.3)
is surely the Ancient of Days of Dan 7[9], and the dragon could be
the Leviathan of Hermes' Vision *(Vis* IV).   In the *Passio* the
"leaders" and "righteous men in Paradise" (Rev 20) are martyrs,

1. *Ibid.*, 3.5.
2. *Ibid.*, 4.2.
3. *Ibid.*, 17.2.
4. *Ibid.*, 18.8.
5. *Apoc of Peter*, 16 (ed M. R. James, Oxford, 1926).   In Saturus' vision *(Passio*
11-13), the ideas seem very close to this Apocalypse.

the true leaders of the Church.   Clergy (unless they are martyrs) are kept outside (*Passio* 13)[1].   The curious detail in Perpetua's dream of her fight with the Egyptian that "she became male", might be Pythagorean,[2] but could also be a reminiscence from the Logion of the *Gospel of Thomas* that refers to "the inside becoming the outside" and the ending of all sexual differences at the end of the world (*Logion* 23), while in a second *Logion* (*Logion* 112), Jesus states, "for every woman who makes herself a man shall enter the Kingdom of Heaven".   This is precisely what Perpetua dreamt had happened to her before her combat with the Devil in the form of an Egyptian.   It was the climax of *Thomas'* eschatology.

At Lyon, there is also late-Jewish inspiration but of a different sort.   The survivors' record of the events must have the story of the heroic Maccabaean mother and her sons defying Antiochus IV, as he wrote about Blandina[3].   She is "the noble mother", who like her Maccabaean predecessor, "encouraged her children, sent them forth triumphant to the King and then, duplicating in her own body all her children's sufferings, she hastened to rejoin them"[4]. As the mother of the Maccabees, she dies last encouraging the youngest of the confessors to be steadfast.   One can point to other resemblances to II Maccabees which the author may have had in mind, when he wrote of Vettius Epagathus who came forward to plead for the Christians after their arrest.   He may be perhaps compared with Razis of II *Macc* 14[37] the one "advocate of the Christians", the other "the father of the Jews"[5], both ready to give their lives in defiance of an idolatrous tyrant.   The restoration to the confessors of their vigour after torture, their resistance to suffering, insensibility to pain, the defeat of the desperate strength of the executioners are all features in the story that point to the Maccabees as recorded in II and IV *Macc* as sources of their ready acceptance of martyrdom[6].

In both *Acta*, therefore, one may point to a late-Jewish legacy, and it is within that framework that the question of Montanist

---

1. *Passio*, 13: See also, TERTULLIAN, *De Anima* 55.

2. Thus, Urbanilla on the third century sepulchral mosaic from Lambiridi in Numidia, see J. CARCOPINO, *Aspects mystiques de la Rome paienne*, Paris, 1941, pp. 281-4. The texts from the *Gospel of Thomas* are taken from the Grant and Freedman ed, Fontana, London 1960.

3. See FREND, *Martyrdom and Persecution*, pp. 19-20 (with references on p. 29).

4. EUSEBIUS, *H.E.*, V.1.55.   Compare *II Macc* 7[41-3].

5. *Ibid.*, 1.10.   Compare II *Macc* 14[37].

6. See the discussion by O. PERLER, *Das vierte Makkabaerbuch, Ignatius von Antiochien und die ältesten Martyrerberichte*, *Rivista di archeologia cristiana* 25, 1949, 47-72.

influence should be viewed[1].   While this is undeniable in the
Passio Perpetuae, it would seem more relevant to suggest that
Montanism itself, and the *Acta Martyrum* from Lyon and Carthage
all point to a movement within Christianity in the last quarter of
the second century based on a profound conviction of the approaching end of the existing age and the glorification of the role of the
confessor and martyr as vehicles of the Holy Spirit in bringing
that about.   The Roman authorities were cast in the role of the
Seleucid kings, as servants of the Devil and oppressive idolators.

Within this general framework there are, however, significant
differences between the two *Acta* and their heroines.   At Lyon,
the confessors are defiant to the end and reject in the amphitheatre charges of cannibalism against them[2], but they die without
visions of Paradise and hopes of vengeance.   The emphasis
throughout lies on positive imitation of Christ, the one true
perfected martyr, and in his and the protomartyr Stephen's
example of loving and forgiving their enemies[3].   Among themselves, it is said "peace they had always loved and it was peace they
commended to us for ever"[4].   They "bound none and loosed all"[5],
while it is assumed that they possessed these powers as confessors.
Apostates only, they regarded as "sons of perdition"[6].   Theirs
was certainly a religion of protest, for they had little use for the
"wild and barbarous people" among whom they lived[7].   They felt
superior to them, but they were not active opponents, asking only
to be allowed to worship God in truth.   Blandina suffers, but does
not threaten her torturers with punishment hereafter.   Her
reward is her opportunity of complete imitation of Christ and
identification with His own perfect martyrdom.

Perpetua shows us a different side of this same sectarian
Christianity.   Hers is a situation more like that described by
Celsus, of profound rejection of the values of the pagan and of her
family's religious tradition.   What led to the family crisis we shall
never know, but there is a real poignancy in her father's continuous
efforts to save her from humiliating death as a result of which the
family itself would hardly recover.   "Give up your pride.   You

---

1. On Montanism in these *Acta*, see the old but excellent discussion in
P. DE LABRIOLLE, *La Crise Montaniste*, Paris, 1913, p. 220 ff, and J. Armitage
ROBINSON, The Passion of St Perpetua, in *Cambridge Texts and Studies*, 1, 1891,
pp. 50-2.
2. EUSEBIUS, *H.E.*, V.1.52.
3. *Ibid.*, 2.5.
4. *Ibid.*, 2.7.
5. *Ibid.*, 2.5.
6. *Ibid.*, 1.48.
7. *Ibid.*, 1.57.

will destroy us all. None of us will be able to speak freely again if anything happens to you"[1]. Perpetua was obviously an adored only daughter who grew up into a spoilt and wilful young woman, but in her case, her frustrations drove her into fanatical adherence to an apocalyptic form of Christianity and hostility to the society in which she had been reared. Though she is fighting the powers of Satan rather than imperial Rome, there is a contempt and sarcasm for the empire and its rulers in her remark to the military tribune. "Why can't you allow us to refresh ourselves at all? We are the most distinguished criminals (noxiis nobilissimis). We are Caesar's and we are due to fight on his very birthday. Would it not be to your credit if we were produced on the day in a fatter condition (pinguiores)[2]?" She shared with her confessor, Saturus, open rejection of the "golden age" of the Severi.

Her story and that of Blandina tell us much about the spirit of Christianity in the last quarter of the second century. They bear out Celsus' attack on the Christians as subversives who deserved the persecutions that befell them. They show, too, a Christianity still drawing much of its inspiration from late-Jewish apocalyptic and Maccabaean defiance of the idolatrous rulers of this world. It is a Christianity whose adherents awaited eagerly the Judgment and the end of the Age. At the same time, for reasons which are still obscure this outlook reflected a deep dissatisfaction with the apparent prosperity of the period. The new religion was not confined to slaves and freedmen. Those who joined found themselves in a close-knit society without social or sex distinction. Blandina and her mistress are both confessors and die in the same persecution. Perpetua and her slave Felicitas also perish together. Christianity provided scope for the human need of achievement and daring for a cause. In the equality practised by the Christians many women found their chance of self-fulfilment. Isis-worship could sustain the mother but not the intellectual and would-be leader. Flora, the correspondent of the Gnostic, Ptolemaeus, probing into the true worth of the Old Testament, Marcellina a Gnostic leader at Rome, Blandina and Perpetua all found scope for leadership and a cause to fight for, which pagan society could not provide. Amid the light and shade of second century Christianity, its mixture of idealism, search for truth, self delusion and angry protest, Blandina and Perpetua stand out as examples of the spirit that resulted in the ultimate triumph of the faith.

1. *Passio*, 3.3, 5.1-4, 6.5.
2. *Ibid.*, 16.3.

95

Résumé

Blandine et Perpétue : deux héroïnes chrétiennes des premiers siècles

Le Christianisme fit partie de l'opposition culturelle et peut-être aussi politique à l'Empire romain des Antonins et des Sévères. Les deux martyres, Blandine et Perpétue appartiennent à cette opposition et montrent leur défiance aux autorités jusqu'au bout. Pourquoi? Quand on analyse les textes des deux *Acta Martyrum*, on trouve des perspectives semblables. Toutes les deux attendent ardemment les Derniers Jours. Toutes les deux pensaient combattre contre le Diable lui-même dans l'amphithéâtre. Toutes les deux appartiennent même de façon différente à la tendance montaniste de l'Église à la fin du IIe siècle. L'inspiration en chaque cas semble venir plutôt du judaïsme tardif et judéo-chrétien que de l'enseignement des Évangiles.

Mais il y a aussi des différences : l'histoire de Blandine est inspirée des livres des Macabées (II et IV) alors que l'histoire de Perpétue doit beaucoup aux textes apocalyptiques comme l'Apocalypse de Pierre. Blandine ne pense pas à la vengeance mais seulement à l'imitation la plus étroite de Jésus. Elle pense à ses compagnons surtout à la paix ; Perpétue est plus fanatique et s'insurge contre les autorités.

Le Christianisme de la fin du IIe siècle fit appel aux femmes de foi et vigoureuses. Isis était pour les mères, le Christianisme pour les « suffragettes ».

DISCUSSION DE LA COMMUNICATION DE M. FREND

M. Fishwick : « Je voudrais faire allusion à l'une des remarques faites par M. Frend. J'ai la traduction sous les yeux. Il dit que : « Il fait peu de doute que sa moindre reconnaissance du génie de l'empereur eût été accueillie avec des soupirs de soulagement ». Il parle ici de Blandine. Il me semble qu'évoquer la reconnaissance du génie de l'empereur est une erreur. Le génie de l'empereur, du moins tel que je le comprends moi-même, est d'ordinaire une statue montrant l'empereur en train de sacrifier, avec des cornes d'abondance, etc. S'il s'était agi d'une statue du génie de l'empereur, les choses auraient été moins difficiles pour une chrétienne, car après tout on devait retrouver plus tard ce génie dans l'idée chrétienne du droit divin de l'empereur, puis dans l'idée chrétienne de l'ange gardien. Mais Pline nous dit : *imaginem tuam simulacraque deorum*. Or *imaginem* est un terme qui s'applique à l'empereur en tant qu'être humain. Il est clair, d'après Pline, que l'image de l'empereur, en particulier son buste, et les simulacres des dieux sont du même ordre. Mais c'est l'empereur en tant qu'être humain qui reçoit les droits revenant aux dieux. Pour les Grecs, c'était je crois une idée acceptable, cette distinction imparfaite entre l'adoration d'une part et l'hommage d'autre part. Les Romains la trouvaient difficile ; ils l'appelaient *adulatio*. Mais pour les chrétiens, cela était complètement impossible, car on rendait ainsi à un homme ce qui était réservé seulement à un dieu. Je pense donc que l'erreur théologique revient entièrement aux chrétiens et que ce que nous devrions dire ici, ce n'est pas que le génie de l'empereur devait être reconnu, mais plutôt que c'est l'empereur en personne, représenté par son buste, à qui les chrétiens devaient verser des libations ou brûler quelques grains d'encens.

M. FREND *(per epistolam)* : D'abord je parlais bien sûr de Perpétue et non de Blandine, et c'est là que réside toute la différence. On aurait pu la placer simplement dans la catégorie des malfaiteurs, mais Perpétue appartenait à une famille assez importante de Carthage. Son père savait que, si elle s'obstinait et était condamnée à l'amphithéâtre, non seulement elle se trouverait déshonorée, mais toute sa famille le serait avec elle (en faisant frapper son père, le Procurateur avait rendu les choses bien claires). Dans ces circonstances, le problème technique de savoir si c'est ou non l'*imago* de l'empereur qu'elle refusait d'adorer, n'a guère de signification. J'ai choisi comme exemple cette forme d'adoration, car elle est formellement rejetée par Tertullien (Apol. 32, 2-3) ; mais ce que voulaient les autorités, et la famille en proie aux tourments, c'est que Perpétue fît quelque chose — peu importe quoi — pour montrer qu'elle ne se révoltait pas contre sa famille et l'autorité de Rome. Elle refusa la moindre concession, et son attitude se comprend peut-être vaguement si on la replace dans le contexte de la psychologie de la jeune génération instruite après guerre, en révolte contre les sociétés établies.

Acts of the Women Martyrs

FRANCINE CARDMAN*

The martyr's confession of faith, enacted through the body, is both the culmination of bodily existence and its end. The completion of the body's plunge into the waters of baptism, martyrdom is at once confirmation and contradiction of the "natural" range of human experience. In early Christian martyr accounts, both women and men willingly die in order to live everlastingly. But it is in the acts of the women martyrs that the complexity of this endeavor is most clearly manifest. There, the inherent ambiguity of martyrdom is dramatically displayed in women's bodies with a directness unmatched in the case of men. Analysis of the acts of the women martyrs and comparison with those of the men with whom they almost always appear will suggest the range of motivation and meaning as well as the significance of the differences in their experience of martyrdom.[1]

In martyr accounts from the second to the fourth centuries, the stories of women are usually told in conjunction with those of men, even when, as in the *Passion of Sts. Perpetua and Felicitas*, the account takes its name from the women. Only two accounts are solely about women. In the titles of the acts, women are infrequently named and are often subsumed among the "companions" of a particular martyr.[2] Regardless of

* *Editor's Note:* Francine Cardman is associate professor of historical theology at Weston School of Theology in Cambridge, Massachusetts.

[1] Works considered here are acts devoted solely to women, and those about both women and men. They are (followed by probable date of martyrdom and shortened title): *Acts of Justin and Companions* (c. 165; three recensions: *Justin* A, B, C); *Martyrs of Lyons and Vienne* (177; *Lyons*); *Acts of the Scillitan Martyrs* (180; *Scilli*); *Martyrdom of Sts. Carpus, Papylus, and Agathonice* (c. 180?; Greek and Latin recensions: *Carpus* A, B); *Passion of Sts. Perpetua and Felicitas* (202/3; *Perpetua*); *Martyrdom of Potamiaena and Basilides* (c. 205?; *Potamiaena*); *Martyrdom of Pionius the Presbyter and His Companions* (c. 250; *Pionius*); *Martyrdom of Agape, Irene, Chione, and Companions* (c. 304; *Agape*); *Martyrdom of St. Crispina* (304; *Crispina*); For convenience, the texts and translations are those of Herbert Musurillo, *Acts of the Christian Martyrs*, Oxford Early Christian Texts (Oxford: Clarendon, 1972). References are to chapter or section number of the work.

[2] Only the *Martyrdom of Agape, Irene and Chione* and the *Martyrdom of Crispina* are about women alone. In the *Passion of Sts. Perpetua and Felicitas*, several chapters are devoted to Saturus, though Perpetua dominates the narrative and Felicitas occupies a chapter. In the *Martyrdom of Potamiaena and Basilides*, it is the example of Potamiaena's death and her intercession for him that leads to Basilides' conversion and subsequent martyrdom. In the *Martyrdom of Pionius and Companions*, the former slave Sabina, who had escaped or was freed from her evil mistress, is martyred along with Pionius, with whom she lived.

how they are titled or whom they include, the acts of the martyrs do not allow direct access to the experience of those memorialized. Rather, the reader views their passion through the scrim of the authors' sensibilities—their perceptions of the martyrs and their estimate of their audience's expectations. Nevertheless, within these accounts the portrayal of women and men is noticeably different, and the most striking differences occur in the two narratives (the *Passion of Sts. Perpetua and Felicitas* and the *Martyrdom of Pionius*) most likely to have drawn on material provided by their protagonists. In assessing the significance of these differences and the degree to which they may reach back behind the redactors' vantage point to the martyrs' own experience, I will consider the following features of the narratives: (1) type of confession, (2) social relationships, (3) athletic and combat imagery, (4) physical and sexual abuse, (5) pregnancy and motherhood.

1. The simple confession, "I am a Christian," is uttered repeatedly by women and men alike. "My first and most distinctive name is that of a Christian," asserts one martyr, "but if you want my name in the world, it is Carpus."[3] Perpetua instructs her father that, just as a vase cannot be called by any other name than what it is, neither can she be "called anything other than what I am, a Christian."[4] The primary identity of both women and men is as Christians. Yet, in this new situation, old patterns persist.

For men, their worldly status often continues to carry weight with Roman officials, local notables, and even the crowd, a point recorded with some satisfaction by the authors. Thus Justin's influence as a teacher is a cause of concern to the prefect Rusticus, and numerous well-placed citizens, out of regard for Pionius' "character and righteousness," attempt to dissuade him from going to his death. When women receive such attention from the crowd or from officials, it is generally on account of their youth or their beauty or their responsibilities to their children.[5]

It is not surprising, therefore, that the prosecutors find it difficult to credit the women with the integrity of their own convictions. Perhaps hoping to undermine their determination, the interrogators pressed the women on their relationships to their teachers and presbyters. Thus, Charito is asked whether she was deceived by the words of Justin and other Christians; Agathonice, whether she would follow her teachers' decision not to sacrifice; Chione is questioned about who gave her these

---

[3]   *Carpus* A.3.
[4]   *Perpetua* 3.
[5]   *Justin* A.3-4, B.3-4, C.2-3; *Pionius* 5; *Carpus* B.6 (Agathonice); *Perpetua* 20; *Crispina* 3.

ideas and counseled her in such folly; and Irene is asked who advised her to keep the outlawed scriptures in her possession.[6]

When called upon to declare or deny their faith, the men are more prone to adorn their testimony with didactic or polemical speeches, while the women are given to formulaic confessions and occasional brief exchanges with their antagonists. Under interrogation, Sabina replies briefly and directly to the questions put to her; her companion Pionius, however, discourses at length on Christian doctrine in general and against the Jews in particular. Potamiaena's reply to her tormentors is reported only to have impressed them as contrary to their religion; whereas the soldier Basilides, subsequently converted through her prayer and example, is said to have persistently assured his questioners about his new religious convictions.[7] Even in the scant *Acts of the Scillitan Martyrs*, the men's responses are more extended than the women's. In the longer accounts of women's martyrdoms, Perpetua's confession is a succinct "Yes, I am [a Christian]." Blandina's is scarcely much longer: "I am a Christian; we do nothing to be ashamed of." Only Crispina engages in any sustained exchange with her judges, forcefully asserting her reasons for refusing to sacrifice.[8]

The obstinacy and impiety of the Christians arouse the ire of the Roman officials, who find the women's contumacy particularly aggravating. Sabina is reprimanded and threatened simply for smiling, although Pionius is permitted to berate his captors for exceeding their authority by trying to force the prisoners to sacrifice. "You are a stubborn and insolent woman," exclaims the proconsul Annulinus to Crispina; later he demands to know why he should "suffer this impious Christian woman any further." Similarly, the prefect Dulcitius taxes Irene with her foolish persistence, her unwillingness to keep the terror of death before her eyes, and her lack of submission.[9]

The discomfited Roman officials testify to the anomalies created by the situation of martyrdom. Typical patterns of male-female interaction persist in the differential treatment by both officials and onlookers of women and men under interrogation. Defiance of the conventions of female behavior is even more disturbing to the authorities than the Christians' refusal to submit to their directives. The greater range allowed to men's voices than to women's reflects an assumption about the propriety of public speech likely to have been shared by the prosecutors and the defendants, as well as by the authors of the acts.

---

[6] *Justin* C.3; *Carpus* B.6; *Agape* 4, 5.
[7] *Justin*, A.3, B.3, C.2; *Pionius* 5, 10 and 4, 13-14; *Potamiaena* 2, 5; *Scilli passim*.
[8] *Perpetua* 3; *Lyons* 19; *Crispina passim*.
[9] *Pionius* 7, 15-16; *Crispina* 1, 4; *Agape* 5, 6.

2. At the same time as the patterns of social and political interaction are being disturbed, the constraints of familial relationships are often dramatically disregarded, if not destroyed. Daughters oppose and humiliate their fathers; wives appear without their husbands; mothers abandon their children; offspring fear betrayal by their families; slaves denounce their owners as Christians, or, being Christians themselves, either elude their mistresses or accompany them to a martyr's death.[10] Poignantly demonstrating the disruptive effect Christianity could have on families, Perpetua's father begs her to take pity on her infant son, to have some regard for the reputation and fortune of the family, and to save herself. His plea is a prayer of supplication, addressed to Perpetua, whose hands he kisses. By her own admission, he regards her *iam non filiam . . . sed dominam:* "no longer a daughter but a mistress" (i.e., an adult woman), perhaps even a goddess.[11] But to no avail. Neither the authority of the father nor the claim of the male child can deter Perpetua from her confession. Similarly, Felicitas gladly gives up her prematurely born daughter, and Agathonice is unmoved by the crowd's appeal that she have pity on her child(ren).[12] Filial ties no longer bind the martyrs to their parents or to their own offspring.

The order of the household is further shaken as distinctions between female servants and their mistresses are blurred or overturned. Blandina's personal power and sheer physical endurance stand in sharp contrast to the fear and weakness of her mistress as they both await martyrdom. Perpetua and her slave Felicitas endure the wild beasts together and support each other through the Gates of Life. Sabina, a former (perhaps escaped?) slave sheltered by the presbyter Pionius, identifies herself by the pseudonym "Theodote" in order to avoid discovery by the mistress who had left her bound and exposed on a mountainside in hopes of turning her away from Christianity. Social, political, and familial relationships are thus profoundly disturbed. Conversion to Christianity, especially by women, begins the dismantling of the patriarchal household; impending martyrdom hastens its disintegration.

3. The further rending of the social fabric is vividly displayed in the martyrs' deaths, as the most intimate of bodily choices is exposed in the public spectacle of their suffering. To a public accustomed to the

---

[10] Daughters: *Perpetua* 3, 5, 6; wives: *Perpetua* 2, *Agape* 3 (Eutychia); mothers: *Perpetua* 6, *Perpetua* 15 (Felicitas), *Carpus* A.43-44, B.6 (Agathonice); offspring: *Agape* 5; slaves: *Lyons* 14, *Pionius* 9 (Sabina), *Perpetua* 1, 20 (Felicitas), *Lyons* 17-18, 55ff (Blandina).

[11] Jan den Boeft and Jan Bremmer, "Notiunculae Martyrologicae II," *Vigiliae Christianae* 36 (1982): 387–89, argue convincingly for the supplicatory prayer form and for a more forceful translation than Musurillo's lame "no longer a daughter but a woman."

[12] *Perpetua* 15; *Carpus* A.43, B.6.

physicality of the athletic contest or the brutality of gladiatorial combat, this practice is not particularly shocking in itself. But the introduction of women into this essentially male context is. To see Blandina or Perpetua as athletes engaged in mortal combat is strangely unsettling, not only for contemporary readers, but also for second- and third-century witnesses. Their physical endurance is astonishing to the crowd, a point of pride and perhaps uneasiness to the authors of the acts. Blandina's tormentors are defeated in their first attempts to kill her; when she finally gives herself over to death, even "the pagans themselves admitted that no woman had ever suffered so much in their experience."[13] Perpetua's youthful beauty and Felicitas' recent childbirth arouse the pity and horror of the spectators, as does Agathonice's beauty and her willingness to die.[14] The public violence of contest and combat is not the usual context of women's bodies. Already out of place in that world, women marytrs pass beyond its confines with a shattering of sensibilities.

4. The dissolution of the social body is mirrored in the destruction of the martyrs' own bodies. Death by beheading, being burned alive, run through with the sword, or tossed to the beasts is inflicted on both women and men. To Potamiaena belongs the distinction of being the first martyr known to have suffered the agonies of having boiling pitch slowly poured over different parts of her body. Unlike the men, many of the women martyrs are threatened with sexual innuendo or abuse during their interrogation, sentencing, or execution. The chastity of the women, much praised by the authors of the acts, is a point of extreme vulnerability before their persecutors. The women are attacked verbally by the crowd and by various officials. Charito is accused by the prefect of not being of good repute; Potamiaena suffers the insults and vulgar remarks of the spectators. The threat of sexual abuse is joined with the physical torment of the proceedings. Having directed Potamiaena's torture, a judge threatens to hand her over to the gladiators for physical, quite possibly sexual, assault.[15] Similarly, Sabina is threatened with prostitution: "You are going to suffer something you do not like. Women who refuse to sacrifice are put into a brothel." Although Sabina is presumably spared this fate (the account tells only of Pionius' death, not Sabina's or the others'), Irene is actually delivered naked to the brothel, where, through the grace of the Holy Spirit, none dared approach or even insult her. Later she is burned alive, as were her sisters before her.[16]

---

[13] *Lyons* 19, 56.

[14] *Perpetua* 20; *Carpus* A.45 (as she threw herself on the stake, witnesses lamented, "It is a terrible sentence . . . "), B.6 (the crowd grieved in mourning for her beauty).

[15] *Justin* C.3; *Potamiaena* 2.

[16] *Pionius* 7; *Agape* 5–7.

The physical beauty of the women heightens the awfulness of their deaths. Perpetua and Felicitas are at first sent naked into the arena, but even the crowd was horrified at this, so they were allowed to put on unbelted tunics. When her tunic is torn in the struggle with the mad heifer (chosen, the author notes, so that its sex might match the women's), Perpetua, "thinking more of her modesty than of her pain," rearranges her clothing so that her thighs are covered. Agathonice removes her clothes before being tied to the stake to be burned, and the crowd grieves for her beauty. Before her beheading, Crispina is threatened with having her head shaved, to shame her beauty. In a deliberate reversal of this theme, the writer of the letter of the churches of Lyons and Vienne describes Blandina as having proved that, through Christ, "the things that men think cheap, ugly and contemptuous are deemed worthy of glory before God."[17]

The body is adorned, rather than defiled, by suffering. This is true for men as well as for women, though there are far fewer direct references in the martyr accounts to men's bodies than to women's. Nevertheless, it is Pionius rather than any of the women who offers the outstanding example of the body's triumph through martyrdom. Having finally reached the amphitheatre, "he gladly removed his clothes as the prison-keeper stood by. Then, realizing the holiness and dignity of his own body, he was filled with great joy. . . ." His body is not destroyed but perfected by the fire, so that "those of us who were present saw his body like that of an athlete in full array at the height of his powers."[18] In the context of martyrdom, it may, in fact, be easier to affirm men's bodies than women's. More commonly associated with situations of public violence and death, not as easily defiled sexually, and untouched by the expectations of giving birth and mothering, the male body is a far less ambiguous symbol than the female.[19]

5. This symbolism may account for the ease with which the experience of mothering is ascribed to men as well as to women in the acts of the martyrs. Imprisoned and awaiting execution, both women and men labor to bring forth in themselves the strength and determination to proceed to the death that is their "birthday." Both serve as midwives and nurses to others on their way to this new life, even bringing those "stillborn" to rebirth. To the onlookers in Lyons, for instance, Alexander "was as one

---

[17] *Perpetua* 20; *Carpus* B.6; *Crispina* 3; *Lyons* 17.
[18] *Pionius* 21, 22.
[19] Although Blandina is hung "in the form of a cross" on a post as bait for wild animals, and her companions saw in her "him who was crucified for them," it is not her body which is being praised, but her endurance and fervent prayer. She signifies Christ in spite of, rather than because of her body: "Tiny, weak and insignificant as she was," she inspired the others, "for she had put on Christ" (*Lyons* 41, 42).

who was giving birth," and Blandina "like a noble mother encouraging her children."[20] For men, the translation of mothering into a spiritual reality is an expansion of their bodily experience, and a freeing from their dependence on women for giving life. For women, however, the detachment of motherhood from the female body is a constriction, even a contradiction, of their experience.

In both the maternal and the social body, the demands of mothering exert a pull away from martyrdom, and so must be denied in order for women to enact their final confession of faith. Their ability to overcome the limitations of their bodies and the restrictions of cultural assumptions about women's responsibilities for nurturing life creates a terrible irony as death displaces birth as the passageway to life. Yet in some accounts the bodies of pregnant or lactating women are made to conform almost effortlessly to the exigencies of martyrdom. Perpetua, initally anxious to nurse her baby and keep him with her in prison, is quickly reconciled to his removal by her father, who has tried to use him as a bargaining piece. Surprisingly, her breasts do not pain her after the sudden weaning.[21] Similarly, Felicitas' pregnancy threatens to delay her martyrdom, but the timely delivery of a daughter at the end of the eighth month offers deliverance to the mother as well.[22] Only when pregnancy, childbirth, and motherhood are wrenched from their bodily context and cease to be natural experiences do they become spiritual possibilities for women. For those who would mother the martyr in themselves or in others, the maternal body is perceived as a distinct liability, a natural impediment to the supernatural birthing process.

In their passage from death to life, women martyrs profoundly unsettled the social and familial relationships on which their world had depended for its coherence. Cultural sensibilities were shattered by the graphic demonstration of women's suffering and the toleration of public violence against their bodies. The ambiguities of female sexuality—its beauty, vulnerability, and reproductive capacity—were heightened as female bodily experience was both confirmed and contradicted in martyrdom. For women especially, the making of a martyr meant the unmaking of the body—her own, as well as her world's.

---

[20] *Lyons* 49, 55. Cf. 45: "The dead were restored to life through the living; the martyrs brought favor to those who bore no witness, and the virgin Mother experienced much joy in recovering alive those whom she had cast forth stillborn."

[21] *Perpetua* 3, 6.

[22] *Perpetua* 15.

The Role of Martyrdom and Persecution in Developing the Priestly Authority of Women in Early Christianity: A Case Study of Montanism

FREDERICK C. KLAWITER

Recently, attention has been given to understanding the status of woman in early Christianity. As expected, the light has been focused on Saint Paul, Saint Jerome and Saint Augustine, but so far, no one has examined one of the most fascinating movements of the second century—Montanism.[1] Perhaps this is because Tertullian is remembered as both a Montanist and a notorious misogynist. Given the boldness and originality of Tertullian's thought, however, it would be perilous to assume that Tertullian's view of women was identical to that originally held by the Montanists of Asia Minor. Indeed, as this study of Montanism in Asia Minor will show, it is highly probable that from the beginnings of Montanism, women were permitted to rise to ministerial status through their role as confessor-martyrs in the early Christian church.[2]

Montanism, or the New Prophecy (its self-appellation), appeared in the area of Phrygia, Asia Minor, sometime around A.D. 165–170. The central leaders were Montanus and two women, Priscilla and Maximilla. They claimed to have received the Holy Spirit, spoke in tongues, enthusiastically

*I am very grateful to Augustana College for the summer grant (1979) which enabled me to complete this article and to Mr. Robert Grant for his constructive criticism of my argument.

1. For Saint Paul, see Wayne Meeks, "The Image of Androgyne: Some Uses of a Symbol in Earliest Christianity," *History of Religions* 13 (February 1974): 165–208. For Saint Jerome and Saint Augustine, see Rosemary Radford Reuther, "Misogynism and Virginal Feminism in the Fathers of the Church," in *Religion and Sexism*, Rosemary Radford Reuther, ed. (New York, 1974), pp. 150–183.
2. An important source for Montanist oracles is Epiphanius, bishop of Cyprus about 375. His knowledge of Montanism was dependent on a lost work (*Syntagma*) by Hippolytus, a Roman presbyter who wrote against Montanists about 215, and on "hear-say" (δι'ἀκοῆς) of those who had contact with Asia Minor Montanists of the fourth century. See Epiphanius, *Panarion* 1.1.2; 48.15.1; 49.2.3-4 (hereafter cited as *Pan.*) and Pierre De Labriolle, *Les sources de l'histoire du Montanisme* (Paris, 1913), pp. xxxvii–xlvii. Epiphanius says that in Montanism there were female presbyters and bishops (*Pan.* 49.2.1-5). The point in question is whether this reflects fourth-century polity or the polity of original Montanism in Asia Minor. Part of the burden of this essay is to establish that such a polity does indeed go back to the origins of Montanism. All translations of Greek and Latin texts into English in this paper are mine.

Mr. Klawiter is associate professor of religion in Augustana College, Sioux Falls, South Dakota.

251

witnessed to their faith, proclaimed a message of repentance and joy, and were media for the voice of the Christian God among his people.

> *Montanus:* I am the Lord God omnipotent dwelling in a human.

> *Montanus:* I am neither an angel nor an envoy, but I the Lord God, the Father, have come.

> *Montanus:* Behold, the human is as a lyre, and I rush on him as a plectrum. The human sleeps and I keep awake. Behold the one who is ecstatically changing the hearts of humans and giving to humans [new] hearts is the Lord.

> *Maximilla:* I am driven away and persecuted as a wolf from the sheep. I am not a wolf. I am word and spirit and power.[3]

Having experienced the ecstasy of the Spirit and new birth, Montanus, Priscilla and Maximilla became revealers and interpreters of God's word to his people. Maximilla, for example, understood herself to be chosen by God in order to proclaim his covenant and promise to Christian people.

> The Lord of this work and covenant and promise sent me as its elector and revealer and interpreter, as one who had been compelled willingly and unwillingly to learn the knowledge of God.[4]

What had these prophets and prophetesses learned, and what was the content of their message? Certainly, their message must have been controversial yet attractive and persuasive, for the New Prophecy was not an insignificant movement in early Christianity. By 177 it had split Christians in Asia and Phrygia and forced no less a figure than Irenaeus to intercede with a letter of peace written by the confessor-martyrs of the churches of Lyons and Vienne in Gaul.[5] Around 200 the bishop of Rome sent a letter of peace to the churches in Asia and Phrygia, recognizing the New Prophecy, but on the advice of a certain Praxeas, the bishop changed his mind and recalled the letter.[6]

---

3. The word Montanism was not coined until the fourth century. It appears first in the writings of Cyril of Jerusalem (*Catecheses*, 16.8; see Labriolle, *Les sources*, p. 89). For the term "the New Prophecy," see the Anonymous, a source written by an unknown contemporary of the first generation of the New Prophecy, and the testimony of Serapion, bishop of Antioch (192–202). Both sources are utilized by Eusebius in his *Historia Ecclesia* (hereafter cited as *HE*); see *HE* 5.16.4; 5.19.2. For the date of the New Prophecy, see Timothy D. Barnes, "The Chronology of Montanism," *Journal of Theological Studies* 21, no. 2 (1970): 403–408. For a description of traits of the New Prophecy, see the Anonymous, *HE* 5.16.7, 9, 12. For the above oracles, see Epiphanius, *Pan.* 48.11.1, 9; 48.4.1; and the Anonymous, *HE* 5.16.17.
4. *Pan.* 48.13.1.
5. *HE* 5.3.4; 5.4.1–2. I am convinced by Pierre Nautin's argument in his *Lettres et écrivains chrétiens des ii' et iii' siècles* (Paris, 1961), pp. 56–59, that Irenaeus is the author of the letter.
6. Tertullian, *Adversus Praxean* 1.5. The identity of Praxeas is not known; Tertullian describes him as a confessor from Asia. Some scholars doubt the reliability of Tertullian's testimony about this Roman attitude. It seems to me that what Tertullian describes is historically plausible.

What was the crisis of the New Prophecy? Central to its message were the hope of the imminent end of the world, the descent of the heavenly Jerusalem and the duty of Christians to confess the name publicly in the midst of persecution. Such a hope was based on a revelation of Christ which Priscilla had received in a dream:

> Christ came to me in the form of a woman clothed with a long, gleaming, flowing robe, and placed wisdom in me and revealed to me that this place is sacred and that in this place the heavenly Jerusalem shall descend.[7]

If apocalyptic hope is interpreted as a political image, then it is not surprising that the desire for martyrdom or what has been called voluntary martyrdom was an important feature in the New Prophecy. The presence of apocalyptic hope and martyrdom clearly indicates that the oppressive condition of persecution created the atmosphere in which the flame of the New Prophecy burned brightly. Two oracles of the New Prophecy are crucial to this point:

> Be exposed to the public [publicaris]; it is for your good. For he who is not publicly exposed [publicatur] by humans is publicly exposed by God. Do not be confused; righteousness is drawing you forth into the midst [of humans]. Why are you confused since you are acquiring and showing forth glory? Power comes when you are seen by humans. . . . Do not wish to die in bed or in miscarriages or gentle fevers, but in martyrdom in order that he who has died for you might be glorified.[8]

Such oracles spoken with the absolute authority of God through prophets and prophetesses must have wielded considerable influence on the minds and hearts of simple Christians, especially in a time when the Roman policy towards Christians was changing. Early in the second century, the emperor Trajan had decreed that Christians were not to be sought out for persecution;[9] by 175 provincial officials were pursuing Christians openly.[10]

How were Christians to respond to this new situation? The answer of the New Prophecy was clear: God's will was that a Christian come forth publicly, witness to the faith and voluntarily hand himself or herself over to the authorities.[11] The reward for such action would be participation in the

---

7. *Pan.* 49.1.3. Maximilla had predicted that the end (συντέλεια) would follow after her own death (*Pan.* 48.2.4).
8. Tertullian, *De Fuga* 9.4. Tertullian does not indicate which leader of the New Prophecy spoke these oracles.
9. Trajan to Pliny, *Letters of Pliny* 10.97.2.
10. Melito, bishop of Sardis in Lydia, wrote an *Apology* (*HE* 4.26.5) about 175 in which he expressed shock and disbelief over the new decrees (καινὰ δόγματα) which were permitting provincials to openly (φανερῶς) plunder and kill Christians throughout Asia. For the date of the *Apology*, see Robert M. Grant, *Augustus to Constantine* (New York, 1970), pp. 90–92.
11. *The Martyrdom of Polycarp* (4.1) depicts the problem of the voluntary martyr in the figure of Quintus and passes harsh judgment on such action. More than likely, Quintus is an anti-Montanist interpolation of the late second or early third century. See Hans von Campenhausen, *Bearbeitungen und Interpolationen der Polycarpmartyriums* (Heidelberg, 1957), p. 20.

transcendent power and glory of Christ himself when he came to establish his kingdom on earth.

The point to be made here is that the New Prophecy in Asia Minor, unlike Gnosticism or Marcionism, the other two movements which were such threats to the church in the second century, was not rejected by the church because it was theologically unorthodox. The New Prophecy was rejected because in the new situation in which Christians were openly pursued, it took a position on martyrdom which the church deemed to be suicidal, irrational and destructive to the life of the church.[12] Thus, the extreme position of voluntary martyrdom distinguishes the New Prophecy from its ecclesiastical opponents.

Likewise, the value the New Prophecy placed on martyrdom explains why women could attain ministerial status within its ranks. It is well known that in early Christianity, martyrs awaiting death could exercise and manifest extraordinary power. They even had the power of the keys, that is, the power to forgive the sins of those who had denied the faith and were therefore thought to have lost salvation. By exercising this power to forgive, the martyr was able to restore a lapsed person back into communion with Christ and his church. Since the power of the keys had been traditionally in the hands of the bishop-presbyter, anyone who exercised such power was thereby demonstrating a ministerial power. Strict logic would lead one to conclude that an imprisoned confessor could have the status of a minister. And, indeed, by 190 a male confessor released from prison automatically had the status of a presbyter in the Roman church.[13] The act of confession followed by imprisonment was one way to acquire ministerial rank.

In the New Prophecy, released confessors had a status not unlike that of released confessors at Rome. Reading between the lines of Irenaeus's *Letter*

12. According to the Anonymous (*HE* 5.16.9), the success of the New Prophecy was due to "the greatness of the promises" which the leaders made to the faithful—promises which certainly had to do with participation in divine glory and power by either confession-martyrdom or the saving experience of heavenly ascent through ecstasy. According to Montanus (*Pan.* 48.10.3), "the one who is saved transcends a human ... and will shine one hundred times brighter than the sun." Theodotus, the first treasurer of the New Prophecy, experienced heavenly ascent through ecstasy (the Anonymous, *HE* 5.16.14); and Priscilla, who had been extolled as a virgin, said that sexual purity allows one to "see visions and ... hear distinct voices which are as saving [*salutares*] as they are mysterious [*occultas*]." See Tertullian, *De Exhortatione Castitatis* 10.5.

The New Prophecy was rejected because the form (ecstasy) of the message was irrational, and as such, an expression of a mind-deceiving spirit. Ecstasy per se was demonic. But why? The probable answer is that the form (ecstasy) of the New Prophecy had become inseparable from its substance (voluntary martyrdom), and the opponents of the New Prophecy judged voluntary martyrdom to be irrational and insane. (Compare the Anonymous, *HE* 5.16.12-13, 20-21; 5.17.2-3).

13. Hippolytus, *Apostolic Tradition* 10.1. Hippolytus's account of Callistus's rise to the Roman episcopate reflects chagrin over Callistus's acquisition of presbyter rank by claiming to have been imprisoned on account of the name rather than the real reason (according to Hippolytus) which was the crime of embezzlement. This happened in the episcopate of Victor (189-199); see Hippolytus, *Refutatio Omnium Haeresium* 9.12.1-13.

of the Churches of Vienne and Lyons to the churches of Asia and Phrygia in 177 reveals that these released confessors were creating a problem for the ecclesiastical opponents of the New Prophecy in Asia Minor. The purpose of the letter was to recount the noble acts of the martyrs of Gaul so that through their examples and their authority, they might act as ambassadors ($\pi\rho\acute{\epsilon}\sigma\beta\upsilon\omicron\iota$) "for the sake of the peace [$\epsilon\acute{\iota}\rho\acute{\eta}\nu\eta$] of the churches."[14]

In the letter Irenaeus makes a sharp distinction between a confessor ($\acute{o}\mu\acute{o}\lambda o\gamma o\varsigma$) and a martyr ($\mu\acute{a}\rho\tau\upsilon\varsigma$). A confessor is one who confesses the name and is consequently imprisoned; a martyr is a confessor who seals the confession with his or her death. The title martyr should never be given to the confessor until the confessor has been put to death.[15] Nevertheless, while awaiting death the imprisoned confessor can exercise "the power of martyrdom" ($\delta\acute{\upsilon}\nu\alpha\mu\iota\varsigma$ $\tau\tilde{\eta}\varsigma$ $\mu\alpha\rho\tau\upsilon\rho\acute{\iota}\alpha\varsigma$). For Irenaeus, the greatest victory of this power was the act in which the martyrs of Gaul with a "mother's love" ($\mu\eta\tau\rho\iota\kappa\acute{a}$ $\sigma\pi\lambda\acute{a}\gamma\chi\nu\alpha$) prayed and shed tears to the Father, interceding for the return of life to those Christians who had denied the faith because of persecution.[16] The Father heard their prayer and "the immeasurable mercy of Christ" was manifested: the martyrs were giving grace ($\acute{\epsilon}\chi\alpha\rho\acute{\iota}\zeta o\nu\tau o$) to the lapsed and there was "deep joy to the *Virgin Mother* who had miscarried [with the lapsed] as though they were dead but now was receiving them back again as living. . . . On account of the living [martyrs], the dead were being made alive."[17]

In encouraging reconciliation, Irenaeus asserts that imprisoned confessors awaiting martyrdom of death have the power of binding and loosing; in particular, the confessor-martyrs of Gaul exercised the power of the keys by praying to the Father for forgiveness of the lapsed. But why the need to make a distinction between confessor and martyr? Did the members of the New Prophecy in Asia Minor have a different view of the confessor-martyr which necessitated this distinction by Irenaeus?

Two leaders of the New Prophecy—Themiso, a first generation leader, and Alexander, probably of the second generation—shed light on why Irenaeus made such a distinction between confessor and martyr. Both of them were released confessors who yet claimed to have the title of martyr. As a released confessor-martyr, Alexander exercised the power to bind and loose sin; in addition, Themiso sought to establish his authority by composing a catholic epistle.[18]

---

14. See n. 5; the quotation is from *HE* 5.3.4. Presumably the martyrdoms took place in the same year that the letter was written.
15. *HE* 5.2.2–3.
16. *HE* 5.2.6.
17. *HE* 5.1.45; 5.2.7. The italics are mine.
18. The Anonymous, *HE* 5.16.16–17; Apollonius, *HE* 5.18.5–10. Evidently on the same occasion, Zoticus of Cumane debated both Maximilla and "the party of Themiso" ($o\grave{\iota}$ $\pi\epsilon\rho\grave{\iota}$ $\theta\epsilon\mu\acute{\iota}\sigma\omega\nu\alpha$). Alexander cannot be dated, but he is described by Apollonius, who was writing forty years after the appearance of Montanus.

In light of the activity of such figures as Alexander and Themiso, it is reasonable to assume that Irenaeus's distinction between confessor and martyr was made in order to undercut the authority of released confessors who claimed the title of martyr and the power of binding and loosing intrinsic to such status. Irenaeus's point must be that only imprisoned confessor-martyrs have the power of the keys; once a confessor is released, he or she can no longer claim the title of martyr or the power inherent in such a title. Moreover, Irenaeus's confessor-martyrs are held up as models of leniency in the exercise of the power of the keys, whereas it seems certain that confessor-martyrs of the first generation of the New Prophecy were more stringent, that is, they refused to give forgiveness to those who lapsed during persecution.[19] No doubt, Irenaeus sought to encourage in the New Prophecy a more compassionate attitude towards lapsed Christians by extolling the power and virtue of the Gaulish confessor-martyrs' gracious compassion and intercessory prayer in behalf of the lapsed.

The conclusion seems unavoidable: in the New Prophecy, one road to the power of the keys was by way of confession and imprisonment. When the confessor was released, he (or she?) still retained his (or her?) power of the keys as well as the title of martyr.

Before we examine whether this situation pertained to women as well as men in the New Prophecy, one last question is in order: was confession, followed by imprisonment, simply an example of an extraordinary situation whereby the "priestly" power of the keys was exercised rather than an avenue to priestly office, as such? Unfortunately, there are no texts of the New Prophecy in Asia Minor which answer this question. Two things, however, can be noted. First, even after the extraordinary situation ceased, that is, when imprisonment and persecution ended, the confessor still retained the title of martyr and the power of the keys. Second, among catholic Christians in Rome, the example of Callistus is indisputable evidence that as early as A.D. 189–199, a released confessor was automatically given the title of presbyter. And this avenue to the priesthood was part of the *Apostolic Tradition* of Rome.[20] It may be that Roman Christians gave more importance to titles than did catholic Christians from Gaul or Asia Minor;[21] still, it seems more than likely that released confessors in the New Prophecy were claiming to have a rank or title equal to that of ordained ministers among catholic Christians in Asia Minor. And given the Roman practice, it is highly

19. Irenaeus says of the confessor-martyrs: "They were releasing [ἔλυον] all [of the lapsed] and binding [ἐδέσμευον] no one" (*HE* 5.2.5). On the other hand, among the original leaders of the New Prophecy the power of the keys was utilized to bind sin rather than to loose it. This is how I construe the oracle which Tertullian cites as the word of the Spirit through the New Prophecy: "The church is able to forgive sins; but I will not, lest they also commit others" (Tertullian, *De Pudicitia* 21.7). I assume that all of the oracles which Tertullian cites go back to either Montanus, Priscilla or Maximilla. Hence, this oracle may be used as evidence for the views of the New Prophecy of Asia Minor.
20. See n. 13.
21. See *HE* 5.4.2.

probable that Christians of the New Prophecy also accepted confession and imprisonment as the means of attaining this ministerial rank.

For our case to be persuasive, we still need to show that this priestly power was exercised by female confessors as well as by male confessors in the New Prophecy. The best evidence for this conclusion is the figure of Perpetua, who was martyred at Carthage in 203. The account of her martyrdom with other Carthaginian Christians is given in *The Acts of St. Perpetua and St. Felicitas*, an eloquent and moving testimony to the power and courage of the noble martyrs. The dramatic impact of the document is heightened by the fact that the visions of Perpetua and Saturus in sections 3-10 and 11-13 are firsthand accounts which the anonymous author has excerpted from their prison diaries.[22]

Without a doubt the document was authored by a member of the New Prophecy, and Perpetua and Saturus stand forth as noble martyrs in that movement.[23] It is significant that even as late as the fifth century, Perpetua was remembered as a martyr in both the catholic and Montanist communities of North Africa. Very probably, the persecution of 203 happened when the New Prophecy had not yet been rejected by the Carthaginian catholic community.

The visions of both Perpetua and Saturus reveal that the imprisoned confessor possessed the priestly power of the keys. One day while praying with other confessors in prison, Perpetua realized that she was intended to pray for her brother Dinocrates, who had died of cancer at the age of seven. She prayed for him with deep sighs before the Lord. That night she was given a vision: she saw Dinocrates, parched, dirty and thirsty, coming out of a dark place; there was a pool of water above him, just beyond his reach. The cancerous wound was on his face, and she knew that he was still suffering. She awoke, confident that she could help her brother. And so (in her own words) "I prayed for him day and night, sighing and shedding tears, that he might be pardoned for me." Days later she had another vision: there was Dinocrates, "washed clean, well dressed and refreshed [*refrigerantem*]." The wound had healed; the pool of water was within his reach, and he was drinking from a golden bowl of water. He drank as much as he wanted, but

---

22. For Latin text and English translation, see Herbert Musurillo, ed., *The Acts of the Christian Martyrs* (Oxford, 1972), pp. 106-131. For the dating of the martyrdom of St. Perpetua, see Timothy D. Barnes, "Pre-Decian Acta Martyrum," *Journal of Theological Studies* 19 (1968): 521-525. Both Barnes (p. 521) and J. Armitage Robinson (*The Passion of S. Perpetua* [Cambridge, 1891], pp. 43-47) think that the difference in style of sections 3-10 and 11-13 from the rest of the martyr act confirms the author's statement about their diary accounts. See *Passio SS. Perpetuae et Felicitatis* 2.

23. In the preface of the document the author identifies his community as "we, who acknowledge and honor, as equally promised anew, new visions as well as [new] prophecies" ("nos, qui sicut prophetias ita et visiones novas pariter repromissas et agnoscimus et honoramus") 1.4. In her first vision Perpetua learned that Saturus would be privileged to be the first to ascend to heaven by martyrdom "because although he was not present when we were arrested, later on he, on our account, voluntarily handed himself over and strengthened us" (4.5). Here, the pre-eminence of the voluntary martyr is clear.

the bowl remained full. After drinking his fill, Dinocrates played like a child. Perpetua awoke and knew that Dinocrates had been delivered from his punishment (*poena*).[24]

Through Perpetua's intercessory prayers and tears, her brother was pardoned and given the full forgiveness of sins by the living water of baptism, the water which previously had been out of reach because he had died as a pagan. Was this an exercise of Perpetua's power of the keys?

Here we need to recall Irenaeus's description of the confessor-martyrs of Gaul who "were releasing [ἔλυον] all, and binding [ἐδέσμευον] no one; . . . with a mother's love . . . they were shedding tears to the Father; they prayed [ᾐτήσαντο] for life [for the apostates] and [the Father] gave it to them. . . . They constantly loved peace."[25] For Irenaeus the power of intercessory prayers and tears was certainly part of the process whereby the apostates were given forgiveness and life. Likewise, through tears and prayers, the confessor-martyr Perpetua brought life and forgiveness to her brother. In this episode, although the language of binding and loosing is not employed with regard to Perpetua, would not any reader in Irenaeus's audience have logically inferred from this picture of Perpetua's intercessory power that as an imprisoned confessor-martyr she had in fact exercised the power of the keys in behalf of a condemned person?[26]

The vision of Saturus implies a similar view of the power of martyrdom. In a vision Saturus saw himself and the other martyrs transported to paradise after death. They were carried by angels to a place whose walls were made of light. Upon entering they heard voices chanting endlessly in unison, making but one sound: "Holy, holy, holy." As the martyrs stood before a throne, angels lifted them up to kiss an aged man of youthful countenance, who touched their faces with his hand. Then they were commanded to go and play. They went out before the gates and saw their bishop Optatus and the presbyter Aspasius approaching them. Optatus and Aspasius were apart from one another and very sad. Throwing themselves at the feet of Perpetua and Saturus, they said: "Make peace between us, for you departed and left us thus." Perpetua and Saturus embraced them and began to talk to them; however, they were interrupted by angels who scolded the bishop and presbyter, instructing them to settle their own quarrels and advising the bishop about shepherding his flock. The angels thought that

---

24. See *Passio SS. Perpetuae et Felicitatis* 7–8. The crucial sentence is "et feci pro illo orationem die et nocte gemens et lacrimans ut mihi donaretur" (7.10). Musurillo's translation (p. 117), "And I prayed for my brother day and night with tears and sighs that this favor might be granted me," leaves open what, specifically, the favor was. Since the episode reveals that Perpetua prayed for her brother and that he was pardoned, my translation seeks to bring out the sense of "to pardon" in *donare* and assumes that the subject of the third person *donaretur* is *he*, which refers back to Dinocrates (*illo*).

25. *HE* 5.2.5–7.

26. Tertullian's catholic letter, *To the Martyrs* (*Ad Martyras* 1.6), demonstrates the view of Carthaginian catholics that imprisoned confessors did possess the power of the keys.

Perpetua and Saturus should be allowed to rest (*refrigerare*), and in addition, it was time "to close the gates [*claudere portas*]. . . ."[27]

This episode could be interpreted as teaching that once put to death, the martyr can no longer bestow peace (through the power of the keys) on Christians who have fallen out of fellowship because of sin. Christians are to work out their own problems and not pray to martyrs. Perhaps this is the meaning. Yet Saturus and Perpetua "were very moved and embraced" (*moti et conplexi sunt*) the bishop and presbyter.[28] Evidently, they were not displeased that the two had come to them for a resolution.

Clearly, there is more to this issue than the text indicates. Whatever the full meaning of the episode, it seems to imply at least that one destined for martyrdom has the power of the keys and can utilize it to bestow peace on other Christians. Perhaps, once the martyr enters into peace through death, he or she is no longer to be approached in prayer by Christians on earth. But that view itself rests on the assumption that while alive the destined martyr has the priestly power of the keys.[29]

Thus far this study has shown that the power of the keys in the New Prophecy was held by released male confessors in Asia Minor. Although the sources tell us nothing about the status of released female confessors in Asia Minor, given the status that women had in this movement, one might expect to find this power held by them as well. But the historian is limited by a paucity of sources for the New Prophecy in Asia Minor. However, *The Acts of Perpetua and Felicitas* shows that, indeed, both male and female imprisoned confessors in the New Prophecy of North Africa did have this power (although the document tells us nothing about the status of a released confessor). If during imprisonment female confessors of the New Prophecy in North Africa had the power of the keys, then it is almost certain that this feature goes back to an original characteristic of the New Prophecy in Asia Minor. (Indeed, it is probably also a characteristic of catholic Christianity since in Irenaeus's portrayal of the power of the keys there is no explicit limitation of this power to males only). Epiphanius's testimony that women in the New Prophecy were ordained as ministers is a description of a feature in fourth-century Montanism. But the historical questions are how far back does this feature go and what conditions explain its origin? It is more plausible that this feature goes back to the very origins of a movement in which it is certain that from the beginning women played a prominent role

---

27. *Passio SS. Perpetuae et Felicitatis* 12–13.
28. Ibid., 13.1.
29. Certainly the view in this episode is not that a confessor can bestow peace only after becoming a martyr (i.e., by dying), for Carthaginian catholics assumed that imprisoned confessors could exercise the power of the keys (see n. 26). The reasonable view is that Perpetua and Saturus had departed by death before Aspasius and Optatus were able to approach them in order to receive peace. Thus, this situation compelled the bishop and presbyter to approach them through prayer after Perpetua and Saturus had died.

than that such a feature was a development in the late third or fourth
century.

This essay has argued that the conditions which explain the ministerial
status of women in the New Prophecy of Asia Minor are confession,
imprisonment and martyrdom. In that situation, women as well as men
exercised the power of the keys, a power held also by presbyters and bishops.
About the time that the New Prophecy emerged, catholic Christians at Rome
maintained that a confessor by virtue of imprisonment acquired the status of
presbyter and, further, that such status was retained even upon release.

It is certain that when male confessors in the New Prophecy were
released, they retained the power of the keys. What better explains the origin
of the ministerial status of women in the New Prophecy than that they too, as
released confessors, retained the priestly power which had been given them
by virtue of confession and imprisonment? The conclusion is almost
unavoidable: in the New Prophecy of Asia Minor, women received
ministerial status because suffering in prison for the name was a form of
martyrdom; such suffering allowed one to participate in the "power of
martyrdom"—that is, the priestly power of the keys.

If it is true, as one scholar has asserted, that in the Hellenistic society of the
Roman Empire "the differentiation and ranking of women and men became
a potent symbol for the stability of the world order," then the relationship
between persecution, martyrdom and the ministerial rank of women in the
New Prophecy becomes understandable.[30] Persecution and the resultant
heightened consciousness that the old world order was coming to an end led
Christians in the New Prophecy to envision the appearance of a new world, a
world symbolized by the unity of male and female in Christ, a world in
which Christ appeared to them in the form of a woman as well as in the form
of a man.[31]

Indeed, martyrs of the catholic church and members of the New Prophecy
may have been in agreement on this point; according to Irenaeus, the martyrs
of Gaul in their compassion for others reflected the "maternal love . . . of the
Virgin Mother [church]"—a love which encouraged other Christians in the
struggle against death.[32] One such martyr was the courageous woman
Blandina who was impaled on a stake in the form of a cross and because of
her continuous prayer was likened to a "noble mother encouraging her
children and sending them forth as ones bringing a victory to the king." They
looked at her and *saw in her* "the one [Christ] who had been crucified in
behalf of them. . . . She had put on the invincible athlete, Christ."[33]

30. See Meeks, "The Image of Androgyne," p. 180.
31. Recall that in Priscilla's vision, Christ comes to her in the form of a woman. See n. 7. What
    a Freudian psychoanalyst would make of this is open to question; I take the vision to signify,
    at the very least, that the feminine dimension of God was not denied by members of the New
    Prophecy.
32. The *Letter of Churches of Vienne and Lyons, HE* 5.1.45; 5.2.6.
33. *HE* 5.1.41–42; 5.1.55.

The catholic vision is a vision of the church, the Virgin Mother who in maternal love bears the crucified Christ to the world through the crucified form of female martyrs (as well as male martyrs). The New Prophecy reflects another, yet not dissimilar ideal: the virgin woman who sees Christ in the form of a woman (or a man) and who, as a woman, represents Christ to the world.[34]

The essential difference between the catholic and the New Prophecy's view of the priestly authority of women may not be in the relation of persecution and martyrdom to Christian authority, for here they probably agreed that Christ communicates his priestly authority through woman. Rather, the difference was more than likely this: for the catholic church only the baptism of the Spirit on the way to actual martyrdom bestowed this authority, but for the New Prophecy the authority which comes from being baptized into Christ's suffering by virtue of imprisonment was adequate to satisfy the requirements for the baptism of the Spirit.[35] Upon release, the confessor still retained the credentials of such a baptism of the Spirit.

Or if we were to put the difference in modern terms, perhaps the following may be ventured: In the catholic church woman was "liberated" to become a minister as long as she participated in the suffering of Christ. The moment she was set free from the suffering of prison, she was placed back into the "imprisoning" role of female subordinate to male. In the New Prophecy, liberation also came by participating in the suffering of prison on account of the name, but a release from such suffering did not mean a retreat to the former role of subordinate female prior to the prison experience. The vision of a new creation which resulted from the experience of suffering in Christ was strong enough to live beyond the circumstance of persecution which had occasioned it. Perhaps there is an important lesson here for the Christian feminists of our own time.

---

34. Recall that Priscilla was extolled as a virgin by the New Prophecy. See n. 12 and Apollonius, *HE* 5.18.3.

35. At Carthage, Gaul and Rome, martyrdom was viewed as a second baptism. See *Passio SS. Pereptuae et Felicitatis* 21.2; *The Letter of the Churches of Vienne and Lyons, HE* 5.2.3 (the use of ἐπισφραγίξειν with regard to martyrdom); Hermas, *Similitudes* 9.28.3–8; Hippolytus, *Apost. Trad.* 19.2.

This belief is significant for our argument if Meeks ("The Image of Androgyne," pp. 180–182) is correct in his argument that Gal. 3.28 was a "baptismal re-unification formula" confessed in Pauline churches during the baptismal ceremony in which the catechumen came out of the water naked and put on a white gown symbolizing "being clothed with Christ" (Gal. 3.27). Meeks suggests that baptism meant taking on the form of Christ in which male and female were one. We have seen that the New Prophecy stressed the descent of the Spirit, being clothed with the form of Christ and martyrdom as a second baptism. It is indeed tempting to conclude that in the New Prophecy martyrdom underscored the unity of male and female in baptism and the ordination of women followed as a consequence. Or perhaps the rite of baptism and martyrdom as baptism were both instrumental in creating the vision of the unity of male and female in the New Prophecy. At any rate, Epiphanius does say that the right of women to be presbyters and bishops (in the New Prophecy) was based on Gal. 3.28. (See *Pan.* 49.2.1–5).

Église et Théologie, 9 (1978), p. 51-101

The Fathers on Women
and Women's Ordination

The accumulated literature on the admissibility of women to priestly ordination will make new acquisitions as a direct result of the *Declaration* under study in this volume; and doubtless a portion of these acquisitions will be devoted to what history can tell us as we face the questions of women's ordination[1] and of women's place in Christianity in general.[2] Many of those historical studies yet to come will have enjoyed a longer interval for reflection on the *Declaration* and its implications; and this longer reflection will, if coupled with real competence, produce the further light still needed to treat these questions with the attention and objectivity they deserve.

The present writer is well aware that he has cornered the market on neither reflection nor competence. Nevertheless he has devoted sufficient time and study to the *Declaration* since its appearance to make some comment on at least one particular aspect

---

[1] To date the best work on women's ministry in the Church of the Fathers is by R. GRYSON, *Le ministère des femmes dans l'Eglise ancienne (Recherches et Synthèses*, Section d'histoire, IV: Gembloux: J. Duculot, 1972); also helpful is H. van der MEER, *Priestertum der Frau? Eine theologiegeschichtliche Untersuchung (Quæstiones Disputatæ*, 42: Freiburg: Herder, 1969). Both works exist in English translation. Michael SLUSSER's article, "Fathers and Priestesses: Footnotes to the Roman Declaration," in *Worship*, 51 (Collegeville: 1977), pp. 434-45, appeared just as my own was being completed, and I can do no more than refer to it here: but I am under the impression that Slusser's findings agree with some of my own.

[2] The more important pre-Declaration works on this theme are: G. H. TAVARD, *Woman in the Christian Tradition* (Notre Dame: University Press, 1973); R. R. RUETHER (ed), *Religion and Sexism. Images of Woman in the Jewish and Christian Traditions* (New York: Simon and Schuster, 1974); and J.-M. AUBERT, *La femme. Antiféminisme et christianisme* (Paris: Cerf/Desclée, 1975).

117

of the argument that "the Catholic Church has never felt that priestly or episcopal ordination can be validly conferred on women";[3] and this is the aspect of what the *Declaration* terms "the Church's constant tradition", as this tradition has been expressed by the writings of the patristic period on which the *Declaration* calls for support.[4] Note that there is no intention here of offering positive proofs that the Church of the patristic period was open to the idea of ordaining women to priesthood; there is only one of examining the patristic arguments brought forward by the *Declaration* in support of the assertion that the idea must be presently excluded, and of examining the claim that such arguments were, at their origin, made outside the influence of anti-feminine prejudice. This article will therefore be in two parts: the first part will examine the general claim; the second will deal with the particular references given in Footnotes 7 and 8 of the *Declaration*, and with some of the attitudes towards women of the sources there invoked.

A. THE FATHERS AND PREJUDICE AGAINST WOMEN

The *Declaration* makes the claim that

> It is true that in the writings of the Fathers one will find the undeniable influence of prejudices unfavourable to women, but nevertheless, it should be noted that these prejudices had hardly any influence on their pastoral activity, and still less on their spiritual direction.[5]

---

[3] *Declaratio "Inter insigniores", Acta Apostolicæ Sedis,* 69 (1977), p. 101 (§ 6): "Numquam Ecclesia catholica sensit presbyteralem vel episcopalem ordinationem mulieribus valide conferri posse." The English rendition of this and all other passages from the *Declaration* is from the translation authorized by the United States Catholic Conference.

[4] The title of the *Declaration*'s first section (p. 101): "Traditio perpetuo ab Ecclesia servata". This section begins after the statement that "the Sacred Congregation for the Doctrine of the Faith judges it necessary to recall that the Church, in fidelity to the example of the Lord, does not consider herself authorized to admit women to priestly ordination" (p. 100, § 5: "...Sacra hæc Congregatio pro Doctrina Fidei [...] censet nunc resumendum: Ecclesiam, quæ Domini exemplo fidelis manere intendit, auctoritatem sibi non agnoscere admittendi mulieres ad sacerdotalem ordinationem").

[5] *Declaration*, p. 101 (§ 6): "Sane in eorundem Patrum scriptis haud dissimulanda percipitur contagio præiudicatarum opinionum circa muliebrem sexum non æquarum, quæ tamen fere nihil in eorum pastoralem actuositatem et etiam minus in eorum spiritalem directionem influxerunt."

While the problem of how someone admittedly prejudiced becomes somehow free of prejudice, at the moment of turning to the two areas of concern named, is in itself an interesting object of study,[6] it is the *but* clause of the statement that will be the immediate object of attention here. Cultural influence is at work in some of the basic anthropological statements of Scripture.[7] It would then seem reasonable to suppose that we will find it at work in theology as well, even in the theology of the Fathers; and if in their theology, then surely on their pastoral activity and spiritual direction — unless the claim is to be made that these two areas were divorced from theology?

On the basis of some of those same culturally-influenced statements in Scripture (*Genesis* 1-3), Clement of Alexandria (+ *ca.* 215) feels that a man (*anēr,* the Greek term for the male of the human species, as opposed to the female) is naturally superior to a woman (*gunē),* and that this superiority is manifest in everything about him, including his beard:

> His beard, then, is the badge of a man and shows him to be unmistakably a man. It is older than Eve and is the symbol of the stronger nature. By God's decree, hairiness is one of man's conspicuous qualities — his hairiness is, in fact, distributed over his whole body. Whatever smoothness or softness there was in him was taken from him by God when he fashioned the delicate Eve from his rib to be the receptacle of his seed, his assistant in procreating and in managing the home. What was left — remembering that he had lost all hairlessness — was man (*anēr*) and reveals man (*anēr*). It is his hallmark to be active, as hers is to be passive. For what is hairy is by nature drier and warmer than what is bare. Therefore the male is hairier and more warm-blooded than the female, the uncastrated than the castrated, the mature than the immature.[8]

---

[6] The *Declaration*'s statement is paraphrased in the official *Commentary* released by the same Congregation (original French text in *La Documentation Catholique,* no. 1714 (Paris: 20 fév. 1977); English translation in *Origins. NC Documentary Service,* vol. 6, no. 33 (Washington, Feb. 3, 1977), p. 526): "It is true that we find in the Father's writings the undeniable influence of prejudices against women. But it must be carefully noted that these passages had very little influence on their pastoral activity, still less on their spiritual direction, as we can see by glancing through their correspondence that has come down to us."

[7] Cf. R. GRYSON, *Le ministère...,* esp. pp. 19-33; also J.-P. MICHAUD, "Marie et la femme selon saint Jean," in *Eglise et Théologie,* 7 (Ottawa: 1976), pp. 387 and 391.

[8] CLEMENT OF ALEXANDRIA, *Paidagōgos,* III, 3: 19, 1 (*GCS* 12, p. 247. 15).

Leaving aside the interesting probability of Clement's own hirsute appearance (no male being likely to extol that much hairiness unless he enjoyed it in abundance), there is Clement's basic theology of woman, expressed here in his curious physiology. The *anēr* already had a complete human nature in himself before Eve was created. The woman — whom Clement regards as the origin of sin[9] — shares human nature with the man; but the nature's completeness resides only in the man, the *anēr,* who is therefore more *anthrōpos* (Man, in the generic sense) than is the *gunē.*[10] The *raison d'être* of the woman is to receive the man's semen and to assist in the management of the house — a view that describes fairly well the situation of woman in hellenic culture at the time of Clement and for centuries before.

And, in both East and West, for a long time to follow. For if the Roman woman was somewhat more emancipated than her Greek sisters,[11] the more lenient status was not necessarily reflected in Western ecclesiastical circles. At Rome between 370 and 382 the unknown author of a series of biblical commentaries, called Ambrosiaster, asserts categorically that the man alone *(uir = anēr),* not the woman *(mulier),* has been made in the image of God — a conclusion he reaches from those contemporary Roman civil laws that are less flattering to woman, that see her as a perpetual minor, never free of the legal custody of a man, be he father, husband, relative or guardian.[12] And, says Ambrosiaster, since woman as a minor can possess no authority in civil society, she should have none in the Church, either:

> For how can it be said of woman that she is the image of God, she who has been constituted as being subject to the mastery of the man and as having no authority? She cannot teach nor be a court

---

[9] CLEM. ALEX., *Protrepticus,* 11 *(GCS* 12, p. 78. 25). The same idea exists elsewhere: cf. THEOPHILUS OF ANTIOCH, *Ad Autolycum,* II, 28 *(PG* 6, col. 1097 A).

[10] In the *Stromata,* IV, 8 *(PG* 8, col. 1272), Clement also says that a man steeped in vice is still superior to a virtuous woman.

[11] Cf. J. GAUDEMET, "Le statut de la Femme dans l'Empire romain", in *La Femme (Recueils de la Société Jean Bodin,* vol. 11; Brussels: Editions de la Librairie Encyclopédique, 1959), pp. 191-222.

[12] *Ibid.,* pp. 194-8.

witness, cannot take an oath nor pass judgment. Still less can she govern![13]

But Ambrosiaster goes even further. Not only is a woman not made in the image of God; she never possessed this image, not even before the Fall.[14] Misreading *Gen* 1: 28, he says that the *uir* alone has *by nature* dominion over all creatures, and that the *mulier* is *by nature* included among all those other creatures which are subject to the *uir*. He comes to this conclusion in a commentary on *1 Cor* 14: 34-35:

"Let your women be silent in the assemblies" (*1 Cor* 14: 34). Now [Paul] treats what he left out earlier. Earlier he commanded that women be veiled in church — or rather, he now shows that they ought to be quiet and discreet *because* they are veiled, that the act may have its logical outcome. For if the image of God is the man, not the woman (*femina*), and if she is subject to the man by the law of nature, how much more should they be subject in church, out of reverence for the one who is the legate of Him who is the head of the man. "For it is not permitted to them to speak, but to remain in silence, as the law says" (*1 Cor* 14: 34). What does the law say? "Your turning shall be to your man, yet he shall have mastery over you" (*Gn* 3: 16). This is a special law [...]

Though she is one flesh [with her man], there are two reasons why she is ordered to be subject [to him]: because she originates from the man, and because sin made its entry by her. "If they wish instruction on some point, let them ask their men at home; for it is improper for women to speak in an assembly" (*1 Cor* 14: 35). It is improper because it would be contrary to the rule that in the house of God, who has prescribed that they be subject to their men, they presume to speak of the Law. They ought to know that the first place there goes to the men, and that they would be better off, in the house of God, passing the time in prayer, keeping their tongue still and their ears open, that they may hear how through Christ the mercy of God has conquered

---

[13] *Liber quæstionum ueteris et noui testamenti,* 45: 3 (*CSEL* 50, p. 83. 4): "Quo modo enim potest de muliere dici, quia imago dei est, quam constat dominio uiri subiectam et nullam auctoritatem habere? nec docere enim potest nec testis esse neque fidem dicere nec iudicare: quanto magis imperare!" Little doubt now remains that the author of the work here cited and the author of the work referred to below (note 15) as Ambrosiaster are one and the same. Cf. the introduction by A. SOUTER to *CSEL,* vol. 50, pp. xii and xxiii.

[14] *Liber quæst. uet. et noui test.,* 21 and 45: 3 (*CSEL* 50, pp. 47. 27 and 82. 20). Cf. also *Comment. in I*[am] *epist. ad Cor.* 11: 7 (*CSEL* 81, 2, p. 121. 24): "Vir enim ad imaginem dei factus est, non mulier."

death, which established its reign through Eve. It would be shameful if they dared speak out in church. They are veiled precisely for this, to show their subjection: yet see how they flaunt their lack of discretion! That is a reason for their husbands to be humiliated as well; for the insolence of wives rebounds on the reputation of those to whom they are married.[15]

Again we see how Ambrosiaster launches his argument from a *fait accompli*. Women are not now subject because the Bible says so; rather, the Bible states the necessary subjection of women after recognizing that such is the way things ought to be. As Gryson notes, in this whole discussion "le mot-clé..., c'est soumission".[16]

His starting-point is not the only flaw in his argument; the manner in which he handles the Scritpure he cites is also questionable. The context for *1 Cor* 14: 34-35 indicates that it probably refers to wives in relationship to their husbands, not necessarily to women in general. Recognizing this (as his closing sentence reveals), Ambrosiaster indulges in a little word-juggling. Where the text he cites speaks of *mulieres* in relation to their *uiri* at home, he leads us to believe that the text applies to any *femina,* because, after all, a woman is not made in God's image, regardless of whether or not she is married. More, he takes it for granted that the biblical text refers to all situations "in church", whereas present-day scholars will point out that the prohibition there is against unwarranted out-

---

[15] AMBROSIASTER, *Comm. in I^am epist. ad Cor.* 14: 34-35 (*CSEL* 81, 2, p. 163. 3): "*Mulieres uestræ in ecclesiis taceant.* nunc tradit quod prætermiserat. superius enim uelari mulieres in ecclesia præcepit: modo ut quietæ sint et uerecundæ ostendit, ut operæ pretium sit, quia uelantur. si enim imago dei uir est, non femina, et uiro subiecta est lege naturæ, quanto magis in ecclesia debent esse subiectæ propter reuerentiam eius, qui illius legatus est, qui etiam uiri caput est. *Non enim permittitur illis loqui, sed esse in silentio, sicut et lex dicit.* Quid dicit lex? *Ad uirum tuum conuersio tua et ipse tui dominabitur.* Lex hæc specialis est [...] quamuis una caro sit, sed duabus ex causis iubetur esse subiecta, quia et ex uiro est et per ipsam intrauit peccatum. *Si quid autem discere uolunt, domi uiros suos interrogent; turpe est enim mulieribus in ecclesia loqui.* Turpe est, quia contra disciplinam est, ut in domo dei, qui eas subiectas uiris suis esse præcepit, de lege loqui præsumant, cum sciant illic uiros habere primatum et sibi magis competere, ut in domo dei precibus uacent linguam retinentes, aures aperiant ut audiant quomodo misericordia dei mortem uicit per Christum, quæ per Euam regnauit. nam si audeant in ecclesia loqui, dedecus est, quia idcirco uelantur, ut humiliatæ appareant. illæ autem se inuerecundæ ostendunt, quod et uiris obprobrium est. in mulierum enim insolentia etiam mariti notantur."

[16] R. GRYSON, *Le ministère...,* p. 153, who says (pp. 155-7 and 164) that the passages cited in notes 15 and 20 are probably against Montanism.

bursts "in the assemblies".[17] Finally, the two most popular modern interpretations of these verses in *1 Corinthians* see them either as a Judaeo-Christian interpolation,[18] or as expressing a general, but culturally-conditioned, attitude toward women on the part of Paul.[19]

In any case, it is clear that Ambrosiaster is operating from a highly misogynistic view which colours his scriptural interpretation. This can also be seen in his commentary on a passage from *1 Timothy,* in which he invokes the "order of creation" theme:

> [The Apostle] puts the man before the woman (cf. *1 Tim* 2: 13-14) for the simple reason that he was created first. The result is that the woman is inferior, because she was created after the man and from him. He adds something else: it was not the man whom the devil seduced, but the woman, and by her agency the man was tricked. That is why no concession is to be made to her impudence, but she is to remain in humility, for by her death entered the world (cf. *Rom* 5: 12).[20]

The use of Scripture to justify a pre-conceived conclusion is even more blatant here than in the passages cited earlier, for here Ambrosiaster misquotes. The language of the scriptural allusion in Ambrosiaster's closing line can only refer to the *Romans* passage; but *Rom* 5: 12 says that sin (and through sin, death) entered the world through one *human being* (in Latin, *homo = anthrōpos*). This would be, of course, unacceptable to Ambrosiaster, since for him the

---

[17] Cf. H. van der MEER, *Priestertum...*, pp. 21-31.
[18] The theory proposed by G. FITZER, *"Das Weib schweige in der Gemeinde". Ueber den unpaulinischen Charakter der mulier-taceat-Verse in 1. Korinther 14 (Theologische Existenz Heute,* N.F. 110; Munich: Chr. Kaiser Verlag, 1963). A résumé is given by R. GRYSON, *Le ministère...*, pp. 27-9. H. van der MEER, who published his work in 1969, actually wrote it as a doctoral thesis in 1962, and so is unaware of the study of Fitzer. Cf. *infra,* n. 83.
[19] So P. de LABRIOLLE, " 'Mulieres in Ecclesia taceant'. Un aspect de la lutte anti-montaniste," in *Bulletin d'ancienne littérature et d'archéologie chrétiennes* (Paris: 1911), p. 13: "L'exclusion de la femme du droit d'enseigner devant tous sur les choses de la foi n'est qu'une application particulière de la conception que Paul s'est formée des droits et des devoirs de la femme". Cf. also R. GRYSON, *Le ministère...*, pp. 25-33.
[20] AMBROSIASTER, *Comment. in Iᵃᵐ epist. ad Tim.* 2: 13-15 (*CSEL* 81, 3, p. 264. 3): "Præfert uirum mulieri, propter quod primus creatus est, ut inferior sit mulier, quia post uirum et ex uiro creata est. adicit et aliud, quia diabolus non uirum seduxit, sed mulierem, uir autem per mulierem deceptus est. ac per hoc nulla illi concedenda audacia est, sed esse debet in humilitate, quia per illam mors intrauit in mundum." The author concludes (p. 267. 28) that there can be no such a thing as deaconesses — in ignorance of the fact that the East possesses them: cf. the statement by EPIPHANIUS, *infra*, p. 83; also p. 85.

man, not the woman, is the human being *par excellence;*[21] so, unless the Pauline text can be doctored, responsibility for sin would logically have to be pinned squarely on the man (as it is in *Rom* 5: 14). Whether the doctoring has been done consciously or not is beside the point. Either way we have a further example of how Ambrosiaster's prejudice affects his interpretation of Scripture, not to mention his reading of the very text.

Because he holds the woman mainly responsible for sin, the man is at most a half-willing accomplice. Her role in involving the man is much the same as was the devil's in involving her; but at the Fall she was *seduced (seduxit):* the man was merely *tricked (deceptus est).* The consequences were not nearly so deep in him as they were in the woman, because his involvement was less direct. It is all her fault, and everything necessary will be done and said to see to it that she never forgets it.

Ambrosiaster's views are shared by many of his contemporaries. Among others,[22] there is Diodore of Tarsus (+ 390) who, commenting on *Gen* 1: 26, says:

> Why does Paul in fact say that the man (*anēr*), and not the woman as well, is the image of God, if Man (*ho anthrōpos*) is the image of God at the level of the soul? For he says, "A man (*anēr*), being the image and glory of God, should not veil his head; but a woman is the glory of the man (*anēr*)" (*1 Cor* 11: 7). Therefore if an image of God should not veil his head, then it is evident that a female, because she is veiled, is not an image of God, not even as regards her soul. So, then, in what way is Man (*ho anthrōpos*) the image of God? According to power, according to authority; and the witness thereof is the voice of God itself, saying, "Let us make Man (*anthrōpos*) according to our image and according to our likeness" (*Gen* 1: 26). And the voice goes on to show how this is to be applied: "And let him have dominion over the fish of the sea, the birds of the air, and the beasts of the earth", and so on. Like the God of all, Man (*ho anthrōpos*) also reigns over the things of the earth. Why, then, does the woman not have dominion over these creatures that have been mentioned? But for her head, which dominates everything else, she has the man (*anēr*); the man was

---

[21] Cf. *Liber quæst. uet. et noui test.,* 21 (*CSEL* 50, pp. 47-8).

[22] PELAGIUS (+ after 418) says that it is "against nature and the law" ("contra ordinem est naturæ uel leges") that women speak in assemblies when men are present (*In Iam epist. ad Cor.* 14: 34-35, *PLS* 1, col. 1227). But he does not prohibit women from privately teaching other women (*In epist. ad Titum* 2: 4, *PLS* 1, col. 1370) or even male relatives (*In Iam epist. ad Tim.* 2: 12, *PLS* 1, col. 1349).

not made subject to the woman. Wherefore the blessed Paul rightly says that only the man (*anēr*) is the image and glory of God, and that the woman is the glory of the man.[23]

This statement deserves no more than a reminder that the "theology" of woman as naturally inferior and as not made in God's image was flatly contradicted close to our own day by the highest of Church authorities.[24] But one cannot help wondering how the good Bishop of Tarsus avoided manifesting this view in his "pastoral activity" among and "spiritual direction" of women.

About the same time as Diodore a well-known Latin Father made the following observation about an even better-known passage in the Letter to the *Ephesians:*

> As long as woman exists for birth and children, she is as different from man (*uir*) as body is from soul. But once she wishes to serve Christ more than the world, she will cease to be a woman and will be called "man" (*uir*), since we all desire to progress "to the perfect man".[25]

So a woman reaches completion by becoming the perfect *uir* (cf. *Eph* 4: 13), which is a notion the author of the scriptural passage probably did not have in mind. It can be argued that Jerome is employing hyperbole to make his point, which is that virginity is superior to marriage: "I praise weddings, I praise marriage", he says elsewhere, "because they produce virgins".[26] But the notion of virginity's automatic superiority[27] is a problem in itself, and anyway

---

[23] DIODORE, *Fragmentum in Gen.* 1: 26 (*PG* 33, col. 1564 C).

[24] PIUS XII, "Allocution à l'Union Mondiale des Organisations féminines catholiques" (29 Sept., 1957), in *Acta Apostolicæ Sedis,* 49 (Rome: 1957), p. 909: "L'homme et la femme sont les images de personnes égales en dignité et possédant les mêmes droits, sans qu'on puisse soutenir en aucune manière que la femme soit inférieure."

[25] JEROME, *In epist. ad Ephes.* 5: 28, III, 5 (*PL* 26, col. 533 B): "Quamdiu mulier partui seruit et liberis, hanc habet ad uirum differentiam, quam corpus ad animam. sin autem Christo magis uoluerit seruire quam sæculo, mulier esse cessabit, et dicetur uir, quia omnes *in perfectum uirum* cupimus occurrere". AUGUSTINE speaks of his own mother in similar terms (*De beata uita,* 2: 10, *CSEL* 63, p. 97. 9: "...ut obliti penitus sexus eius magnum aliquem uirum considere nobiscum crederemus").

[26] JEROME, *Epist.* 22 ad Eustochium, 20: 1 (*CSEL* 54, p. 170. 7): "Laudo nuptias, laudo coniugium, sed quia mihi uirgines generant."

[27] On this theme cf. J. BUGGE, *Virginitas. An Essay in the History of a Medieval Ideal* (International Archives of the History of Ideas, Series Minor, 17; The Hague: Martinus Nijhoff, 1975); also J. E. KERNS, *The Theology of Marriage. The Historical Development of Christian Attitudes Toward Sex and Sanctity in Marriage* (New York: Sheed & Ward, 1964), pp. 141-77.

it cannot be divorced in Jerome from his view of woman as a threat to chastity in others and as prone to weakness in herself.[28]

There are passages in Jerome which lead to the conclusion that marriage can be justified only insofar as having babies can be justified.[29] For this women are necessary — at least, some women are. But a woman who chooses a life of chastity chooses a better way; so much better, that by virginity a woman is given the chance of overcoming her own nature and receiving a better one, that of a man.

These ideas cannot be ascribed to Jerome's particular temperament alone, for we find them elsewhere.[30] Ambrose of Milan has some fairly positive statements on women,[31] but he also says:

> A female non-believer is a *woman* and is designated by her physical sex; for she who believes progresses "to the perfect man, to the measure of the maturity of Christ" (cf. *Eph* 4: 13). Then she dispenses with her worldly label, with the sex of her body...[32]

To be a woman is thus inferior to being a man, a *uir,* a thought that Ambrose makes explicit.[33] Ever mindful of this inferiority, a woman must be careful to keep silence, especially in church.[34] For if the *uir* did not maintain his mastery over the woman, she would fall again, as once she fell in Paradise,[35] and she would once more draw the *uir* with her down to degradation.[36] Besides, women

---

[28] JEROME, *Aduersus Iouinianum,* 1: 28 (*PL* 23, 250 B): "Non hic (Pro. 33: 16) de meretrice, non de adultera dicitur, sed amor mulieris generaliter accusatur, qui semper insatiabilis est, qui exstinctus accenditur, et post copiam rursus inops est, animumque uirilem effeminat, et excepta passione quam sustinet, aliud non sinit cogitare."

[29] Cf. JEROME, *Epist. 22 ad Eustochium,* 19 (*CSEL* 54, pp. 168-70). For a similar notion in AUGUSTINE, cf. *De Genesi ad litteram,* VIII, 5-8 (*CSEL* 28, 1, pp. 273-6). Actually, Augustine is more radical: bearing children justifies not only marriage, but woman's very *existence.*

[30] Sources in J.-M. AUBERT, *La femme...,* p. 72. Cf. also J.-C. GUY and F. REFOULÉ, *Chrétiennes des premiers temps* (Paris: Cerf, 1965), pp. 22-4.

[31] Cf. G.-H. TAVARD, *Woman...,* pp. 102-9.

[32] AMBROSE, *Expositio euang. sec. Luc.,* X, 161 (*CSEL* 32, 4, p. 517. 6): "Quæ non credit mulier est et adhuc corporei sexus appellatione signatur; nam quæ credit occurrit *in uirum perfectum, in mensuram ætatis plenitudinis Christi,* carens iam nomine sæculi, corporis sexu..."

[33] AMBROSE, *De paradiso,* 4: 24 (*CSEL* 32, 1, p. 280. 17): "Vir melior inuenitur et illa [...] est inferior". Cf. also *Explanatio ps. 1,* 14 (*CSEL* 64, p. 11. 23).

[34] AMBROSE, *De uirginibus,* III, 3: 9-11 (*PL* 16, cols. 222-3).

[35] AMBROSE, *Exameron,* V, 7: 18 (*CSEL* 32, 1, p. 153. 23).

[36] AMBROSE, *De uirginitate,* I, 6: 24-27 (*PL* 16, cols. 195-6); *Exhortatio uirginitatis,* 6: 36 (*PL* 16, col. 346 C).

cannot proclaim the Gospel for the further reason that they are too unstable to preach it and too weak to have it put into practice.[37]

It is less surprising to find such ideas in Augustine: his notions on sex, marriage and women have been written about too often to require any treatment here.[38] But he has received a great amount of attention because of the extensive influence he exercised in these areas on Western Church thinking, and because he represents the culmination of attitudes that at least partly consider sex as suspect and women as naturally inferior to men, to whom they are subjected by divine decree, and as responsible for original sin.[39] Where these notions are found, their biblical foundation is usually the passages we have already come across, from *Gen* 3 or the writings ascribed to Paul;[40] but the tone in which these notions are often expressed indicates that the foundation is used to maintain the convenient cultural and social *status quo,* in both civil and church life. Those same notions betray their possessors as torn between two views on marriage (and, by implication, sex and women), both of them something less than positive:[41] if marriage

---

[37] AMBROSE, *Expos. eu. sec. Luc.,* X, 157 (*CSEL* 32, 4, p. 515. 1): "Quia constantia ad prædicandum inferior, sexus ad exsequendum infirmior, uiris euangelizandi mandatur officium."

[38] Cf. K. E. BØRRESEN, *Subordination et équivalence. Nature et rôle de la femme d'après Augustin et Thomas d'Aquin* (Oslo-Paris: Universitetsforlaget, 1968), pp. 15-113; D. S. BAILEY, *The Man-Woman Relation in Christian Thought* (London: Longmans, 1959), pp. 50-61.

[39] For such texts in AUGUSTINE, cf. *supra,* notes 25 and 29. He claims (*Quæst. in Heptateuchum,* I, 103, *PL* 34, col. 590) that woman is intellectually inferior to man. Hence, when he states (*De Genesi ad litteram,* III, 22: 34, *CSEL* 28, 1, pp. 88-90) that woman is in the image of God, this is only in regard to her power to reason. The man alone is in the image of God in terms of both body and soul (cf. K. E. BØRRESEN, *Subordination...,* pp. 34-8). And it is always degrading to the man's soul to yield to a woman's enticements (for it is always the woman who entices) — even within the context of marriage (*Soliloquia,* I, 10, *PL* 32, col. 878).

[40] On these passages and their cultural connotations, cf. H. van der MEER, *Priestertum...,* pp. 15-59; J. R. DONAHUE, "Women, Priesthood and the Vatican," in *America,* vol. 136, no. 13 (New York: April 2, 1977), p. 287; J. J. O'ROURKE, "Women and the Reception of Orders," in *Revue de l'Université d'Ottawa,* 38 (Ottawa: 1968), pp. 291-4; and J. REUMANN, "What in Scripture Speaks to the Ordination of Women?", in *Concordia Theological Monthly,* 44 (St. Louis: 1973), pp. 15-22.

[41] What J. BUGGE (*Virginitas...,* p. 6) has to say about patristic views of the Fall is also applicable here: "It is a striking fact that commentators occupied with the first things seem to align themselves with one or the other of two quite distinct persuasions over the problem of sexuality in the Garden of Eden. First, there are those whose conclusions show a remarkable affinity to those of heterodox gnosticism, and who might, therefore, be regarded as

is a good, it is a lesser good, made necessary by woman, because of whom there must now be childbearing;[42] but sometimes marriage is seen rather as an evil — again because of woman, who (to the minds of some) is a symbol for evil.[43]

These are not the only views one finds, of course. The patristic corpus also contains positive things, even beautiful things, said of both marriage and women (even apart from a Marian context).[44] Yet these two views remained in force, alongside more positive ones, "woman as evil slowly casting her shadow over woman redeemed".[45] Logically such a process had to lead, not to the ordination of women,[46] but to the endorsement of celibacy for men about to be or already ordained.[47]

---

members of a 'Christian gnostic tradition' [...] On the other side, fundamentally opposed to these Christian gnostics, are certain Fathers of the Church whose ideas on the original nature of man are less austere and uncompromising; their most important spokesman is Augustine." For a wide selection of texts that express the two views on marriage, cf. J. E. KERNS, *The Theology..., passim;* D. S. BAILEY, *The Man-Woman Relation...,* pp. 19-28 and 43-62; D. F. WINSLOW, "Sex and Anti-Sex in the Early Church Fathers," in R. T. BARNHOUSE and U. T. HOLMES III (ed.), *Male and Female. Christian Approaches to Sexuality* (New York: Seabury Press, 1976), pp. 28-38; and the texts collected by F. QUÉRÉ-JAULMES, *La Femme. Les grands textes des Pères de l'Eglise* (*Lettres Chrétiennes,* 12; Paris: Editions du Centurion, 1968). Cf. also L. LELOIR, "La femme et les Pères du Désert," in *Collectanea Cisterciana,* 39 (Chimay: 1977), pp. 149-59; and the works referred to *supra,* note 2.

[42] JEROME says (*Epist.* 22 and Eustochium, 19, *CSEL* 54, p. 169. 5): "...et ut scias uirginitatem esse naturæ, nuptias post delictum." For similar statements in the Fathers, consult J.-M. AUBERT, *La femme...,* pp. 60-9; J. BUGGE, *Virginitas...,* pp. 16-9; J. E. KERNS, *The Theology...,* pp. 31-8 and 41-51; and G.-H. TAVARD, *Woman...,* pp. 67-8, 76-7 and 86-7.

[43] This is particularly true of Judæo-Christian circles. Cf. J. BUGGE, *Virginitas...,* pp. 6-21 (on the Gnostics); and G. H. TAVARD, *Woman...,* pp. 50-1.

[44] Cf. J. E. KERNS, *The Theology...,* pp. 13-27, 197-246 and *passim;* also J.-C. GUY and F. REFOULÉ, *Chrétiennes...,* pp. 25-8.

[45] G. H. TAVARD, *Woman...,* p. 72. See also J.-M. AUBERT, *La femme...,* p. 56; D. S. BAILEY, *The Man-Woman Relation...,* pp. 62-4; H. van der MEER, *Priestertum...,* pp. 90-101; and K. THRAEDE, "Frau" in *Reallexikon für Antike und Christentum,* 8 (Stuttgart: Hiersemann, 1973), cols. 242-3 and 254-60.

[46] An expression of this logical outcome is a statute by the Synod of Orleans (can. 18) of 533: "From now on the diaconal blessing is to be given to no woman, because of the weakness of her nature" (*CCL* 148A, p. 101. 70: "Placuit etiam, ut nulli postmodum fœminæ diaconalis benedictio pro conditionis huius fragilitate credatur").

[47] Cf. D. S. BAILEY, *The Man-Woman Relation...,* pp. 28-34; G. H. TAVARD, *Woman...,* p. 119; H. van der MEER, *Priestertum...,* pp. 118-20; B. COOKE, *Ministry to Word and Sacrament. History and Theology* (Philadelphia: Fortress, 1976), pp. 545 and 588-9; and J. A. RANGE, "Legal Exclusion of Women from Church Office," in *The Jurist,* 34 (Washington: 1974), pp. 112-27, esp. 114-6.

Even this brief glance over the available evidence justifies the need to qualify the statement that "in the writings of the Fathers [...] prejudices unfavourable to women [...] had hardly any influence on their pastoral activity, and still less on their spiritual direction". If their theology was influenced, then so was their pastoral activity, so was their spiritual direction. And, in the case of the writers we have thus far seen, their theology *was* influenced by these prejudices.[48]

So, too, was the theology of the patristic sources to which the *Declaration* explicitly refers in its argument against ordaining women to priesthood.

B. THE FATHERS INVOKED

There are eight such references, grouped in two footnotes (7 and 8). The first group of five references is called upon to support the statement that

> a few heretical sects in the first centuries, especially Gnostic ones, entrusted the exercise of the priestly ministry to women: this innovation was immediately noted and condemned by the Fathers, who considered it as unacceptable in the Church;

and the last three references are meant to illustrate the claim that

> over and above considerations inspired by the spirit of the times, one finds expressed — especially in the canonical documents of the Antiochian and Egyptian traditions — this essential reason, namely, that by calling only men to the priestly Order and ministry in its true sense,

---

[48] So P. de LABRIOLLE, "Mulieres...", pp. 114-5: "Il est curieux de constater à quel point les plus ouverts même, parmi les champions de l'orthodoxie, deviennent sensibles et chatouilleux, dès qu'ils sentent poindre la menace de l'indiscrétion féminine. Saint Jean Chrysostome nous fournit de cette susceptibilité une exemple significatif. A l'instant où Jean vient de rappeler avec admiration le rôle prépondérant de Priscilla, femme d'Aquila, dans la conversion d'Apollo, d'après le récit des Actes des Apôtres (xviii, 24 et s.), une inquiétude s'empare de lui et il se croit obligé de couper court à toute équivoque." For some the obligation had further ramifications. In a synod held at Auxerre some time between 561 and 605, a canon was passed forbidding women to receive Communion (in the hand) with uncovered hands (can. 36, *CCL* 148 A, p. 269. 101: "Non licet mulieri nudam manum eucharistiam accipere"). For a contemporary Eastern ruling along the same line, cf. the Synod of Laodicea (between 343 and 381), can. 44 (C. J. HEFELE, *Histoire des Conciles d'après les documents originaux*, tome 1, 2e partie [Paris: Letouzey et Ané, 1907], p. 1020).

the Church intends to remain faithful to the type of ordained ministry willed by the Lord Jesus Christ and carefully maintained by the Apostles.[49]

But do these references actually prove the claims they are intended to support? To answer this, we must try to determine what the texts referred to really *say,* the *circumstances* which provoke them to say it, and the *purpose* they hope to accomplish by saying it. These considerations will be kept in mind as each reference is examined, in the order in which the references are given in Footnotes 7 and 8 of the *Declaration.*[50]

1. IRENAEUS, *Aduersus hæreses,* 1, 13: 2

Bishop of Lyons from 177 or 178 to *circa* 202, Irenaeus was a prolific writer, but only two of his works have survived. Of these, *The Detection and Overthrow of the Pretended but False Gnosis* — or *Aduersus hæreses,* as it is more commonly known — now exists in its original Greek only in some parts, the text cited by the *Declaration* being one of those parts. That text belongs to the refutation of a Gnostic sect led by one Markos, and in the course of the refutation Irenaeus says:

> Pretending to consecrate (*eucharistein*) drinking-cups [containing] wine mixed [with water?], and dragging out the words of invocation (*epiklēsis*) over a long period of time, he [Markos] causes [the contents] to turn red and purple, so that Charis, one of those who are above all, may seem to let her own blood drop into that cup through his invocation, and so that all present, longing for that drink, may rejoice that Charis, contained within this sorcerer, will flow into them as well. Again he offers the cup of mixed drink, this time to women, whom

---

[49] *Declaration,* p. 101 (§ 6): "Fuerunt quidem primis sæculis nonnullæ sectæ hæreticæ præsertim gnosticæ, quæ mulieribus sacerdotale ministerium committere agressæ sunt: quod statim Patres animadversum vituperaverunt, utpote quod novum atque in Ecclesia minime accipiendum iudicarent [...] At prætermissis hisce commentationibus, illius temporis ingenio afflante concitatis, aperte legitur, præcipue in monumentis iuris ecclesiastici, quæ Antiochena et Aegyptiaca traditio servavit, ob eam propriam præcipue causam solos viros ad ordinem ministeriumque vere sacerdotale vocari, quia Ecclesia fideliter servare intendit exemplar illud sacerdotalis ministerii, quod Dominus Iesus Christus voluit quodque Apostoli accurate custodierunt."

[50] The history of the terms *episkopos, presbuteros, diakonos* is such (cf. B. COOKE, *Ministry...,* pp. 420-2, 444-7, 530-4 and *passim*) that I prefer to leave them in these forms, rather than risk translating them by the equivalents: bishop, priest, deacon. Be it added that all translations of patristic texts are my own.

he urges to consecrate in front of him. Once this has been done, he produces another drinking-cup much larger than that consecrated by the woman he has deluded; then, pouring from the smaller one — the one consecrated by the woman — into the one presented by himself, at the same time he exclaims, "May Charis, who is before all, Charis, the incomprehensible and unutterable, satisfy your inner man (*anthrōpos*) and bring the knowledge concerning her to completion in you, sowing the mustard-seed in good ground". And as he says such things he drives this miserable woman into a frenzy and appears to be a wonder-worker, since the large cup is filled from the small to the point where it has been made to overflow. And, by doing other things of this kind for them, he has completely deceived many and led them after himself into error.[51]

Of this Markos nothing is known besides what Irenaeus tells us.[52] The following chapters (3-7) make the claim that Markos was a 'ladies' man' who exploited women in a variety of ways. So the crux of the matter seems to be that this was one of those ways: a *man* makes a woman carry out the *pretense* of "eucharistizing". Irenaeus' indignation is directed at Markos, not the woman, who is presented as a victim. The clearest indication of this is the attention given to what *Markos* does: in a mockery of the Great Church's liturgy, he performs acts which purport to be *of themselves* sufficient for salvation (following a general Gnostic tendency at the end of the II century),[53] therefore even more efficacious than their sacramental equivalent in the Church which Irenaeus represents.

---

[51] *PG* 7, cols. 580-1.

[52] The brief notices by HIPPOLYTUS (*Philosophoumena,* VI, 42, *GCS* 26, pp. 173-5) and EPIPHANIUS (*Panarion,* 34: 1, *GCS* 31, pp. 5-6) are dependent on Irenæus. On Markos and the Markosians, cf. also E. de FAYE, *Gnostiques et Gnosticisme. Etude critique des documents du Gnosticisme chrétien aux IIe et IIIe siècles (Bibliothèque de l'Ecole des Hautes Etudes,* Sciences Religieuses, 27; Paris: E. Leroux, 1913), pp. 313-25; F.-M.-M. SAGNARD, *La Gnose valentinienne et le témoignage de saint Irénée (Etudes de Philosophie Médiévale,* XXXVI; Paris: J. Vrin, 1947), pp. 358-86; and L. ZSCHARNACK, *Der Dienst der Frau in den ersten Jahrhunderten der christlichen Kirche* (Göttingen: Vandenhoeck & Ruprecht, 1902), pp. 171-3.

[53] Cf. E. de FAYE, *Gnostiques...,* pp. 324-5: "Les écrits gnostiques coptes nous ont permis de constater qu'il se produit, vers le commencement du IIIe siècle, un changement profond au sein même du gnosticisme. Il est incontestable que, dans les sectes dont proviennent les documents coptes, on faisait dépendre le salut bien plus du rite que de la gnose. Le baptême et l'eucharistie sont maintenant des sacrements dont l'efficacité s'étend jusque dans l'au-delà. Il n'est pas douteux, d'autre part, que les gnostiques du IIe siècle, notamment les hommes des deux premières générations, aient fait très exclusivement consister la rédemption dans la possession d'une gnose transcendante. Les causes qui ont amené la substitution graduelle du rite à la gnose ont été sans doute

We might be able to say more with certainty if we knew more about Irenaeus' sources.[54] We know that *Aduersus haereses* was written between 180 and 190, which was well after Irenaeus left Asia Minor, where Markos and his followers were. There is no reason to believe that Irenaeus ever had a chance to observe Markos at firsthand, and perhaps his only source of information about him was women who had once belonged to the sect.[55]

In any case, the text in question cannot be used as an argument against the priestly ordination of women. Not only is ordination not mentioned, it is not even implied. What *is* implied is the exploitation of women in the name of religion — in fact, the exploitation of women *and* men.[56] Implied, too, is the general theme in *Aduersus haereses,* which is Irenaeus' anti-Gnosticism. Markos' actions involve the female deity *Charis* (Grace), and he has women join him in his 'liturgy' to heighten the symbolism. In the beginning of his work Irenaeus tells us that Charis — identified with *Sigē* (Silence) or *Ennoia* (Thought) — is consort of the Gnostic supreme deity, *Buthos* (Abyss), whose supremacy she shares.[57] In Irenaeus' eyes the entire framework of the Markosian activity — no matter whom it involves — would therefore lack validity, because for him the supreme deity has no consort.

Even were one able to find in Irenaeus' writings an explicit denunciation of the ordination of women, it would have to be employed with caution. For Irenaeus has to be counted among those Fathers whose feelings about women are sometimes less than

---

diverses [...] Les marcosiens ont ceci d'intéressant qu'ils marquent le moment où se fait la transition. L'idée sacramentelle commence à pénétrer parmi eux. Il s'y trouve des gens qui attribuent une efficace spéciale au baptême, et qui voudraient donner à la cérémonie une importance et un éclat qu'elle n'avait pas encore [...] Au IIIᵉ siècle, presque dans toutes les sectes gnostiques, la gnose est reléguée au second plan; le rite est au premier. La révolution est faite."

[54] Cf. J. SOBOSAN, "The Role of the Presbyter. An Investigation into the *Advertus Hæreses* of Saint Irenaeus," in *Scottish Journal of Theology,* 27 (Edinburgh: 1974), p. 130: "In writing the *Adversus Hæreses,* Irenaeus relied on treatises written by others; since most of these sources are no longer extant, the due proportion between the originality of Irenaeus as weighed against his dependence on earlier writers is a matter of conjecture."

[55] Cf. IRENAEUS, *Adu. hær.,* I, 13: 4 (*PG* 7, col. 586 A).

[56] Cf. *ibid.,* I, 13: 1 (col. 577 B): "*...gunaia kai andras hup'auto peplanēmena.*"

[57] *Ibid.,* I, 1: 1 (col. 445 A).

positive. He considers Eve to be the cause of death, in herself and in all humanity.[58] Adam was merely misguided; he fell only because of betrayal by Eve,[59] who is not made in God's image.[60] This is probably a factor to consider whenever we find Irenaeus talking about women: but, while the text we have been examining does speak (marginally) of them, it has no bearing on the question of their ordination to priestly ministry.

2. TERTULLIAN, *De præscriptione hæreticorum,* 41: 5

Though he ended his days outside the Catholic Church, Tertullian (+ *ca.* 220) remains among the most influential of early Christian Latin writers. His works are usually categorized into those composed in his Catholic period, those written during his transition to Montanism, and those penned while he was a Montanist. *De præscriptione (ca.* 206) belongs to the middle category. In the brief passage from it to which the *Declaration* refers, Tertullian says:

> How impudent those heretical women who would dare to teach, to engage in disputation, to perform exorcisms, to promise healings — perhaps even to baptize![61]

Once more it is Gnosticism that is under attack, this time a branch of the Marcionites. This should immediately put us on our guard against making too much of these few words. They reveal that Tertullian's source of information is not firsthand, since they express uncertainty about just what it is these "heretical women" do: *perhaps (fortasse an)* they baptize.[62] The words reveal little else,

---

[58] *Ibid.,* III, 22: 4 (*Sources Chrétiennes,* 211, p. 440. 65) and V, 19: 1 (*SC* 153, p. 248. 6).

[59] *Ibid.,* III, 23: 5 (*SC* 211, p. 460. 125).

[60] *Ibid.,* III, 23: 2 (p. 448. 30); cf. also *Epideixis,* 11 (*SC* 62, pp. 48-50).

[61] *CCL* 1, p. 221. 13 (also *CSEL* 70, p. 53. 13): "Ipsæ mulieres hæreticæ, quam procaces! quæ audeant docere, contendere, exorcismos agere, curationes repromittere, fortasse an et tingere."

[62] The manner in which Tertullian expresses himself here belies the interpretation of R. GRYSON, *Le ministère...,* p. 42: "La restriction qu'introduit à cet endroit Tertullien, — *'peut-être* même baptiser', — semble indiquer que cet abus n'était guère répandu et que l'auteur l'envisage plutôt comme une hypothèse que comme un fait avéré." Tertullian may not be dealing with an established fact, but he is not dealing with a mere hypothesis, either. He is basing himself on secondhand knowledge, and the information was garbled enough to make the item about possible baptism unclear. But the possibility was there, as the contemporary *De baptismo* (17: 4, *CCL* 1, p. 291. 20) affirms.

except Tertullian's usual irritation with the disorderly nature of most Gnostic expressions of cult.[63] Certainly the passage cannot be used to prove that women should not be admitted to ordination, about which there is no mention.[64] Even the argument that Tertullian's prohibition to women to teach and so on implies that they cannot be ordained loses a great deal of its force when thrown up against his well-known antipathy to women and to their involvement in *any* aspect of church life. The classic example of this antipathy is a passage from a work contemporary to *De præscriptione*:

> You give birth in sorrows and anxieties, O woman, and your yearning is for your husband (*uir*) and he lords it over you (cf. *Gen* 3: 16); and you don't know that you are an Eve? The sentence God passed on that sex lives on in the present age; so it must be that the guilt for the sin lives on as well. You are the devil's gateway, you are the violator of the tree, you are the first deserter of God's law; you are the one who duped him whom the devil was not powerful enough to assault; you shattered so easily God's image, man (*homo*). On account of the death you richly deserved, even the Son of God had to die...[65]

How would it be possible for Tertullian to divorce this fundamental attitude from any dealings with women? As far as

---

[63] Cf. P. de Labriolle, *La crise montaniste* (Paris: E. Leroux, 1913), p. 304: "Tertullien avait un goût natif pour les organisations régulières, où chaque fonction et nettement définie et où les droits acquis sont sûrs d'être respectés. Autant que l'absence de règle dans l'ordre intellectuel, l'incohérence dans l'ordre pratique lui infligeait un véritable malaise. Au fond, en cet homme si fécond en outrances, si complaisant aux paradoxes, se cachait l'âme d'un consciencieux administrateur, pour qui une exacte hiérarchie est la condition absolue du bon fonctionnement des services. De là venait pour une large part son antipathie contre les hérétiques de son temps, gens *sine grauitate, sine auctoritate, sine disciplina*, chez qui aucune ordonnance fixe ne réglait la place réservée à chacun."

[64] Cf. P.-H. Lafontaine, "Le sexe masculin, condition de l'accession aux ordres, aux IVᵉ et Vᵉ siècles," in *Revue de l'Université d'Ottawa*, Section spéciale, 31 (Ottawa: 1961), p. 141*, n. 9: "Les sources n'établissent pas d'une façon suffisamment spécifique la participation des femmes à la liturgie ou au magistère dans le marcionisme pour que nous en traitions ici, même si cette participation est très probable."

[65] Tertullian, *De cultu feminarum*, I, 1: 1-2 (*CCL* 1, p. 343. 13): "In doloribus et anxietatibus paris, mulier, et ad uirum tuum conuersio tua, et ille dominatur tui: et Euam te esse nescis? uiuit sententia dei super sexum istum in hoc sæculo: uiuat et reatus necesse est. tu es diaboli ianua, tu es arboris illius resignatrix, tu es diuinæ legis prima desertrix; tu es quæ eum suasisti, quem diabolus aggredi non ualuit; tu imaginem dei hominem tam facile elisisti; propter tuum meritum, id est mortem, etiam filium dei mori habuit..." I have substituted the word *tam* (so), which is the reading of all the manuscripts, for *Adam*, which is the conjecture in both *CCL* and *CSEL* (vol. 70).

he is concerned, God's curse on Eve lives on in all her daughters, even those who have been baptized. And through her daughters — even after baptism — Eve remains the temptress, still the occasion of sin.[66] This view breaks out even in Tertullian's more positive statements about marriage, which is nonetheless always a sign of fallen mankind's weakness.[67] People do not so much marry as "fall into" marriage,[68] and second marriages are to be avoided at all costs.[69]

These are less conclusions he has arrived at from his study of Scripture, than they are the bases on which he approaches it. Such texts as *Gen* 3: 16 are used here to bolster a position already held,[70] and to reinforce, particularly in conjunction with *I Cor* 14: 34-35, Tertullian's conviction that women are to be permitted no office in church.[71] But that conviction is itself based on a doubtful premise — woman as the unceasing occasion of sin.

3. FIRMILIAN of CAESAREA

In or about 256 this bishop wrote a letter to Cyprian of Carthage. This letter of Firmilian (+ 268), which is now preserved

---

[66] *Ibid.*, II, 2: 1 (*CCL* 1, p. 354. 1); cf. also *De patientia, 5:* 10 (*CCL* 1, p. 329. 36).

[67] See the references given by G. H. TAVARD, *Woman...*, pp. 59-61.

[68] TERTULLIAN, *De uirginibus uelandis,* 17: 1 (*CCL* 2, p. 1225. 2).

[69] TERTULLIAN, *De monogamia,* 16: 1 (*CCL* 2, p. 1251. 2.). Cf. P. de LABRIOLLE, "Un épisode de l'histoire de la morale chrétienne. La lutte de Tertullien contre les secondes noces," in *Annales de philosophie chrétienne,* IVᵉ série, tome 4 (Paris: avril-septembre 1907), pp. 362-88.

[70] Cf. G. H. TAVARD, *Woman...*, pp. 57-8: "Previous authors were anxious to stress the historical differences between the Old and the New Covenants. Tertullian makes little distinction between the two moments of the Revelation when he is looking for texts supporting his doctrines. And once he is convinced of the sense and value of a text, he pushes its logic to the end with what may be called fanatical zeal. What the Book of Genesis says, for instance, about Eve, is the ultimate truth about every woman. Paul's direction about the veiling of women in church stands for all times, all places, and all conditions of womanhood. His views of marriage and continence are not a counsel but a decree from which no exception is admissible."

[71] Cf. TERTULLIAN, *De baptismo, 17:* 4, 4 (*CCL* 1, p. 291. 20), and *De cultu feminarum,* 13: 7 (*CCL* 1, p. 370. 36). As a Montanist, Tertullian relaxed his opposition somewhat to church office for women, for he then granted them a prophetic function, in contrast to his pre-Montanist stance. Compare the Montanist works *De anima* (9: 4, *CCL* 2, p. 792. 24) and *De uirginibus uelandis* (9: 1, *CCL* 2, p. 1218. 4) with *Aduersus Marcionem,* written just prior to leaving Catholicism (V, 8: 11, *CCL* 1, p. 688. 7). On the change, cf. P. de LABRIOLLE, *La crise...*, pp. 300-4 and 318-22; also "Mulieres...", pp. 107-8.

among the letters written by Cyprian himself, gives an account of an incident witnessed by the writer in Palestine nearly twenty-two years before. During one of the intermittent persecutions against Christians, there suddenly appeared in the district a woman from Cappadocia. Calling herself a prophetess, and claiming to be filled with the Holy Spirit, she worked wonders, and she said she had the power even to cause an earthquake. Through the lies she told — or rather, amends Firmilian, through the lies of the demon within her — she gathered a large following. She had even managed to win over a priest and a deacon, before an exorcist unmasked her as the possessed woman she was.

Then comes the segment of the letter to which the *Declaration* refers:

> Through the demon's tricks and illusions this woman had previously been working at deceiving the faithful in a variety of ways. Among those means with which she had duped many, what she frequently dared to do was this: using the proper invocation, she pretended to sanctify bread and to consecrate it; she offered sacrifice to the Lord in an act of liturgy celebrated according to an approved rite; and she baptized many, making use of the traditional and legitimate wording of the interrogation. And she did all this in such a manner that in no way did she seem to deviate from the rule set down by the Church.[72]

A threefold liturgical activity is reported in this account. The woman *(illa mulier)* pronounced the proper words *(inuocatio)* of the preparatory *epiclesis* and of the consecration *(sanctificare se panem et eucharistiam facere);* she offered sacrifice (i.e. consecrated bread and wine) to the Lord *(sacrificium domino offerret);* and she baptized *(baptizaret).* Firmilian stresses that in all three instances she followed the proper procedure and used the accepted formulae, so as to appear to be in complete conformity with what the Church has prescribed *(ut nihil discrepare ab ecclesiastica regula uideretur)*: she consecrated with the right words *(inuocatione non*

---

[72] *Inter epistulas Cypriani, 75,* 10: 1 *(CSEL* 3, p. 817. 28): "Atqui illa mulier quæ prius per præstigias et fallacias dæmonis multa ad deceptionem fidelium moliebatur, inter cetera quibus plurimos deceperat etiam hoc frequenter ausa est, ut et inuocatione non contemptibili sanctificare se panem et eucharistiam facere simularet et sacrificium domino [non] sine sacramento solitæ prædicationis offerret, baptizaret quoque multos usitata et legitima uerba interrogationis usurpans, ut nihil discrepare ab ecclesiastica regula uideretur."

contemptibili); she offered the consecrated gifts with the proper *anamnēsis ([non] sine sacramento solitæ prædicationis);*[73] and she baptized after putting the proper series of questions to the candidates *(usitata et legitima uerba interrogationis usurpans).*[74]

If the example of Firmilian himself is anything to go by, what he says here cannot be employed as indicative of the patristic stance against ordaining women. His reason for the narrative becomes clear in the commentary that follows, and it is a reason that has nothing to do with ordination:

> What, then, are we to say about such a baptism, in which a wicked demon baptized through a woman? Do Stephen and those who side with him condone this, particularly since neither the trinitarian creed nor the legitimate interrogation was lacking? Can it really be believed that the forgiveness of sins took place or that the saving rebirth by water (*Tit* 3: 5) was properly accomplished, since everything had been done in a semblance of truth but actually through a demon? Unless those who acknowledge baptism by heretics are claiming that a demon could have conferred the grace of baptism, in the name of the Father and of the Son and of the Holy Spirit! But doubtless the same error, the same demonic trickery, is in them that is in the heretics, from whom the Holy Spirit is totally absent.[75]

The reader is immediately struck by a curious omission: of the three acts ascribed to the woman, only baptism receives attention. But if Firmilian's intent is to fulminate against "women

---

[73] G. HARTEL omits *non* in *CSEL* 3; but the entire phrase, in order to fit its context, requires changing *sine* to *siue* or the addition of *non* to *sine.* Cf. P. de LABRIOLLE, "Mulieres...", p. 121, n. 1.

[74] It should not be forgotten that this letter was probably written originally in Greek. In any case, the Latin terms employed here in reference to liturgical acts would be a translation of terminology with which Firmilian was familiar in Palestine. On this terminology cf. C. BAYARD, *Saint Cyprien. Correspondance,* t. II (Paris: Société d'Edition "Les Belles Lettres", 1925), p. 297, n. 1; this should be read in conjunction with P.-H. LAFONTAINE, "Le sexe masculin...", p. 142*, n. 11.

[75] *Inter epistulas Cypriani,* 75, 10: 2 (*CSEL* 3, p. 818. 8): "Quid igitur de huius baptismo dicemus, quo nequissimus dæmon per mulierem baptizauit? numquid et hoc Stephanus et qui illi consentiunt conprobant, maxime cui nec symbolum trinitatis nec interrogatio legitima et ecclesiastica defuit? potest credi aut remissio peccatorum data aut lauacri salutaris regeneratio rite perfecta, ubi omnia quamuis ad imaginem ueritatis tamen per dæmonem gesta sunt? nisi si et dæmonem in nomine patris et filii et spiritus sancti gratiam baptismi dedisse contendunt qui hæreticorum baptismata adserunt, apud quos sine dubio idem error est, dæmonum fallacia ipsa est, quando apud illos omnino sanctus spiritus non est."

priests", we would expect him to deal now with all three of those acts — especially the two he omits.

To the omission add a contradiction: the woman is not the central figure in the commentary, but the "wicked demon" who baptized (and performed the other acts) through her is the real cause of Firmilian's indignation. We understand why when the circumstances of Firmilian's letter are explained.

His purpose in writing to Cyprian is to offer support to the latter in his famous quarrel with Pope Stephen over heretical baptisms. Stephen is prepared to accept the validity of such baptisms, Cyprian is not. In his letter Firmilian is endorsing Cyprian's contention that no baptism — and *a fortiori* no other sacrament — administered by heretics can be valid, since the Holy Spirit will not be found among heretics *(quando apud illos omnino sanctus spiritus non est).*[76] The woman's activities are thus repudiated, not because she is a woman, but because she is a heretic, and as such filled with a demon rather than with the Holy Spirit. This forms the basis for the rest of Firmilian's argument. The demon performed all the actions, using the woman as his instrument; but he was careful to perform them according to the rite established by the Great Church. If Stephen and his cohorts are ready to recognize the validity of baptisms conferred by heretics, so long as they have been conferred according to the prescribed rite, they should also be ready to accept as valid the actions of this demon.

Far from being an argument against women's ordination (of which Firmilian makes no mention), the passage to which the *Declaration* refers us can only be used for what it is: an illustration of Cyprian's quarrel with Pope Stephen.[77]

---

[76] Here Firmilian echoes the same argument employed by Cyprian himself (*Epist.* 74, 4, *CSEL* 3, p. 802. 17): one cannot transmit the Spirit who does not possess the Spirit.

[77] P.-H. LAFONTAINE *("Le sexe masculin...",* p. 148*) extracts more from the passage than it has to offer when he concludes (emphasis mine): "Firmilien de Césarée ne fait que décrire la conduite de la prophétesse de Cappadoce. Mais son langage *laisse entendre* qu'il s'agit de simulation et, par voie de conséquence, *suppose* l'incapacité radicale de la femme d'accéder au vrai sacerdoce." This conclusion can only be reached by ignoring the whole background of the polemic against Stephen.

4. ORIGEN, *Commentarium in I^am epist. ad Corinthios,* 14: 34-35

The passage from Origen to which the *Declaration* calls attention belongs to a collection of fragments found in an eleventh-century manuscript in the Vatican.[78] In this commentary on a passage that is classic when the more misogynistic Fathers are discussing women,[79] Origen (+ *ca.* 250) attempts to illustrate the consequences when women disobey Paul's injunction to keep silent in assemblies. The example he produces is one we shall encounter again, that of the Montanist prophetesses Priscilla and Maximilla. To justify the prophetic activity of these women, their disciples, says Origen, employ the following line of reasoning:

> They say that Philip the Evangelist had four daughters who prophesied (cf. *Acts* 21: 9): now, if these prophesied, why should it be out of place for our own prophetesses — as they call them — to prophesy also?

> Let us unravel this tangled assertion. First of all, since you say, "Our own women prophesied", prove that the marks of prophecy were in them. Secondly, Philip's daughters may indeed have prophesied, but it was not in assemblies that they spoke; we have no such case in the Acts of the Apostles nor, for that matter, anywhere in the Old Testament. It is testified that Deborah was a prophetess (cf. *Judges* 4: 4). Aaron's sister Miriam stepped forward from the women's ranks, her tambourine in her hand (cf. *Ex* 15: 20-21). But it so happens that we do not find Deborah delivering public speeches to the people, in the manner of a Jeremiah or an Isaiah. We do not find Huldah, who was a prophetess, making an address to the people, but rather to an individual man who had come to her home seeking her out (cf. *2 Kings* 22: 14-20). In the Gospel there is an account of the prophetess Anna, daughter of Phanuel, of the tribe of Asher (cf. *Luke* 2: 36), but it was not in an assembly that she spoke out. Even if (on the basis of the prophetic mark) it is granted that a woman is a prophetess, she is still not permitted to speak out in an assembly. When the prophetess Miriam spoke out, it was as the leader of certain women. "For it is not right for a woman to speak out in an assembly" (*1 Cor* 14: 35) and "I am not giving permission for a woman to teach", still less "to tell a man what to do" (*1 Tim* 2: 12).

---

[78] Codex Vat. gr. 762, published by C. JENKINS, "Origen on I. Corinthians," IV, in *Journal of Theological Studies,* 10 (Oxford: 1908-09). The text in question is Fragment 74 (pp. 41-2).

[79] Cf. *supra,* pp. 55-6.

I will go on proving this from yet another source, even though what has already been quoted states in a more categorical way that a woman is not to make herself by her words the guide of a man. "The older women should behave like women who are religious; they are to be the teachers of right behaviour, and to show the younger women how to act with moderation" (cf. *Tit* 2: 3-4), not simply are they "to be the teachers": for women should stick steadfastly to "teaching right behaviour", but not in such a way that men are seated and listening to women, as though there were not enough men capable of mediating the word of God.

"If they have any questions to ask, they should ask their own men at home; for it is not right for a woman to speak out in an assembly" (*1 Cor* 14: 35). It seems to me that the phrase "their own men" does not refer to husbands alone. If it did, virgins would either be speaking out in an assembly, or be without anyone to teach them, and the same would be true of widows. Cannot "their own men" also include brother, kinsman, son?

In summary, a woman should acquire her information from "her man", "man" being understood here as a general term contrasted to "woman". "For it is not right for a woman to speak out in an assembly", no matter what she says; even if she utters marvellous things, holy things, the fact remains that all of it is only coming from the mouth of a woman. It is clear that "a woman in an assembly" is pronounced to be "not right" as an indictment against the assembly as a whole.

Can this passage rightfully be invoked as a patristic prohibition against priestly ministry for women? To teach *(didaskein)* or to mediate the word of God *(presbeuein ton tou theou logon)* are, it might be argued, priestly functions, and certainly Origen, on the basis of Scripture,[80] is forbidding those functions to women. But to follow that argument would be, in Origen's case at least, to put the cart before the horse. Aside from the fact that it would only apply to the exclusion of laypersons *as such,* men *or* women, from the exercise of functions which properly pertain to an ordained

---

[80] Generally I follow the Bible of Jerusalem translation (BJ), but the way in which Origen uses his scriptural references sometimes necessitates taking liberties with the text. "It is not right" fits Origen's usage better than BJ's less dogmatic "it does not seem right", though both phrases translate the Greek *aischron*. For a similar reason, I have rendered *en ekklēsia lalein* as "to speak out in an assembly" where BJ has "to raise her voice at meetings", because Origen has in mind something more formal than simple meetings and something more solemn than simply raising one's voice. Finally, it was necessary to render *tous idious andras eperōtatōsan* as "ask their own men" instead of "husbands", because Origen's argumentation would otherwise make no sense.

priesthood, there is the consideration of the main issue at hand. For Origen that issue is not priesthood at all, but *prophecy* — not only whether it was valid in the case of Priscilla or Maximilla, but whether, since the close of the Old Testament, it is *ever valid at all.* So far as he is concerned, the time for prophecy is now over;[81] any attempt to revive it, no matter by whom, is bound to encounter Origen's suspicion.[82] If such an attempt can be undermined by Scripture, so much the better; and it does not really seem to matter to Origen that *1 Cor* 14: 34-35 (leaving aside the questions of its interpretation and authenticity)[83] is not in reference to prophecy at all, or that Paul distinguished teaching and prophecy and treated them as separate charisms (cf. *Rom* 12: 6-7 and *1 Cor* 12: 4-10 and 28). Hence his argumentation against prophecy (for anyone, male or female) in the Christian era is untenable. But, even if it were not, it could not be used against the admission of women to priesthood for two reasons: Origen does not discuss the subject at all in this passage; and Paul makes a further distinction between those he terms "prophets" and those he calls "apostles", the latter possibly meaning a more 'sacerdotal' ministry (cf. *1 Cor* 12: 28 and *Eph* 4: 11).

With all of this said, it should be added that this passage reveals a certain anti-feminine prejudice. Having denied that prophecy exists anywhere, let alone in the Montanist women Priscilla and Maximilla, Origen applies the *coup de grâce:* "the fact remains that all of it is only coming from the mouth of a woman"

---

[81] So J. L. ASH, Jr., "The Decline of Ecstatic Prophecy in the Early Church," in *Theological Studies,* 37 (Baltimore: 1976), pp. 247-8.

[82] *Ibid.,* p. 248: "For Origen, then, Montanist prophets were heretical simply because prophets did not properly belong to the Christian era." It is a mystery to me how P.-L. CARLE can say, "La femme et les ministères pastoraux d'après la tradition," in *Nova et Vetera,* 47 (Geneva: 1972), p. 282, that "nul n'élève la voix pour exclure le prophétisme féminin", citing this fragment (p. 282, n. 2) as one of the indications that "les voix sont convergentes en faveur du prophétisme féminin". Though Origen was primarily occupied with proving the extinction of prophecy among Jews, he would never have agreed with Justin (*Dial. cum Tryphone,* 82) that it has now been transferred to *Christians.*

[83] Cf. J. J. O'ROURKE, *Women...",* pp. 291-2; also J. REUMANN, "What in Scripture...", p. 19: "Because of this likely limitation to wives (not a general rule for women), the puzzling relation to *1 Cor* 11 (and *Gal* 3: 28), and the possibility involved of interpolation (in the opinion of some), this verse today makes a much less certain basis for forbidding ordination of women than it often has seemed in past usage." Cf. also *supra,* p. 57.

(monon de apo stomatos gunaikeiou exerchētai). This remark is not inextricably linked to Origen's stance on prophecy, but reveals an attitude scattered throughout his extant writings.[84] Commenting elsewhere on *1 Cor* 14: 35, he maintains that God would not lower himself to look at what is corporeal or what is feminine:[85] that is why a woman, when she wishes to partake of the Body of Christ, has to have in herself "a manly soul".[86] Origen is among those who see virginity as the original state of mankind, and original sin as the soul's fall from pure spiritual existence into flesh.[87] In fact, woman becomes for him the symbol of a soul unable to resist temptation.[88]

With this negative approach, it is difficult to see how Origen could maintain his objectivity when speaking about women, no matter what the context. From that regard alone the passage that has been studied here would be subject to some doubt. More to the point is that the passage cannot be invoked to forbid ordination to women; it can only be used to illustrate Origen's antipathy to prophecy.

5. Epiphanius of Salamis, *Panarion*

The *Declaration* gives three references to the "Medicine Chest", written between 374 and 377. As the passages are rather long, they will be quoted and dealt with individually.

---

[84] As G. H. Tavard says, *Woman...,* pp. 68-9: "One of his chief objections to Montanism was that the Cata-Phrygians did not leave woman where she belongs." Cf. also P. de Labriolle, "Mulieres...", pp. 23-4 and 109-11; and H. Crouzel, *Virginité et mariage selon Origène* (Paris-Bruges: Desclée de Brouwer, 1962), pp. 135-9.

[85] Origen, *Selecta in Exodum,* 23: 17 (*PG* 12, col. 297 A). Cf. H. Crouzel, *Virginité...,* pp. 49-53.

[86] Origen, *Hom. in Leuiticum,* IV, 8 (*GCS* 28, p. 328. 10). Cf. also *Hom. in Iosue,* IX, 9 (*GCS* 8, p. 356. 3).

[87] In another fragment of his commentary on I Corinthians, Origen says that the curse on the woman reported in *Gen* 3: 16 is lifted from a Christian woman — not by marriage, but by virginity: cf. C. Jenkins, "Origen...", III, in *Journal of Theological Studies,* 9 (1907-08), p. 510. This idea can be traced back to his notion (engendered by Middle Platonism and shared by many Christian writers) that the flesh — and therefore male/female sex differentiation — is itself a punishment for the Fall: cf. *Hom. 14 in Lucam 2* (*PG* 13, cols. 1836-7). On the Platonist view, cf. R. A. Baer, Jr., *Philo's Use of the Categories Male and Female (Arbeiten zur Literatur und Geschichte des hellenistischen Judentums,* III; Leiden: Brill, 1970).

[88] Origen, *Hom. in Leuiticum,* II, 5 (*GCS* 29, p. 298. 5); *Hom in Num.,* I, 1 (*GCS* 30, p. 3. 6).

a) 49: 2-3

This concerns a group linked to the "Cataphrygians" (Montanists)[89] and called "Quintillians". The terms are so reminiscent of Origen that he could well be the source here.[90] In any case, what Epiphanius has to say about them is this:

> They, too, make use of both the Old and the New Testament, and they likewise affirm the resurrection of the dead. They regard Quintilla as a foundress, along with Priscilla (who is also regarded as such by the Cataphrygians). They make many false claims, as when they affirm that Eve was the first to eat of the Tree of Knowledge, or when, to justify admitting women into their clergy, they say that the sister of Moses was a prophetess and that Philip had four daughters who prophesied. Frequently a group of seven virgins, clad in white and bearing lamps, will appear before their assemblies: they have actually come to prophesy to the people! To give the people the impression that they are inspired, they create illusions, give false impressions, and make the audience break into tears and perform all kinds of penances to obtain mercy. The women themselves shed tears and lament, with suitable gestures, over the life of mankind. Among them are women *episkopoi*, women *presbuteroi* and the like. They say there should be no distinction, "For in Christ Jesus there is neither male nor female" (*Gal* 3: 28).

> These are the data we have been able to collect.

Though he makes an allusion to women bishops and priests, it is already clear that, like Origen, Epiphanius has here for his main concern the question of *prophecy*,[91] unlike Origen, he recognizes the continued presence of prophecy in the Church, but he sees it as absorbed by the *episcopal* role.[92] This is the only use that can be made of Epiphanius' text, but the rest of the passage is interesting, because it points to his general feeling on women and ministry:

> The full scorn of mankind should be poured on him who deviates from the true faith and abandons himself to a multiplicity of frenzied

---

[89] Treated by EPIPHANIUS in *Panarion*, 48 (*GCS* 31, pp. 219-41). It is not clear just how Cataphrygians differed from Quintillians. Cf. P. de LABRIOLLE, *La crise...*, p. 585.

[90] K. HOLL notes a resemblance (*GCS* 31, p. 243, note). In turn, AUGUSTINE, *De hæresibus*, 26-28 (*CCL* 46, pp. 302-3) and JOHN DAMASCENE, *De hæresibus*, 49 (*PG* 94, col. 767 A) draw on Epiphanius.

[91] Explicit in *Panarion*, 49: 1 (*GCS* 31, p. 242. 10): "*Gunaikes goun par' autois kalountai prophētides.*"

[92] Cf J. L. ASH, "The Decline...", p. 239-41 and 248-52; B. COOKE, *Ministry...*, Chapter 10.

and orgiastic behaviour. For such notions always turn mad those who
do not keep a firm grip on the anchor of truth, but let themselves
go adrift, to be carried away by whatever wind happens along. If their
view is that because of Eve women can be admitted to the office of
episkopos and *presbuteros,* they have heard the word of the Lord saying,
"Your yearning shall be for your husband, yet he shall lord it over you"
(*Gen* 3: 16). To them as well is addressed the apostle's saying, "I do
not permit a woman to speak out nor to tell a man what to do" (cf.
1 Tim 2: 12), and again, "For the man did not come from the woman,
but the woman came from the man" (*1 Cor* 11: 8), and further, "It
was not Adam who was led astray, but Eve who was the first to be
led astray and into sin" (*1 Tim* 2: 14). Oh, the manifold wickedness
of this world![93]

We must not be diverted by the explicit mention here of
women's admission to priesthood and episcopacy. Though later
citations from Epiphanius will make it clear that such admission
is unacceptable to him, in the present text the main point is that
this Montanist group's cardinal sin is Montanism: the reference to
roles filled by women is to illustrate how far into heresy the group
has sunk.[94] His diatribe against a bit of hearsay — for in his case
it cannot be more than that[95] — calls on every scriptural source
available, including the *loci classici* against female involvement:
Gen 3: 16, *1 Cor* 11: 8; *1 Tim* 2: 12-14. But in *1 Tim* 2: 12 he has
suppressed the specific "teach" *(didaskein),* substituting the more
general "speak out" *(lalein)* borrowed from *1 Cor* 14: 35; and, like
Origen, he has conveniently forgotten the distinctions made in *1
Cor* 12: 4 and 28. This eclectic use of Scripture — and the anti-
feminism which it expresses — is more clearly seen in the other
passages from the *Panarion* still to be studied.

---

93 *GCS* 31, p. 242. 13 — p. 244. 7.
94 HIPPOLYTUS, *Philosophoumena,* 8: 19 (*GCS* 26, p. 238. 4) mocks the
"Phrygians" for letting themselves fall under the thumbs of *gunaia.*
95 P.-H. LAFONTAINE, "Le sexe masculin...", pp. 145*-7*, holds for the
veracity of Epiphanius' account, but admits that he is the only source to
speak of Montanist women being ordained to priesthood. He concludes,
rather lamely: "Il est possible que ses sources fussent plutôt orales qu'écrites,
mais ses exposés sont reconnus comme fidèles. La présence du sacerdoce féminin dans la secte montaniste nous paraît donc reposer sur l'honnêteté d'E-
piphane dans l'utilisation des sources — ni son génie ni son caractère, sur
lesquels on pourrait faire des réserves, ne sont ici en jeu — puis sur le caractère général de la secte montaniste et seulement en dernier lieu sur la
forme historique de la religion en Phrygie." Against the historicity of "diese
apokryphe Quintilla" — and with better arguments — is L. ZSCHARNACK,
Der Dienst..., pp. 182-3.

b) 78: 23

Chapter 78 of the *Panarion* deals with the *Antidicomarianites*, who — as this label given them by Epiphanius implies — failed to show due honour to Mary (specifically, by denying her perpetual virginity). This group tried to justify itself by pointing to an example of what happens when Marian devotion gets out of hand, that of the "Collyridians". Epiphanius therefore takes a little time to speak of this second group, by quoting a letter he wrote sometime around 367 (the year he became a bishop):

> It is related that certain women there in Arabia had brought this absurd doctrine from Thrace: how in the name of the Ever-Virgin they make an offering (*epitelein*) of small loaves (*kollurida*), and under that same name hold their gatherings, and how in the Holy Virgin's name they attempt something far beyond what is permissible. In an unlawful and blasphemous ceremony they ordain (*epicherein*) women and through them make offerings (*hierourgein*) in her name. This means that the entire business is wicked and criminal, a perversion of the Holy Spirit's preaching — indeed, that the whole affair is diabolical and a teaching of the spirit of uncleanness. For in them is fulfilled the saying about how "some depart from sound teaching, paying attention to fables and demons' doctrines" (cf. *1 Tim* 4: 1; *2 Tim* 4: 3-4). They will be, it is said, "worshippers of the dead", as once there were such worshippers in Israel. This has taken place at its appointed time that the glory of the saints in God may come to those others who refuse to perceive truth in what is false.[96]

As the next text to be studied deals with the Collyridians at some length, only two brief remarks need be made here.

First, it is noteworthy that Epiphanius here refrains from making any specific denunciation of the *fact* that women were 'ordained' or that they exercised some sort of 'priestly' function. He is, as he himself admits, accusing on the basis of hearsay; but that hearsay seems to have included dark rumours about the nature of the 'ordination': it was an "unlawful and blasphemous ceremony" (*athemitō kai blasphēmō pragmati*). If it is the idea of ordaining women that is the main cause of his upset, he devotes precious little attention to it. It may be objected that here he is dealing primarily with another group, and with the Collyridians only

---

[96] *GCS* 37, p. 473, lines 8-21.

marginally; one might therefore expect a more lengthy treatment on ordaining 'women priests' when Epiphanius devotes his attention directly to the Collyridians.

This brings me to the second remark: for it will become clear that in Chapter 79 (where the Collyridians are given their fair share of attention) the main issue is — as it is in the present passage — the attribution of divinity to Mary. In fact, the Marian aspect is the only Christian note in the whole account. But it seems fairly certain that the excessive devotion accorded Mary by the Collyridians was simply the christianization of a popular pre-Christian cult among Semitic peoples, including those of "Arabia" (i.e., the Roman province of that name to the northeast of Palestine). This is substantiated by the odd manner in which Epiphanius applies the passage from Timothy, by the oblique reference to *Rom* 1: 25 ("worshipped in Israel"; cf. *Jeremiah* 7: 18 and 44: 19), and by the clearer allusion to a theme found in the *Didachē* and elsewhere ("worshippers of the dead").[97] Hence we have to deal, not only with the probability that Epiphanius' real concern is undue devotion to Mary, but also with the pagan origins of this devotion. This is clarified by some remarks Epiphanius makes in his next chapter.

c) 79: 2-4

The opening paragraph of Chapter 79 of the *Panarion* is not referred to by the *Declaration,* and the text will not be given here. Substantially, Epiphanius provides the same information there that he supplied in 78: 23: that the Collyridian heresy was introduced into "Arabia" from Thrace and Upper Scythia; that those who belong to it are known mainly for a rite in which they present to the gaze of the faithful, at a makeshift altar, small loaves *(kollurida);*[98] and that these loaves are offered in sacrifice "to the name of Mary" before they are distributed to those in attendance.

This time there is no mention of ordination: Epiphanius deals with it later, but not as an aspect of "Collyridianism". Even if an

---

[97] *Wisdom* 15: 17; cf. *Didachè,* 6: 3; *Letter to Diognetus,* 2: 4-6; *Second Letter of Clement,* 3: 1.

[98] The term *kolluris* is discussed by F. J. DÖLGER, "Die eigenartige Marienverehrung der Philomarianiten oder Kollyridianer in Arabien", in his *Antike und Christentum,* vol. I (Münster: Aschendorff, 1929², reprinted in 1974), pp. 130-8.

ordination were part of the issue here, it could not be applied to the question of women's ministry in the Great Church. What Epiphanius describes is a thin veneer of Christianity on an ancient cult that apparently involved the same elements he mentions: makeshift altar, small loaves or cakes, female deity.[99] At this stage of his exposé it is the 'heretical' (read: pagan) aspect that is uppermost in Epiphanius' mind. Though he is our only source of information about the Collyridians,[100] Epiphanius himself admits that he really knows very little about them, and that only by hearsay;[101] yet he feels he can confidently assert that (as in all heresies) the devil operates through them, as he did in the case of Quintilla, Priscilla and Maximilla. What the Collyridians teach, he continues, is propagated by a few females and by no one else — by the "fickle female species, unreliable and low on intelligence" (gunaikōn gar to genos euolisthon, sphaleron de kai tapeinon tō phronēmati). His anti-heretical polemic is thus heightened by a factor that we have seen already and will see again: his view of women in general as not intellectually or emotionally qualified to teach (didaskein) anything at all, at least publicly.

In the next section — the first of those referred to from Chapter 79 by the Declaration — Epiphanius gets down to the specifics of "Mariolatry' (tōn huper to deon doxazontōn). This is the background for the following statements — and note the contrast between manly (i.e., orthodox) attitudes and "women's notion":

> Be on your guard, therefore, servants of God. Let us put on a manly attitude (andrikon phronēma), let us disperse the mania of these women. For it is all women's notion, the sickness of the seduced Eve all over again; or rather, the deceitful promise of the serpent, through whom so many things are distorted, convulsing and babbling within her, bringing nothing salutary and carrying out none of his promises, but bringing to fulfillment only death, calling real beings things that do

---

[99] On the custom of offering small loaves or cakes to the supreme female deity, cf. P.-H. LAFONTAINE, "Le sexe masculin...", pp. 143-4. On the substitution of Mary for this deity, cf. P. G. M. ALBARELLI, "L'eresia dei 'Colliridiani' ed il culto paleo-cristiano di Maria," in Marianum, 3 (Rome: 1941), pp. 187-91; and J. DANIÉLOU, "Le culte marial et le paganisme," in H. du MANOIR (ed.), Maria. Etudes sur la Sainte Vierge, t. I (Paris: Beauchesne, 1949), pp. 161-81 (esp. 174-9).
[100] Cf. F. J. DÖLGER, "Die eigenartige...", pp. 107-42.
[101] EPIPHANIUS, Panarion, 79: 1 (GCS 37, p. 476. 1.).

not exist, and building, in the guise of the tree, disobedience and deviation from the truth.[102]

It is only after a few more sentences in a similar vein that Epiphanius turns his attention to the question of women's admission to priesthood. He begins with an appeal to the Old Testament:

> Never from the beginning has a woman offered sacrifice (*hierateusen*) to God — not even Eve, although she had committed the transgression: but she did not dare attempt something so sacrilegious. Nor did any of her daughters...[103]

Then Epiphanius gives examples of all those (males) in the Old Testament who exercised a true priestly function, beginning with Cain and Abel. "And never", he sums up, "did a woman offer sacrifice" *(kai oudamou gunē hierateusen)*.[104] But there is a serious flaw in this approach, because it is entirely linked to Old Testament sacrifices, sacrifices unceasingly denied by Christians from the beginning of their era as having any claims on the "New Israel". If there is no longer a need for a temple in Jerusalem or for bloody sacrifices, there is also no need of a temple priesthood, and no argument that justifies itself on the basis of that example can be valid for the new situation: the hereditary, levitical priesthood has been completely superseded, and can provide no proofs against admitting women to the Christian priestly ministry.[105]

But now Epiphanius turns his attention to an argument based on the New Testament. Of all the references to the Fathers given by the *Declaration,* this is the only passage which gives support to the claim that women may not be admitted to priestly ministry. It therefore merits close attention. The argument begins with the example of Jesus' Mother:

> If women had been directed by God to offer sacrifice (*hierateuein*) or to perform some ecclesiastical office, it would have been more proper

---

[102] *Ibid.,* 79: 2 (p. 476. 6).
[103] *Ibid.* (p. 477. 6).
[104] *Ibid.* (p. 477. 26).
[105] Cf. J. M. FORD, "Biblical Material Relevant to the Ordination of Women," in *Journal of Ecumenical Studies,* 10 (Philadelphia: 1973), p. 686: "Perhaps the only two points of identity between priesthood in the Old Testament and in the present Christian Church are the limitation of the priesthood to males and, until recently, the retention of the prohibition against handicapped people being ordained, Canon Law being remarkably close to Lev. 21: 16-24."

to Mary than to anyone else in the New Testament to exercise a priestly role...[106]

Actually, the example of Mary (employed also by the *Declaration)*[107] only proves that holiness is not dependent on whether or not one has received the sacrament of Order, that ordination would have added nothing to the excellence Mary already had, and that no one can claim a *right* to be ordained. Such considerations do not trouble Epiphanius, as he goes on to point out what are admittedly the facts (but are not useful as arguments, for the reasons just mentioned): that Mary was not entrusted with baptizing as was John the Baptizer, nor with being an apostle as were the Twelve, nor with being "in charge of the mysteries" *(mustērion archēgetai)* as was James, first *episkopos* of Jerusalem. Epiphanius develops this last train of thought:

> From this *episkopos* and the aforementioned apostles were established successions of *episkopoi* and *presbuteroi* in the house of God; and never was a woman appointed among them *(kai oudamou gunē en toutois katestathē)*. It is said that Philip the Evangelist had four daughters who prophesied (cf. *Acts* 21: 9) — but they did not carry out priestly functions *(ou mēn hierourgousai)*; and that Anna, the daughter of Phanuel, was a prophetess (cf. *Luke* 2: 36) — but she was not entrusted with priestly office *(ouch hierateian pepisteumenē)*: rather, there had to be fulfilled [the saying], "Your sons will prophesy, and your daughters will dream dreams, and your young men will see visions".
>
> In the Church there can also be perceived the rank of deaconesses *(diakonissōn tagma)*; this is not, however, conferred *(epitrepetai)* for offering sacrifice *(hierateuein)* nor for consecrating *(epicheirein)*, but rather for preserving the modesty of the female sex when baptism is to be conferred or when sickness or injury has to be treated. This is so that, when a woman's body is uncovered in such instances, it will not be looked at by men of the priestly order but by the woman attendant *(hupo tēs diakonousēs)* assigned by the bishop *(hiereus)* to help a woman who requests it when she is undressing; this is to keep the requirements of propriety and of church discipline, as is prescribed by those canons which provide safeguards against excess.
>
> Therefore the Word of God does not permit a woman to "speak out" (cf. *1 Cor* 14: 34) in church, nor to "have authority over a man" (cf. *1 Tim* 2: 12). Concerning this much more could be said.[108]

---

[106] EPIPHANIUS, *Panarion*, 79: 3 (*GCS* 37, p. 477. 27).
[107] Cf. *Declaration*, p. 103 (§ 13).
[108] EPIPHANIUS, *Panarion*, 79: 3 (*GCS* 37, p. 478. 9).

Besides the use of texts familiar when the Fathers are speaking of women's place in the Church, Epiphanius introduces into Chapter 79 an argument not seen in other authors we have examined: the argument that women cannot be ordained because it has never been done, an assertion he does not allow to be overturned by the examples of Anna and Philip's daughters. It is interesting to note how consistently Epiphanius avoids the Pauline distinction between prophecy and other forms of ministry; because this distinction was ignored in other places where it would have hurt his argument, it cannot be invoked now when it would come to his aid. So he invents another "scriptural" counter-attack: Anna and Philip's daughters were needed, he says, to fulfill Scripture's saying (a prophecy!) about women and prophecy. He appeals to *Joel* 3: 1 (repeated in *Acts* 2: 17): but we notice that, in the process of being quoted, something has happened to his text, which (in the Septuagint) should read:

Prophēteusousin hoi huioi humōn kai hai thugateres humōn,	Your sons and daughters will prophesy,
kai hoi presbuteroi humōn enupnia enupniasthēsontai,	and your old men will dream dreams,
kai hoi neaniskoi humōn horaseis opsontai.	and your young men will see visions.

Epiphanius has substituted "daughters" for "old men", and has suppressed the mention of the old men altogether. Intentionally or inadvertently? The word suppressed is in Greek *presbuteroi;* this, coupled with the fact that there is no variant reading of *Joel* 3: 1 or *Acts* 2: 17 as Epiphanius renders it, justifies the suspicion that he has doctored his text so as not to give the impression that "daughters" and "presbyters" can share similar powers, "daughters" prophesying and "presbyters" dreaming dreams. Yet he needs the mention of "daughters" in order to make his point. His point would be better made, of course, if he remained faithful to the scriptural text and left the "daughters" prophesying; but he needs a replacement for the suppressed *presbuteroi,* and he chooses to make the replacement with "daughters". Now they only "dream dreams": the *real* (and now sole) "prophesiers" are the "sons", i.e., males. The fact that all this scriptural juggling has ruined his own "proof" appears to have escaped Epiphanius' notice. Certainly, it does not prove why Anna and the daughters of Philip prophesy; logically, they should be "dreaming dreams". Still less, of course, does it prove why women should not be ordained.

But Epiphanius is not finished yet. He is sure enough of his position to feel that it is not disturbed by the objection that the Church has deaconesses:

> It should be carefully noted that only the Church's good order made necessary the rank of deaconesses (*diakonissōn tagma*). True, the Church named [some women] "widows" (*chēras*), and among the widows it termed the older ones "elders" (*presbutidas*: cf. *Tit* 2: 3); but never did it appoint (*prosetaxe*) "presbyteresses" (*presbuteridas*) or bishopesses" (*hierissas*). For not even *diakonoi* were entrusted with the exercise of some particular liturgical function (*mustērion*) in the ecclesiastical order, but only with assisting (*diakonein*) at such functions.

So where does this new myth among us come from? Whence this vanity of women and womanish madness? What feeds the malice whereby a female notion is foisted on our intellects, making every effort to turn us away from what has been revealed and so leave our miserable humanity entirely on its own? But now let us make our own the firm attitude of that athlete, Job; let us arm ourselves by having his righteous response on our lips, that we too may say, "You have been talking like one of those silly women" (*Job* 2: 10). How could anyone who possesses intelligence and has acquired [right-mindedness?] in God not be astonished by this? In what sense is this practice not idol-fashioning, its operation not devilish? For the devil always sneaks into the mind under the cloak of righteousness and, making mortal nature look godlike to human eyes, draws skilful, colourful portraits that really look like men. Those worshipped have died, but their effigies — which never lived, for dead things can never be called living ones — are presented as objects deserving of worship by the adulterous mind, [once it has turned away?] from the one and only God, like the common whore who instigates all sorts of unnatural sexual indulgence and obliterates the chastity of lawful, faithful marriages.

I agree that Mary had a holy body — but she was not divine; I agree that she was a virgin, worthy of veneration — but she was not given to us as a cult-object. Rather, she herself worshipped the one born of her flesh, he who came forth from heaven, out of the bosom of the Father. And now he guards us from falling, through that Gospel passage where he says — it is the Lord himself who speaks — "Woman, what is that to me and to you? My hour has not yet come" (*John* 2: 4). So that no one would jump from this phrase, "Woman, what is that to me and to you", to the conclusion that the holy Virgin was anything above and beyond that, he called her "woman", as though prophesying that there would eventually be schisms and heresies of this type upon the earth; and he called her "woman" so that no one would go to the extreme of adoring Mary, thereby falling into this heresy's particular nonsense.[109]

The closing lines of this final passage from Epiphanius re-enforce what has been maintained all along: that the main issue, in those sections where he specifically speaks out against ordaining women, is not their ordination but what he calls here "the extreme of adoring Mary" *(huperbolē thaumasantes tēn hagian)*. We do not know if in fact any sort of "ordination" of women was ever involved nor, if there was, whether Epiphanius objected to the idea itself or to the manner in which (he thought) it was done. His prime target is mariolatry, against which any seemingly useful argument is employed, sometimes uncritically. Due reflection might have led Epiphanius to see that his exegesis of the Johannine verse is curious, to say the least. It might also have led him to admit that there is a reference in some ancient texts to deaconesses as really ordained *(cheirotonein)*,[110] which makes his argumentation on that point somewhat less simple than he might wish.[111]

If, on the issue of women's ordination itself, we consider all the weaknesses in Epiphanius' objections, and if we set aside the

---

[109] *Ibid.,* 79: 4 (p. 478. 27). Words between [ ] are my conjectures, since they are missing from the Greek text. On the etymological difference between *presbutidas* and *presbuteridas,* cf. R. GRYSON, *Le ministère...,* pp. 93-4.

[110] For the texts cf. A. KALSBACH, *Die altkirchliche Einrichtung der Diakonissen bis zu ihrem Erlöschen (Römische Quartalschrift,* Supplementheft 22; Freiburg: Herder, 1926), condensed in "Diakonisse", in *Reallexikon für Antike und Christentum,* 3 (Stuttgart: Hiersemann, 1957), cols. 917-28. Also helpful are: P.-L. CARLE, "La femme...", pp. 277-82; J. PARISOT, "Les diaconesses," in *Revue des Sciences Ecclésiastiques,* 79 (Paris: 1899), pp. 289-304, 481-496; and 80 (1899), pp. 193-209; J. FORGET, "Diaconesses," in *Dictionnaire de Théologie Catholique,* 4 (Paris: Letouzey et Ané, 1911), cols. 685-703; H. LECLERCQ, "Diaconesse," in *Dictionnaire d'Archéologie Chrétienne et de Liturgie,* 4 (Paris: Letouzey et Ané, 1920), cols. 725-33; J. MAYER, *Monumenta de viduis, diaconissis virginibusque tractantia (Florilegium Patristicum,* XLII; Bonn: Hanstein, 1938); and R. GRYSON, "L'ordination des diaconesses d'après les Constitutions Apostoliques," in *Mélanges de Science Religieuse,* 31 (Lille: 1974), pp. 41-5. J. DANIÉLOU, "Le ministère des femmes dans l'Eglise ancienne," in *La Maison-Dieu,* 61 (Paris: 1960), pp. 70-96, and C. R. MEYER, "Ordained Women in the Early Church," in *Chicago Studies,* 4 (Chicago: 1965), pp. 285-308, tend to read too much into their sources.

[111] That the *Declaration* deliberately avoided the issue of diaconal ordination for women is confirmed by the *Commentary,* p. 526 (full reference to the English translation, *supra,* n. 6): "In the past there had been deaconesses: had they received true sacramental ordination? [...] It is a question that must be taken up fully by direct study of the texts, without preconceived ideas; hence the Sacred Congregation for the Doctrine of the Faith has judged that it should be kept for the future and not touched upon in the present document."

verbal smokescreen (but substantial enough from a cultural point of view) of "vanity of women and womanish madness", "female notion", "silly women", idolators and whores,[112] the objections are consistently reduced to one: it has never been done. Epiphanius never offers a truly theological argument.[113] But then, though he is acknowledged as a bishop, as a historical source (if not a historian), and (because he falls into that period) as a 'Father', few would willingly grace him with the title of theologian.[114]

6-7. *Didascalia apostolorum,* 15 and *Constitutiones apostolicæ,* III, 6 and 9

Because the *Constitutiones* contain essentially the same ideas in the passages referred to by the *Declaration* as does the *Didascalia,* on which they are based, we can study the two together.

---

[112] On the label of "whoredom" applied by the Fathers to heresy, cf. K. THRAEDE, "Frau", *RAC,* 8, cols. 264-5; also the apt remarks of L. ZSCHAR-NACK, *Der Dienst...,* p. 78: "So suchte man die Frauen ihres Unrechts zu über-führen und konnte ihr Gebahren als 'ungesetzlich und unfromm" hinstellen. Daneben hatte man, falls das weibliche Geschlecht sich nicht durch mehr oder minder freundliche Worte bekehren liess, noch einen anderen Weg, der gewiss ans Ziel führte, wenn man ihn mit Energie verfolgte; man musste Frauenwort bei den männlichen Zuhören diskreditieren, 'lächerlich' machen und als Teufelswerk hinstellen. Zu welcher Meisterschaft man auch hier gelangen konnte, zeigt uns Epiphanius in jenem Kapitel über die Lehre und den Kult der Kollyridianerinnen, indem er nicht müde wird, auf die leichte Verführbarkeit der Frau und deren Mangel an vernünftiger Be-sonnenheit hinzuweisen."

[113] Pointed out by H. van der MEER, *Priestertum...,* pp. 64-5: "Was ist nun zu all dem zu sagen? Sicher ist Epiphanius ein Zeuge dafür, das [sic] es nie weibliche Priester gegeben hat und dass man sie auch nicht haben wollte. Wir haben gesehen, dass er zwar Bezug nimmt auf ein (ihm zufolge) allgemeines Prinzip: es hat nie weibliche Priester gegeben, sogar Maria war nicht Priester, Paulus hat es verboten; aber sein Hauptanliegen besteht darin, darzustellen, ein wie grosser Unfug es ist, Maria anzubeten. Man bekommt den unvermeidlichen Eindruck, dass für sein Empfinden 'weibliche Priester in der Kirche' zwangsläufig zur Verehrung einer weiblichen Gottheit führen müssen oder umgekehrt. Seine Ablehnung der weiblichen Gottheit zwingt ihn also, auch weibliche Priester abzuweisen. Das macht u. E. sein Zeugnis aber wieder ziemlich schwach. Man könnte sofort dagegen einwenden: Tatsächlich, falls diese beiden Fragen notwendigerweise zusammenhängen sollten, darf es keine weiblichen Priester geben. Aber wenn dem nicht so ist — die Beweislast liegt auf jeden Fall bei dem, der meint, die Meinung des Epiphanius als einen Beweis für die Ablehnung des weiblichen Priest-ertums anführen zu können —, scheidet schon Epiphanius aus der Kette der patristischen Zeugen aus."

[114] Cf. J. QUASTEN, *Patrology,* vol. III (Utrecht-Antwerp-Westminster [Md.]: Spectrum Publishers/Newman Press, 1960) pp. 384-6.

Both works, as their titles imply, pretend to have been authored by the Apostles. The *Didascalia* is really a series of instructions, loosely strung together, on Church organization and practice. Written originally in Greek, definitely in Syria or Palestine and probably in the early III century, it is extant only in a fourth-century Syriac version and in some Latin and Greek fragments. As these fragments only partially represent the section referred to by the *Declaration,* we will rely mainly on the Syriac.[115]

The *Constitutiones* were composed in Greek between 375 and 400, in Syria or at Constantinople.[116] As much of what they contain is from the *Didascalia,* both texts are presented here in parallel columns for easier comparison. Words and phrases in italics are those that appear only in one of the two documents:

Didascalia, 15[117]	*Constitutiones,* III, 6[118]
It is therefore neither proper nor necessary that women be teachers, *especially concerning the name of Christ and the redemption by his passion; for you have not been appointed to teach, O women, especially you that are widows,* but to pray *and petition the Lord God.* For the Lord *God,* Jesus Christ our Teacher, himself sent us, the Twelve, to instruct the people and the Gentiles; and with us were *women disciples:* Mary Magdalene and Mary, daughter of James, and *the other* Mary. And he did not send them to teach the people with us. For if it were required	*We do not permit* women to teach *in church,* but only to pray *and to hear the teachers.* For our Teacher and Lord, Jesus the Christ, himself sent us, the Twelve, to instruct the people and the Gentiles; but nowhere did he send out women for the preaching — *not, though, because of a lack of women.* For with us were *the Mother of the Lord "and his sisters"* (cf. *Mt* 13: 56), *besides* Mary Magdalene and Mary, [daughter?] of James, *and Martha,* and Mary, *the sister of Lazarus, and Salome, and some others.* For if it were really necessary for

---

115 The most reliable edition is still the one done by P. de LAGARDE in 1854, *Didascalia apostolorum syriace* (photographic reproduction in 1967, at Osnabrück-Wiesbaden). The *Declaration* refers to R. H. CONNOLLY, *Didascalia Apostolorum. The Syriac Version Translated and Accompanied by the Verona Latin Fragments* (Oxford: Clarendon Press, 1929), but — as the subtitle tells us — this is a Latin edition with an English translation from the Syriac.

116 Text edited by F. X. FUNK, *Didascalia et Constitutiones Apostolorum,* vol. I (Paderborn: Schöningh, 1905). Funk is much less reliable for the *Didascalia:* cf. R. H. CONNOLLY, *Didascalia...,* pp. xxiii-iv.

117 P. de LAGARDE, *Didascalia,* p. 63. 27 - p. 64. 10.

118 F. X. FUNK, *Didascalia et Constitutiones...,* p. 191, lines 8-22.

that women teach, *our Teacher himself* would have commanded these to teach with us. But a

widow should know that she is the altar of God. She should *always* remain sitting in her house, and not *go wandering, making the rounds of* the houses of the faithful in order to receive something. For the altar of God never goes wandering *and making the rounds anywhere,* but stays fixed in one place.

women to teach, he would *probably* have *first* ordered them also to catechize the people with us. *For if "the man is head of the woman" (1 Cor 11: 3), it is not right that the rest of the body assume leadership over the head.* The widow ought to know, then, that she is the altar of God. She ought to remain sitting in her house, and not *under any pretext enter* the houses of the faithful in order to receive something. For the altar of God never goes wandering about, but remains in one place.

The first thing that strikes the reader who compares the texts (and this is also true of the next two passages to be compared) is the differences between them, consisting in suppression of phrases in some instances, addition in others, by the author of the *Constitutiones*.[119] The criterion for selection or supplementation in this later document is the strengthening of the exclusion of women from ministerial functions. Thus the qualifications in the opening lines of the *Didascalia* passage have been dropped: now there can be no objection that women might be able to be teachers on other subjects *besides* "the name of Christ and the redemption by his passion"; the *Constitutiones* make it simple: women may not teach in church, period. And this is now not "especially widows", but simply "women" in general. Similarly, the permission to "petition the Lord God" has been rescinded: it would still be too much (liturgical?) involvement.

The additions in the *Constitutiones* also point to the strengthening idea. More women are named, to prove the point, and the whole is capped by *1 Cor 11: 3*. The fact that the context of this Pauline verse is the husband-wife relationship,[120] and the permission given

---

[119] On the changes cf. R. GRYSON, *Le ministère...*, pp. 99-100 (though I do not entirely concur with his translation).
[120] Used elsewhere in this context by both documents: cf. P. de LAGARDE, *Didascalia...*, p. 7. 10 (chap. 1), and F. X. FUNK, *Didascalia...*, p. 21. 16 (I, 8: 1).

by *1 Cor* 11: 5 to a woman to act in public, so long as her head is veiled, bother the author not at all. The Scripture is invoked solely as a "proof-text" to support conclusions already arrived at.

The same mentality is at work in *changes* of wording. What in the *Didascalia* is "neither proper nor necessary"[121] becomes "not permitted"; where women could not teach on certain subjects, now they cannot teach "in church" *(en ekklēsia);* where they could "petition the Lord God", they must now passively "hear the teachers".

But the author of the *Didascalia* is not much less rigid. He shares with the later writer the implicit combination of *1 Tim* 5: 13 with a metaphor from Polycarp, and makes a widow "an altar of God",[122] so it is he who first arrives from this to the conclusion that the widow, being an altar, has to stay fixed in one spot and not go running around! And it is he who leads up to the prohibition against women teaching by arguing that pagans would not accept God's word from one not qualified (i.e., not male), but instead would mock and sneer at the word, "all the more when it is spoken to them by a woman".[123]

A cultural fact is thus taken for granted by both authors.[124] This fact does not, of course, disappear from the two other passages still to be compared:

---

[121] The words "or necessary" were apparently not in the Greek original of the *Didascalia,* to which the phrase "the Lord God Jesus Christ" also appears to have been added by the Syriac. Cf. J. V. BARTLET, "Fragments of the *Didascalia Apostolorum* in Greek," in *Journal of Theological Studies,* 18 (Oxford: 1917), pp. 304 and 307.

[122] Syriac, *mdbḥô dôlohô;* Greek, *thusiastērion theou.* Cf. POLYCARP, *Epist. ad Philippenses,* 4: 3 (*SC* 10, p. 182); also TERTULLIAN, Ad uxorem, I, 7: 4 *(CCL* 1, p. 381. 24), and PSEUDO-IGNATIUS, *Epist. ad Tarsenses,* 9: 1 (in F. X. FUNK and F. DIEKAMP, *Patres Apostolici,* vol. 2 (Tübingen: Laupp, 1913), p. 142. 10). On the institution of "widows", cf. L. ZSCHARNACK, *Der Dienst...,* p. 99-156.

[123] *Didascalia,* 15 (P. de LAGARDE, *Didascalia...,* p. 63. 25).

[124] Of the passage in the *Didascalia* R. GRYSON notes *(Le ministère...,* p. 74): "On sent incontestablement percer ici un certain mépris de la femme, qui n'est pas le fait propre de l'auteur, mais le reflet de la mentalité ambiante." He adds — but does not explain — that "Il ne faudrait pas exagérer cependant l'influence que ce mépris ambiant a pu avoir sur les positions théologiques de l'auteur." Then, at the close of his book (pp. 176-7), he has this to say: "Les considérations qui étayent l'argument de tradition chez les auteurs anciens, reflètent souvent une anthropologie qui ne serait pas unanimement admise aujourd'hui. Pour ces hommes qui ont un senti-

Didascalia, 15[125]	*Constitutiones*, III 9[126]
We do not advise that a woman baptize *or that anyone be baptized by a woman*, because that is *a violation of the commandment and* a great danger, *both* to her who baptizes` *and to him who is baptized.*	Concerning baptizing by a woman, *we make known to you* that it is no small danger for the woman who attempts it; wherefore we do not advise it. *For it can lead to her downfall; more, it is contrary to custom and sacrilegious. For if "the man is head of the woman" (1 Cor* 11: 3) *and he is the one chosen for the priestly office* (hierōsunē), *it is not right that the body, disregarding the procedure followed in creation, forsake its highest point and hurry off to the lowest. For a woman is a man's body, being from his rib* (cf. *Gen* 2: 21) *and being subject to him from whom she was made distinct in order to bear children. For [Scripture] says, "He shall lord it over you" (Gen* 3: 16). *For a woman's highest point is a man, since he is the head. But if in an earlier passage we do not permit them to teach, how can anyone assent to their exercizing a priestly office* (hierateusai) *inconsistent with their nature? For the ordaining of women priests to serve female deities is an ignorant act*

ment très vif du pouvoir quasi-royal qu'exerce l'orateur sur son auditoire, de la supériorité de celui qui enseigne sur celui qui est enseigné, il apparaît inconvenant qu'une femme dispense en public un enseignement à des hommes. De même le sacerdoce, en tant que ministère du salut, leur paraît impliquer une supériorité, dans le chef de celui qui l'exerce, vis-à-vis de celui au profit duquel il est exercé; ils jugent donc normal, comme le dit la *Constitution ecclésiastique des apôtres,* que "le faible soit sauvé par le fort", c'est-à-dire la femme par l'homme, et non l'inverse. Sous-jacente à ces raisonnements, et plus d'une fois exprimée en toutes lettres, on trouve l'idée d'une supériorité et d'une primauté naturelle de l'homme sur la femme, qui se reflète dans la fréquence et la complaisance avec lesquelles on cite des versets bibliques comme celui de la Genèse: "Vers ton homme tu te tourneras, et lui sera ton maître", ou encore la phrase paulinienne: "Le chef de la femme, c'est l'homme", dont on force probablement le sens en en faisant, comme les *Constitutions apostoliques,* le slogan décisif en cette matière."

[125] P. de LAGARDE, *Didascalia...,* p. 67, lines 19-25.
[126] F. X. FUNK, *Didascalia...,* p. 199. 21 - p. 201. 17.

For if it were *permitted* for someone to be baptized by a woman,
our Lord *and Teacher* would have
been baptized by his Mother *Mary*;
in fact, he was baptized by John,
*just like others of the people.
Therefore do not bring danger on
yourselves, brothers and sisters, by
acting outside the Law of the
Gospel.*

*of pagan godlessness, but not a
commandment of Christ. Also,* if
it were proper to be baptized by
women, then certainly the Lord
would have been baptized by his
own Mother, and not by John,
*just as, when he sent us out to
baptize, he would have sent women
along with us for the same purpose. But it so happens that this is
nowhere commanded or set down
in writing, because he knew the
arrangement of nature and the ap-
propriateness of the act, being as
he was the architect of nature and
the legislator of the commandment.*

Again the additions supplied by the *Constitutiones* are meant
to re-enforce the position: not only is baptism by a woman a
"violation of the commandment", it is "contrary to custom and
sacrilegious"; not only is it not found in the example of Jesus, it
is "nowhere commanded or set down in writing" by him; not only
would he have been baptized by Mary, he would *certainly* have been
baptized by her. The added Scripture betrays the same intent:[127]
none of the texts cited comes as a surprise, because we have seen
the same kind of usage before. What *does* bemuse the reader is
that the author thinks he can use *1 Cor* 11: 3 both to stop women
from baptizing and to stop them from teaching, when the original
context of the verse is so different — the man-wife relationship.
Exegetes today would also add that the Genesis references are to
be understood in a similar way.[128]

But the *Didascalia* has a particular use for Scripture, too.
What is this "commandment" that would be violated, the "Law
of the Gospel" that would be transgressed? An earlier argument
employed in the *Didascalia* against baptism by *widows* invokes
Matt 7: 6: "Our Lord said in the Gospel to *widows and to all laymen*: 'Do not cast your pearls before swine, lest they trample on

[127] Cf. R. Gryson's remarks, *supra*, n. 124.
[128] So J.-M. Aubert, *La femme...*, pp. 85-95; G. H. Tavard, *Woman...*,
pp. 3-19; W. Brueggemann, "Of the Same Flesh and Bone *(GN* 2, 23a)," in
Catholic Biblical Quarterly, 32 (Washington: 1970), pp. 532-42; an P. K. Je-
wett, *Man as Male and Female. A Study in Sexual Relationships from a
Theological Point of View* (Grand Rapids: Eerdmans, 1975), pp. 120-8.

them, then turn against you and tear you to pieces'."[129] The author makes no attempt to prove (assuming that he could) that "widows and all laymen" were the intended audience of the Matthaean verse. Even if they were, the verse has nothing to do with women (or anyone else) baptizing. If the same verse is meant here by "commandment" and "Law of the Gospel" — and it seems that it is —, *Didascalia*'s argument rests on a very shaky foundation, indeed.

What is the real issue behind the prohibitions of both the *Didascalia* and the *Constitutiones?* It cannot be to state some irrefutable principle about women's ordination, for the arguments are remarkably weak. "Women priests" are mentioned only once, in connection with pagan cult, and it could be argued that the "pagan connection" is what makes the idea distasteful to the author of the *Constitutiones.* The argument — such as it is — is only that Jesus did not call anyone but men to the ministries of teaching and baptism: but no attempt is made to discover *why* this is so; no account is taken of the distinction made in *1 Cor* 12 between teaching and other forms of ministry (which means that, even if it could be proven that Paul was against women teaching — and *1 Cor* 11: 5 would seem to belie this — it would still have to be proven that they were to be excluded in his view from other ministries as well); and no one would consider the arguments against women baptizing as valid today. In other words, the *Didascalia* and the *Constitutiones* cannot be called upon to support Canon Law's can. 742, 2 (when no one better qualified is present, women can baptize in an emergency); why, then, are they permitted to give support to can. 968, 1 (only a baptized *uir* can validly be ordained)?

So the texts cannot be called upon to refute women's ordination, which in any case is not their main concern. What *is* their main concern is the role of the *bishop,* to whom the functions of teaching and baptizing properly belong.[130] Each document attests

---

[129] *Didascalia,* 15 (P. de LAGARDE, *Didascalia...,* p. 63, lines 21-23).
[130] Chapters 4 through 11 of the *Didascalia* outline the duties of bishops in detail. Cf. also the commentary by H. ACHELIS and J. FLEMMING, *Die ältesten Quellen des orientalischen Kirchenrechts,* zweites Buch: *Die syrische Didaskalia (Texte und Untersuchungen,* 25/2; Leipzig: Hinrichs, 1904), pp. 269-72 and 274-82.

to a different phase of this convention; but generally the *Constitutiones* mark a further intensification of an idea that might on some points still be expressed rather hesitantly by the *Didascalia*.[131] By the time of the later document the involvement of the *episkopos* in administrative functions in quite complete.[132] The accession of a woman to the episcopacy is therefore unthinkable: her social position, which excludes her from all administrative function, would simply not permit it; and her social position is taken for granted, by the Church as well as by society.[133]

Finally, by the time of the *Constitutiones* another process — of which the *Didascalia* also marks an earlier stage — is complete as well. This is the process which relies on "apostolic succession" as the ultimate guarantee for the correct transmission of both word and sacrament.[134] No other person besides the bishop, male or female, can guarantee the transmission, can therefore on his/her own assume such functions as teaching (word) or baptizing (sacrament). It is this position that the two documents just studied are principally maintaining; apart from this position their denial of teaching and baptizing roles to women cannot be properly understood.

8. JOHN CHRYSOSTOM, *De sacerdotio,* 2: 2

The treatise of the future Bishop of Constantinople *On the Priesthood (Peri hierōsunēs)* was penned at Antioch around the time of his ordination to the priesthood in 386. The passage from it to be studied is very brief, and so will be the examination:

---

[131] Such intensification is typical of the *Constitutiones.* Cf. R. GRYSON, *Le ministère...,* pp. 96-104.

[132] Cf. B. COOKE, *Ministry...,* p. 354: "One of the negative results of the new situation that followed Constantine's recognition of Christianity was the increasing involvement of church leadership in state affairs. Even apart from the instances where a civil ruler would utilize the services of a prominent bishop or presbyter to expedite some of his own business, the leaders of the church were in more or less constant interchange with civic authorities. This touched upon the arrangement of Christian property rights, the question of clerical freedom from civil service and taxation, and the involvement of bishops in judicial proceedings. Constantine himself had given recognition to judicial proceedings by the bishop as equivalent to civil court action." Cf. also pp. 431-2.

[133] Cf. the remarks of R. GRYSON, *supra,* n. 124.

[134] Cf. B. COOKE, *Ministry...,* pp. 235-47; and L. ZSCHARNACK, *Der Dienst...,* pp. 78-84.

"Feed my sheep" (*John* 21: 15). For the things I spoke of before are things which many of those in positions of authority, both men and women, might be able to fulfill easily. But whenever it becomes necessary to set someone in charge over a church and to entrust him with the care of so many souls, then the entire feminine sex has to stand back from the magnitude of the task, and the majority of men (*andrōn*) as well.[135]

The operative phrase here is the one I have translated as "has to stand back" (*parachōreitō*). Is Chrysostom stating a simple fact here (no women, and only a few men, are bishops or priests); or is he proclaiming a theological principle? If the latter, the lack of supportive arguments is glaring; and he certainly cannot be made to say that, not only have all women and most men *been excluded from priestly ordination,* they have been excluded *by Jesus.*[136] Nothing is said by Chrysostom about ordination, about exclusion, or about exclusion by Jesus.

There is the fact, however, that he does mention that no woman is entrusted with the "charge over a church" or with the "care of souls", even if it is a fact that he simply takes for granted. Given some of his views, he could hardly be expected to do otherwise. Elsewhere in the same chapter of the same work he reveals his general opinion, not only of women, but of the laity: the difference between shepherds (pastors) and sheep (laity) is as great as that between rational and non-rational creatures. The startling impression this opinion makes can be diluted somewhat by remembering his enthusiasm for his new priesthood, whether soon to be or just received. But it is more difficult to separate his views on priesthood from his enthusiasm for virginity, his endorsement of virginity from his ideas about marriage, and his concept of marriage — "that most bitter slavery" (for the man!)[137] — from

---

[135] *PG* 48, col. 633.

[136] Cf. the *Commentary,* p. 526 (full reference to the English translation, *supra,* n. 6): "St. John Chrysostom, for his part, when commenting on chapter 21 of John, understood well that women's *exclusion from the pastoral office entrusted to Peter* was not based on any natural incapacity, since, as he remarks, 'even the majority of men *have been excluded by Jesus* from this immense task." I do not see how the words I have emphasized here are justified by the text we have seen; nor do I think the claim that Chrysostom's statement — such as it is — has nothing to do with woman's "natural incapacity" is warranted by other texts.

[137] JOHN CHRYSOSTOM, *De uirginitate,* 28: 1 (*SC* 125, p. 182. 14). Cf. also *Hom. 62 in Matt.* 2-3 (*PG* 58, col. 599).

his notions on women in general. Here is another Father who thinks that marriage was not originally *willed* by God, and is now only *permitted* by him — a necessity created from sin.[138] Since the whole sad present state of affairs can be traced back to the action of the first woman, who thereby lost her equality with the man,[139] all women should be regarded with distrust.[140] They are obviously so much weaker, more fickle, more frivolous than men.[141]

Because of woman's connection with the Fall, what *is* willed by God is her present inferior social position. No writing of Chrysostom deals with women in connection with priestly ordination, but it seems safe to say that he would consider the idea as absolutely unthinkable: not only could he never question the rightfulness of her inferiority, he cannot bring himself to admit that woman is made in God's image:

> Otherwise God would have to be not only Man (*ho anthrōpos*), but woman (*gunē*) as well, because both possess the same form (*morphē*). But those who would say this [that woman, too, is made in God's image] are crazy, for listen to what Paul says: "A man (*anēr*) should not cover his head, since he is the image of God and reflects God's glory; but woman is the reflection of man's glory" (*1 Cor* 11: 7)...[142]

The Pauline reference merely confirms what Chrysostom already believes. Women took authority once — reversing the order of creation[143] — and what a mistake *that* was!

> The only time the woman made the husband take her advice she turned everything upside down. That is why the saint says, "You are not to teach!"[144]

With this mentality, Chrysostom could never imagine a different cultural possibility for women, in the Church or anywhere

---

[138] JOHN CHRYS., *De uirginitate*, 15-17 *(SC* 125, pp. 144-54). Cf. also *Hom. 18 in Gen.* 4: 1 *(PG* 53, col. 154); and A. MOULARD, *Saint Jean Chrysostome, le défenseur du mariage et l'apôtre de la virginité* (Paris: Gabalda, 1923), pp. 62-6 and 276-85.

[139] JOHN CHRYS., *Hom. 17 in Gen.* 3: 8, 9 *(PG* 53, col. 145).

[140] JOHN CHRYS., *Ad Theodorum*, 14 *(SC* 117, p. 164.54).

[141] JOHN CHRYS., *Hom. 37 in I*am *epist. ad Cor.* 14: 34, 1 *(PG* 61, cols. 315-6).

[142] JOHN CHRYS., *Hom. 8 in Gen.* 1, 4 *(PG* 53, col. 73). Cf. also *Hom. 9 in I*am *epist. ad Tim.* 2: 11-15, 1 *(PG* 62, cols. 543-5).

[143] JOHN CHRYS., *De uirginitate*, 53 *(SC* 125, p. 298. 3).

[144] JOHN CHRYS., *Hom. 9 in I*am *epist. ad Tim.* 2: 11-15, 1 *(PG* 62, col. 545). Cf. also *Hom. 17 in Gen.* 3, 4 and 8 *(PG* 53, cols. 139 and 144-5).

else.[145] Later on some aspects of his thought were to mellow (on marriage, for instance),[146] but his basic stance on woman herself always remained the same.[147]

C. SOME CONCLUDING OBSERVATIONS

It might be well to synthesize briefly the various considerations pointed out in the course of examining the *Declaration*'s references to the Fathers of the Church, before drawing a general conclusion with regard to the applicability of those references to the *Declaration*'s thesis.

First, since the reflection of various Fathers on woman's involvement in responsibility for the human condition and on her consequent place in the Church (and society) is, to say the least, not entirely free of certain prejudices, it is difficult to see how the "pastoral activity" and "spiritual direction" given by these same Fathers could then be prejudice-free. And every one of the authors cited in Footnotes 7 and 8 of the *Declaration* is imbued with those prejudices.

Secondly, all Christian groups alleged by patristic sources to have had a female priesthood were considered by those same sources to be heretical. That the "women priests" of such groups are repudiated by those sources is undeniable. Yet areas of doubt remain. For the orthodox authors do not seem very sure in what the repudiated phenomenon consists. No source available to us offers any real proof that actual ordinations were involved,[148] or that the groups concerned definitely "entrusted the exercise of the

---

[145] So G. H. TAVARD, *Woman...*, p. 88: "What Chrysostom found in the type of civilization with which he was acquainted colored his understanding of the stable nature of men and women. The feminine activities of which he speaks at length in *On the One Marriage* and in his homilies on marriage have been forced on woman by society [...] From matters of fact in the world of John Chrysostom, these restrictions on women become in his mind eternal decrees enshrined by divine providence in the nature of things." Cf. also the remarks of P. de LABRIOLLE, *supra*, n. 48.

[146] Cf. G. H. TAVARD, *Woman...*, pp. 82-5; and A. MOULARD, *Saint Jean Chrysostome...*, pp. 87-165.

[147] Cf. A. MOULARD, *op. cit.*, pp. 25-37.

[148] Cf. L. ZSCHARNACK, *Der Dienst...*, pp. 156-90.

priestly ministry to women", or, even if they did, that the nature of the women's "ministry" was considered to be "priestly", even by the groups themselves. The lack of detail supplied by the repudiators indicates a wide distance of space or time (or both) between themselves and the groups attacked,[149] and therefore one can hardly speak without qualification of "this innovation" as "immediately noted and condemned".[150] What (eventually) is noticed is primarily the *heterodox* nature of the groups; details about the groups' activities, while they receive some disapproving attention, would be perceived and judged within the light of antiheretical polemic. Where "women priests" are concerned, this raises two possibilities: that their condemnation springs at least in part from cultic activities believed to be connected with "priestesses";[151] or that any idea of a priestly ministry for women in the Great Church is rejected on the grounds that there can be no seeming agreement with heterodox groups that appear to permit such a ministry.[152]

Thirdly, even where there is a repudiation of "women priests", the over-all intent, being something quite different, makes that repudiation incidental. It is never the main point — not even in the case of Epiphanius, who is not only the most lengthy patristic source offered by the *Declaration,* but perhaps also the only one

---

[149] A strange note is that there are no conciliar or synodal decrees from the early Church condemning the practices alleged in the sources reviewed in this article; yet, during the time Epiphanius' "Collyridians" were supposed to be active, bishops from their area ("Arabia") took part in various bishops' gatherings. The Synod of Nîmes in Gaul (396) stands alone in speaking out against the ordination of women, and that is in reference to deaconesses — an institution in the East, but then unknown to the West.

[150] Cf. *supra,* p. 63.

[151] So D. S. BAILEY, *The Man-Woman Relation...*, p. 68: "The prohibitions imposed by the Church were probably designed in part both to minimize the risk of confusion between Christianity and its rivals, and to obviate as far as possible the various abuses which were associated in those days with a female ministry." This is also admitted by the *Commentary,* p. 526 (full reference to the English translation, *supra*. n. 6): "Only within some heretical sects of the early centuries, principally Gnostic ones, do we find attempts to have the priestly ministry exercised by women. It must be further noted that these are very sporadic occurrences and are moreover associated with rather questionable practices."

[152] R. GRYSON, *Le ministère...*, p. 176: "Il est certain que cette intrusion des femmes dans les fonctions ecclésiastiques chez les hérétiques, et les abus auxquels elle a donné lieu, à tout le moins le fait qu'un pareil zèle fût mis au service d'une doctrine hétérodoxe, n'a pas dû encourager l'Eglise à confier de son côté pareilles fonctions aux femmes et a pu alimenter pour une part une certaine défiance à l'égard du sexe féminin." He adds: "Il

to give a clear rejection of priestly ministry for women, and to give it on some other basis than the simple assumption that nature so ordained or Jesus so willed. Yet not even in Epiphanius' case is any real *theological* argument offered;[153] and never is there a serious attempt to declare the non-admissibility of women to ordained priesthood as part of the *depositum fidei*.[154]

Fourthly, though we cannot say that no attempt is made to justify this exclusion on the basis of Scripture, we note that it is always a very narrow range of biblical texts that is cited, and that in no case has the original context a connection with the point that is being "proved".[155] Those texts, in fact, are influenced by cultural contexts of their own.[156] Moreover, there is a careful avoidance of other biblical passages harmful to the cause — most notably *Galatians* 3: 28 —, as well as an ignorance of New Testament concepts of priesthood and ministry.[157]

---

n'apparaît pas, cependant, que ce soit le souci de se distinguer de l'hérésie qui ait été la raison déterminante pour laquelle l'Eglise a cru devoir exclure les femmes de l'enseignement public et des fonctions sacerdotales." However, the heretical framework certainly made its impression. Consider this statement by JEROME, *Epist. 133 ad Ctesiphontem*, 4 *(CSEL* 56, p. 247. 22): "Cum haec se ita habeant, quid uolunt miseræ mulierculæ oneratæ peccatis, quæ circumferuntur omni uento doctrinæ semper discentes et numquam ad scientiam ueritatis peruenientes (cf. II Tim. 3: 6-7) et ceteri muliercularum socii prurientes auribus (cf. II Tim. 4:3) et ignorantes, quid audiant, quid loquantur, qui uetustissimum cænum quasi nouam suscipiant temperaturam, qui iuxta Hezechiel (13: 10) liniunt parietem absque temperamento, qui superueniente ueritatis pluuia dissipatur?" Jerome goes on to give a list of women who became involved in heresy, and he concludes with the jibe, "The two-faced sex trips up both sexes".

[153] Cf. van der MEER, *Priestertum...*, p. 131: "Es ist auffallend, dass die Väter keine eigentlichen Spekulationen über ihre These angestellt haben. Sie berufen sich einfach auf die Tatsache, dass Jesus und die Apostel keine Frauen ausgesandt haben. Oder sie verweisen auf die Paulus-Texte. Das ist gar nicht spekulativ. Nur dort taucht eine Reflexion auf, wo sie sich auf die niedrige Stellung der Frau berufen. Dabei setzen sie natürlich voraus, dass der Priester ein Vorgesetzer ist." Cf. also *supra,* n. 113.

[154] Cf. P. HÜNERMANN, "Roma locuta — causa finita? Zur Argumentation der vatikanischen Erklärung über die Frauenordination" in *Herder Korrespondez,* 31 (Freiburg: 1977), pp. 206-9.

[155] Cf. P. de LABRIOLLE, "Mulieres...", p. 114; also J. REUMANN, "What in Scripture...", pp. 5-30.

[156] Cf. R. GRYSON, *Le ministère...*, pp. 176-8.

[157] For instance, the term *hiereus* is not employed in the New Testament to express some specific ordained priestly "rank" in the Christian community. Such a use comes relatively late, perhaps not until the *Didascalia.* Cf. B. COOKE, *Ministry...*, pp. 33-125 and 537-8; also J. SOBOSAN, "The Role...", *passim.*

Fifthly, the only *firsthand* models of a female priesthood these writers had to go by were to be found in paganism — a fact which could hardly have encouraged Christian emulation.[158]

What then remains of the *Declaration*'s patristic support? No reference supplied can do more than explain how the Church's present-day prohibition of priestly ordination to women has been arrived at. Some of them cannot do even that; and none of them can be employed validly to justify prolonging the prohibition.[159] For while no satisfactory attempt has ever been made to disclaim that "the Catholic Church has never felt that priestly or episcopal ordination can be validly conferred on women",[160] it cannot be simply assumed that a datum with an unbroken history is the same as "the Church's constant tradition",[161] especially when, as in this case, clear and direct documentation is so sparse.

It is true, of course, that this entire issue turns on considerations far more complex than the simple endorsement or refutation of a few ancient texts. But that *caveat* applies to both

---

[158] Cf. J.-M. AUBERT, *La femme...,* pp. 159-60: "Dans le monde antique, romain et christianisé, l'exclusion des femmes de toute vie publique, qui était un des traits caractéristiques de cette société, [...] était transposé spontanément dans les structures de l'Eglise [...] Dans cet univers où la femme était 'privatisée", même si elle était plus libre de mœurs que jadis, l'existence, d'ailleurs limitée, d'un sacerdoce féminin, sans parler de la prostitution sacrée, ne pouvait jouer un rôle de modèle. En effet, l'existence des prêtresses antiques, loin d'avoir dû influencer le christianisme dans le sens d'une imitation, ne pouvait que le renforcer dans le sens d'un refus; car si le paganisme a influencé le christianisme, c'est essentiellement au niveau culturel, du droit, des institutions, des idées générales, et non pas du culte païen réprouvé comme idolâtre." Cf. also R. GRYSON, *Le ministère...,* p. 176.

[159] So J. R. DONAHUE, "Women...", p. 288: "The question of evaluating the tradition of exclusion from ordination [...] is not simply the question of whether the church can be reconciled with the tradition of de facto exclusion. The further problem for the modern church is whether it can be reconciled with the kind of scriptural exegesis, cultural worldview and anthropology in which this tradition grew and flourished." Cf. also R. METZ, "L'accession des femmes aux ministères 'ordonnés'," in *Effort diaconal,* 34-35 (Lyons: 1974), pp. 21-30; and J.R. SHEETS, "Ordination of Women: The Issues", in *American Ecclesiastical Review,* 169 (Washington: 1975), pp. 17-36.

[160] Cf. *supra,* p. 52.

[161] Cf. *supra,* n. 4. In invoking its second group of patristic sources (cf. *supra,* p. 63), the *Declaration* omits all reference to sources from the "Egyptian tradition".

the pro and contra sides in the discussion.[162] It *may be* that divine
law itself excludes women from an ordained priestly ministry. It
may be that this exclusion will be revealed as solidly established in
Scripture and Tradition. It *may be* that further serious research
will lead to a final conclusion not substantially different from the
conclusion already reached by the *Declaration*. But, if texts are
ever found in the Fathers of the Church that give unquestionable
support to that conclusion, we should expect that the sources invoked by the *Declaration* will not be among them.

J. Kevin COYLE, O.S.A.

Saint Paul University

---

[162] The warnings of R. GRYSON, *Le ministère...*, pp. 15-7 and 177-9,
should be read and retained with care.

The "Divine Woman"? Propaganda and the Power of Celibacy in the New Testament Apocrypha: A Reconsideration[1]

GAIL PATERSON CORRINGTON*

Although the claim may still be debated, it is by now virtually a scholarly cliché that one of the paradigms for the early Christian presentation of Jesus was that of the "divine man" (*theios anēr*), whose authority is validated by pointing to its divine source in the working of miracles. This paradigm, whose origins appear to be Greek and which was absorbed and modified in Hellenistic Judaism, has three general manifestations: the wise man (*sophos*), the charismatic religious leader (*theios anthrōpos*), and the possessor and manipulator of spiritual powers (*magos*). These types are frequently conflated, especially in the popular imagination, because they are all legitimated through miracles as a means of demonstrating their access to a transcendent power. The miracles of Jesus were often perceived as the result of his possession of such a divine power. For example, in Jn 3:2, Nicodemus "knows" that Jesus is a teacher "come from God," because the "signs" he performs indicate "God is with him." For the author of the canonical Acts, not only is Jesus "attested by God with powerful deeds and wonders and signs" (Acts 2:22), but Jesus' disciples (the apostles) also possess this divine power, demonstrating it through similar *dynameis* ("mighty acts"), *terata* ("wonders"), and *sēmeia* ("signs"). Miracle-stories thus served the same purpose in early Christianity as they did in the rest of the Greco-Roman world: they were a form of popular religious propaganda, used to win converts to a particular way of life by showing its power.[2] Moreover, because of the propagandistic

---

* *Editor's Note:* Gail Paterson Corrington teaches at Pennsylvania State University. She is the author of The "Divine Man": His Origin and Function in Hellenistic Popular Religion (Lang, 1986). During 1988–89, she is visiting lecturer and research associate in women's studies in New Testament at Harvard Divinity School.

[1] The present article represents the development of ideas first presented in a paper entitled "Salvation, Celibacy, and Power," delivered to the Greco-Roman Religions Group at the 1985 Annual Meeting of the Society of Biblical Literature. That paper was subsequently published in a greatly revised and expanded version in a special issue on Women in Antiquity of the classical journal *Helios* (vol. 13, no. 2, 1986). This article is itself a revision of a paper presented at the SBL Annual Meeting, 5–8 December 1987, before the Consultation on Ascetic Behavior in Greco-Roman Antiquity.

[2] Elisabeth Schüssler Fiorenza, "Miracles, Mission, and Apologetics," in *Aspects of*

207

function of this material, the "divine man" became crystallized as a literary *type,* whatever social reality the preacher and the audience experienced.

If we continue tracing the trajectory of this paradigm beyond the NT canon, we may discover that the apostles are even more clearly portrayed as divine men in the apocryphal Acts of the Apostles [or *AAA,* for convenience hereafter]. The miracle-stories of these "forgotten novels of the early church," as Dennis MacDonald has called them,[3] served both to provide propaganda for conversion to the "higher power" afforded by Christianity and to provide edifying tales for converts. In this second- to fourth-century popular literature, moreover, a new dimension of the divine-man paradigm emerges when the charismatic teacher and miracle-worker is combined with the ascetic "holy man" of later antiquity.[4]

Another, parallel paradigm may be discerned in the *AAA,* a paradigm I call "the divine woman" *(theia gynē),* a female apostle whose ability to work or to cause miracles appears in every case to depend on her celibacy. In certain of the *AAA*—the *Acts of Andrew* (Coptic), *Acts of Paul and Thecla, Acts of John,* and *Acts of Thomas*—the miracles function as propaganda for female conversion, not simply to Christianity, but to the celibate life, its inevitable consequence. Moreover, like the miracle-stories of the male apostles, these *Acts* probably serve also for the edification of female converts. In each of these stories, despite resistance to the adoption of celibacy by the woman's family, husband (or fiancé), male civic authority, or even a male apostle, the woman, with the help of divine power, wins approval of her choice.[5] In addition, the equality of the female convert to the male apostle is frequently demonstrated both by her assumption of his role and functions (teaching, baptizing, preaching) and by the continuity of her apostolic work without his assistance. Thecla in the *Acts of Paul and Thecla* is herself an apostle; Drusiana in the *Acts of John* and the unnamed ascetic "virgin" of the Coptic *Acts of Andrew* are exorcists; Mygdonia of the *Acts of Thomas* and Thecla teach and baptize. The pseudonymity of these stories, their popular nature, and their later condemnation by the church fathers indicate that the forms of behavior extolled by the *AAA* were considered at variance with the prevailing social and religious values of second- to fourth-century Greco-

---

Religious Propaganda in Judaism and Early Christianity, ed. Robert L. Wilken (Notre Dame, Ind.: Univ. of Notre Dame Press, 1976), 7.

[3]   Dennis R. MacDonald, "The Forgotten Novels of the Early Church," in *The Apocryphal Acts of the Apostles,* ed. D. R. MacDonald, Semeia 38 (Decatur, Ga.: Scholars Press, 1986), 5.

[4]   Peter Brown, *Society and the Holy in Late Antiquity* (Berkeley: University of California Press, 1981), 131f.

[5]   Virginia Burrus, "Chastity as Autonomy: Women in the Stories of the Apocryphal Acts," *Apocryphal Acts,* 105f.

Roman society, pagan and Christian.[6] Many scholars have suggested that what was unacceptable about the behavior of these Christian heroines was that they were both celibate and authoritative, and that they experienced celibacy as a "liberating option" from the social roles expected of them.[7] Further, because these women were idealized, literary types, they provided ideals and models for real women who wished, in a similar way, to break through their own constricting social roles.[8]

Several questions have been raised in the course of the exploration of this paradigm, but they stem from two main issues: the question of parallels to the "divine woman" paradigm and the question of what authority this paradigm claims for women. First, since the divine-man paradigm existed before its Christian application to Jesus and the apostles, was there a similar pre-Christian model for the proposed "divine woman" paradigm? Second, in what way did the miraculous occurrences associated with these divine women function as "dramas of authority,"[9] in relation to the Christian communities in which these stories developed? These questions, like the paradigms to which they refer, are related to the larger question of the dimensions of power in the Greco-Roman and early Christian worlds, power as it operated within social position and power which, coming from a source outside social position, transformed or challenged it. The question of power is particularly relevant to the situation of women within those worlds and their ability to achieve empowerment, their choices being limited by law and by tradition because of their gender. This ability is in turn associated with the issue of control, especially control over oneself and one's situation in life. The literary heroine manages to achieve a form of control, providing a model (or perhaps functioning as a projection of desire) for women who had little of such control.

The arena in which power was exercised, in the transition from the

---

[6]   Gerd Theissen, *The Miracle Stories of the Early Christian Tradition*, trans. Francis McDonagh (Philadelphia: Fortress, 1983), 268.

[7]   Rosemary R. Ruether, "Mother of the Church: Ascetic Women in the Late Patristic Age," in *Women of Spirit: Female Leadership in the Jewish and Christian Traditions*, ed. Ruether and Eleanor McLaughlin (New York: Simon & Schuster, 1979), 73; Jo Ann McNamara, *A New Song: Celibate Women in the First Three Christian Centuries* (New York: Institute for Research in History/Haworth, 1983), 43; Ross N. Kraemer, "The Conversion of Women to Ascetic Forms of Christianity," *Signs* 6 (1980): 301; Elisabeth Schüssler Fiorenza, *In Memory of Her: A Feminist Theological Reconstruction of Christian Origins* (New York: Crossroad, 1983), 184; Gail Paterson Corrington, "The Divine Woman? Propaganda and the Power of Chastity in the NT Apocrypha," *Helios* 13 (1986): 151–62.

[8]   The chart following this article shows, in schematic fashion, the way in which the heroine's choice of celibacy is opposed in the *AAA*, and the way in which the conflict is resolved by her assumption of some form of power or authority, usually vindicated by divine approval in the form of a miracle.

[9]   Brown, *The Cult of the Saints: Its Rise and Function in Latin Christianity*, Haskell Lectures 2 (Chicago: University of Chicago Press, 1981), 93.

Hellenistic to the Greco-Roman period and thence to the early Christian, was increasingly less public and more private. The political changes which occurred in the Mediterranean basin in the fourth century BCE brought to an end the possibility of direct involvement in the government of the city-state. The rise of the Roman republic, culminating in its victory over most of the Greek world in 146 BCE, again fostered the idea of involvement (at least for upper-class males) in the public life of the city-state. This hope, too, collapsed, with the beginnings of the Empire under Augustus in 27 BCE. These changes had a great deal of influence on the preoccupation of the Greco-Roman world with power and its manifestations. "It is within this horizon that the concept of the 'embodied power' of the *theios anēr* is to be found. . . . The control over or display of power seemed . . . to be evidence of the divine,"[10] because it was not a power ordinary mortals, even the traditional holders of power, appeared to possess.

I would here like to suggest that, judging from the literature relating to women in the Greco-Roman and early Christian worlds, there appear to be three models of female empowerment: *enthousiasmos* ("embodied power" through possession by a male deity); martyrdom (another form of *askēsis*, by which a woman "symbolically becomes male");[11] and asceticism as a form of self-mastery, by which a woman needs also to become, like a male, an "athlete" in training to become a champion (cf. *Acts of Andrew* [Coptic] 10.6–8, 25–30). Therefore, if a woman is not to be "mastered" by a male, she must become a male or adopt a male paradigm of empowerment.

Let us deal first with the most traditional forms of female empowerment, which is quite literally that of being filled with the power of the deity (*enthousiasmos*). The most famous example is that of the Pythia, the priestess of Apollo at Delphi. According to myth, she was originally a virgin, but because of the seduction of an early Pythia, the office was reserved for older women, who, even if they were married at the time of their election, were required to observe ritual purity (*hagneia*) to serve the god. The Pythia's prophecies were attributed to Apollo, who "entered her," causing her to speak with a *pneuma enthousiastikon* (Strabo, *Geog.* 9.3.5).[12] A connection between female sexuality and prophetic spirit

---

[10] Corrington, "Power and the Man of Power in the Context of Hellenistic Popular Belief," *SBL Seminar Papers 1984* (Chico, Calif.: Scholars Press, 1984), 257f.

[11] McNamara, *New Song*, 88; Marie-Luise von Franz, *The Passion of Perpetua* (Irving, Tex.: Spring, 1980), 59; Elizabeth Clark, *Jerome, Chrysostom, and Friends: Essays and Translations*, Studies in Women and Religion 2 (New York: Mellen, 1979), 16.

[12] It is probable that the Pythia never "raved" in an uncontrollable frenzy, as later generations assumed she did. Cf. Joseph Fontenrose, *The Delphic Oracle: Its Responses and Operations, with a Catalogue of Responses* (Berkeley: University of California, 1978), 196ff.

subsequently arose in the Greco-Roman world out of a negative attitude towards female sexual freedom and the male need to control it. Although it might be expected that a church father like John Chrysostom would attribute the Pythia's inspiration to an evil spirit, which he says entered her genitals while she was seated on her prophetic tripod,[13] Chrysostom evokes the connection between inspiration and male-controlled female sexuality made by the first-century Roman poet Lucan, who described the Pythia's prophecy as the result of being raped by the god [*Bell. civ.* 5.166f). The great Roman epic poet Vergil also described as rape the process by which another virgin prophetess of Apollo, the Cumean Sibyl, was inspired (*Aeneid* 6.77–82). Indeed, Apollo as the god of prophecy was usually described in myth as raping his prophetesses. This view of female enthusiasm perhaps lies behind the reason that the Montanist prophetesses, who claimed authority as embodied *pneuma*, were suspected of sexual debauchery. Certainly an attempt was made to bring the female "enthusiasts" in the Christian congregation at Corinth under "control" rather quickly (1 Cor 11:4–16), and it is also interesting to note that the slave-girl with the *pneuma pythona* who follows Paul and Barnabas in the canonical Acts (16:16–18) is "exorcised" by Paul. In conclusion, then, this form of female claim to divine empowerment was seen as either a violation of the woman, who was nevertheless still under male control, or as an invitation to sexual license.[14] In the *AAA*, the celibate woman's husband or fiancé assumes that she has separated from him (left his control) because she is "possessed" by (under the power of) another male.

All too briefly, let us turn to the second "option" for female empowerment: martyrdom. Lest this seem too far-fetched an alternative, let us consider that, even in the chastity romances, death was preferable to marriage or its symbolic equivalent, rape. This motif appears even more strongly in accounts of female martyrdoms. As Susan Ashbrook Harvey and Sebastian Brock note in their commentary on the accounts of the Persian martyrs, these Christian women prefer death to the violation that even an earthly marriage would mean. The graphic sexual mutilation that appears in these stories, rare in martyrologies of men, serves, as does the transvestitism in the stories of penitents, to "destroy their identity as women and take on that of men."[15] Even in the early third-century *Passio Perpetuae*, possibly written in great part by the martyr Vibia Perpetua herself,

---

[13]   John Chrysostom, *Ep. 1 ad Cor. Hom.* 29.1 (*PG* 61:242), cited by Fontenrose, *Delphic Oracle*, 210.

[14]   See parallels with the Bacchic mysteries in Livy, *Urb. cond.* 40.43.1; *Pythagorean Treatise*, in Mary R. Lefkowitz and Maureen B. Fant, *Women's Life in Greece and Rome* (London: Duckworth, 1981), 104; cf. Thecla's "freedom" seen as license by Alexander (*Acts of Paul and Thecla* 36).

[15]   "Introduction," *Holy Women of the Syrian Orient*, trans. Sebastian P. Brock and Susan Ashbrook Harvey (Berkeley: University of California Press, 1987), 25.

her identity as a woman is gradually transformed into that of a man. During her imprisonment, she sends her infant son away, and her breast-milk dries up. She rejects the control of her father, when she refuses to recant. In the fourth and last of a series of visions, she actually loses her female identity. Stripped of her female garments, Perpetua is changed into a male gladiator in order to fight the Egyptian, symbol of demonic power. In the account of her actual martyrdom, her clothing is literally torn off her, and she is about to be killed in a man's death,[16] by the sword of a gladiator being thrust into her side, although she herself guides it to her throat in a form of death considered in literature "appropriate" for a woman. (As the commentator notes, however, she could not have been killed, as female or male, unless she herself "willed" it.) In the case of *enthousiasmos*, control is forced on the woman: in the martyrdom stories, she resists control by death, a death through which she ceases to be a woman. In both cases, the battleground is the woman's body.

Turning to the third alternative model for female empowerment within the Greco-Roman and early Christian world—asceticism—we must note that here, too, there were serious obstacles to a woman's choice, obstacles graphically portrayed in the *AAA* as attempts by the woman's family and civil authorities to force her to accept marriage and family life as the social norm. Life-long female celibacy was not an option in the social sphere from Solonic Greece to fourth-century Rome, since the woman's duty—indeed, a daughter's very reason for existence—was to marry and have children, thus assuring the preservation and proper transfer of private property. Thus, although virginity was often portrayed as being an attractive state of affairs to a young woman, persisting in it to the denial of family life was an object of reproach.[17] Marriage was itself considered a form of "mastering" or "taming" women by men (cf. Sophocles. *Antigone* 578f; *Trachiniae* 143–50), unmarried women being referred to as "unmastered" (*adamatos*), while a wife was referred to as *damar*, "mastered." In numbers of Roman wedding-songs, women were shown as experiencing this mastery as rape (cf. Catullus 61.3–4; 62.20–24),[18] a violation that was not only symbolic but actual, since a man was expected either forcibly to deflower his wife on her wedding-night or, sparing her feelings, to sodomize her.[19] It is no wonder that the "freedom of the apostle" preached by Paul and other Christian missionaries would have been interpreted as did Thecla, the aristocratic virgin from Iconium,

---

[16]   Nicole Loraux, *Tragic Ways of Killing a Woman*, trans. Anthony Forster (Cambridge, Mass.: Harvard University Press, 1987), 50ff.

[17]   Cf. Eva Stehle Stigers, "Retreat from the Male: Catullus 62 and Sappho's Erotic Flowers," *Ramus* 6 (1977): 83–102.

[18]   Ibid.; Corrington, "Divine Woman," 159.

[19]   Paul Veyne, "The Roman Empire," in *A History of Private Life 1: From Pagan Rome to Byzantium*, ed. Paul Veyne (Cambridge, Mass.: Harvard University Press, 1987), 35.

especially in view of her impending marriage. Indeed, in the *AAA*, as in the martyrdoms, the attempt either to conclude a marriage or to rape is often portrayed as the action of "demonic" forces, which the woman must fight off.

The traditional religious practices that supported this social order, whether Greek, Hellenistic, or Roman, afforded equally small opportunity for female celibacy. Ritual purity (*hagneia*) in Greece might mean sexual abstinence for a period of time, the duration of priestly office, of a particular festival, or of a period of initiation.[20] In classical Greece, virginity was viewed as a liminal state prior to "initiation" into marriage, as in the case of the "she-bears of Artemis" at Brauron. Virgins were barred, however, from participating in certain women's festivals like the Thesmophoria.[21] Although the priestesses who served the mother-goddess Demeter were unmarried, perhaps representing the state of her daughter, Korē, before her rape by Hades, those who served the virgin deities Hestia, Athene, and Artemis were women no longer capable of marriage, but those for whom marriage was presupposed.[22] Those who served Vesta, Hestia's Roman counterpart, the Vestal Virgins, were required to remain celibate for a specific period of time, during which they shared many of the "privileges" of married women, while the honor of being a Vestal was sometimes granted to married women of the imperial household.[23]

Hence, it would appear that "withdrawal" from fulfillment of one's obligation (indeed, the only public obligation Greco-Roman women were expected to fulfill) was the prerogative of men. Michel Foucault has noted that the idea of self-sovereignty, that Stoic/Cynic ideal so popular in the first centuries of the imperial era, became even more popular when the traditional holders of public authority were excluded from the center of power at the beginning of the Imperial period. As he notes, "The Greco-Roman ideal of self-discipline and autonomy was associated with the desire to exert power in public life."[24] The ascetic life practiced by the neo-Pythagoreans, if we can believe the third-century evidence of Iamblichus for practices of the first two centuries, represented a withdrawal from public life and the formation of an alternative community (*Vit. Pyth.* 21.95–100). The Epicureans, also noted for recommending

---

[20] Walter Burkert, *Greek Religion*, trans. John Raffan (Cambridge, Mass.: Harvard University Press, 1985), 78.

[21] Ibid., 242.

[22] Ibid., 221, 224.

[23] Mary Beard, "Sexual Status of Vestal Virgins," *Journal of Roman Studies* 70 (1980): 12ff.

[24] Michel Foucault, quoted in Veyne, "The Roman Empire," 36.

withdrawal from public life, were according to Numenius associated with an alternative *politeia*.[25]

Such withdrawal, or such self-discipline as a form of autonomy, seems in general to have been a possibility only for the upper-class Greco-Roman gentlemen who had previously had control not only over their own lives but also over those of others. In late Republican and early imperial Rome, private life became the arena in which control was exercised. As a special result of the idea of Stoic self-mastery, marriage in these periods became an "issue" which, according to Paul Veyne, "created the illusion of a 'marriage crisis,' a spread of [male] celibacy."[26] This illusory "crisis" was addressed by the Augustan marriage-legislation (18 BCE, *Lex Julia de maritandis ordinibus;* 9 CE, *Lex Papia Poppaea*),[27] which was intended to direct the attention of good citizens toward their minimal obligation to the Roman state: producing children.

This obligation, in early Republican times, was seen as a "burden" even for men.[28] For women, however, marriage was not even a burden that might be assumed out of Stoic duty, but a necessity that was social, familial, and legal. This situation certainly sheds light upon the reasons why the celibate life is represented as having appealed so readily to the female Christian converts of the *AAA*. It also explains why this choice was made over "the strenuous objections of the family."[29] The perilous nature of this choice is graphically portrayed in the *Acts of Paul and Thecla,* in which Thecla's own mother, Theokleia, urges the governor of Iconium to have the "un-bride" (*anymphon*) burned (*APT* 20). Such episodes suggest that conversion to celibacy was an affront to the Greco-Roman social order because it appeared to be a denial of heteronomy (outside control) and an assertion of autonomy (self-control). In setting forth the reasons why it was so, we shall answer the first question raised, viz., whether there are any parallels in antiquity for the divine-woman paradigm, as there are for the divine man.

To answer this question succinctly, there are no pre-Christian female parallels. But to come to this conclusion requires both an exploration of possible parallels and a distinction that must be drawn between the terms "celibacy" and "chastity," especially as they relate to women. Even though "celibacy" to Greco-Roman society carried the meaning of the "unmarried" state (much as *partheneia* originally did to the Greek), I use

[25] Wayne Meeks, *The First Urban Christians* (New Haven: Yale University Press, 1984), 83.
[26] Veyne, "Roman Empire," 38.
[27] Beryl Rawson, "The Roman Family," in *The Family in Ancient Rome: New Perspectives,* ed. B. Rawson (Ithaca: Cornell University Press, 1986), 9f.
[28] Ibid., 11.
[29] Ann Yarbrough, "Christianization in the Fourth Century: The Example of Roman Women," *Church History* 45 (1976): 154.

it to refer to the complete abstinence from sexual relations like that practiced by the wives and virgins of the *AAA*, since they live "as if" they were unmarried. Single women, unlike single men, were expected by both societies not to have engaged in sexual intercourse before marriage. Chastity, on the other hand, meant a state of being "pure in respect to the marriage-bed,"[30] a private manifestation of the *pietas*, or loyalty, expected of the citizen. The hypothesized Roman ideals of Castitas and Pudicitia (Chastity and Modesty) were held up for emulation by Vestal Virgins and married women alike.[31]

It is necessary to have drawn this distinction before proceeding to an examination of possible antecedents or parallels to the portrayal of the divine woman of the *AAA*, since the most often cited parallels are the heroines of the Hellenistic "chastity romances," Chariton of Aphrodisias' *Chaereas and Callirhoe*, Xenophon of Ephesus' *Ephesiaca*, Heliodorus of Emesa's *Ethiopica*, Achilles Tatius' *Leucippe and Clitophon*, and Longus' *Daphnis and Chloe*.[32] Although the extant romances belong to the second to fourth centuries CE, as do the *AAA*, they arose in the first century, primarily out of the stories of parted and reunited lovers and their tribulations dramatized in Greek New Comedy.[33] The salient feature of these romances is the "laudable fidelity" of parted lovers, usually amid "fearsome and protracted" vicissitudes.[34] A great deal of emphasis, however, is placed upon the chastity of the woman, which she defends against many threats to her person, and which is continually being put to the test. In the third-century *Ethiopica* of Heliodorus, the heroine, Chariclea, faces at least ten trials of her chastity, beginning at the precocious age of seven.[35] Such is the power of her resolve to remain chaste until marriage that she defends her chastity even in the face of death. So high a value does the author place upon her chastity that several miraculous occurrences assist Chariclea, both in proving and in defending that chastity: another woman is mistakenly slain; an amethyst magically appears to pay her ransom; the fires to which she is condemned will not burn her because of her "innocence and piety." Leucippe, the heroine of Achilles Tatius' second-century romance, *Leucippe and Clitophon*, likewise protects and is magically protected by her chastity, to which the virgin goddess Diana has called her. Threatened with torture, Leucippe says she will bear the rack, the fire, and decapitation because of the

---

[30]   *Pythagorean Treatise*, in Lefkowitz and Fant, *Women's Life*, 104.
[31]   Rawson, "Roman Family," 25.
[32]   Burrus, "Chastity as Autonomy," 103.
[33]   Jacqueline de Romilly, *A Short History of Greek Literature*, trans. Lilian Doherty (Chicago: University of Chicago Press, 1980), 205.
[34]   Ibid.
[35]   Cf. the trials of Peter's daughter in *Acts of Peter* (Berlin Coptic Papyrus 8502, pp. 128–32, 135–41), which begin when she is ten.

"freedom of her spirit," rather than face the loss of her chastity. Her virginity is finally divinely tested and proven by the magical sounding of a syrinx from Diana's cave.

Despite the dissimilarity noted by Virginia Burrus between the narrative structure of these and other Hellenistic chastity romances and the chastity stories in the AAA,[36] there are some apparent similarities, especially in their emphasis on female chastity, the empowerment of the woman for the purpose of defending that chastity, often with magical or miraculous aid, and the quasi-magical power of that chastity itself to defend her. Yet there are some major differences, which would preclude the heroines of these romances from providing a true parallel for those of the AAA. In the first place, the heroine of the Hellenistic romances preserves her virginity for marriage with her sundered beloved. Thus, her chastity before marriage presages her fidelity to her prospective husband. In this respect, the martyrdoms of the ascetic Syrian women, with their emphasis on the testing of the women's celibacy as proof of their fidelity to the Heavenly Bridegroom, Christ, exhibit a closer parallel to the Greek romances than do the AAA.[37] Second, the miraculous occurrences connected with the chastity of the Greek romantic heroine do not function as "dramas of authority" by which she takes control of her own identity, but as "rescue" miracles, which preserve her chastity for its proper destiny: marriage. Unreasonable as she may seem to her putative suitors (most of whom have marriage as an object), she does not violate the norms of acceptable Greco-Roman social behavior.

When we examine the status of women in those philosophic associations which might be expected to support forms of behavior contrary to those generally accepted by the social order, the situation is not very much different. The Epicureans admitted women to their "commonwealth" on the same terms as they did men, and the male Cynics frequently had women as their partners in *autarkeia*, with or without a formally recognized marriage.[38] Nevertheless, as previously observed, a third-century BCE Pythagorean treatise enjoins chastity on married women as purity "with respect to the marriage-bed."[39] Only the Therapeutidae of Philo of Alexandria's *De vita contemplativa* are described as *parthenoi*, their purity (*hagneia*) compared to that of "some of the priestesses among the Greeks" (*Vit contemp.* 68), but the lack of contemporary parallels, either to the Therapeutidae or their male counterparts, is frustrating and well known, and has led to the supposition of

---

[36] Burrus, "Chastity as Autonomy," 105f.
[37] Brock and Harvey, "Introduction," *Holy Women of the Syrian Orient*, 8f.
[38] Schüssler Fiorenza, *In Memory of Her*, 213; Meeks, *First Urban Christians*, 84.
[39] Lefkowitz and Fant, *Women's Life*, 104.

the pseudonymous and late authorship of the *Vita*.[40] In any case, as Wayne Meeks has pointed out, the philosophical communities themselves took "the form of modified households or voluntary associations,"[41] a model that the Christian communities adopted only as a form of integration into the prevailing social order and that was equally oppressive to women.[42]

The only other possible non-Christian parallel to the divine woman paradigm comes from Eunapius' *Lives of the Philosophers*; it is the philosophic teacher, Sosipatra, who is hailed as a teacher of "inspired" (*enthousiasmon*) wisdom and as a goddess (*thea*). Her prophetic powers and the miraculous episodes of her life are the equals of any of the divine women of the *AAA*, but her power comes, not from her celibacy, but from her "surpassing wisdom." She is married to a philosopher, Eustathius (even though she surpasses him in wisdom), and dutifully has three children, each of whom is divinely prophetic as well. Even if we excepted the celibacy motif, this fourth-century account does not seem to have preceded those of the women of the *AAA*, but may even have been presented as a rival to those stories, its author's opinion of Christians, particularly celibate ones, being what it was: negative in the extreme.[43]

In conclusion, the sort of authority the women of the *AAA* sought, and the reason for their willingness to fly in the face of the "intentions of the existing law and the general cultural ethos" of Greco-Roman society,[44] is the authority to make choices about their bodily destiny, which was possible only for the males of that society. Hence, it must be admitted that the "divine woman" paradigm is derived from a male model, the "divine man" paradigm of the male apostles. Women experienced the ascetic life as a new alternative, a chosen liberation from the social roles, and the "mastery" marriage and family life demanded of them, a form of autonomy with the highest sanction, that of God.[45] Christianity, from its very inception as a prophetic-charismatic religion, had opposed itself to the structures of the social order and of the family. This freedom from social ties was also necessary for the spread of the gospel, an idea succinctly expressed by Paul, whose vaunted "freedom of the apostle" (1 Cor 9:19) was apparently understood in the type of Christian circles that produced the *Acts of Paul and Thecla* as the freedom of the

---

[40]   F. H. Colson, "Introduction," *Philo*, vol. IV, Loeb Classical Library (Cambridge, Mass.: Harvard University Press, 1941), 105–7.

[41]   Meeks, *First Urban Christians*, 84.

[42]   Schüssler Fiorenza, *In Memory of Her*, 249.

[43]   Philip Rousseau, *Ascetics, Authority, and the Church* (Oxford: Oxford University Press, 1978), 9f; Eunapius, *Vit. Phil.* 6.11.

[44]   Schüssler Fiorenza, *In Memory of Her*, 225.

[45]   Ruether, "Mothers of the Church," 73; McNamara, *New Song*, 43; Schüssler Fiorenza, *In Memory of Her*, 225.

unmarried (*parthenoi*, 1 Cor 7:26). To be an *apostolē*, therefore, a woman had to be free of the yoke of social and sexual dominance. In the stories of the celibate women in the *AAA*, the miracles serve, as Gerd Theissen has noted, as "symbolic actions of human subjectivity in which the real negativity of existence is transcended," giving, as is true of other miracles, authority of a transcendent kind to those whose beliefs were at variance with those of the prevailing social order.[46] It is both ironic and tragic that these women, like other female saints, in rejecting the roles imposed upon them by that social order, adopted an ideal that men had originally chosen and promoted for themselves. As William Davis has observed of the ascetic saints of the Middle Ages, "On the one hand, the saintly women struggled desperately to free themselves of the shackles of male authority. Yet in doing so, they may have unwittingly colluded with the very forces they were attempting to bypass."[47]

---

[46] Theissen, *Miracle Stories*, 268.

[47] William N. Davis, "Epilogue," in Rudolph M. Bell, *Holy Anorexia* (Chicago: University of Chicago Press, 1985), 285.

RELATIONSHIP OF WOMEN TO POWER AND AUTONOMY IN THE SECOND-THIRD
CENTURY *APOCRYPHAL ACTS OF THE APOSTLES*

TEXT	WOMAN	OPPONENT (threatens chastity/celibacy)	FORM OF POWER Authoritative role (A) Assumption of power (P) Miracle (M) Rescue miracle (R)
Acts of John (H–S 2:215–58)	Drusiana	Andronicus (husband)	Persuades him to release her (A)
		Callimachus (suitor), aided by Fortunatus	Bitten by snake (R) Bitten by snake (R) Raised by Drusiana (M)
Acts of Peter I (Berl. Copt. Pap. 8502, pp. 128–32, 135–41)(H–S 2:276–78)	Peter's daughter	Ptolemaeus (suitor)	Vision from God and divine warning (R)
II (Actus Vercellenses, 9) (H–S 2:314–22)	Agrippina Nicaria Euphemia Doris (concubines)	Agrippa (master; prefect)	Survive "every injury . . . strengthened by the power of Jesus" (P; R)
	Xanthippe	Albinus (husband)	Separation (P) Informs Pt. of plot (A)
Acts of Paul and Thecla (AA 1:235–69; H–S 2:353–64)	Thecla	Thamyris (betrothed)	Fire is put out (R)
		Theocleia (mother)	Governor of Iconium "marvels at the power . . . in her." (P)
		Alexander (suitor)	Lioness defends her (R) Baptizes herself; seals are killed (A;R) Rescued from bulls (R) Seeks Paul, dressed as a man (A) Converts mother (A)
Acts of Paul (PH, 1–5; H–S 2:369–73)	Artemilla	Hieronymus (husband; governor)	A. "dismissed to her husband" (neg. A)
	Eubula	Diophantes (husband)	H. is stricken with ear infection, healed by "Paul's God" (M) [Conversion?]
Acts of Andrew I (Pap. Copt. Utrecht I, Quispel & Zandee) (H–S 2:403–8)	"Virgin"	Young magician (suitor), with assistance of Semmath (demon)	Demon defeated (M; P) Demon cast out of brother (M; P; A)
II (Codex Vat. 808) (H–S 2: 408–16)	Maximilla	Aegeates (husband, judge)	Resists (P) "Lives apart"; rejects A.'s promise of "control over his affairs" (*Narr.* 36; *Mart.* II.10; *Ep.Gr.*15) (P; A) Aegeates commits suicide (R)

continued

Acts of Thomas (AA II.2:99–287; H–S 2:442–531)	Mygdonia	Charisius (husband)	"Parted from her husband" (A) Anoints and baptizes women (A)
	Marcia Tertia	(master) Misdaeus (husband, king)	Mygdonia, Marcia, Tertia "shut up" in prison by Charisius, Misdaeus, but miraculously freed (M; R)
	Mnesara	(Resists chaste marriage with husband)	Healed of disease (M); becomes celibate.

Eng. trans. of texts based on Edgar Hennecke, *New Testament Apocrypha*, Vol. 2: *Writings Relating to the Apostles, Apocalypses, and Related Subjects*, ed. Wilhelm Schneemelcher, trans. ed. R. McL. Wilson (Philadelphia: Westminster, 1964); abbreviated H-S. Other abbreviations: AA = *Acta Apostolorum Apocrypha*, ed. R.A. Lipsius and M. Bonnet (Braunschweig: Schwetschke, 1883–90; Darmstadt: Wiss. Buchgesellschaft, 1959); PH = Hamburg Papyrus.

Libertine or Liberated: Women in the So-called Libertine Gnostic Communities

Recent studies have brought into focus the special attraction that Gnosticism and asceticism offered to women of the early centuries C.E. It has been recognized that women found opportunities in gnostic communities that were closed to them in the "orthodox" church. This is seen not only in the number of female leaders in gnostic circles but also in the prominence given to the feminine in gnostic sources.[1] Similarly, it has been argued that women discovered in the ascetic life style a path through which to escape from the gender-defined constraints imposed upon them by Roman society. This path supplied an alternative to marriage through which a woman could use her talent and power to God's and her own glory.[2] While the significance of these conclusions for women's existence in the Roman world is under debate,[3] the reality of the appeal of these ideologies to certain women is beyond dispute.

1. E. Pagels, *The Gnostic Gospels*, 57–83; idem, "What Became of God the Mother?" 293–303; K. Rudolph, *Gnosis: The Nature and History*, 211–12, 270–72; and R. Mortley, *Womanhood*. The bibliography on the various feminine aeons in Gnosticism is large. References may be found in the standard bibliographies on Gnosticism. David M. Scholer, *Nag Hammadi Bibliography 1948-1969*. This bibliography is supplemented yearly in *NovT*.
2. E. A. Clark, "Ascetic Renunciation and Feminine Advancement: A Paradox of Late Ancient Christianity," *ATR* 63 (1981) 240–57; R. Kraemer, "The Conversion of Women to Ascetic Forms of Christianity," *Signs* 6 (1980/81) 298–307; R. R. Ruether, "Mothers of the Church: Ascetic Women in the Late Patristic Age," in *Women of Spirit: Female Leaders in the Jewish and Christian Traditions* (ed. Ruether and McLaughlin), 71–98; A. Yarbrough, "Christianization in the Fourth Century: The Example of Roman Women," *CH* 45 (1976) 149–65.
3. Elizabeth Anne Castelli, "Virginity and Its Meaning for Women's Sexuality in Early Christianity," *Journal of Feminist Studies in Religion* 2 (1986) 61–88.

Given that many gnostic communities expressed their hostility toward creation through the practice of asceticism, the attraction of women to Gnosticism may have been in part a result of their attraction to asceticism. Not all Gnostics, however, expressed their opposition to the created world through asceticism. Some gnostic individuals and communities expressed their beliefs through a practice that underscored their absolute freedom from the created order, a stance most often termed libertine.[4] It is clear from the reports of the heresiologists that the participation of women in these so-called libertine gnostic communities was as extensive as in the ascetic branches of Gnosticism. Irenaeus reports, for example, that the proselytizing success of the Valentinian Marcus in Lyon involved his special attraction to many women with whom the bishop charges he had illicit sexual affairs.[5] According to the same bishop, it was the woman Marcellina who first brought the teachings of the Carpocratians to Rome.[6] Epiphanius's encounter with the Phibionites in Alexandria in his youth involved the attempt of a number of the women of the community to seduce him.[7]

Scholars have not distinguished in the past between the libertine and ascetic branches of Gnosticism in their discussion of its attraction to women in the Roman world. In fact, the attraction of women to libertine gnostic movements and the roles that they assumed in them have not been dealt with in the literature, to the best of my knowledge.[8]

The place and function of women in such communities, however, is not easily recovered. The role of libertine gnostic women is distorted not only by those factors which distort women's history in gnostic communities in general—namely, the biases of the patriarchal sources and the

4. While the term 'libertine' derives from the Latin for freedperson, it has come to connote deviation from the accepted sexual mores of a society. One has only to note the synonyms for libertinism given in Roget's Thesaurus (profligacy, dissoluteness, licentiousness, wildness, debauchery, venery, wenching, and whoring) to recognize the modern connotation of the term. This derogatory sense necessarily affects the view of the groups that the term is used to describe. As such, it uncritically perpetuates the presentation of these groups found in the heresiologists. I shall use the term in this essay for lack of a better alternative, though it is to be understood throughout in a neutral sense of liberty from the customary laws of nature and society.

5. Irenaeus *Adv. haer.* 1.7.1–6.

6. Irenaeus *Adv. haer.* 1.25.6; cf. Origen *Contra Celsum* 5.62; Epiphanius *Haer.* 27.6.1; and Augustine *De haeresibus* 7.

7. Epiphanius *Haer.* 26.17.4–9.

8. Rudolph (*Gnosis*, 211), e.g., uses side by side the Carpocratian Marcellina and the possible Valentinian convert "sister Flora," to whom Ptolemaeus wrote his famous letter, as examples of the major role played by women in Gnosticism. No discussion or distinction of the appeal of the libertine teachings of the Carpocratians over against the more ascetic stance of Ptolemaeus's letter is presented. The distinction is simply not recognized in connection with the appeal of Gnosticism to women.

opposition of the communities' "orthodox" opponents—but also by the opposition of the society in general to the communities' breach of customary law.[9] The fact that this opposition to custom involved deviation from sexual norms served only to heighten the passion of their opponents and thus further distort the reports about these communities and individuals.

This societal opposition to sexual deviation is not unique to these early gnostic communities. Opposition to a group whose practices involve supposed or real deviation from the accepted sexual behavior of the larger society invariably focuses on this behavior. Sexuality underlies the fabric of a society and must be controlled if the society is to maintain the status quo. To permit a group to redefine sexual practice and law is to permit it to challenge the social structure of the society at its very core. Opposition to the group is demanded.

The reality of this dynamic is observed again and again throughout history. The introduction of the Bacchic religion in Italy drew angry opposition from the conservative Roman senate. Its attraction to women and its challenge to the accepted sexual norms of Roman society are underscored in Livy's account.[10] The cult of Antinous in Antinoopolis, Egypt, in the second century C.E. was condemned by Celsus along with Christianity for its immorality.[11] In the Middle Ages the charge of sexual libertinism was widely used by the church against various groups that challenged its authority. The attraction of women to the movement of Priscillian brought with it widespread charges of sexual license.[12] The

---

9. The frequent charges of immorality leveled against the paganism of late antiquity in general have been recognized as an oversimplification of the situation based on Christian biases. Adultery and fornication are treated very seriously by Roman law (Lefkowitz and Fant, eds., *Women's Life in Greece and Rome*, 181–89). While the free expression of sexuality existed in certain circles, it is incorrect to conclude that it had the full and widespread support of the entire society (R. F. Hock, "The Will of God and Sexual Morality: I Thessalonians 4.3–8 in Its Social and Intellectual Context," unpublished). The common charge of sexual immorality used by pagans against their Christian opponents underscores the pagan opposition to such practices.

10. Livy 39.8–18.

11. Origen *Contra Celsum* 5.63; cf. 3.36–38. The practice of libertine sexual rites by some Christians may ultimately depend in part upon similar pagan practices. Likewise the significant role of women in such groups may represent a continuity with women's involvement in magic and witchcraft. Cf. M. Smith, *Clement of Alexandria and a Secret Gospel of Mark*, 270.

12. H. Chadwick, *Priscillian of Avila: The Occult and the Charismatic in the Early Church*, 37, 47–56, 143. The charge of immorality was supported by the association of the Priscillian movement with magic and nighttime gatherings. Priscillian was identified by his opponents as a crypto-Manichean, and charges of sexual immorality were part of the standard attack on the Manichean religion by this time (Ambrose *Ep.* 50.14; Augustine *De moribus* 2.19–20, 67–75; *De haeresibus* 46).

Bogomils, whose early theology appears diametrically opposed to libertinism, are nonetheless so charged.[13] The Cathars and Free Thinkers are likewise rebuked for their practice of sexual freedom, though recent studies have again questioned the extent and meaning of such practices as charged by their opponents.[14] Even the apparent references in their own surviving literature are open to the question of the relationship between spiritual language and physical practice.[15]

Here of course one confronts the major methodological problem in interpreting the surviving evidence from these so-called libertine groups. The charge of sexual deviance is part of the rhetoric of opposition. What appears most often to be the case, however, when one has evidence from the group itself is that the opposition has distorted the facts. The group's use of sexual language on a spiritual plane may thus be distorted by its incorrect translation to the physical level of ritual. In such a case, the charge is unfounded and represents a complete distortion of the group's practice.[16] It may also be but one of a stock set of charges aimed against an opponent, much as the charge of Manicheism became a standard part of the heresiological vocabulary of the Middle Ages.[17] It may, on the other hand, be a misrepresentation of the practice and its meaning within the group's theology. The fact of sexual deviation is all that matters to the opponent, who then proceeds to interpret that fact through his or her own theology instead of through the theology of the practicing group. Given the ascetic stance of "orthodox"

13. D. Obolensky, The Bogomils: A Study in Balkan Neo-Manichaeism, 150–52.

14. Cathars: M. D. Lambert, Medieval Heresy: Popular Movements from Bogomil to Hus, 131; E. L. Ladurie, Montaillou: The Promised Land of Error, 139–203; H. G. Kippenberg, "Gnostiker zweiten Ranges: Zur Institutionalisierung gnostischer Ideen als Anthropolatrie," Numen 30 (1983) 147–48, 170 n. 4. Freethinkers: Lambert, Medieval Heresy, 178–81; and R. E. Lerner, The Heresy of the Free Spirit in the Later Middle Ages.

15. Lambert, Medieval Heresy, 178. Sexual language and imagery is common in Gnosticism (cf. Exeg. Soul, NHC II,6). The spiritual bridal chamber found in the Nag Hammadi Gospel of Philip may have been translated among certain gnostic groups into a physical rite that involved sex. Whether it did so or not, the heresiologists found in the language ready ammunition for such an understanding (below, pp. 334–35).

16. The orthodox Christians well knew the specious use of such charges in religious debate. The pagan opponents of Christianity had early brought such charges against the Christians: Athenagoras 32–35; Justin Martyr 1 Apology 26; Tertullian Apology 4.7; Minucius Felix Octavius 9; cf. Pliny Epp. 10.6; R. L. Wilken, The Christians as the Romans Saw Them, 15–25.

17. The unfounded charge of Manicheism was basic to the orthodox attack on Priscillian (Chadwick, Priscillian of Avila, 55–56, 98–99, 143–44). It was commonly used to describe any dualist heresy (Lambert, Medieval Heresy, 13, 32–33, 63, 143). It becomes such a standard label for wrong thinking that Gregory of Tours can report that there are some who believe that Pontius Pilate was a Manichean (Historiae Francorum 1.24).

Christianity in such matters, such interpretations inevitably represent the basis of the sexual deviation in terms of lust. The nineteenth-century utopian Oneida community was originally driven out of Vermont on such charges connected with its founder's ideas on communal marriage. We know now from the community's own literature that, while the practice was a part of their belief structure, it was carefully controlled. It was not a matter of orgies for the sake of sexual pleasure, as their opponents asserted, but a practice based on ideas of utopian communism.[18] The Mormon practice of polygamy produced similar charges from the non-Mormon community.[19] Finally, the distortion of such groups may involve the universalized interpretation of deviation within a smaller subgroup as representative of the group as a whole or the translation of a later development within the group as indicative of the group's beliefs and practices from the start.[20]

What do these factors mean for our interpretation of the varied gnostic libertine communities? First, there are no recognizable sources from these communities themselves through which to test the accounts of the heresiologists.[21] One sees them only through the eyes of their self-

18. R. DeMaria, *Communal Love at Oneida: A Perfectionist Vision of Authority, Property, and Sexual Order*; and M. L. Carden, *Oneida: Utopian Community to Modern Corporation.*

19. Early anti-Mormon invective often charges that polygamy was called forth by lust. An example of such invective is found in J. H. Beadle, *Life in Utah; or, the Mysteries and Crimes of Mormonism*, 349–50. Beadle begins his account of polygamy (332–33) by revealing the typical association of sexual deviation and heresy in the mind of the "orthodox," in this case clearly Protestant, heresiologist. He states that "gross forms of religious error seem almost invariably to lead to sensuality, to some singular perversion of the marriage relation or the sexual instinct; probably because the same constitution of mind and temperament which gives rise to the one, powerfully disposes toward the other. The fanatic is of logical necessity either an ascetic or a sensualist; healthy moderation is foreign alike to his speculative faith and social practice. He either gives full rein to his baser propensities under the specious name of 'Christian liberty,' or with a little more conscientiousness, swings to the opposite extreme and forbids those innocent gratifications prompted by nature and permitted by God. Of the former class are the Mormons, Noyesites of Oneida, the Antinomians, and the followers of St. John of Leyden; of the latter the Shakers, Harmonists, monks and nuns, and a score of orders of celibate priests."

20. Charges leveled against Christians by their pagan opponents, including the charge of infanticide, may be dependent in part on the pagans' attribution to Christianity in general of practices limited to a small minority, i.e., the Phibionites and their kind (W. Speyer, "Zu den Vorwürfen der Heiden gegen die Christen," *Jahrbuch für Antike und Christentum* 6 [1963] 129–35). Late charges of libertinism were leveled against the Bogomils in general in spite of the fact that their early theology was diametrically opposed to it (Obolensky, *The Bogomils*, 150–52).

21. While it is true that no source exists today that derives recognizably from a libertine gnostic group, it by no means follows that we possess no gnostic source used by a libertine group. Gnostic sources rarely deal with gnostic ritual, and even when a source does, e.g., the *Gospel of Philip* from Nag Hammadi, the references do not make

righteous and ascetically oriented opponents. Hence it is only through an understanding of the character of their opponents and the nature of the rhetoric of opposition that one can begin to unravel the reality and meaning of their practices and the significance of these practices for the women who participated in these communities.

I want now to look briefly at two rather distinct cases labeled by opponents in some way as libertine: the prophet Marcus of Lyon and the Phibionite community in Alexandria. The "libertine" charges against the Valentinian Marcus in Lyon seem to involve, as those brought somewhat later against Priscillian,[22] the teacher's particular attraction to the wealthier women of the community. They are directed more against the individual and his behavior than against the beliefs and practices of the group at large. On the other hand, Epiphanius attacks the Phibionite community in terms of their ritual.

It was in the middle of the second century in the upper Rhone valley at Lyon in Gaul that a Valentinian prophet named Marcus appeared and sought to convert members of the Christian community to his particular brand of the Christian religion.[23] He taught a Valentinian Gnosticism transformed through sophisticated number speculation and alphabet mysticism. His followers participated in a developed system of prophecy and ritual.[24] While the complex nature of his speculative thought might seem to have doomed his efforts among the general population from the beginning, the ritual dimension appears to have led to his considerable

the ritual itself very clear. Various gnostic texts known to us may have been used by libertine groups as well as by the original ascetic gnostic communities that produced them. Sexual language used to discuss spiritual matters is not uncommon in the preserved gnostic sources. The translation of spiritual practices into physical rites by certain groups may well account for many libertine sects (Rudolph, *Gnosis*, 251). The Phibionite community used books about Ialdabaoth and Seth and employed the figure of Barbelo extensively in its mythology (below, p. 341). From this it is not inconceivable that these gnostic libertines used various texts that we today label Sethian. We know that they used other books not originally theirs in their religion, namely, the Old and New Testaments. Jürgen Dummer, "Die Angaben über die gnostische Literatur bei Epiphanius, Pan. Haer. 26," in *Koptologische Studien in der DDR zusammengestellt und herausgegeben vom Institut für Byzantinistik der Martin-Luther-Universität Halle-Wittenberg*, 205–8; cf. S. Benko, "The Libertine Gnostic Sect of the Phibionites According to Epiphanius," *VC* 21 (1967) 103–19.

22. See n. 12, above. Jerome understood the patronage of heretics by well-to-do women as a general phenomenon (*Ep.* 133; Chadwick, *Priscillian of Avila*, 37).

23. The account of Marcus's activity in Lyon is preserved by Irenaeus in his *Adversus haereses*. The text is found in Harvey, ed., *Sancti Irenaei, Episcopi Lugdunensis, Libros quinque adversus haereses*, 1:114–88. Rudolph offers a good account of Marcus's activity (*Gnosis*, 213–15, 241–42, 324–25).

24. Irenaeus *Adv. haer.* 1.7.2; 1.14.1–2.

success.[25] Irenaeus, the "orthodox" bishop of Lyon, reports that many men and women converted to Marcus's cause.[26]

The role played by women in the Marcosian movement was significant, to judge from Irenaeus's report. The nature of their participation, however, has been distorted by the bishop's opposition to the movement, his cultural conservatism, and his patriarchal biases. For Irenaeus, women who truly possess the fear of God are not deluded by Marcus but rather abhor him.[27] The women who succumb to his teachings, on the other hand, are deluded and wicked. They are, in fact, less than real women (γυναικάρια).[28]

Marcus attracted many women from the wealthier elements in the community.[29] While Irenaeus uses this evidence to attack Marcus, presumably to suggest his greed, one recalls the similar appeal of early Christian asceticism among the aristocratic women of Rome.[30] It may be that Marcus offered these women, in particular, a means to express their religious convictions outside the more typically patriarchal structure of the church. They represented the class of women who had the time and the means to explore the alternatives.

Irenaeus accuses Marcus of seducing these women through the use of deceit and magic. He reports that the seduction involved the use of ritual. His understanding of the Marcosian rituals, however, is inadequate. He first reports that Marcus "goaded the women on to ecstatic prophecy" through the use of a eucharistic rite that involved the par-

25. The ritual dimension of Gnosticism surely accounts in part for its widespread success. Irenaeus's account of the success of Marcus reveals the important role that ritual played in gnostic missionary activity. While a detailed account of the speculative Marcosian theology is given, one meets the converts within the discussion of the ritual dimension of the movement. They are not present to discuss or debate subtleties of the theology (though many undoubtedly did) but to participate in the sacraments and to receive the gift of prophecy.

26. Irenaeus Adv. haer. 1.7.1. Irenaeus of course reports their conversion in terms of their "having been led astray" (πεπλανημένα). The extent of the bishop's rebuttal underscores the serious nature of Marcus's challenge to the Christian community in Lyon. One might suspect that it was this experience that convinced Irenaeus of the need to compose and circulate his Adversus haereses.

27. Irenaeus Adv. haer. 1.7.3. Even here, however, Irenaeus seems to say that these women accepted Marcus at first and only then had the "good" sense to return to his flock.

28. Irenaeus Adv. haer. 1.7.2, 5. Γυναικάρια appears as mulierculas in the Latin version. The negative sense of simple or silly is clear. The faithful women are called simply γυναί (1.7.3). In Epiphanius's account of the Phibionites, the men and women of the sect are labeled γυναικάρια καὶ ἀνθρωπάρια (Haer. 26.5.8).

29. Irenaeus Adv. haer. 1.7.2.

30. Clark, "Ascetic Renunciation and Feminine Advancement," 240–57; Yarbrough, "Christianization in the Fourth Century," 149–65.

taking of the blood of Charis.[31] In the next paragraph, however, Irenaeus relates that the Charis is received by the women through a ritual of the bridal chamber. He offers the following citation of Marcus's seductive words:

> I wish to share my Charis with you, since the Father of all sees your angel continually before his face. The place of the greatness is in us. We must be united.[32] Receive the Charis first from me and through me. Adorn yourself as a bride awaiting her bridegroom, so that you may be what I am and I what you are. Establish the seed of light in your bridal chamber. Receive the bridegroom from me and contain him and be contained in him. Behold the Charis has descended upon you. Open your mouth and prophesy.[33]

The language is Valentinian, with its notion of the heavenly counterpart of the Gnostic's soul. Irenaeus uses it to suggest the physical nature of the rite of the bridal chamber. The first person singular suggests Marcus's involvement in the ritual, which Irenaeus wants the reader to assume involved sexual intercourse. It is interesting to note, however, that Irenaeus reports shortly after this point that it is only after the woman prophesies that she yields up to him her person.[34]

At the very least it would seem that Irenaeus has confused the Marcosian practices here in his attempt to equate the religious and sexual "seduction" of the women. In fact, the eucharist and the bridal chamber were two distinct rituals which may have represented different stages of initiation. It is possible that Irenaeus is correct in asserting that the Charis and gift of prophecy were bestowed by both rituals, though this fact may also represent his own confusion.

The nature of the ritual of the bridal chamber must remain uncertain. At a later point when he is describing the ritual in more abstract terms, Irenaeus says that the Marcosians assert that it is a spiritual marriage (πνευματικὸν γάμον).[35] There is no hint at this point that the rite involved sexual intercourse. It is only when Irenaeus moves from the abstract to concrete examples that he reports the rite in terms of seduction and sexual intercourse. For Irenaeus, the bridal chamber was simply a vehicle of seduction. While all of the individual accounts that are

---

31. Irenaeus *Adv. haer.* 1.7.2.
32. The text is supplied from the Latin, *oportet nos in unum convenire.* The Greek text is given by Harvey as follows: ὁ δὲ τόπος τοῦ μεγέθους ἐν ἡμῖν ἐστι δι' ἡμᾶς ἐγκαταστῆσαι [1. δεῖ ἡμᾶς ἐν καταστῆσαι].
33. Irenaeus *Adv. haer.* 1.7.2. The translation is mine.
34. Irenaeus *Adv. haer.* 1.7.2.
35. Irenaeus *Adv. haer.* 1.14.2.

reported involve only Marcus, Irenaeus does note that Marcus's disciples likewise deceived and defiled many women.[36]

It is difficult to interpret this evidence. The Marcosian theology that is preserved by Irenaeus does not in itself suggest a libertine dimension to the bridal chamber. It is a spiritual marriage, a ritual union with one's heavenly counterpart. If Irenaeus is correct in his assertion that the rite involved sexual intercourse, the theological undergirding behind the practice was certainly more significant than he portrays. It is doubtful that Marcus was the charlatan that Irenaeus wants the reader to believe. This portrayal of the teacher is more likely to be attributed to Irenaeus's rhetoric of opposition and the bishop's view of women as simpletons who can be seduced in great flocks by clever sophistries.

The recognition of the heresiologist's biases, however, does not automatically translate into a more objective definition of women's participation in the movement. One may speculate about the alternatives, but one cannot claim the opposite reality simply on the basis of a single witness's biases. Nonetheless, the silence of the groups themselves and the obvious biases of the opposing witnesses demand an exploration of the alternatives, if only to counter our own inherent patriarchal biases that accept too readily those of the ancient heresiologists.

The Marcosian system is complex. Irenaeus records it in great detail. Yet he seems to suggest that Marcus attracted his male disciples through the teaching and that together they seduced the women into participation. The bias is obvious. Women and sex are limited in Irenaeus's account to the beginning, where he reports the rituals or concrete activity of Marcus and his followers. They are absent from the major portion of his account wherein he records the movement's theology. This division surely reveals more about the bishop's view of women than about their role in the Marcosian movement. The role played by women, whether the movement actually involved sexual intercourse or not, was a major one. This Irenaeus cannot deny. Rather, he counters it by trying to show that their involvement was superficial, an involvement based not on intellectual acceptance of the complex Marcosian theology but on sexual seduction.[37]

If indeed women were as prominent in the Marcosian movement as

36. Irenaeus *Adv. haer.* 1.7.5.
37. It is undoubtedly true that there were those who joined libertine communities for less than respectable reasons. The reasons for joining the movement or being "seduced" into joining, however, are not gender-defined. It is most likely true, because of the patriarchal nature of ancient society, that more women than men were "seduced" or compelled into joining the movement.

the evidence suggests, one may speculate that on occasion they too converted male members of the wider community to the movement. Irenaeus cannot suggest this, however, because he cannot conceive of the women in a dominant role. His rhetoric of opposition is based on his portrayal of the women as simpletons who were seduced because of their sexual nature through rituals that involved sex. To suggest that they converted or even "seduced" men into the Marcosian movement would run counter to this portrayal.

The latter image of women as those who used their sex to seduce men away from "orthodoxy" is not unknown in the heresiological literature. The account of the Phibionite community in Alexandria includes such a report. Its author, Epiphanius, presents the participation of the female members of this community in its rituals as dependent on their "natural" sexual appetite. The women are viewed as sexual beings whose lust led them even to attempt to seduce the "righteous" Epiphanius himself.[38]

The Phibionites (also called Gnostics or Borborites) are known chiefly through the account preserved by Epiphanius in his *Panarion haereses*.[39] This account conflates his own experience of a group in Egypt (probably in or near Alexandria)[40] with materials that he gleaned from elsewhere. He presents the group as a generic sect. He recognizes different names for the organization in different geographical areas and in the account often refers to "others" ($\H{a}\lambda\lambda o\iota$ $\delta\acute{e}$) as a designation for different segments of the generic group.[41]

It must be pointed out that scholars are not unanimous in their acceptance of Epiphanius's report. Many view his explicit descriptions of the Phibionites' sexually based rituals as a heresiological invention designed to discredit the sect. In spite of Epiphanius's statement of his own youthful contact with the group, it is argued that any such involvement would have been superficial and would not have given

38. One must point out that Epiphanius considers all members of the community, both male and female, as driven by sexual lust. Yet of course it is the women who seek to seduce him.

39. Epiphanius *Haer.* 25—26. Epiphanius offers chap. 26 as his account of the Phibionites and their kind. He presents chap. 25 as an account of the Nicolaitans. It has been demonstrated, however, that the material used in chaps. 25 and 26 properly belong together. Epiphanius's description of the Nicolaitans in chap. 25 is designed to link the Phibionites with this archetypical libertine gnostic group. Dummer, "Die Angaben über die gnostische Literatur," 194–95; C. Schmidt, *Gnostische Schriften aus koptischer Sprache*, 570–73; and de Faye, *Gnostiques*, 423.

40. Epiphanius *Haer.* 26.17.4–8. The reference to the expulsion of eighty Phibionites from the city ($\tau\hat{\eta}s$ $\pi\acute{o}\lambda\epsilon\omega s$) suggests that the events took place in or near Alexandria. Schmidt, *Gnostische Schriften*, 575; L. Fendt, *Gnostische Mysterien: Ein Beitrag zur Geschichte des christlichen Gottesdienstes*, 12; and idem, "Borborianer," *RAC* 2.511.

41. Epiphanius *Haer.* 26.2.5–6, 3.7.

him access to their inner rituals. His descriptions are thus rhetorical inventions, or at best a product of his imagination which was influenced by the sexual imagery that he found in their sacred texts.[42]

Others have been more convinced of the basic accuracy of Epiphanius's report.[43] These scholars argue that the rituals presented by Epiphanius are to be understood in relation to the reconstructed theology of the group.[44] The detail and complexity of Epiphanius's account, the inner continuity between Phibionite theology and ritual, and the scriptural support of their practices cited by the heresiologist suggest to this author a reality behind his presentation. This conclusion is supported by the fact that the practices of the Phibionites and the resultant horror in which the group was held are documented outside Epiphanius's account.[45] While it was certainly not a mainstream movement, we must not let our own puritanism or the more ascetic nature of the surviving gnostic sources preclude our openness to such libertine alternatives.[46]

Epiphanius reports that the Phibionites reject the stance of the "orthodox" church with respect to the understanding of the body. They are not ascetic in even the most limited sense of the word. Fasting

42. J. L. Jacobi ("Gnosis," *Realencyklopädie für protestantische Theologie und Kirche* [2d ed.], 5:246–47) asserts with respect to Phibionite rituals that "trotz Epiphanius Versicherung sie kaum für möglich halten möchte." More recently Kraft has doubted the reliability of the accounts (H. Kraft, "Gnostisches Gemeinschaftleben: Untersuchungen zu den Gemeinschafts- und Lebensformen häretischer christlicher Gnosis des zweiten Jahrhunderts," 77–83, 158). Koschorke, under the influence of the Nag Hammadi texts, questions in general the reliability of the patristic evidence for libertine Gnosticism (K. Koschorke, *Die Polemik der Gnostiker gegen das kirchliche Christentum,* 123–24); Wilken (*The Christians,* 20–21) is cautious, but unwilling to "dismiss such reports out of hand."

43. Fendt, *Gnostische Mysterien,* 3–22; idem, "Borborianer," 510–13; Benko, "The Libertine Gnostic Sect," 103–19; idem, "Pagan Criticism of Christianity During the First Two Centuries A.D.," *ANRW* 23:2 (1980) 1081–89; S. Gero, "With Walter Bauer on the Tigris: Encratite Orthodoxy and Libertine Heresy in Syro-Mesopotamian Christianity," in *Nag Hammadi, Gnosticism, and Early Christianity* (ed. Hedrick and Hodgson, Jr.) 287–307; F. E. Williams ("Were There 'Immoral' Forms of Gnosticism?" [paper presented at the "Rediscovery of Gnosticism" conference at Yale University, March 1978]) offers a careful discussion of Epiphanius's reliability; Rudolph, *Gnosis,* 247–50; Schmidt, *Gnostische Schriften,* 566–76, esp. 573–74; de Faye, *Gnostiques,* 421–28, esp. 423–24; Gaffron, "Studien," 355 n. 4; Dummer, "Die Angaben über die gnostische Literatur," 191–219; Speyer, "Zu den Vorwürfen der Heiden," 129–35; and H. J. Schoeps, *Aus frühchristlicher Zeit: Religionsgeschichtliche Untersuchungen,* 260–65.

44. Fendt, *Gnostische Mysterien,* 3–22; and Benko, "The Libertine Gnostic Sect," 103–19.

45. *Pistis Sophia* 147; *Second Book of Jeu* 43; cf. Clement of Alexandria, *Stromateis* 2.2; Minucius Felix *Octavius* 9. A detailed account of the Syro-Mesopotamian evidence has been supplied by Gero ("With Walter Bauer").

46. Gero ("With Walter Bauer," 306) suggests that "the Borborites constituted for the most part a secret society that led a clandestine existence within other Christian groups."

belongs to the archon of this world, and care and adornment of the body are not scorned (*Haer.* 26.5.8, 13.1, 17.8). One must be careful, however, in moving beyond this stance to Epiphanius's interpretation of it as one of whoring and drunkenness (κοίταις τε καὶ μέθαις σχολάζοντες).[47] The sect does practice an elaborate table fellowship which Epiphanius charges is followed by an orgiastic sharing of sex partners (*Haer.* 26.4.3). The Phibionites term this after-dinner fellowship the Agape. It involves the sharing of sexual mates and a sacrifice of the male semen and female menstrual blood which is apparently modeled on the Christian eucharist.[48] The semen is taken in the hands, offered in prayer as the body of Christ, and eaten with the words of supplication: "This is the body of Christ; and this is the Pascha, because of which our bodies suffer and are made to acknowledge the passion of Christ" (*Haer.* 26.4.7). The menses is likewise offered up as the blood of Christ (*Haer.* 26.4.8). In the heterosexual Agape, *coitus interruptus* was practiced in order to avoid procreation and gather the semen for the sacrifice. If conception did take place, the group performed an abortion and made a meal of the fetus (*Haer.* 26.5.4–6). The gathering of the semen was also accomplished, according to Epiphanius, through masturbation and homosexual practices (*Haer.* 26.5.7, 11.1, 7).

Epiphanius is, of course, scandalized by these practices and portrays the members as persons seeking only sexual self-gratification (*Haer.* 26.5.2; etc.). The practice of *coitus interruptus* and the use of abortion suggest rather that their theology (a matter of little interest to Epiphanius) centered on the avoidance of procreation (*Haer.* 26.5.2, 16.4). Space here does not permit a detailed analysis of Phibionite theology.[49] It is sufficient to point out that the negative stance toward creation coupled to the identification of the human sexual emissions with the element of the divine in humanity accounts for the Phibionite practices. The separation of the original Adam into male and female worked to divide further the divine "light" caught in the material creation and hence hinder its eventual reunification into the pleromatic realm. Procreation was the demiurge's device to effect this further division. The

47. Epiphanius *Haer.* 26.5.8. Such descriptions are clearly dependent on Epiphanius's rhetoric of opposition.

48. Fendt (*Gnostische Mysterien*, 3–22) offers the fullest study of the sacramental nature of the cult. He believes that it represents the christianization of an originally pagan cultus (p. 14).

49. A number of good accounts exist: Rudolph, *Gnosis*, 247–50; Schmidt, *Gnostische Schriften*, 566–77; Benko, "The Libertine Gnostic Sect," 103–19; Fendt, "Borborianer," 510–13; idem, *Gnostische Mysterien*, 3–22; and de Faye, *Gnostiques*, 419–28.

Phibionite practice represents a short-circuiting of this process. The "light" of the pleroma, which is drawn out of individuals in their sexual emissions, is gathered and offered to the divine. The practice is a ritual enactment of conclusions drawn from this basic gnostic theological conception. It is not, as Epiphanius presents it, simply a group seeking fulfillment of sexual fantasies.

It is interesting in this light to reevaluate the role of women in this particular "libertine" group. Epiphanius would have his readers believe that the women were simpletons, used by the male members of the sect as sacrifices to the archons (*Haer.* 26.9.6). Women are deceived by the men (*Haer.* 26.11.9) and made foolish (*Haer.* 26.9.8). In the Agape rite, it is the male members who give their wives to other brothers (*Haer.* 26.4.4). At best, the women are victims (*Haer.* 26.9.8).

Closer examination of the material suggests that Epiphanius's presentation of the female members of this group suffers as much distortion as a result of his patriarchal biases as his presentation of the group's practices suffers from his "orthodox" assumptions. It is interesting in this connection to examine Epiphanius's account of his own encounter with the group in his youth (*Haer.* 26.17.4–9). He emphasizes the fact that the Phibionite women tried to seduce him, which corresponds well with his general presentation of the group. Yet it is an interesting fact that it is precisely and only the female members who first speak to the young Epiphanius of the group's theology (*Haer.* 26.17.4) and then attempt as part of the conversion process to involve him in the Agape.[50] It is understandable that the old Epiphanius would view this as an attempted seduction. It was in all likelihood understood by the women involved as part of the salvation process, an attempt to win a convert and gather more "light" for God.

This fact raises in turn the question of Epiphanius's presentation of the role of women in the sect's rituals in general. One might suspect, for instance, that the sharing of sexual partners in the Agape was not simply a case of husbands' giving of their wives to other brothers but rather a free communal interchange. Why could not women also take the initiative in the exchange? It is only Epiphanius's patriarchal conservatism that leads him to ignore this possibility.

Various factors in Epiphanius's account point to the high regard in which the feminine was held by the Phibionites. Thus the incorporation of the menses as the blood of Christ alongside the semen as the body of

---

50. This may be in part a result of his desire to stress the sexual nature of the group. Yet it is significant that the women took the initiative.

Christ in the Phibionite ritual underscores the positive involvement of
the women. According to Aristotle's account of the reproductive process, the contribution of the female, represented in the menses, was the
material portion of the new creature. The male semen contributed the
soul.[51] On the basis of this theory, the Gnostic might be expected to
show interest only in the semen, which represented the portion of
humanity that required salvation. While the Phibionite inclusion of the
menses in their ritual may be in part a result of the influence of the
eucharistic pattern of "body and blood," it nonetheless argues for the
high regard of the female partner. She is not just a victim used to
withdraw the male element. She too contains a part of the divine which
must and can be gathered!

While Epiphanius does not report on the writings and myths of the
group in any detail, he does offer enough material to reveal the importance of the feminine in the Phibionite texts. The list of books with
which he associates these groups in his chapter 26 is already fascinating
in this regard. They include *Noria* (26.1.3), a *Gospel of Perfection* (26.2.5),
a *Gospel of Eve* (26.2.6), *Questions of Mary* (26.8.1), *Greater Questions of
Mary* (26.8.2), *Lesser Questions of Mary* (26.8.2), the *Birth of Mary*
(26.12.2), a *Gospel of Philip* (26.13.2), books about Ialdabaoth (26.8.1;
25.3.5), and books in the name of Seth (26.8.1).[52] The number of these
books attributed to women or about women is indeed remarkable.
While we cannot know the titles of the books about Ialdabaoth and
Seth, six of the remaining eight titles bear the name of a woman.[53]

While the Phibionite cosmogony includes a large array of aeons (*Haer.*
26.9.6, 10.1–4), the place of the feminine aeon Barbelo appears from
Epiphanius's account to be foremost in the sect's understanding of its
ritual life. Barbelo occupies the eighth and highest heaven (*Haer.*
26.10.4). She is the one from the powers on high, the opposite of the
archon (*Haer.* 26.1.9). What has been taken from the Barbelo, the mother
on high, by the demiurge, that is, the "light," is that which must be
gathered by the Phibionites in their Agape ritual (*Haer.* 26.1.9).

The Phibionite practice is in fact an earthly rendition of the seduction
of the archons, which Barbelo herself performs in the heavenly realm
(*Haer.* 25.2.4).[54] As the beauty of the Phibionite women (*Haer.* 26.17.7–8)

---

51. Aristotle *Gen. an.* 738B, 26–28.
52. They also use the Old and New Testaments (26.6.1).
53. It is to be recognized that the *Lesser and Greater Questions of Mary* (26.8.2) may be
identical with the *Questions of Mary* mentioned earlier (26.8.1).
54. Fendt, *Gnostische Mysterien*, 6–7; and de Faye, *Gnostiques*, 422.

is designed to "seduce" the men into releasing their "light" in the form of the ejaculation of semen, so Barbelo's beautiful form brings the archons to climax and ejaculation, through which she recovers her power (*Haer.* 25.2.4). As such it is the role of the woman which, though a role of seduction, mirrors the pattern of the divine Barbelo. It is as positive a pattern in Phibionite mythology as it is negative for Epiphanius. Epiphanius's patriarchal orthodoxy with its emphasis on an ascetical approach to the world simply precluded the recognition or in any event the acceptance of any alternative interpretation to the Phibionite practices other than his own.

While each of the points made above with respect to the Phibionite women require further investigation, it seems clear that the presentation of them by Epiphanius is distorted by his own view of women. He presents the Phibionite women as "orthodox" women gone astray. They are simple and theologically naive. They have been misled by the male Phibionite members to whom Epiphanius surely credits the theology of the group.

We have seen that Phibionite theology places a strong emphasis on the feminine aeon of Barbelo and that the books of the group were predominantly attributed to women. The practice of the Agape, which Epiphanius viewed as the unregulated use of the women by the male members, was more likely a practice that involved both sexes equally in the communal recovery of the lost "light" in the semen and menses. The "seduction" of men by Phibionite women, evidence of their depravity to Epiphanius, was more likely understood within the Phibionite community as an earthly reenactment of Barbelo's seduction of the archons.

What does this mean for the women in these libertine gnostic communities? I suspect that many women who joined the Phibionite community did so with a full awareness of the theological foundation of the group. They were not simply led astray or lured into the community by lustful men. This is not to deny that many women may well have been taken advantage of by the male members of the sect or by their husbands who chose to join the group. It is, rather, to argue that the distinction between "simple" members who were deceived by others and more astute devotees who developed the theology and practice of the group is not a division that breaks down on sexual lines. The sexual definition of that division represents, rather, the interpretation of the patriarchal Epiphanius. He could understand it in no other way. Certainly there were as well simple men who were "deceived." Epiphanius himself in his youth apparently came close to the "fall." Likewise there were certainly women in such groups, particularly judging from the theological emphases, who were theologically astute.

Thus, were the libertine gnostic women liberated? One should not use terms loaded with modern ideas to label persons from the past. It is fair to say that there were Phibionite women who were instrumental in the group's development and that they found in the group an avenue to express their release from the societal constraints imposed upon them by their sex. The libertine path offered this possibility to some women in much the same way that the ascetic path did for others.

If indeed the Phibionite Agape is understood as an earthly reenactment of the seduction of the archons by Barbelo, then the role of women in this rite takes on heightened significance. It has been argued that in asceticism women remained bound to the patriarchal past, since they simply replaced an earthly husband with a heavenly male Christ.[55] In the Phibionite system they function in the dominant role. The Phibionite women are the earthly representative of the Mother who recovers her lost power through the seduction of the male archons.[56]

55. Castelli, "Virginity and Its Meaning."
56. The fact that the Phibionites borrowed the figure of Barbelo from another group (Fendt, *Gnostische Mysterien*, 9) is of little relevance.

SEX AND SALVATION IN TERTULLIAN

F. Forrester Church

Cambridge, Massachusetts 02138

Though often remembered for something he never said,[1]
Tertullian did contribute a few bold lines to his own caricature.
Take for instance the famous, "*Quid ergo Athenis et
Hierosolymis?*"[2] It has come to symbolize Tertullian's wholesale
rejection of philosophy.[3] In fact, his indebtedness to the matter
and methods of his classical heritage is profound.[4] Today, by the
same token, his ability to coin a striking phrase is earning for
Tertullian yet another reputation he does not deserve. In the first
book of *De cultu feminarum*, a withering attack on female
fashions, Tertullian invokes the curse of Eve by means of a cruel
and impressive metaphor: "*Tu es diaboli ianua*," he writes; "You
are the devil's gateway."[5] At once provocative of timely
indignation and attractive as a foil, this single utterance is alone
responsible for perhaps as much popular notoriety as Tertullian
has ever been afforded.[6] The following is offered in the hope that a
more extensive examination of his attitude toward women may

[1]"*Credo quia absurdum.*" Timothy Barnes notes, "the passage is frequently
invoked to prove his irrationality, or that he viewed religion as the realm of
subjective and unreasoning emotion. If that was his true attitude, why did he
ever descend to apparently rational argument?" (*Tertullian: a Historical and
Literary Study* [Oxford: Clarendon, 1971] 223).

[2]*De praescriptione haereticorum* 7. 9 (*Tertulliani opera, CCL* I, II [Turnhout:
1954]).

[3]E.g., Charles Cochrane's chapter "Quid Athenae Hierosolymis? The Impasse
of Constantinianism," in *Christianity and Classical Culture* (1940; reprint,
Oxford: University Press, 1972) 213ff.

[4]Recent scholarship has overthrown the previous notion entirely; see in
particular: Stephen Otto, *Natura und Dispositio: Untersuchung zum
Naturbegriff und zur Denkform Tertullians* (München: Hueber, 1960); Richard
Klein, *Tertullian und das römische Reich* (Heidelberg: Winter, 1968); Robert
Sider, *Ancient Rhetoric and the Art of Tertullian* (London: Oxford University
Press, 1971); Jean-Claude Fredouille, *Tertullien et la conversion de la culture
antique* (Paris: Etudes Augustiniennes, 1972); Justo L. González, "Athens and
Jerusalem Revisited: Reason and Authority in Tertullian," *Church History*, 43
(1974) 17-25; and, Barnes, *Tertullian*, who provides perhaps the finest and
certainly the most provocative single study of Tertullian available.

[5]*De cultu feminarum* I. 1. 2.

[6]To give but a sampling of those recent publications in which this text is so
utilized: Nancy van Vuuren, *The Subversion of Women as Practiced by*

serve both to correct such misconceptions as have been drawn from the famous "gateway passage," and also to clarify some of the ambiguities inherent in the *Frauenfragen* for early Christians.

While no single study has been devoted to Tertullian's "misogyny," his attitude toward women is generally characterized as such.[7] Paul Monceaux, the great scholar of African Christianity, has made the case as forcibly as any: "These minute precautions and railleries betray a singular defiance with regard to woman. Tertullian is the first of the great Christian misogynists. In advance of the medieval theologians, he considers woman as the principal obstacle of salvation. He precludes her from any active role in the Church, and seeks to restrict her to the home. He sharply summons her to modesty, to a consciousness of her weakness and of her eternal misery, which renders her forever responsible for the unhappiness of humanity."[8] When isolated from his other writings on the subject, the *locus classicus* of Tertullian's misogyny does seem to bear these observations out. Due to its importance, I quote it in full.

> If faith on earth were as great as the reward expected in heaven, my well beloved sisters, not one of you from the moment when you came to know the living God and recognized your own state, that is, the condition of all women, would have desired too gay, not to say too ostentatious, an apparel. Rather, you would have gone about in humble dress, even preferring to affect squalor, that you might, by donning every sort of penitential garb and acting the part of mourning and repentant Eve, expiate more fully that which woman derives from Eve, the ignominy, I mean, of the first sin, and the odium of human perdition. "In sorrow and anxiety you will bring forth, O woman, and you shall incline toward your husband, and he will be your master." Are you not aware that you are each an Eve? The sentence of God on this sex of yours lives on in our own time; the guilt must then, of necessity, live on also. You are the devil's gateway. You first plucked the forbidden fruit and first deserted the

Churches, Witch-hunters, and Other Sexists (Philadelphia: Westminster, 1973) 29; Vern L. Bullough, *The Subordinate Sex: a History of Attitudes toward Women* (1973; reprint, Boston: Beacon, 1974) 114; Mary Daly, *Beyond God the Father* (1973; reprint, Boston: Beacon, 1974) 44; Rosemary Ruether, "Misogynism and Virginal Feminism in the Fathers of the Church," *Religion and Sexism: Images of Woman in the Jewish and Christian Tradition*, ed. Rosemary Ruether (New York: Simon and Schuster, 1974) 157.

[7]Even George Tavard, whose book *Woman in Christian Tradition* ([Notre Dame: University of Notre Dame Press, 1973] 59) offers perhaps the most balanced treatment of the subject available, goes no further than to admit that "Tertullian is no ordinary misogynist."

[8]*Histoire littéraire de l'Afrique chrétienne* I: *Tertullien et les origines* (1901; reprint, Brussels: Culture et civilisation, 1963) 387.

divine law. You are she who persuaded him whom the devil was not brave enough to attack. It was you who so readily destroyed the image of God, man. By virtue of your just desert, that is, death, even the Son of God had to die. And you still think of putting adornments over the animal skins that cover you![9]

Even allowing for considerable hyperbole, Tertullian's indictment strikes one as exceptionally vicious. Most disconcerting of all is the damning implication that woman was, is, and shall continue to be, little more than a millstone around man's neck. Again to cite Monceaux: "Woman is the devil's ally on earth against man; her weaknesses, her seductions, and her coquetries are nothing but stratagems of hell. She cannot hope for her forgiveness and her salvation except on the condition of renouncing the graces of her sex. And man, if he wishes to please God, must separate himself as much as possible from woman."[10]

Placing the "gateway passage" in perspective should help to answer such criticism as has been generalized from it. To this end, Tertullian's conception of woman must be clarified. Did he consistently blame woman for the fall? Is her natural status held to be inferior to that of man? Does Tertullian apply an ethical double standard when instructing women and men in matters of discipline? Are women really represented in his writings as "the weaker sex?" Since each of these questions touches on the problem of sex as it affects salvation, they will be considered with an eye to Tertullian's various schemes of redemption. Beginning with the fall, I shall proceed by examining, with regard to their respective efficacy for women and men, three means of exculpation available to Christians: sanctification by water, by moral discipline, and by blood. A brief section on the kingdom, with special note taken of the resurrected body, will bring this study to a close.

I. *Diaboli ianua*: the Devil's Gateway

The section on Tertullian in a recent treatment of the doctrine of original sin opens with the following pertinent caveat: "When one attempts to reconstruct his ideas about the primitive state of man, Adam's sin and its consequences, one must guard against isolating certain texts, no doubt important, but lost in the mass of works in which the object is quite otherwise."[11] Though our text is

[9]*Cult.* I. 1. 1-2.
[10]Monceaux, *Histoire littéraire*, 388.
[11]H. Rondet, "Le péché originel dans la tradition," *Bulletin de littérature*

not singled out for mention, it might well have been. The "gateway passage" is the only place in all Tertullian where the exclusive culpability of Eve is spelled out.[12] To account for this singular discrepancy, we may consider for a moment a second anomalous passage, in which the fall is attributed to gluttony.

> Adam had received from God the law that he not taste of the tree of recognition of good and evil, with death to follow should he taste of it. But even he, reverting to the condition of a psychic, . . . and no longer being capable of the things which were the spirit's, yielded more readily to his belly than to God. Heeding the pablum rather than the precept, he sold salvation for his gullet.[13]

Here, the issue at hand is fasting. Tertullian invests it with great significance by blaming the fall on unbridled appetite. In *De cultu* he employs a like device to persuade women to dress modestly. To establish the salvific importance of his subject, he hearkens back to Eve. Her complicity in the fall is then utilized to produce upon his listeners the desired effect, which he provokes by means of a pointed and highly rhetorical *ad feminam* argument. While details of his invective cannot be attributed entirely to rhetorical invention, one must always keep in mind that in Tertullian a given problem, such as the fall, may be adapted freely to the requirements both of subject and of audience.[14]

The extent to which this is the case in *De cultu* can be shown by a brief review of several other passages where Tertullian's notion of the fall is revealed. In an elemental form it appears in the second chapter of *Adversus Iudaeos*. Adam and Eve, ordered to abstain from a given tree's fruit or die, break the primordial law by yielding to the persuasion of the serpent. In this interpretation both are made partners with the devil. Adam is his ally no less than Eve. In *De patientia*, where the entire undoing is ascribed to

---

ecclesiastique, 67 (1966) 115.

[12]Citing this fact with reference to the same article by Rondet, Marie Turcan, in her edition of *De cultu* (*Tertullien: La toilette de femmes*, Sources chrétiennes, No. 173 [Paris: Les editions du Cerf, 1971] 37, n. 3) notes that in every other instance, "C'est toujours Adam qui est sur la sellette."

[13]*De jejunio* 3. 2.

[14]The "gateway passage" and its immediate context, constituting the *exordium* of *De cultu* I, are replete with *ethos* and *pathos*, which were the favored means of proof for an introduction. Sider (*Ancient Rhetoric*, 21) describes the *exordium* as an attempt "to set the audience in a receptive mood by an immediate appeal to considerations of an ethical and emotional character." His important study contributes substantially to our appreciation of the influence of rhetoric on Tertullian's theological methodology.

impatience on the part of the principals, their mutual complicity is further underscored. While Eve's sin is acknowledged to be prior to that of Adam, the two share a common frailty for having sinned in the same manner. Even the devil, in whom Tertullian had perceived "the nativity of impatience," is guilty of the weakness he inspired.[15] In *Adversus Marcionem*, Tertullian acknowledges Eve in the context of Adam's not concealing from God "her who had done the beguiling,"[16] but in the final analysis he dismisses implicitly the importance of any mediating role she may have played. "It was the man who brought upon himself the indignity of death, . . . for even if it was an angel that beguiled him, he who was beguiled was a free man and master of himself."[17] The same note is struck in *De exhortatione castitatis*: "Adam, the founder of our race and first to sin, willed the sin which he committed, for the devil did not impose the will to sin upon him, but simply subministered material to that will."[18] In the words of Rondet, "Adam is, therefore, very much at fault. Having been advised that on the day he would eat of the fruits of the tree of knowledge he would die, he transgressed the divine law. Therefore, he is clearly the one responsible for the entry of death into the world."[19]

That Eve's participation in the fall was of minor moment to Tertullian can be confirmed by evidence drawn from his two principal programs for salvation. While in each of these Eve figures only incidentally, either Adam or the devil plays a central part. In the one, Adam's responsibility for the fall is crucial to the subsequent process of redemption; in the other, the corruptive influence of the devil anticipates and predicates the Christian's struggle with the powers of evil in the world. The former, built around Christ's atonement, is heavily dependent upon Tertullian's notion of traducianism. Inherited sin, passed on through the process of generation, stems directly from Adam. When he was given over to death on account of his sin, "the whole human race, infected with his seed, were made the carrier of his condemnation."[20] This process is reversed by the action of Christ as conferred upon the individual Christian through baptism in the

[15] *Pat.* 5. 5.
[16] *Marc.* II. 2. 7.
[17] *Marc.* II. 8. 2.
[18] *Exhort. cast.* 2. 5.
[19] "Le péché originel," 118.
[20] *De testimonio animae* 3. 2.

Holy Spirit. Accordingly, "every soul is therefore reckoned in Adam until it is reckoned anew in Christ."[21] In a different vein entirely, the latter program provides for sanctity to be earned and maintained by personal discipline. Here, for Tertullian, one's struggle is with the devil, "the author of error, the corrupter of the whole world."[22] Citing Adam's disobedience, he warns:

> In like manner you too, if you should disobey the Lord who has instructed you by placing before you the precept of free action, will, through the freedom of your will, slip into willing that which God does not permit. . . . Thus, the devil's only task is to try to make you will that which it rests with you to will. But when you have, it follows that he subjects you to himself.[23]

Here too, although other disconcerting conclusions might be drawn from the fact, Eve is peripheral to Tertullian's conception of the fall. According to him, the devil is to blame for the woes of humankind, and Adam is responsible.

II. *Ignoscentiae ianua*: the Gateway of Forgiveness

Baptism. Simone de Beauvoir was perhaps the first in this century to give the "gateway passage" wide public notice. In her influential work, *The Second Sex*, it is twice alluded to; once, in a manner reminiscent of Gibbon, to juxtapose Christianity with barbarism, and later to demonstrate the practical application of dualism in early Christian thought. On this second occasion she introduces the passage in the following manner: "Evil is an absolute reality; and the flesh is sin. And of course, since woman remains always the Other, it is not held that reciprocally male and female are both flesh: the flesh that for the Christian is the hostile Other is precisely woman."[24] This interpretation raises two questions regarding Tertullian's anthropology. First, has he really this low an estimation of the flesh; and, are women actually relegated by Tertullian to a natural status inferior to that of men?

Simply to place these questions in the context of redemption and salvation is to answer them. Adam's sin, issuing in the mortality of the flesh and passed on by fleshly means in

---

[21] *De anima* 40. 1. In contrast, the Eve/Mary motif is utilized but slightly by Tertullian. In *De carne Christi* 17, where it finds its fullest expression, the argument appears to be derivative (compare Justin Martyr, *Dialogue with Trypho* 100; Irenaeus, *Adversus haereses* III. 22. 4).

[22] *Test. an.* 3. 2.

[23] *Exhort. cast.* 2. 6-7.

[24] Tr. H. M. Parshley (New York: Knopf, 1953) 167.

procreation, established the flesh to be sinful. The reversal of this process demands that this same flesh be cleansed of sin that it may again be found suitable for eternal life. Tertullian writes that "for humankind to be saved it was necessary for Christ to come forth in the very state that humankind had entered upon its condemnation."[25] By this model, and in the words of Tertullian, "the flesh, in fact, is the hinge of salvation."[26] In *De resurrectione*, he elaborates on this:

> Since the soul, in consequence of its salvation, is chosen to the service of God, it is the flesh which actually renders it capable of such service. The flesh indeed, is washed, in order that the soul may be cleansed; the flesh is anointed, that the soul may be consecrated; the flesh is signed with the cross, that the soul too may be fortified; the flesh is shadowed with the imposition of hands, that the soul also may be illuminated by the Spirit; the flesh feeds on the body and blood of Christ that the soul likewise may fatten on its God. They cannot then be separated in their recompense, when they are united in their service.[27]

There is no dualism here of flesh and soul, much less of fleshly women and high-minded men, but rather a sharp differentiation between those who remain in Adam and all who have come to live in Christ. "Whatever flesh lives in Christ . . . is already a different substance, emerging in a new state, no longer generated of the filth of the seed, nor of the ordure of concupiscence, but of the pure water and a clean spirit."[28]

Even this weight of evidence may not satisfy those who would place the burden of proof on a single text or two that seem to imply the opposite. It will be recalled that Tertullian in *De cultu* I.2. claims of woman, "it was you who so readily destroyed the image of God, man." The inference to be made is that she is considered something less than the image of God, which grounds Tertullian's bias in the supposed spiritual deficiency of womankind. By way of corroboration a second passage can be adduced which concerns the veiling of virgins. It is Tertullian's contention that female virgins should not be made any more conspicuous than male. As the latter are distinguished by no sign, the former must also conform to the standard of their sex and be veiled. In an *a fortiori* argument, he asks how God, if he truly had intended for women to be so privileged, would have failed also to

[25]*De carne* 17. 6.
[26]*De resurrectione mortuorum* 8. 2.
[27]Ibid. 8. 2-3.
[28]*De pudicitia* 6. 16.

make such a concession to men, "either on account of their higher claim to intimacy, for having been created in his image, or due to the more strenuous nature of their work."[29] Michel Spanneut for one, in his recent book, *Tertullien et les premiers moralistes africains*, cites this text as proof of Tertullian's disregard for women. "He seems clearly to say, even more plainly in *De virginibus velandis*, that man alone is the glory and image of God, and that woman destroyed this image. Consequently, she must be veiled and dressed very modestly, and she cannot have the same familiarity with God that man can."[30] While forced to admit that "this restriction does not prevent Tertullian elsewhere from calling upon woman to respect the image of God within her," Spanneut makes no attempt to reconcile this fact with the passage at hand.[31]

Allowing for the sake of argument that Tertullian did believe man alone to have been formed in the image of God, how does this affect my contention that Tertullian held baptism in the Spirit to be efficacious for both women and men? First of all, the "image" (*imago*) and "likeness" (*similitudo*) of God must be differentiated. The former is an external resemblance to God, the latter, an internalization of God's very Spirit. In the act of creation the flesh was formed by the divine creator, "in the image of God, which he animated from his own breath into the likeness of his own vital vigor."[32] In yielding to the spirit of evil, humankind was deprived of its likeness to God; God's image, being formal in character, was retained despite the fall from grace. With the action of Christ came forgiveness of sins and redemption through the agency of the Holy Spirit. By accepting Christ, one was restored "to God's likeness, who formerly existed in his image (the 'image' reckoned in form; the 'likeness' for eternity) for he again receives that Spirit of God which he once had received from his breath, but later had lost through sin."[33]

---

[29] *De virginibus velandis* 10. 4. See Christoph Stücklin's edition (Frankfurt / M.: Herbert Lang Bern, 1974), in which is contained a considerable essay on "Die Stellung der Frau in der Gemeinde nach der Schleierschrift." Stücklin makes more of the first two chapters of Genesis than Tertullian does, writing (p. 187) that "Schöpfungs- und Sündenfallgeschichte haben in seinen Augen das Verhältnis der Frau zum Manne und ebenso ihre Stellung vor Gott irreversibel determiniert."

[30] (Gembloux: Editions J. Duculot; Paris: P. Lethielleux, 1969) 45.

[31] Ibid., n. 2.

[32] *Res. mort.* 9. 1.

[33] *De baptismo* 5. 7.

Now, even if Tertullian actually believed that woman was not formed in the "image" of God, this is demonstrably not the case with respect to God's "likeness." Although holding that her flesh was long without specific form, Tertullian argues that "even so, she was a living soul, since in my opinion she was then a part of Adam's soul. Besides, God's breath would have animated her too, if woman had not received, along with his flesh, a transmission of his soul."[34]

It seems certain that Tertullian, having acknowledged the eternal "likeness" to God in woman, would not need begrudge her the formal "image." If he actually does, it is either as a function of rhetorical expedience, or as required by literal exegesis of the scriptures. Either way, extensive reading in Tertullian bears out in principle Henry Chadwick's observation that while "Christianity did not give political emancipation to either women or slaves, . . . it did much to elevate their domestic status by its doctrine that all . . . are created in God's image and all alike redeemed in Christ."[35]

Modesty and Chastity. Rather than faith, hope, and charity, in Tertullian the principal Christian virtues are modesty, chastity, and sanctity. The third and greatest of these was bestowed by the Holy Spirit through the redemptive act of baptism as a consequence of God's forgiveness. However, once the sin inherited from Adam had been absolved in the baptismal ablution, the gateway of forgiveness (*ignoscentiae ianua*) was closed and bolted fast.[36] The Christian was now responsible for all his or her actions just as Adam had been before the fall. With little recourse offered should one sin after baptism, the sanctity sealed by it had to be maintained intact for salvation to be assured. This required strict discipline, which for Tertullian consisted principally in the exercise of modesty and chastity, or continence. Thus, it is on theological grounds that Tertullian presents his case

---

[34] *De anima* 36. 4.

[35] *The Early Church* (Baltimore: Penguin, 1967) 59.

[36] *De Paenitentia* 7. 10. To Tertullian, an opening for repentance seemed little more than an invitation to sin. A single second repentance, which had at first been sactioned by him (*Paen.* 7. 10), was later admitted only in the case of lesser offenses (*Pud.* 1. 10). Two ramifications of this are first, the disapprobation of pedobaptism — one should postpone baptism until one's faith is sound and one's lustfulness contained, as by marriage, or abated, as by continence (*Bapt.* 18); second, the insistence upon moral purity — one must refrain from sin in order not to fall from grace.

(*pro pudicitia, pro castitate, pro sanctitate*) for moral purity.[37]

Opening book two of *De cultu feminarum*, Tertullian strikes a note of promise and compassion very different from that searing admonition of woman with which the first began.

> Handmaids of the living God, my fellow-servants and sisters, by the right which I, the least consequential of persons, enjoy with you, by the right of fellow-servantship and brotherhood, I make bold to address to you a discourse, not out of affectation but rather in affection, for the cause of your salvation. That salvation, not only of women, but also of men, consists primarily in the exhibition of modesty.[38]

In stressing the importance of modesty, Tertullian is urging his listeners to look to their own best interest. He asks them to consider "whether you will rise with your powder and rouge and perfume, and with your fancy hairdos; whether it will be women thus made up whom the angels will carry into the clouds to meet Christ."[39] In addition, he makes a point to generalize his remarks:

[37] *Pud.* 17. 1.

[38] *Cult.* II. 1. The difference of tone between the two proems has led some scholars, most recently Timothy Barnes (*Tertullian*, 137), to conclude that the two books must be independent works, written as many as ten years apart, during which time Tertullian's antipathy for women markedly increased. His chronology is adapted from G. Säflund, *De Pallio und die stilistische Entwicklung Tertullians* (Lund: 1955) 106ff., with Barnes dating II in 197, and I in c. 205/6. Marie Turcan, in her new edition of *De cultu* (p. 20ff), disagrees, as does René Braun in "Le problème des deux livres du *De cultu feminarum*," *Studia patristica* VII (Berlin: Akademie, 1966) 133-42. The single most convincing factor in their arguments is that Tertullian gives a summary of his subject in I. 4. 1-2, making a division of the *"habitus feminae"* into two parts roughly corresponding to matters discussed in I and II respectively. *"Habitus feminae duplicem speciem circumfert, cultum et ornatum. Cultum dicimus quem mundum muliebrem vocant, ornatum quem immundum muliebrem convenit dici. Ille in auro et argento et gemmis et vestibus deputatur, iste in cura capilli et cutis et earum partium corporis quae oculos trahunt."* While it is dangerous to argue, as does Turcan, that the plan is entirely consistent with its execution, it is clear that the first book will not stand alone, given the statement of intention in I. 4. Braun, while defending his earlier opinion that the two books belong together (*Deus Christianorum* [Paris: Presses universitaires de France, 1962] 571), suggests that what we have represents an expansion of a sermon (originally II) into a tractate (I and II). This serves to explain those aspects of I that indicated to Säflund that it was prior, especially the elaboration in I of certain points only touched on in II (e.g., II. 10 as presupposed in I. 2 and 7). A third possibility would be that Tertullian consolidated two addresses into a single tractate. Regardless, there is no reason to assume that the two are distanced from one another by a decade in order to rationalize any implicit differences between them.

[39] *Cult.* II. 7. 3; compare *Cult.* I. 2. 5, where it is claimed that all artificial

they pertain to men as well. Men have "deceptive trickeries of form peculiar to their own sex," such as enhancing the shape of the beard by severe trimming, selective plucking, and shaving around the mouth.[40] Tertullian has to remind his brothers that "since the knowledge of God has put to an end every desire to please by means of voluptuous attraction, all these things are rejected as frivolous, as hostile to modesty."[41] On the other hand, he warns women that "attractiveness is not to be censured, as being a bodily happiness, . . . but is to be feared, on account of the effrontery and violence of suitors."[42] In *De pudicitia*, a treatise devoted to the claims of modesty (depicted therein as the "*flos morum, honor corporum, decor sexuum, . . . fundamentum sanctitatis*"[43]), this same concern is expressed. There Tertullian writes that "it makes no difference whether a man assault another's bride or widow, provided she be other than his own wife, just as it makes no difference where, whether it be in chambers or towers that modesty is massacred."[44]

Along with modesty, chastity too is cited for its services as a handmaiden to sanctity. Through chaste living, "we, God's image, become also his likeness, that we can be holy just as he himself is holy."[45] While such a statement seems, on the face of it,

---

adornments originated with the devil, and consequently must be shunned by self-respecting Christians, who aspire to salvation. Noting *De cultu* in particular, Sider (*Ancient Rhetoric*, 120) remarks, "how pliant the topics of deliberative and epideictic rhetoric were in his hands. . . At every point, he casts aspersion upon, he vituperates, the various parts of dress on the grounds of their origin and utility. By thus bringing together two themes appropriate each to a different genre, he has been able to write an exhibition piece that carries at the same time an honest hortatory purpose."

[40]*Cult.* II. 8. 2. Moreover, it is the same motive, *ambitio*, that impels both men and women to dress fashionably. "Vanity" drives men to exchange the mantle for the toga (*De pallio* 4. 10), as much as it does women to bedeck themselves with jewels (*Cult.* I. 2. 4).

[41]*Cult.* II. 8. 2. In *De spectaculis* (25. 2) Tertullian notes that among the devil's things there will be met with no greater stumbling-block than "*ille ipse mulierum et uirorum accuratior cultus.*"

[42]*Cult.* II. 2. 6.

[43]*Pud.* 1. 1.

[44]Ibid. 4. 3.

[45]*Exhort. cast.* 1. 3. This kind of emulative sanctification, part and parcel of a works-righteousness, has, as is evident from the language, many constitutive elements in common with Tertullian's theory of atonement. It might be said to represent a post-baptismal extension of the means by which humankind was made pure, as adapted to the requirements that attend to the maintenance of that same purity. While Christ plays an exemplary role in this second scheme, humankind is left, for all intents and purposes, to atone for itself.

straightforward enough, Tertullian's advocacy of continence has been characterized as not only "a repudiation of sex, but also of women."[46] A simple comparison of *Ad Uxorem* I, in which Tertullian advises his wife against remarrying if she should happen to outlive him, and *De exhortatione castitatis*, addressed to a recently widowed friend and instructing him in the same manner, demonstrates that the latter assumption simply is not so. Even Monceaux admits that Tertullian's advice to widows applies equally to widowers.[47] This is emphasized in a third and later tract against remarriage, where Tertullian is careful lest it be inferred that he is speaking only to one sex, in this case women: "we address both sexes, even if we mention here but one, since a single discipline applies to both."[48]

[46]Katharine M. Rogers, *The Troublesome Helpmate: a History of Misogyny in Literature* (Seattle: University of Washington Press, 1966) 14. Generalized, the argument reads as follows: "What the early Christians did was to strike the male out of the definition of man, and human being out of the definition of woman. Man was a human being made for the highest and noblest purposes; woman was a female made only to serve one. She was on the earth to inflame the heart of man with every evil passion." James Donaldson, *Woman: her Position and Influence in Ancient Greece and Rome, and among the early Christians* (London: Longmans, Green, and Co., 1907) 182, cited by Chapman Cohen, *Woman and Christianity: the Subjection and Exploitation of a Sex* (London: Pioneer Press, 1919) 46.

[47]*Histoire littéraire*, 391. Henry Chadwick (*The Early Church*, 59) writes, "The Christian sex ethic differed from the conventional standards of pagan society in that it regarded unchastity in a husband as no less serious a breach of loyalty and untrust than unfaithfulness in a wife. The apostle's doctrine that in Christ there is neither male nor female (Gal. iii, 28) was not taken to mean a programme of political emancipation, which in antiquity would have been unthinkable. The social role of women remained that of the homemaker and wife. At the same time, Christianity cut across ordinary social patterns more deeply than any other religion, and encouraged the notion of the responsibility of individual moral choice in a way that was quite exceptional."

[48]*De monogamia* 10. 7. Monceaux (*Histoire littéraire*, 191) suggests that Tertullian's interest in his wife's future continence is occasioned by proleptic jealousy, noting that, "il proteste aussitôt qu'il ne lui donne pas ce conseil par une sorte de jalousie anticipée, mais il proteste de telle sorte, et avec tant d'insistance, qu'il trahit justement son involontaire préoccupation." However, in the three tracts treating of the question, only in the one addressed to his wife is allowance made for the contingency that she may, regardless of his wishes, decide to remarry. If she should, he requires only that she remarry within the faith. This is just an intimation of the dangers to be incurred by the first who is trepidatious enough to attempt a psycho-historical study of Tertullian. Timothy Barnes (*Tertullian*, 136) states the problem nicely and makes a few sound conjectures, noting that "some explanation must be attempted for his repeated discussion of women and marriage." It is hoped that this article will contribute a

It is also claimed, by Michel Spanneut among others, that "what Tertullian says about chastity lets it be understood that he does not have a high opinion of marriage."[49] Spanneut cites Tertullian's antipathy to women as responsible for this. However, the basis for his original assumption is undermined by one remarkable piece of evidence, the closing chapter of Tertullian's *Ad uxorem*:

> What kind of yoke is that of two believers, sharing one hope, one desire, one discipline, one and the same service? Both are brethren, both fellow-servants; there is no difference of spirit or of flesh. They truly are two in one flesh, and where the flesh is one, the spirit is one also. Together they pray, together prostrate themselves, together perform their fasts; mutually teaching, mutually exhorting, mutually sustaining. Equally are both in the Church of God; equally at the banquet of God; equally in straits, in persecutions, in refreshments. Neither keeps secrets from the other; neither shuns the other; neither is troublesome to the other. . . . Between the two echo psalms and hymns; and they mutually challenge each other as to which shall better chant to their Lord. When Christ sees and hears such things, he rejoices. To these he sends his own peace. Where two are, he is also there. Where he is, the evil one is not.[50]

Here we have as explicit an acknowledgement of the equality of partners in Christian marriage, and as moving a tribute to matrimony itself, as is to be found anywhere in early Christian literature. Actually, Tertullian only denigrates marriage when contrasting it with his higher call of continence. Both are prophylactics to the devil, and his emphasis upon the latter may best be appreciated in light of his respect for the former. As much opposed to the proscription of marriage as to its permitted recurrence, Tertullian reminds the Marcionite that "if there is to be no marriage, there is no sanctity."[51]

As in the case of modesty, it is Tertullian's belief that "continence has been shown us by the Lord as an instrument for attaining to eternity."[52] This helps to explain his passionate

---

few theological points to that explanation, as well as a warning to any who would take too many liberties with this admittedly provocative material.

[49] He continues, "En effet, il est sévère pour la femme qui doit porter l'expiation de son péché, elle qui a été 'la première à déserter la loi divine' et qui a brisé l'image de Dieu, condamnant a mort le Fils de Dieu," (*Tertullien*, 45).

[50] *Ux*. II. 8. 7-9. This and two analogous tracts are conveniently collected in W. P. LeSaint, *Tertullian. Treatises on Marriage and Remarriage: To his Wife; An Exhortation to Chastity; Monogamy*, Ancient Christian Writers 13 (Westminster, Md.: Newman Press, 1951).

[51] *Marc*. I. 29. 5.

[52] Three forms of celibacy are reckoned accountable for sanctification:

insistency in arguing on its behalf. To his recently widowed friend he exclaims,

> How many men and women there are whose position in ecclesiastical orders is due to continence, who preferred to be wedded to God, who restored the honor of their flesh, and who already have declared themselves to be children of eternity, by slaying in themselves the concupiscence of lust, and all else that could not be admitted within paradise. . . . All who wish to be received into paradise ought at least to begin to cease from that thing from which paradise is preserved.[53]

The importance of the flesh to one of Tertullian's schemes of redemption has already been discussed. Here it serves a somewhat different function through being maintained in the same sanctified state into which it will be received. If mortification of the flesh is to a certain extent required by such a system, Tertullian's ultimate intention is quite the opposite. One must take into consideration both the practical consequences and the desired results of Tertullian's relentless rigorism. However, whether rooted in a fear of human sexuality, or chiefly inspired by the promise of eternal life, his preoccupation with the claims of modesty and chastity on Christians of both sexes cannot be ascribed to a simple disdain for women. One need not embrace Tertullian's deprecations in order to appreciate the consistency with which they are enjoined on each and all alike.

Martyrdom. In his book *Tertullians Ethik*, Theodor Brandt describes as paradoxical Tertullian's image of woman. "There are two clear ideas here which cannot be easily reconciled: her sin and weakness, on the one hand, and her creation and answerability to the same moral law, on the other."[54] Brandt's reference is to *De cultu* I.1: "Here woman clearly proves herself to be the weaker party."[55] In a note he defends this as "on the whole, Tertullian's point of view," citing only a single indecisive passage for

---

virginity from birth; virginity from rebirth, that is, from the moment of baptism; and, chaste monogamy, often initiated upon the death of one's spouse and maintained by continence thereafter.

[53]*Exhort. cast.* 13. 4.

[54](Gütersloh: Bertelsmann, 1929) 194. Stücklin (ed. *De virginibus velandis*, 205) poses the problem in similar terms: "Hinsichtlich der Stellung der Frau in der Gemeinde nimmt Tertullian eine Stellung ein, die wiederum von zwei Faktoren bestimmt ist: Einerseits anerkennt er die Frau als gleichwertige Glaubensschwester, andrerseits scheint ihm das weibliche Geschlecht besonders schuldbeladen, da alle Frauen an der Ursünde ihrer Stammutter Eva teilhaben."

[55]Brandt, *Tertullians Ethik*, 193.

corroboration.[56] But Tertullian makes no allowance for this supposed weakness when it comes to martyrdom. "I fear the neck, strung with pearl and emerald nooses, will give no place for the sword," he writes. "Wherefore, O blessed ones, let us meditate on hardships and we shall not feel them; let us abandon luxuries and we shall not desire them. Let us stand prepared for every violence, possessing nothing that we fear to leave behind."[57]

To Tertullian, "weakness" and "strength" are the respective attributes not of women and men, but of flesh and spirit. To a mix of Christian prisoners awaiting martyrdom he writes:

> Perhaps the flesh will dread the heavy sword, and the elevated cross, and the beasts' mad rage, and the capital punishment of flames, and all the executioner's talent for torture. But let the spirit respond to itself and to the flesh, that these things, while very painful, have, even so, been received with equanimity and with acute desire for the sake of fame and glory, not only by men, but also by women, that you, O blessed ones, too may be worthy of your sex.[58]

Challenging the assumption that martyrdom may be too much to ask of women, Tertullian inspires them to fulfill a promise equal to that of men. This he does in part by choosing pertinent exempla from history. Exactly half of his illustrations in Ad martyras, each a model of fortitude, are of women. This same pattern is adapted elsewhere by Tertullian to the specific requirements of like passages in Ad nationes and the Apology.[59]

As the ultimate sanctification, martyrdom is commended by Tertullian to each and all alike as a more perfect baptism. "Uncleanness," he writes, "is washed away in baptism, of course, but the stains of it are made immaculately white through martyrdom."[60] While it is far from clear, Tertullian may even have believed that martyrs alone were resurrected directly, all other Christians being obliged to wait in Hades for the judgment

[56] Ibid., n. 2.
[57] Cult. II. 13. 4-5.
[58] Ad Martyras 4. 2-3.
[59] Nat. I. 18; Apol. 50. The most striking of Tertullian's exempla is that of Dido, whose story he tells in its Carthaginian rather than Roman version. That is, she preferred to burn rather than remarry (Apol. 50. 5). On one occasion Tertullian even presents her as a judge of Christians less protective than she of their sanctity (Mon. 17. 2). Such is the virtue of continence and the efficacy of martyrdom, that a pagan queen, dead centuries before the birth of Christ, should be accorded priority over baptised Christians, who, interpreting the word of the apostle, chose rather to remarry than to burn.
[60] Scorpiace 12. 10.

day.[61] He claims that Perpetua, martyred early in the third century in Carthage, had envisioned only martyrs in paradise, adding, "the key to unlocking paradise completely is your own blood."[62] The consequence would seem to be salvation by works alone, and Tertullian's teachings on martyrdom represent the furthest extension of his system of sanctification by moral purity. In any event, sex proves in no way a qualifying factor for what is considered by Tertullian the most difficult and glorious of all endeavors. Just as he refuses to acknowledge human claims of weakness, of the flesh for instance, as extenuating factors, there is certainly no provision taken for a weaker sex by one who writes, "seek not to die on cosey couches, nor in miscarriages, nor in soft fevers, but to die the martyr's death."[63]

III. *Regni ianua*: the Gateway to the Kingdom

We are distanced from Tertullian by many things, not the least of them his rigorism. As indicated above, its theological roots can be traced to his conception of the history of salvation.[64] On the one hand, he perceives the same forces at work in his own day that conspired to precipitate the original falling from grace. That is, he believes that Christians, having also been promised eternal life

[61]*An.* 55.

[62]Ibid. 55. 5.

[63]*De fuga in persecutione* 9. 3: evidently a dictum of the New Prophecy. Two aspects of Tertullian's acceptance of the paraclete are of particular relevance to the question of his attitude toward women. First is the role of the coming of the paraclete in the unfolding drama of salvation history. Since Christ had already done what he could in making sanctification for Christians through baptism possible, Tertullian might look to the paraclete for such revelations as would confirm Christians in their determination to persist in a manner befitting their sanctity, through modesty, continence, martyrdom, etc. Second, in the words of R. Gregor Smith, the paraclete "liberated his thought with regard to the work of the Holy Spirit. The grand conception that the Spirit is utterly free in His workings, and that the Church is consequently a living company capable of being led into all truth is the assumption underlying all of Tertullian's work" ("Tertullian and Montanism," *Theology* 46 [1943] 134). While precipitating his rift from the Church, this principle contributes directly to Tertullian's enormous respect for the spiritual authority of individual believers. By virtue of his respect for the pure who see visions (*Exhort. cast.* 10. 5), he derives both personal inspiration and matter for his teachings from such individuals as Perpetua, the Montanist prophetesses Prisca and Maximilla, and the woman in his congregation who saw visions during worship, such as that of the corporeal soul (*An.* 9. 4).

[64]See Fredouille, *Tertullien*, 235-300, for a valuable assessment of the history of salvation in Tertullian's thought.

through the redeeming action of Christ, are in danger of relapsing into sin and death. A major difference between the two situations is that one now supposedly knows what Adam did not, and should therefore be expected to act more prudently than he. Enhanced vigilance comes with the knowledge of what this penalty death actually entails. One grows to appreciate the very real consequences attendant upon the breaking of God's ordinances. On the other hand, Tertullian makes bold to postulate the future in order that his fellow Christians can anticipate in their own lives the promise of the Kingdom. He teaches that the more one conforms to the set standards of heaven, the closer one comes to an assurance of salvation. That which in heaven one will cease to desire, one must check one's longing for while still on earth. In practice this means a gradual self-perfection in emulation of angelic likeness. Flesh immortal neither marries, nor has sex, nor wears jewels; flesh redeemed, stamped with the baptismal seal, must adhere to the same high standards, or squander, with its sanctity, its claim to eternal life.

As conceived by Tertullian, the emoluments of salvation justify each of the various stages leading up to it, including the first. By this token the fall becomes a requisite part of salvation history. While Adam's sin introduced the need for redemption, it also made salvation possible. In fact, the final victory over the devil occasions a return from this present life to a paradise even more glorious than that which was forfeited.[65] Tertullian's treatise devoted to paradise is not extant, but there remain several hints in his other writings that will give us an inkling of his impressions. In *De resurrectione*, to those who would contend that the second paradise is none other than the first, Tertullian responds, "even so, a restoration of paradise will seem to be promised to the flesh, whose lot it was to dwell there and tend it."[66] In *Adversus Marcionem*, he claims that the resurrected flesh is itself, "the gate through which one enters into the kingdom (*ianua regni*)."[67] To make this passage good, the risen flesh is changed; humankind is suited for immortality, "translated, in fact, into the condition and sanctity of angels," as Tertullian describes it to his wife.[68] This does not imply a loss of humanity, but a heightening of it. "Christ said not 'They shall *be* angels,'" he writes elsewhere, "but he said,

[65] *Marc.* II. 10.
[66] *Res. mort.* 26. 14.
[67] *Marc.* V. 10. 13.
[68] *Ux.* I. 1. 5.

'They shall be equal unto the angels,' that he might preserve their humanity unimpaired. When he ascribed an angelic likeness to the flesh, he did not take from it its proper substance."[69]

How does all of this affect the status of the sexes? In *De cultu* I, following upon the "gateway passage," Tertullian reminds his listeners that "you too have as your promise the same angelic nature, the same sex, and the same advancement to the dignity of judging as do men."[70] This does not mean that in heaven women will finally become men, any more than it does that they both will become angels. Rather, it indicates that, according to Tertullian, everyone in heaven assumes an angelic likeness, which is understood to mean a loss of specific sexuality for women and men alike. When contesting the elaborate speculations of the Valentinian gnostics, Tertullian states his own expectation unequivocally.

> After I die I must return to that place where no one marries, where I must be clothed rather than stripped, where, even if I am stripped of my sex, I am classed among the angels, not as a male or female one. No one then will make a thing of me, in which they will discover masculinity.[71]

It has not been my purpose in this paper to suggest that Tertullian was a champion for woman's rights as understood today. A literalist in his interpretation of the scriptures, he was no different from others who followed the letter in respect to such matters as a woman's subordination to her husband, silence in church, or ordination to baptise and teach. However, the only liberation he knew was liberation in Christ from the limitations imposed by this age and the curse of mortality. I argue simply that Tertullian believed women and men to be equally capable of that liberation, both while on earth and also in heaven. That such a statement needed to be made is due in large measure to the ever more frequent citation of a single passage, *De cultu* I.1-2, which, abstracted from its context, and with no reference given to Tertullian's motives, can be employed to depict him as a misogynist. But this is to mistake concern, here with respect to woman's salvation, for belief, as inferred from the specific language through which that concern is expressed. Naturally it is difficult, at a remove of almost two millenia, to recover from

[69] *Res. mort.* 62. 4.
[70] *Cult.* I. 2. 5.
[71] *Adversus Valentinianos* 32. 5.

rhetoric the motive that informs it. It is even more so when the arguments advanced are alien and often offensive to modern sensibilities. However, to a certain extent, Tertullian faced the same problem in his own time. To those whom he could not expect to understand the theological grounds for his concern, pagans with little patience for Christian speculation, he provides a comprehensible motive for the tenor and scope of his prescribed morality. Perhaps we may profit in our own understanding of Tertullian by the words he offers them.

> Though the things we maintain be deemed false and idle fancies, nevertheless they are necessary; though deemed absurd, they are useful: for they compel all who believe in them to be made better people, through the fear of eternal punishment and the hope of eternal bliss.[72]

[72]*Apol.* 49. 2.

SEXUAL EQUALITY AND THE CULT OF VIRGINITY IN EARLY CHRISTIAN THOUGHT

Jo Ann McNamara

Early Christianity grew out of a religious milieu that was rarely favorable to women. Some pagan sects wove fears and prejudices about the functions of women into the fabric of their beliefs. Others excluded them from worship altogether. Judaism also took a dim view of the sex which, through Eve, had supplied the instrument of humanity's downfall. Women were excluded from most acts of public worship and subjected to rituals which assumed that they were polluted by nature. The early Christians were not exempt from the predispositions of their contemporaries. There were no mothers of the Church and most of the fathers confined their procreative instincts to the products of the intellect, eschewing the sexual society of women. It would be all too easy to gather a large body of evidence exposing their fear of the seductions of women and their revulsion against her physical functions. In moments of moral passion, normally prudent preachers and writers were all too prone to lapse into diatribes against the offensive behavior and questionable moral capacity of women. I need not labor the point. For some time now, both feminist and anticlerical writers have made this literature familiar to us all.

Despite these predispositions, however, patristic writers were committed to the doctrine that with God there is neither male nor female. Thus, despite the personal proclivities of many of its formulators, the logic of Christian doctrine required a commitment to sexual equality. Nevertheless, before the achievement of that state of bliss in which sexual differences were to be erased in the mind of God, Christian women and men were to resolve the real and apparent differences that determined their earthly condition. The curses laid on Adam and Eve still burdened humanity in its mortal state and the makers of Christian doctrine were much concerned with the reconciliation of the doctrine of spiritual equality with the practical conditions of life.

It cannot be said that Christianity always moved in a direction favorable to the aspirations of women. In the primitive community, Christian women appear to have enjoyed a better relationship with their brethren than they were to have in later centuries. In the earliest writing produced by the new religion, Paul assumed that women and men men would worship together.[1] His instruction that women must be veiled when praying and prophesying implied that the segregation to which they had formerly been subjected would be replaced by a simple difference of clothing.[2] Prophetesses continued to teach until the third century when the activities of free-lance teachers of both sexes began to fall into disrepute.[3] The earliest constitutions of the church formalized the

219

equal position of women as members of the congregation.[4] On the other side, however, women were totally excluded from the ranks of the emerging priesthood, which constituted a major loss of position in the community. In at least one case, this exclusion was defended on the grounds that the natural pollution of the female body rendered women ineligible to participate in the sacrifice of the altar.[5]

This argument exposes a predisposition among early Christians to denigrate the very nature of women. Patristic writers ultimately condemned this tendency but it was never entirely expunged from their minds. Paul himself had likened the inferior relationship of the wife to the husband as a parallel to the inferiority of the flesh to the spirit.[6] His successors, through the fifth century, sought to deal with this dichotomy in a variety of ways. Substantial numbers of Christians embraced the extremist position that women were to be identified with the flesh, the flesh with the world, and the world with evil itself.[7] Procreation in particular was viewed as the instrument of the devil in his eternal struggle with God.[8] These views, however, were unequivocally condemned by the fathers, who fought grimly against the heretical tendency to weaken God's claim to be the sole creative power in the universe. The orthodox view of the nature of God and the necessary goodness of his creative design implied an intrinsic defense of the nature of women.[9] Moreover, the inherent demands of their logic imposed a recognition of the fact that woman differs from man only in the functions attendant upon her as wife and mothers:

> For if the God of both is one, the master of both is also one; one church, one temperament, one modesty; their food is common, marriage an equal yoke; respiration, sight, hearing, knowledge, hope, obedience, love, all alike. And those whose life is common have common graces and a salvation in common; common to them are love and training. "For in this world," He says, "they marry and are given in marriage," (Luke 20-34) in which alone the female is distinguished from the male. Common therefore, too, to men and women is the name of man.[10]

The Pauline metaphor was attacked and its contradictions resolved in two ways by the fifth century. Augustine's exegesis denied that Paul had ever intended to equate the wife with the flesh except to command that men should love their wives as they love their own bodies:

> And yet the woman received not the pattern from the body, or flesh, to be so subject to the husband as the flesh is to the spirit; ... but the man did, for this reason: because although the spirit lusteth against the flesh, even in this it consults for the good of the flesh; not likewise, the flesh lusting against the spirit, for such opposition consults neither for the good of the spirit nor for its own.[11]

A simpler, if less ingenious, formulation was devised by Paulinus of Nola in a letter to a married men: "You are her head in Christ and she is your foundation."[12] The same bishop summarized the Christian opinion on the spiritual equality of women and men by pointing out that God chose to incarnate himself as a man and to be born of a woman "so that the creator of both sexes might make both holy."[13]

The same writers who defended the intrinsic equality of the spiritual natures of women and men were not backward in granting a large measure of equality to their physical capacities as well. The intellectual abilities of women were also generally admitted and their capacity to study and teach both women and men was often admired.[14] Indeed, the fourth-century biographer of the eastern saints, Palladius, went so far as to criticize St. Jerome for having thwarted the genius of his assistant, Paula, by subjecting to his own scholarly pursuits "a mind that was well able to surpass everyone else."[15] Women were further conceded to be capable of considerable effectiveness in warfare and politics. The controversial Byzantine bishop Chrysostom was the exception in his belief that women were suited only to the lesser and more delicate activity of the home.[16] In the world of the late Roman Empire, no one had very far to look if they wished to discover women occupying influential positions. Indeed, Chrysostom himself paid dearly for his failure to respect the power of the Empress. Moreover, the Old Testament provided a wealth of historical examples.[17] Justin Martyr considered the study of classical literature, with its rich testimony to the powers of women at court and in battle, unsuitable for Christians because of the unseemliness of the models. But he never doubted that women could and did participate effectively in politics and war.[18] Clement of Alexandria devoted a lengthy passage to the military achievements of pagan and barbarian women, but concluded: "We do not train our women like the Amazons to manliness in war for we wish even our men to be peaceable."[19] Such reservations were nullified when the physical courage of the battlefield was transformed into that of the martyrs. In the late second century, the spokesman for the martyrs of Lyon paid special tribute to the Christian women who heroically passed through the ordeals of the arena to win the crown of martyrdom. The long ordeal of the slave woman, Blandina, was singled out to prove "that the things among men which appear mean and obscure and contemptible, with God are deemed worthy of the greatest glory. . . . For although small and weak and greatly despised she put on the great and invincible athlete Christ and in many contests overcame the adversary."[20]

With such standards before their eyes, the fathers had little patience with arguments drawn from assertions about the weaknesses of women to excuse them from the more rigorous demands of religion. Tertullian, who argued that a second marriage should be regarded as adultery, scoffed at the excuse that a woman needed the protection of a man.[21] When young women and men consecrated to virginity excused their practice of setting up joint households on the grounds that the women were thus protected from the corrupting atmosphere of the market place, Chrysostom pointed out that the market place was full of women buying and selling and that if, perhaps, it was not the best place for a virgin, it was certainly preferable to the proposed alternative.[22] Jerome showed similar misgivings about the propriety, but not the capacity of women to operate in the market place: "I certainly do not know if she who is engaged in shop keeping remains a virgin in body, but I do know that she does not remain a virgin in spirit."[23] The argument of propriety was always subject to consideration of the alternatives and the motives of the individual. Thus a certain Amanda, who took charge of the administration of her own estates and those of her husband, was praised for "interposing her holy slavery" between her husband and the world, "confronting worldly needs as a tower founded on unbudging rock confronts the storm," in order to free her husband for a life of contemplation.[24]

From these examples, we can already perceive that although the fathers put few limitations on what women could do, they were much more restrictive in their view of what they should do. Their idea of the life suitable to Christian women relied on two models: Martha and Mary, the one busy with the cares of the household and the other sitting rapt at the feet of Jesus among the apostles. Then, as now, they could reasonably expect the majority of women to take up the life of Martha, the wife and mother.

As we have seen, Paul instructed married women to be subject to their husbands.[25] This was reiterated in one of the earliest pieces of post-Apostolic writing: "You exhorted girls to do their duty with a blameless, modest, and pure conscience. And you taught married women to love their husbands as they should, to be subject to them according to the laws of obedience and to manage their homes with much piety and wisdom."[26] The subjection of wives, as envisaged by the patristic writers, was never intended to be total or unquestioning. Even in the ordinary course of marriage, the husband's superiority was limited by the claims of love and duty, as Ambrose of Milan preached: "You are not her lord but her husband; and she is not the maidservant but your wife. God desires that you guide the inferior sex, not dominate it."[27] Moreover, the husband's role of guide did not confer a one-sided power upon him. Paul ordered each partner to give the other her or his due sexually: "For the wife does not rule over her own body, but the husband does; likewise, the husband does not rule over his own body, but the wife does."[28] Between married persons, this claim took precedence over almost all others. Even the desire of one partner to embrace a life of celibacy could not not free them from the power of the spouse. Saint Melania obeyed her husband to the extent of bearing two children before she could persuade him to abandon the marriage bed.[29] Augustine advised a man who had broken a vow of continence in order to marry to urge his wife to join him in celibacy. But, he concluded, if she were not willing to do so, the husband must maintain his conjugal fidelity and hope that God would forgive him for the broken vow.[30]

Within marriage, the most substantial distinction between the partners, aside from the obvious physical differences, was in the type of labor apportioned to each. In this respect, Christian thinking was generally very conservative. The *Apostolic Constitution* devoted an entire section to a discussion of the labor suitable to women and its claim to honor.[31] One of the few married fathers, Clement of Alexandria, gave immediacy to this general picture with his portrait of the Christian family sitting together on a winter's evening: he with his books and she at her spinning, "each with his proper occupation."[32] Jerome, who approved of marriage only because it produced new virgins, never tired of describing the never-ending hectic round of activities that must fill the days of a busy wife.[33] The virtuous and hard-working wife, however, was not to be denigrated. Writing to his own wife, Tertullian described the union of "two who are one in hope, one in desire, one in the way of life they follow, one in the religion they practice. They are in very truth two in one flesh and where there is but one flesh there is also but one spirit."[34] Martha had her place and it was not without honor. But, by virtue of the married state, Martha also had her subjection to bear: "A woman is not inferior in her own person. It is because of her condition, not her nature, that she is subjected to man and ordered to fear him."[35]

The condition of the married woman was, after all, only a temporal condition. It would cease to be when the soul was released from the greater bondage of life on earth. Meanwhile, the nature of women, like that of man, was essentially spiritual. The restrictions of marriage were dissolved if they conflicted with the demands of morality which the fathers assumed to be binding equally on both sexes. Occasionally, they felt the need to remind the reader that women were included under the category "man" where no specific distinction was made.[36] More commonly, they were compelled to remind men that they were obligated to the same sexual restrictions as women. Modesty, simplicity of dress, decorum in behavior, avoidance of temptation and care not to be tempting oneself, were standards for both sexes.[37] Ambrose was simply repeating a Christian truism when he stated that "all sexual violation is adultery and what is not allowed to a woman is also not allowed to a man."[38] Caesarius of Arles spelled this out at length in a sermon addressed to men who thought that sexual lapses were unimportant as long as they were not committed by a woman. He bade the man tormented by hot blood to cool himself with fasting, and specifically prohibited sexual relations with prostitutes and concubines, women taken as booty in war, or slaves. Adulterous men were to be subjected to the same penalties as adulterous women and men who demanded virgin brides must themselves be virginal. Caesarius viewed the double standard as an outrage:

As though God gave two commandments, one for men and another for women! . . . How is it that some men are so insolent that they say cruel vice is lawful for men but not for women! They do not reflect that men and women have been redeemed equally by Christ's blood, have been cleansed by the very same baptism, approach the Lord's altar to receive his body and blood together, and that with God there are no distinctions of male or female.[39]

Furthermore, no one doubted that in practice, the woman might be the moral superior of the man. This was considered by Paul in discussing the problem of the Christian wife of a pagan husband, whom he advised to save her husband if she could.[40] In dealing with the same problem, Tertullian dwelt on the dangers for the Christian wife: "Every Christian woman is obliged to obey the will of God. Yet how can she serve two masters, the Lord and her husband . . . ? Let her take care how she discharges her duties to her husband."[41] Even between Christians, a virtuous woman might find herself joined to a vicious man. Arguing that women and men have equal capacities for perfection, Clement of Alexandria advised the virtuous woman to make every effort to persuade her husband to unite with her in pursuit of the good. If she failed, she might then ask permission of him to proceed alone. But at the last, if necessary, she must disobey her husband rather than turn from the path of virtue.[42]

This was no simple-minded preaching, for these fathers wrote in dangerous days when women were paying the price of blood for the rewards of virtue. In the second century, Justin Martyr described the death of a woman who was betrayed to the persecutors by a husband who refused to support her efforts to reform a dissolute life.[43] A century later, Cyprian of Carthage described the similar case of a lady named Bona "who was dragged by her husband to sacrifice, who did not pollute her conscience.

but as those holding her hands sacrificed, she herself began to cry out against this: 'I have not done it!' "[44] She and her sisters in the arena had earned the right to say, with the slave martyr Ariadne, that her masters might command her body but not her soul.[45]

In less dramatic circumstances, it was taken for granted that a wife should play an active and, where necessary, leading part in the joint effort to win salvation. Chrysostom offered many helpful examples of wives whose advice had led their husbands to the right path.[46] Paulinus of Nola consoled a widower that he had the remainder of his life to strive for equality with the dead woman, "who was mature and complete in Holiness" in the world to come.[47] The biographer of Melania the Younger dwelt at length on the seductions which she practiced to woo her husband to a life of celibacy and to keep him faithful to it. With Melania, however, we are introduced to a new idea whose attraction proved compelling to many women of the fourth century. On their wedding day, she said to her husband:

If you wish, my lord, to practice chastity with me and live with me under the law of continence, I will recognize you as lord and master of my whole life; but if that seems too heavy, if you cannot support the ardor of youth, here are all my goods at your feet to use, as master, however you will. Only free my body, so that I may present it with my soul unblemished to Christ on the redoubtable day.[48]

The proposition, however, came too late. Melania had entered into the subjection of the marriage bond and it was only after she had borne two children that she finally succeeded in winning her husband's cooperation in undertaking the celibate life. For many of her contemporaries, however, no claims of mastery or conjugal duties stood in their way. From the outset they gave themselves to the life of virginity.

Many social conditions and psychological pressures united with the religious attitudes at the base of the ascetic movement. But as it reached its flowering, Christian women were presented with one over-riding and consistent argument. The life of Martha was one of honor and salvation was well within her grasp. But Mary had chosen the better part and, as Christ had promised, it should not be taken from her. The sweet yoke which which bound two souls in love was still a yoke. As Ambrose said, married women and men could at best be one flesh and one spirit, but neither could ever be free.[49] The classic statement of the problem was drawn from Paul:

But I would have you to be free from cares. He that is unmarried is careful for the things of the Lord; but he that is married is careful for the things of the world, how he may please his wife. And there is a difference also between the wife and the virgin. She that is unmarried is careful for the things of the Lord, that she may be holy both in body and spirit; but she that is married is careful for the things of the world, how she may please her husband.[50]

For centuries thereafter, the growing literature in praise of virginity reverted to this rule, repeated it and refined upon it. The image of marriage as bondage was elaborated in the most uncompromising detail. For example, the process of entering the bond in the the first place was likened to being placed in the slave market:

How miserable is she who, to find a husband is put up, as it were, for sale, so that the one who offers the highest bribe obtains her. Slaves are sold for better terms, for they often choose their masters; if a virgin chooses her husband it is an offence, but if she is not chosen, it is an insult. And, though she is fair and beautiful, she both fears and wishes to be seen. She wishes to be seen so that she may fetch a better price; she fears to be seen lest the very fact of her being seen should not be fitting. What fears and suspicions she experiences as to how her suitors will turn out? She is afraid that a poor man may trick her or a noble one despise her.[51]

And once married, what could the wife hope for? At best, she must endure a constant round of harassment in the wearing care of her household and children, seeking to please her husband and accomplish all her work.[52] The horrors of childbearing with its danger and pain were dwelt on in the most lurid detail. Saint Melania, who had suffered two extraordinarily agonizing births before being released to the chaste life, brought her company of virgins with her when called to assist in a difficult labor so that they might see what afflictions attended life in the world.[53] Both Tertullian and Gregory of of Nyssa, who were married, stressed that the very happiness of marriage was ultimately rooted in misery. The more two people loved one another, the greater their anxiety that they lose one another must be. The "bitter pleasure of children," too, brought only fear of loss and failure.[54] Even in the best of marriages, the happiness of the wife was fraught with anxiety for her husband:

And since, according to the divine plan, the wife does not govern herself, but has her place of refuge in the one who has power over her through marriage, if she is separated from him for even a short time, it is as if she has been deprived of her head. She cannot endure the separation . . . she keeps her eyes glued to the door, full of worry and fright. She pays too much attention to gossip. Her heart is scourged by fear, tortured even before any news is brought back. At the door there is only knocking, real or imagined, as if some messenger of evil had suddenly and violently shaken her soul. . . . Such is the life of the happy pair!

And as for the others:

Come to the law courts, read the marriage laws. See there the abominations of marriage. For just as when you hear the doctor's description of various diseases, you recognize the wretchedness of the human body, since you learn what evils it can be afflicted with, so when you read the marriage laws and discover the many illegalities of marriage for which fines are inflicted, you perceive clearly the circumstances of marriage.[55]

The conclusion is obvious. From best to worst, marriage is a state of bondage from which the only escape is celibacy. Happy the woman or man who had never been subjected at all but had preserved her or his virginity! These praises of the virginal state were not the result of an attitude antithetical to sexual relations in themselves. The same writers produced a considerable literature defending the claims of marriage as a virtuous and worthwhile state.[56] Nor did they proceed from enmity toward women; the same literature was addressed to men. Virginity was presented as an ideal higher state of being for all and, practically considered, as an opportunity to obtain freedom from that condition which alone defined the inferior status of the female.

At the very least, the virgin woman could expect release from the governance of a husband and the chains of children. She was free of the burden of worldly cares and responsibilities that weighed her sisters down. On a higher plane, she was almost free of the mortal coil itself:

Those who refrain from procreation of death by preventing it from advancing further because of them, and, by setting themselves up as a kind of boundary stone between life and death, they keep death from going forward. If, then, death is not able to outwit virginity, but through it comes to an end and ceases to be, this is clear proof that virginity is stronger than death.[57]

And, again, in giving instruction to a consecrated girl, Jerome stated:

I would not have you subject to that sentence whereby condemnation has been passed upon mankind. When God said to Eve, "In pain and sorrow thou shalt bring forth children," say to yourself, "That is a law for married women, not for me." . . . And when last of all, he says, "Thou shalt surely die" once more, say, "Marriage indeed must end in death; but the life on which I have resolved is independent of sex. Let those who are wives keep the place and the time that properly belong to them."[58]

Examples of Christian virgins go back, of course, to the foundation of the religion - to the Virgin Mary herself. Legend provided Paul with a virgin companion who was said to have risked her life to embrace Christianity and flee the married life.[59] From the second century on, the consecrated virgin and the consecrated widow were recognized members of the Christian community and their number multiplied steadily through the fourth and fifth centuries when really large communities of such women were beginning to be established. The reward of their self-denial was social honor and a promise that they would be first in the ranks of the saints in heaven. On earth, they enjoyed the the freedom natural to their state.

The freedom promised by the writers in praise of virginity was no mirage. Critics of the actual behavior of the virgins are almost as plentiful as admirers of their state. Again and again, they were warned against pride and vaingloriousness.[60] They were repeatedly censured for adopting the frivolous dress, language, and deportment of courtesans rather than the decorous manner fitting to the consecrated.[61] We have already seen the reservations of Chrysostom and Jerome regarding the market place as a suitable place for virgins. But Chrysostom was obliged to approve even the market as a superior milieu to the joint households of female and male virgins he saw around him, where the wise women were called in regularly to furnish proof that the virgin was still intact.[62] It is abundantly clear, therefore, that a number of women seized the promise of freedom but used it in a way that was far from the intention of the fathers, for whom the object of the virgin life was to achieve perfection in sanctity. The life of Mary was envisaged as a heroic and self-sacrificing life of prayer, study, and charity, to be embraced only by the wisest and hardest working of women.[63]

Such a woman, with her virgin brother, stood on the most elevated level of the spiritual hierarchy. Since woman's special condition was defined by her status as a wife, the virgin must be viewed as having transcended that condition and therefore the limitations placed on her sex. However, that transcendence was not always easy to express in the linguistic patterns of the fathers. Chrysostom, carried away in praise of female virginity, enthused: "Not until Christ appeared, could women eclipse men in sanctity, fervor, devotion and love of God."[64] On the other side, we can frequently find men being included among the "Brides of Christ." To be sure, the fathers did not forget that the category "man" included woman. But they had an ineradicable tendency to characterize certain psychological qualities as "masculine" and others as "feminine." And, it must be added, that their instinctive tendency was to equate "masculine" with the higher attributes.[65] As a result of these predispositions of style, the sexual equal-ity obtained by virgins was habitually expressed by viewing them as having become men. Thus Gregory of Nazianzus praised the masculine soul of his widowed mother.[66] Gregory of Nyssa wondered whether he could call his sister, Macrina, a woman, since she had "gone beyond the nature of a woman."[67] Of the elder Melania, an admirer wrote: "What a woman she is, if one can call so virile a Christian a woman . . . a soldier of Christ with the virtues of Martin, though she is of the weaker sex . . . as a strong member of the weak sex, she might arraign idle men."[68]

It cannot be denied that such language betrays a deep-seated tendency to despise the nature of women.[69] Like most of their contemporaries, the fathers were infused with age-old prejudices which were heightened in this age by an atmosphere of sexual confusion and uncertainty. They were struggling against their own predispositions in a society that was producing heretical teachers preaching strange and disturbing trans-sexual images of the spiritual world.[70] Men as well as women were going beyond the limits of conventional behavior to escape from the bonds of sexuality. By the third century, the orthodox church had to adopt stringent doctrinal positions against men who too literally followed Christ's suggestion that "some make themselves eunuchs for the sake of heaven."[71] Jerome warned his virginal pupil against emulating those virgins who "change their garb and assume the mien of men, being ashamed of what they were born to be—women. They cut off their hair and are not ashamed to look like enuchs." Conversely, he went on to condemn men who dressed as women and forsook their true nature.[72]

Fourth and fifth century hagiography reflected this trend with the recurring theme of the woman who lived in a monastery as one of the monks. There are many variations on the tale: the imposter might have disguised herself as a man to escape the importun-ities of a suitor, to protect herself while traveling or, straightforwardly, in order to gain admission to the ascetic community. Her sex might be revealed accidentally, or by death, or as a defense against some slanderous sexual charge.[73] Probably we shall never know how much truth is embedded in these romantic fantasies, but Jerome's warning seems to suggest that they were not entirely ill-founded. And yet there were sisterhoods in the desert to which such women might well have gone. The pious folk of that age were at least prepared to believe that holy women might choose to become men and that God would bless them for it. At a somewhat later period, Gregory the Great re-corded the ultimate progress of this tendency in the tale of a widow who was warned by her doctors that if she pursued her determination to live in continence, the super-abundance of heat generated by this repression would cause her to grow a beard like a man. According to Gregory, she gladly accepted that deformity for her soul's good.[73]

Despite the initial confusions in their language and the distortions developed in the minds of the vulgar, it was certainly not the object of the fathers to turn women into men through the virgin life. Rather, they were seeking to express the absolute equality which the two sexes enjoyed outside the limitations of marriage. A monk named Sin-nius formed a brotherhood of women and men where "by his revered way of life, he drove out his own masculine desires and by his mastery he bridled the feminine traits of the women so that the scriptures were fulfilled: In Christ, there is neither male nor female."[74] Even a married couple might aspire to that condition of spiritual equality achieved by virgins if they abstained from sexual relations. Thus Augustine praised such a couple, Aper and Amanda, especially the wife who "did not lead her husband to effeminacy and greed but . . . to self-discipline and courage . . . restored and reinstated into unity with you, for Christ's love joins you with spiritual bonds. . . . You have passed from your own bodies into that of Christ."[75] Melania the Younger's biographer noted that male monks received her into their monasteries as though she were a man, "for she had gone beyond the limits of her sex and acquired a virile mentality." Then, bethinking himself of the implications of this image, he added, "or rather a celestial one."[76] That was the real object of the Christian: to attain the "celestial mentality," the state transcending all sexual differences. It was most easily achieved by virgins who were free from sexual bondage but others were not barred from the attempt.

As a conclusion, I should like to present the personal testimony of one woman who recorded her experiences in prison awaiting martyrdom. Perpetua and her slave girl Felicitas were both mothers and both condemned to the beasts. Even while awaiting the terrible contest, Perpetua complained of the pain of her breasts where the milk was unsuckled, and the pain in her heart for the baby who had been taken away from her. But at night, haunted by the vision of what was awaiting her, she dreamed that she stood in the arena: "And because I knew that I was condemned to the beasts, I marvelled that beasts were not sent out against me. But there came out against me a certain ill-favored Egyptian with his helpers to fight me. . . . And I was stripped, and I became a man. . . ."[77] There follows an account of the dream battle in which she gained the victory. Apparently, Perpetua dreamed of herself as a man because she expected to play the part of a man in battle. Her perception was very like that of Augustine, who preached in praise of her and her companion:

Perpetua and Felicity were not only of the female kind but were very women . . . and mothers likewise, that unto the frailty of that sex might be added a more importunate love.[78]
. . . .

For what thing might there be more glorious than these women, whom men may wonder at sooner than they may imitate? But this is chiefly the glory of Him, in whom they that do believe and they that with holy zeal in his name do contend one with another are indeed, according to the inward man neither male nor female; so that even in them that are women in body the manliness of their souls hideth the sex of their flesh and we may scarce think of that in their bodily condition which they suffered not to appear in their deeds.[79]

The manliness of the virgin woman was a transcendence of the sexual nature itself. In extreme circumstances, it could also be achieved by the nonvirginal. But in essence the equality of which the Christian fathers wrote was a celestial condition, not a temporal one. Social reform was not their object. In general they viewed social inequities, violence, and oppression as evils that grew out of man's original fall from grace. As long as humanity was born in sin and had failed to achieve complete reconciliation with God the world would be afflicted with these evils. Their aim, therefore, was to pursue a system that would free the life of the soul from the world of sin and strife and achieve its ultimate redemption. They sought to bring women and men alike to that state of grace in which there would be neither bond nor free, neither male nor female.

NOTES

[1] *I Corinthians* 11.5. See also Madeleine Boucher, "Some unexplored parallels to I Cor. 11-12 and Galatians 3, 28: The New Testament on the Role of Women," *Catholic Biblical Quarterly* 31 (1969): 50-58. And, for a more general view: Johannes Leipoldt, *Die Frau in der Antiken Welt und in Urchristentum* (Leipzig: Koehler and Amelang, 1954).

[2] The interpretation of Paul's instructions are explored at length by Paulinus of Nola, *Epistola* 23, 24-25, *Patrologia Latina* (*PL*), ed., Jacques P. Migne, 61, 273.

[3] The names of these prophets and prophetesses and their work is preserved by Eusebius, *Historia Ecclesiastica*, 5.17.3, *Sources Chrétiennes* (*SC*) 41, 54.

[4] *Didascalia et Constitutiones Apostolorum*, II, 57, ed., Franciscus X. Funk (Torino: Botteged' eiasmo, 1905), pp. 160-66.

[5] The Apostolic Constitutions, ibid., retain earlier sections which are contradicted in the text. Section 3, 2, p. 208, advised the ordination of deaconesses for the baptism of women, while Section 3, 6, p. 190, prohibited the teaching of women on the grounds that Christ did not include women among the twelve apostles, despite the presence of eligible women among the disciples. Section 3, 9, pp. 198-200, forbade women to perform baptism on the grounds that if Christ had wished to allow it he would have been baptized by his own mother and that a woman in the role of a priest, though known to Gentile paganism, was contrary to the laws of nature. The latter argument was vividly restated by the author of the pseudo-Clementine *Homilies*, 3.24, *Ante-Nicene Christian Library* (*ANCL*), eds., Alexander Roberts and James Donaldson (Edinburgh: T. & T. Clark, 1870), 17, 67. He expressed horror at the sight of women performing sacred rites: "being in her courses . . . [she] is stained with blood; and then she pollutes those who touch her."

[6] *Ephesians* 5.21. The question of the authenticity of the Pauline letters has been much debated. This letter in particular is generally held to be a product of another author. A broader discussion is available in Frederick R. Crownfield, *A Historical Approach to the New Testament* (New York: Harper: 1960), p. 248, who questions even passages in letters conceded to be authentic, where they command the subordination of women. See also Jean J. von Allmen, *Maris et femmes d'après Saint Paul* (Paris: Delachaux et Miestle S. A., 1951) and Else Kähler, *Die Frau in den paulinischen Briefen unter besonderer Berucksichtigung des Begriffes der Unterordnung* (Zurich: Gotthelf, 1960). For the purposes of this article, however, the Pauline letters will be treated as equally authoritative because the patristic authors cited here considered them to have scriptural authority.

[7] For example, the Gospel of the Egyptians, cited by Clement of Alexandria, *Stromata*, 3.9, *ANF*, 2, 392.

[8] This theme runs through the teachings of various gnostics and Manichaeans throughout our period. For further discussion of their ideas, see Joseph C. Plumpe, *Mater Ecclesia: An Inquiry into the Concept of the Church as Mother in Early Christianity* (Washington, D.C.: Catholic University Press, 1943), and, on a more general level, Hans Jonas, *The Gnostic Religion: The Message of the Alien God and the Beginnings of Christianity* (Boston: Beacon Press, 1963). The antifeminist impact is outlined by Jean Leclercq, "Un témoin de l'antiféminisme du moyen age," *Revue Benedictine* 80 (1970): 304-309.

[9] See the treatises written against these heretics by Irenaeus of Lyons, *Adversus Haereses*, *ANF*, 1, Hippolytus, *Refutation of All Heresies*, *ANCL* 6, and others. The limitations of their defense of women are shown by the continuation of superstitions regarding woman's nature and

physique as shown as Vern Bullough, "Medieval Medical and Scientific Views of Women," *Viator* 4 (1973): 484-501.

10Clement of Alexandria, *Paedogogos*, 1.4, trans., Simon P. Wood (New York: Fathers of the Church, 1954), p. 12.

11*De Continentia* 23, *PL* 40, 366.

12*Epistola* 44, 4, *PL* 61, 589.

13*Epistola* 23, 14, *PL* 61, 265.

14Tatian, *Address to the Greeks*, 33, *ANF* 2, 78, defended the philosophic studies of Christian women against the mockery of the Greeks by citing the fame of female philosophers among the pagans and claiming superior wisdom for the Christian women. Eusebius, *Historia*, 6, 4, *SC* 41, 90, praised the female pupils of Origen who suffered martyrdom in the persecution of the third century. A number of individual women were praised for their scholarship in the fourth and fifth centuries, for example, Gregory of Nyssa's praise of his sister Macrina in her biography, *Vie de Sainte Macrina*, *SC*, 178, and his demonstration of her learning in the *Dialogue on the Soul and Resurrection*, included in *Ascetical Works*, trans., Virginia W. Callahan (Washington D.C.: Catholic University Press, 1966). Jerome, who surrounded himself with learned women, wrote: "They will convict themselves of pride, rather than me of folly, who judge of virtue not by the sex but by the mind." *Epistola* 127, *Ad Principiam Virginem de Vita Sanctae Marcellae*, ed., F. A. Wright (Cambridge: Harvard University Press, Loeb Classical Library, 1933), p. 450.

15Palladius, *The Lausiac History*, 141, 2, trans., Robert T. Meyer, *Ancient Christian Writers* (*ACW*). 34 (Westminster, Md.: The Newman Press, 1965).

16*Sur la dignité de mariage*, 4, men and women live in two worlds, public and private and God has introduced the more important and useful to men and the lesser and humbler to women, in France Quéré-Jaulmes, *Le mariage dans l'église ancienne* (Paris: Editions du centurion, 1969).

17Clement of Rome, *Ad Corinthios que dicuntur epistulae*, 55, 4, ed., Oscar Gebhardt and Adolf Harnack, *Patrum Apostolicarum Opera* (Leipzig, 1876), p. 91.

18Justin Martyr, *Discourse to the Greeks*, 2, *ANF* 1, 271.

19*Stromata*, 4, 8, *ANF* 2, 419.

20Eusebius, *Historia Ecclesiastica*, 5, 1, 18-41, *SC*, 41, 10-17.

21*Ad Uxorem*, 1,4, *Corpus Christianorum Series Latina* (*CCSL*), 1, 377.

22*Comment observer la virginité*, 5, ed., J. Dumortier, *Nouvelle Collection de textes et documents* (Paris: Société Guillaume Bude, 1955).

23*Adversus Helvidium: Liber de perpetua virginitate b. Mariae*, 21, *PL* 23, 214.

24Paulinus of Nola, *Epistola* 44, *PL* 61, 388.

25*I Corinthians* 11.1; *Ephesians* 5.21; *Colossians*, 4.1.

26Clement of Rome, *Ad Corinthios*, 10.

27*Hexameron*, 5.7, *PL* 14, 214.

28*I Corinthians* 7:3-14; similar sentiments are expressed in *Ephesians* 5:29.

29*Vie de Sainte Mélanie*, trans., Denys Gorce (Les éditions du cerf: Paris, 1962).

30*Epistola* 127, *PL* 33, 483. This power, however, was broken by death. In urging his wife not to marry again if she should be widowed, Tertullian was anxious to explain that he was not attempting to enforce a proprietary claim on his wife's body, a claim ended forever by death, *Ad Uxorem*, 1, 1, *CCSL* 1, 373. I have further examined the question of celibate marriage in a paper given at the Medieval Institute of Western Michigan, 1974, called "Chaste Marriage and Clerical Celibacy." See also Pierre de Labriolle, "Le mariage spirituel dans l'antiquité chrétienne," *Revue Historique*, 137 (1921): 204-25.

31*Didascalia et Constitutiones Apostolorum*, 1, 3, 8.

32*Stromata* 4, 20, *ANF* 2, 432. A broader discussion of Clement's writings on marriage can be found in Richard B. Tollinton, *Clement of Alexandria: A study in Christian Liberalism* (London: Williams, 1914).

33*Adversus Helvidium*, 20, *PL* 23. 214.

34*Ad Uxorem*, 2, 6, *CCSL* 1, 393.

[35]Ambrose, *Commentaria in epistolam ad Ephesios*, 5, 32, *PL* 17, 399.

[36]For example, Cyprian, *De habitu virginum* 4; *Corpus Scriptorum Ecclesiasticorum Latinorum* (*CSEL*), 3, 190. Christ's praises of virginity were not confined to men alone but to both sexes, for women are part of men. Most exotically, Augustine, *Epistola*, 211, *PL* 33, 964, reminded the nuns that the scriptural saying, "He that hateth his brother is a murderer," was intended to apply also to women who must obey whatever is enjoined upon men.

[37]*Didascalia et Constitutiones Apostolorum*, 1, 2, p. 5-6, enjoined men to be compassionate, bountiful and willing to please their wives while forbidding them to adorn themselves in such a manner as to attract the interest of other women. Ibid., 1, 3, p. 8, says exactly the same commandment is laid on women. Clement of Alexandria *Paedogogos*, 7, *ANF*, 2, 252, warned both young women and men to avoid banquets where they would be beset by temptations and young unmarried men who found themselves obliged to attend were warned to keep their eyes on the ground and otherwise comport themselves in a manner which would keep them out of temptation.

[38]*De Abraham*, 1, 35, *CSEL* 32, 1, 519. See also Jerome, *Epistola 77, Ad Oceanum*, 3, *PL* 22, 691 and the elaborations of Augustine, *De conjugiis adulterinis*, 1, 8, *PL* 40, 456.

[39]Caesarius of Arles, *Sermo* 42, *CCSL* 103, 186.

[40]*I. Corinthians* 7:14.

[41]*Ad Uxorem*, 2, 4, *CCSL* 1, 388.

[42]*Stromata*, 14, 19.

[43]*Second Apology*, 2, *ANF*, 1, 188.

[44]Cyprian, *Epistola*, 24, *CSEL* 3[2], 537.

[45]Cited with other examples by Paul Allard, *Histoire des persecutions* (Paris: V. Lecoffre, 1911).

[46]*Homily 61 on John*, 4, Library of the Fathers, 36 (Oxford: 1852), p. 540.

[47]*Epistola 13*, *PL* 61, 223.

[48]*La Vie de Sainte Mélanie*, 131.

[49]*De institutione virginis*, 1, 6, *PL* 16, 320.

[50]*I Corinthians* 7:32-34.

[51]Ambrose, *De virginibus*, 1, 56, *PL* 16, 215.

[52]Jerome, *Adversus Helvidium*, *PL* 23, 214.

[53]Palladius, *The Lausiac History*, 249.

[54]Tertullian, *Ad Uxorem*, 1, 5, *CCSL*, 1, 374.

[55]Gregory of Nyssa, *Traité de la virginité*, 3, *SC* 114, 290-301.

[56]For example, Augustine *De bono conjugali*, *CSEL* 41. Even Methodius' whose *Symposium* consists of ten monologues delivered by a gathering of women on the subject of chastity, gave over one of the addresses to a defense of the married state and its procreative element, c. 2, *SC* 95, 69.

[57]Gregory of Nyssa, *Traité de la virginité*, 14, *SC* 119, 434 ff.

[58]Jerome, *Ad Eustochium*, 18, *PL* 22, 405.

[59]For a discussion of the various versions of this story see William M. Ramsay, *The Church in the Roman Empire* (London: G. P. Putnam's Sons, 1894), 375 ff.

[60]This trend is summed up by Augustine's warning that the marriage of the faithful is to be set up above the virginity of the impious, *De bono conjugali*, 8, *CSEL*, 41, 198.

[61]For example, Cyprian, *De habitu virginum*, *CSEL* 3[1], 185.

[62]*Comment observer la virginité*, 1-2, p. 100.

[63]Methodius, *Symposium*, 1, *SC* 95, 57.

[64]*PG* 62, 99.

[65]This is most elaborately worked out in a novel of unknown date.dealing with the adventures of Saint Peter and wrongly attributed to his companion, Clement of Rome, *Recognitions*, Homily 3, *ANCL* 17. More typical is the type of remark made by Augustine, *De bono conjugali*, 20, *CSEL* 41, 213, that men's capacity for reproduction is superior to that of women—a man can get children with more women than women with men—which demonstrates the universal power of things principle.

[66]*Epitaph for his mother*, no. 70, *PG* 38, 47.

67*Gregory of Nyssa, Vie de Macrina, SC* 178.

68Paulinus of Nola, *Epistola* 29, *PL* 61, 315. See also T. C. Lawler, "Melania the Elder," *Traditio*, 1947, 59.

69This is the argument advanced by Vern Bullough, "Transvestites in the Middle Ages," *American Journal of Sociology* 79 (May 1974): 1381-94.

70Hippolytus, *Adversus Haereses,* 5, 8, *ANF*, 1, 44, says that the gnostics responsible for the Gospel of Thomas taught that a woman could not enter the kingdom of heaven without first becoming a man. Conversely, however, one of the Montanist prophetesses had a vision of Christ as a woman. Epiphanius, *Haereses*, 49.1. Some of the psychological explanations for these phenomena are discussed by Eric R. Dodds, *Pagan and Christian in an Age of Anxiety* (New York: Cambridge University Press, 1965), p. 112.

71The most famous of the fathers who took this route was Origen. A broader discussion of this problem can be found in Edward Schillebeeckx, *Celibacy* (New York: Sheed and Ward, 1968).

72*Ad Eustochium*, 27, *PL*, 22, 412.

73These tales are included in the hagiographical collections made from the Jacobite (Egyptian) *Synaxarium* and other related material by DeLacy E. O'Leary, *The Saints of Egypt* (London and New York: Macmillan, 1937).

74*Dialogues*, 4, 13, *PL* 77.

75Citing Paul, *Galatians*, 3:28, Palladius, *The Lausiac History*, 132. Paul's dictum was expanded by Peter's companion, Clement of Rome, in his second letter, 12, 72, that when the kingdom of God should come, "the two shall be made one and the outside as the inside and the male with the female." For further material see H. Achelis, *Virgines subintroductae, ein Beitrage zu I. Korinth VIII* (Leipzig, 1902).

76Paulinus of Nola, *Epistola* 44, *PL* 61, 388.

77*Vie de Sainte Mélanie*, 201.

78*Passion of Perpetua and Felicity*, trans., St. W. Shewring (London: Sheed and Ward, 1931), p. 10.

79Augustine, *Sermo 282, PL* 38, 1285 and *Sermo 280, PL* 38, 1281.

Sexual Politics in the Writings of John Chrysostom

"...revolution is always heresy, perhaps sexual revolution most of all." [1]

ELIZABETH A. CLARK *

"HOWEVER muted its present appearance may be, sexual dominion obtains nevertheless as perhaps the most pervasive ideology of our culture and provides its most fundamental concept of power," wrote Kate Millett in *Sexual Politics*. [2] The "caste structure" of society, she claimed — and demonstrated through an examination of a wide variety of literary materials — is based more essentially on distinctions of sex than on those of "wealth or rank." [3] In its struggle to preserve this structure, patriarchy co-opted the Christian God and aligned Him with the immutabilities of "nature," [4] insofar as it decreed that "nature" had foreordained certain prescribed roles and functions for men and complementary ones for women. A student of the New Testament era might rightfully protest that radical potential for the upgrading of female status *had* been present in the primitive Christian message (one thinks immediately of Galatians 3:28); church teaching, nonetheless, rather quickly adjusted itself to the mores of the world and revolutionary changes in women's position were relegated to the eschaton, the afterlife — or to the machinations of the "heretics." [5]

From John Chrysostom, who successively served as deacon and priest in Antioch (381-397) and as bishop of Constantinople (397-407), we have numerous writings which illustrate the theory of "sexual politics" in the early Christian centuries. Chrysostom was an unmarried church father whose beliefs and practices in regard to women were somewhat at variance with each other. He, like Jerome, had a coterie of female

---

* Elizabeth A. Clark is Professor and Chairperson of the Department of Religion at Mary Washington College, Fredericksburg, Virginia.
[1] Kate Millett, *Sexual Politics* (Garden City, N.Y.: Doubleday & Co., 1970), p. 127.
[2] Millet, *Sexual Politics*, p. 25.
[3] Millet, *Sexual Politics*, p. 65.
[4] Millet, *Sexual Politics*, pp. 51, 58.
[5] The church fathers frequently attacked heretical and schismatic groups for their freer attitudes concerning women. See Hippolytus (*Philosophoumena* VIII, 12) and Epiphanius (*Panarion* XLVIII, 2). For a recent discussion of women's roles in early Christian orthodoxy and heterodoxy, see Wayne A. Meeks, "The Image of the Androgyne: Some Uses of a Symbol in Earliest Christianity," *History of Religions* 13 (1973-4): 165-208.

friends, most of whom had dedicated their lives to Christian celibacy; to them he penned dozens of admiring letters, encouraging their devotion to the Christian cause. But in his sermons and treatises, Chrysostom's attitudes toward women emerge as far more ambivalent. The biblical story of Eve's wayward behavior and the assignment of traditional roles to women in the Pastoral Epistles were used by him to enforce a female submissiveness and seclusion somewhat at odds with the picture presented in other parts of the New Testament of the expanded functions permitted women in the infant church. That he would employ theological rationalizations for his conservative views is one of the more interesting — and deadly — manifestations of the workings of "sexual politics."

"Power politics" provide the key to Chrysostom's understanding of all human relationships. His writings abound in images of authority and domination; repeatedly he alludes to the necessity of rulership and submission. It was impossible for Chrysostom to conceive of associations — here on earth, at least — in which equality and democracy might prevail. And the model for his understanding of authority is revealed in that prototypical human "government," the relation between man and woman. God established the male's dominance over the female at the time of the first human couple, Adam and Eve; hence, attempts to alter the civil or social status of women were contraventions of the laws of God and of "nature." But there was, he thought, one way in which female subjection could be partially overcome: through the woman's profession of celibacy, whether in virginity or widowhood. A nobility and freedom awaited women in the celibate life; there the disabilities hampering females in the present order might at least be mitigated and a foretaste of the angelic realms be sampled. And whom should we thank for introducing this new mode of existence? Not the philosophers, whose worthless speculations deserve only mockery; it was Jesus himself who taught us the Christian path of virginity, described by Chrysostom as a "state." He was fond of contrasting Christ's contribution to Plato's on this topic: the former, he asserted, did not idle away his earthly days merely *writing* about a "republic" (*politeia*); he *founded* one.[6] But those who wished to count themselves citizens of the Christian commonwealth must be ready to sacrifice much. Although Chrysostom did not require Christians to embrace virginity in order to enter the Kingdom, he strongly recommended they do so as an aid.[7] For those not willing to espouse the heroic life of abstinence, it was "patriarchy as usual." To

---

[6] Adv. Jud., 5, #3 (PG 48, 886). The section numbers listed for Chrysostom's treatises correspond to the divisions in Migne's *Patrologia Graeca* and are not always the same as those given in various French, English, and German translations.

[7] Virginity was given as a "counsel," not as a "law." De Virg. #9; #34; #41 (PG 48: 239, 557, 564-5).

characterize Chrysostom's position as a form of "sexual politics" is not, then, an anachronism. Rather, the phrase not only neatly sums up his affirmation of the imbalance of power which he saw existing between men and women; it acquires deeper significance when we consider the frequent use he made of the word *politeia* to designate the celibate state which he encouraged his flock to espouse.

I

In all aspects of human life, Chrysostom believed, there must be a ruler and a ruled; otherwise, anarchy would prevail. [8] In the individual's personal life, reason should dominate the senses and lusts of the body, just as a competent charioteer reins in his horses. [9] Inhabitants of a country are to obey their rulers; Chrysostom assured his congregation that Christ in no way intended his followers to "subvert the commonwealth" by stirring up "unnecessary and unprofitable wars." [10] Likewise, the family unit was pictured as a monarchy (*basileia*). Since "equality often produces strife," [11] there could be no peace in a household which attempted to operate on democratic principles (*dēmokratoumenē oikia*). [12] Within the tiny domestic state, the "king" should rule over his subjects, the wife, children, and slaves. [13] Chrysostom was fond of employing these images of dominance and submission to describe the relation of man and woman. Male and female are compared to ruler and subject, head and body (to use Paul's image), teacher and disciple, master and slave [14] — they are even like the strong-willed charioteer and his unruly horses! [15]

Despite Chrysostom's conviction that woman had been subjected to man's authority, he nonetheless wavered considerably when he pondered at what point woman had received her subordinate status. Was Eve inferior to Adam at creation (male dominance would then be "by nature") or was her subjection the penalty for luring Adam into sin? [16] At times,

[8] Hom. 23 Rom., #1 (PG 60, 615).
[9] Hom. 17 I Cor., #5 (PG 61, 144); Hom. 22 Gen., #3 (PG 53, 189). The image is borrowed from the *Phaedrus* 246A-248E.
[10] Hom. 23 Rom., #1 (PG 60, 615). Translation from NPNF, XI, 511.
[11] Hom. 34 I Cor., #3 (PG 61, 289-90).
[12] Hom. 20 Eph., #4 (PG 62, 141).
[13] Hom. 34 I Cor., #3 (PG 61, 289-90); De inani gloria, #23ff. The latter treatise is not contained in Migne's collection of Chrysostom texts.
[14] Slaves are better off than wives are; they at least have the hope of changing masters without death having to intervene, whereas wives do not. De lib. rep., #1 (PG 51, 219).
[15] Hom. 12 Col., #5 (PG 62, 388); Hom. 4 Rom., #1 (PG 60, 417); Hom. 17 Gen., #8 (PG 53, 145); Hom. 20 Eph., #1 and #2 (PG 62, 136-7).
[16] Sometimes Chrysostom espoused both positions at once, for example, in Hom. 9 I Tim., #1 (PG 62, 544): the man has preeminence *both* from his

Chrysostom affirmed the latter. If Eve had not fallen, she and her female descendants would not have been enslaved to the male. [17] Thus Chrysostom can depict God speaking to Eve, "I made you equal in honor to the man. I did not place any authority over you. Resign yourself to your subjection. You did not use your freedom wisely, so accept slavery." [18] This description of woman's position has several merits. First of all, it has biblical authority to support it: consider I Timothy 2:13-14. Moreover, it is in accord with Chrysostom's emphasis that we are personally liable for our actions and their consequences. Sin, he insisted, comes about by our own volition, not by "necessity" or by "nature"; we bear the responsibility for our decisions and their effects. [19] Thus, one might infer, if women are in a state of subjection to men, their unfortunate condition is the penalty for a misdeed on their part; they must have deserved the punitive measures directed against them. Both on biblical and moral grounds, Chrysostom might well have believed that woman's inferior status — far from being the one God intended for her — was the direct result of sin.

This interpretation of Eve's position, however, is not in keeping with one he puts forth elsewhere, which, I would argue, was more central to his thinking: that there was an *original* male preeminence over and

prior creation *and* because of woman's sin. Chrysostom's ambivalence on this point provides a perfect illustration of Rosemary Ruether's thesis that the "double definition of woman as submissive body in the order of nature and 'revolting' body in the disorder of sin, allows the Fathers to slide somewhat inconsistently from the second to the first and attribute woman's inferiority first to sin and then to nature." "Misogynism and Virginal Feminism in the Fathers of the Church," *Religion and Sexism: Images of Woman in the Jewish and Christian Traditions*, ed. R. R. Ruether (New York: Simon & Schuster, 1974), p. 157. For a discussion of the contradictory passages in Chrysostom's writings on this point, see Anatole Moulard, *Saint Jean Chrysostome: sa Vie, son Œuvre* (Paris: Procure Générale du Clergé, 1941), p. 175.

[17]   Serm. 5 Gen., #1 and #3 (PG 54: 599, 602); Hom. 26 I Cor., #2 (PG 61, 215); Hom. 9 I Tim., #1 (PG 62, 544); Hom. 17 Gen., #8 (PG 53, 144). Both George Tavard (*Woman in Christian Tradition* [Notre Dame: University of Notre Dame Press, 1973], p. 89) and Bernard Grillet ("Introduction générale," *Jean Chrysostome: La Virginité* [Paris: Les Éditions du Cerf, 1966], p. 59, n. 2) assume that this is Chrysostom's normative position.

[18]   Serm. 4 Gen., #1 (PG 54, 594).

[19]   Hom. 17 I Cor., #5 (PG 61, 144-6); Hom. 31 I Cor., #2 (PG 61, 258); Hom. 2 Eph., #3 (PG 62, 20); Hom. 33 Heb., #3 (PG 63, 228). For a discussion of Chrysostom's emphasis on "free choice," see, for example, Louis Meyer, "Liberté and Moralisme chrétien dans la Doctrine spirituelle de Saint Jean Chrysostome," *Recherches de Science Religieuse* 23 (1933): 284-5; Jean Dumortier, "Les Idées morales de Saint Jean Chrysostome," *Mélanges de Science Religieuse* 12 (1955): 30; Anne-Marie Malingrey, "Introduction," *Lettres à Olympias* (Paris: Éditions du Cerf, 1947), p. 61; C. Baur, "Das Ideal der christlichen Vollkommenheit nach dem hl. Joh. Chrysostomus," *Theologie und Glaube* 6 (1914): 569; V. J. Stiglmayr, "Zur Aszese des heiligen Chrysostomus," *Zeitschrift für Aszese und Mystik* 4 (1929): 38-9.

domination of the female. This quite different understanding emerges in several of the passages in which Chrysostom discusses Genesis 1 and 2. Surprisingly, we find that he scarcely commented on the production of Eve as it is described in the Genesis 1 story of the simultaneous creation of the sexes, which, had he so chosen, could have served as the basis for a theory of the equality of man and woman. When faced with the obvious difficulty that the female is mentioned along with the male in Genesis 1:27, Chrysostom explained that God was simply referring "ahead of time" to woman's creation, which would not actually take place until the events related in the next chapter; the eyes of the spirit, he piously asserted, are able to see things which do not yet exist. [20] (Chrysostom took Genesis 2 to be a continuation and elaboration of the first chapter's account.) Eve's debut, then, occurs only in the second creation story, which depicts her as being formed out of the male and for him; the man is, quite simply, "that for which everything was made." [21] And the mere "fact" of Adam's prior origin is understood to entail his "headship" and superiority. [22] By affirming that man's rule is "natural," Chrysostom also implied that the man would have been pre-eminent even if the Fall had *not* occurred. [23] In this version of Chrysostom's account, God's *original* intention was that man should be the "head" and woman the "body," a plan which was upset as early in human history as the Garden of Eden, when Eve, like rebellious women of later times, tried to take charge. [24]

The chief point at which Chrysostom's acceptance of traditional notions of primordial male superiority revealed itself most clearly, however, was in his interpretation of the "image of God" (Genesis 1:27). Chrysostom did not view the "image" primarily in terms of man's intelligence or rational faculties, as did many church fathers, but in his ability to exert power, to govern, to dominate, to wield authority. [25] Chrysostom generously allowed the woman to participate to a limited extent in the original "government"; Eve, like Adam, had dominion over the animals — which was the reason, Chrysostom quaintly noted, that she did not flee in fear when the serpent sidled up to her with his provocative questions. [26] But, of course, mere dominion over the animals was not the most important way in which man was to exert his governance; a fuller understanding of man's dominion involves his authority over human

[20]   Hom. 10 Gen., #4 (PG 53, 86).
[21]   Hom. 15 Gen., #3 (PG 53, 122).
[22]   Hom. 14 Gen., #4 (PG 53, 115); Hom. 9 I Tim., #1 (PG 62, 544).
[23]   Hom. 26 I Cor., #4 (PG 61, 218).
[24]   Hom. 17 Gen., #4 and #9 (PG 53: 139, 145).
[25]   Hom. 7 Stat., #2 (PG 49, 93); Serm. 2 Gen., #2 (PG 54, 589); Hom. 26 I Cor., #5 (PG 61, 218); Hom. 10 Gen., #4 (PG 53, 85); Serm. 3 Gen., #1 (PG 54, 591).
[26]   Serm. 3 Gen., #2 (PG 54, 592); Hom. 10 Gen., #4 (PG 53, 86).

beings as well — and the model for all later rulership was that of Adam over Eve. In other words, the "image of God" meant not just government and authority in general; it denoted the subjection of the woman to the man in particular. [27] It is the male who is truly in the "image" of God for Chrysostom, because he is not placed under anyone else here on earth, whereas woman, on the other hand, is submitted to him. Man is like God in this respect: as God rules the heavens and does not recognize a superior being, so man (and by "nature," not by "election") reigns over all earthly creation, [28] and has everything, including the woman, under his authority. [29] Now Chrysostom is quite willing to admit that male and female share the same "substance" (*ousia*); [30] after all, she was fashioned out of him. Likewise, they share a common human form (*morphē*) [31] and both of them are in the "likeness" (*homoiōsis*) of God in that both have the capacity for virtue, can imitate God's goodness. [32] But only the man has the "image" — because he was not "subjected" in the way the woman was — despite their mutual possession of the same *typos* and *charaktēr* and *homoiōsis*. [33] The notion of *power*, in other words, rests with the male alone, despite Chrysostom's half-hearted attempts to affirm an "equality of honor," [34] an ambivalent phrase which he freely admitted did not in any way indicate a genuine parity between them. Equality, as Chrysostom did not tire of saying, caused strife, and hence the woman was "reasonably" subjected to the man. [35]

Once Chrysostom had established the point that it was the man who was in the image of God, ruling over earth as God did over heaven, he could assert that male domination and female subjection were "natural." [36] ("But when I say Nature, I mean God. For He it is who created Nature.") [37] Male and female roles or "spheres of activity" are likewise considered to be "by nature" and to correspond with the diverse, God-given dispositions of male and female. [38] For men, there were public affairs to be managed; for women, the household. (Chrysostom willingly acknowledged that woman's service in the home was beneficial: it en-

---

[27] Hom. 26 I Cor., #5 (PG 61, 218); Serm. 2 Gen., #2 (PG 54, 589); Hom. 8 Gen., #4 (PG 53, 73).

[28] Hom. 7 Stat., #2 (PG 49, 93).

[29] Serm. 2 Gen., #2 (PG 54, 589).

[30] Hom. 15 Gen., #1 (PG 53, 120).

[31] Hom. 8 Gen., #4 (PG 53, 72-3). Here Chrysostom continues that despite the common "form," "the man has the authority and the woman ought to obey."

[32] Serm. 3 Gen., #1 (PG 54, 591).

[33] Serm. 2 Gen., #2 (PG 54, 589).

[34] Serm. 4 Gen., #1 (PG 54, 594).

[35] Hom. 26 I Cor., #2 (PG 61, 215); Quales ducendae, #4 (PG 51, 231).

[36] Hom. 10 Col., #1 (PG 62, 365); Hom. 26 I Cor., #3 (PG 61, 216); Hom. 7 Stat., #2 (PG 49, 93).

[37] Hom. 26 I Cor., #3 (PG 61, 216). Translation NPNF XII, 151.

[38] Hom. 5 Tit., #4 (PG 62, 694); Ep. 170 (PG 52, 709-10).

abled the man to participate in public life.) [39] Even customary types of clothing, such as woman's head covering, were held to be ordained "by nature." [40] Chrysostom's "sexual politics" begin to emerge more clearly: anything which tended to overthrow, rearrange, or even mitigate the power of the male over the female, particularly in marriage, was seen as rebellion against God and against "nature." [41]

In defense of Chrysostom, he thought that there was one point — although he himself admits, *only* one — at which males and females had genuine equality in the marriage relation: extramarital sexual experience was forbidden to the man as well as to the woman. Here their equality was complete. [42] Chrysostom noted that although Roman civil law concerned itself only with the wife's adultery, in the eyes of God, a man's straying was as reprehensible as a woman's; he would be punished by his Creator, if not by the state. [43] The standard for sexual conduct should be the same for both male and female, before marriage [44] as well as after. As D. S. Bailey has pointed out, this aspect of Christian sexual teaching was revolutionary. [45] But we must remember that Chrysostom, even more than Paul before him, thought of marriage as a bondage, not as freedom. [46] It appears to be only on the issue of the single standard of sexual fidelity that Christianity brought any advance to married women — aside, of course, from Christianity's injunctions about kindness in human relations generally. J.P.V.D. Baldsdon has noted that even before the end of the Republic, Roman women had achieved considerable

[39] De Anna 1, #3 and #4 (PG 54, 637-8); Hom. 10 II Tim., #3 (PG 62, 659); Quales ducendae, #4 (PG 51, 231); De non it. conj., #4 (PG 48, 615). Chrysostom hints that sex-role divisions would have existed even if the Fall had not occurred. De non it. conj., #4 (PG 48, 615) and Quales ducendae, #4 (PG 51, 231). Commentators reveal their traditional bias when they make such remarks as the following one by Donald Attwater, *St. John Chrysostom: The Voice of Gold* (Milwaukee: Bruce Publishing Co., 1939), p. 56: Chrysostom "knew nothing about 'feminism,' and any suggestion of identity of function between the sexes would have seemed to him as fantastic as in a well-ordered society it is."

[40] Hom. 26 I Cor., #5 (PG 61, 219).

[41] For Chrysostom's ideas on what constituted behavior "against nature" (including male homosexuality), see Hom. 4 Rom., #3 (PG 60, 419); Hom. 10 Col., #1 (PG 62, 366); Hom. 26 I Cor., #5 (PG 61, 219).

[42] Propter forn., #4 (PG 51, 214); Hom. 19 I Cor., #1 (PG 61, 152).

[43] Hom. 5 I Thess., #2 (PG 62, 425); Propter forn., #4 (PG 51, 214).

[44] De Anna 1, #6 (PG 54, 642-3); Hom. 59 Matt., #7 (PG 58, 582-3); Hom. 5 I Thess., #3 (PG 62, 426); De inani gloria, #53, #81, #82.

[45] Derrick Sherwin Bailey, *Sexual Relation in Christian Thought* (New York: Harper & Row, 1959), p. 11.

[46] Paul's ideas on this topic are discussed by Elaine Pagels, "Paul and Women: A Response to Recent Discussion," *Journal of the American Academy of Religion* 42 (1974): 542.

freedom, especially the freedom to divorce. [47] Although it has been elo-
quently argued that the family circle was the last battleground upon
which paganism and Christianity waged their warfare, [48] it is not evident
that Christianity of the patristic era really contributed much to the
emancipation of women. [49] For Chrysostom, true freedom lay elsewhere
(as we shall see), in the absence of any sexual connection whatsoever. [50]

II

Chrysostom provides us with numerous examples of what decent,
God-ordained behavior for women might be. For him, the married
woman's role revolved around the notion of service. Whereas he praised
the Old Testament men — even the married ones — for their sexual
abstinence and control, [51] the women held up as models for our admiration are those who waited upon their husbands or other men: Sarah, [52]
the widow who provided food for Elijah, [53] and Rebecca, who carried
water for Eliezer and his animals. [54] Domestic aid, however, was not of
much importance in the larger scheme of things, as Chrysostom revealed
in his comments on the story of Mary and Martha. Martha waited upon
Jesus, but Mary, whose action according to Chrysostom was of a more
spiritual sort, receives the higher praise. He even goes so far as to call
Mary a "disciple" (*mathētria*) of Jesus. [55] His discussion of this episode
indicates how low the female attendance to kitchen duties ranked in his

---

[47]   J. P. V. D. Balsdon, *Roman Women: Their History and Habits* (London:
Bodley Head, Ltd., 1962), pp. 14-15.

[48]   Jean Dumortier, "Le Mariage dans les Milieux chrétiens d'Antioche et de
Byzance d'après Saint Jean Chrysostome," *Lettres d'Humanité* 6 (1947): 162.

[49]   Ruether, "Misogynism and Virginal Feminism," p. 165.

[50]   It does not militate against Chrysostom's misogyny that he emphasized
the "sweet side" of woman's subjection. Serm. 4, Gen., #2 (PG 54, 595). His
patriarchal attitudes are clearly revealed in Hom. 20 Eph., #7-9 (PG 62: 145-8).
There Chrysostom depicts the bridegroom lecturing his new bride ("my child")
in a most condescending fashion. It is difficult to imagine a woman of *any* era
responding to this husband with the enthusiastic admiration of Chrysostom's
ideal bride: "What a philosopher this man is!" Nonetheless, commentators such
as Bruno Vandenberghe, "Saint Jean Chrysostome Pasteur des jeunes Époux,"
La Vie spirituelle 89 (1953): 47 think the scene delicately depicted and "charm-
ing."

[51]   For example, Hom. 24 Gen., #1 (PG 53, 207); Hom. 38 Gen., #2
(PG 53, 352); Hom. 24 Heb., #2 (PG 63, 168); Hom. de cont. (PG 56, 292).
Chrysostom's favorite Biblical model of chastity was Joseph, who fled from the
insidious designs of Potiphar's wife.

[52]   Hom. 41 Gen., #5 (PG 53, 381).

[53]   Hom. 42 Gen., #6 (PG 54, 393).

[54]   Hom. 48 Gen., #5 (PG 54, 441).

[55]   Hom. 65 Joa., #2 (PG 59, 362).

scale of values. In marriages of his own day, Chrysostom thought that the man as the "head" contributed spiritual qualities to the relationship, whereas the woman as the "body" could give only the material services appropriate to her station, [56] such as the sexual ones which kept her husband from frequenting prostitutes. [57] Whatever help or aid God had intended woman to provide for the man had been seriously curtailed, limited to things of the present life concerning the family, the calming of sexual desire, and other such items "of little importance." [58]

It was traditionally considered that one of the prime services a married woman rendered her husband was the providing of children. Chrysostom also discussed this female function. He admitted that "Paul's" words in I Timothy 2:14-15 (that women are saved in childbearing) raised some puzzling questions. Why should not a woman's salvation depend on her own personal virtue, rather than being mediated through her offspring? What are we to think about virgins or the barren or widows without children? — surely they are not to be excluded from the possibility of salvation. [59] (Chrysostom, as we might expect, thought that virgins and widows had the opportunity for a higher mode of life than did married women.) But apart from this dilemma, Chrysostom had difficulty with this text on childbirth for two other reasons.

First of all, he did not believe that the bearing of children had been the primary reason for the institution of marriage in the first place; rather, it was intended to tame concupiscence. [60] Only after death (the penalty for sin) entered the world did God allow Adam and Eve to reproduce in a sexual manner; children were a solace, a compensation for the immortality they had forfeited — a notion, Chrysostom believed, unworthy of Christians who now have the hope of resurrection. [61] If God had wished to increase the sinless human race in Paradise, He could have done so by *asexual* means, just as He multiplied the angels. [62] The bearing of children as we know it would never have taken place

---

[56] Hom. 5 II Thess., #5 (PG 62, 500).
[57] Hom. 5 II Thess., #5 (PG 62, 499); Hom. 59 Gen., #3 (PG 54, 518).
[58] De Virg., #46 (PG 48, 568). Women who rejected their humble roles of servitude — such as those who wished to teach or preach or order men about — are severely criticized by Chrysostom. See for example, Hom. 9 I Tim., #1 (PG 62, 545); De Sacerd. 3, #9 (PG 48, 646); De Virg., #53 (PG 48, 576); Hom. 49 Acta, #4 (PG 60, 344).
[59] Hom. 9 I Tim., #1 (PG 62, 545).
[60] Propter forn., #3 (PG 51, 213); Hom. 21 Gen., #4 (PG 53, 180); De Virg., #19 and #25 (PG 48: 547, 550).
[61] Hom. 20 Gen., #1 (PG 53, 167); Hom. 18 Gen., #4 (PG 53, 154); Propter forn., #3 (PG 51, 213).
[62] De Virg., #14 and #17 (PG 48: 544, 546); Hom. 15 Gen., #4 (PG 53, 123).

had Adam and Eve remained innocent. [63] No sexual relations would have occurred, no children would have been born through sexual union.

In addition, Chrysostom could not very genuinely affirm woman's "natural" role as childbearer in any case since he rejected the view that conception and birth are ever simply "natural" events resulting from sexual union. Children are gifts from God, who stirs up nature to produce an infant: such is the moral Chrysostom derived from the numerous Old Testament stories of women who had difficulty in conceiving. [64] Through these tales, God was preparing us to understand the mystery of Christ's virgin birth. If we can believe that a sterile and decrepit woman brought forth, we should find it credible that a virgin did. [65] Chrysostom's comments on these points — the secondary position of reproduction in the scheme of marriage and God's responsibility for the conception of children — place woman's role as childbearer in a rather dubious light. Her status here is fraught with ambivalence. If her services as allayer of male lust and as bearer of children were not part of her original role at creation, but rather were a result of sin, her value to the man in these respects appears somewhat negative.

III

From Chrysostom's point of view, then, God had ordained a certain hierarchy in sexual relations. While man was the glory of creation, woman was to serve, submit, and be silent. Our author was aware, however, that not all of the intellectual giants of the past agreed with that estimate. Plato in particular he singled out as his *bête noire*. In more than a half-dozen passages, Chrysostom took Plato to task for his proposals regarding women in Book 5 of the *Republic*: to imagine women being shared in common or performing traditionally "male" activities rendered human beings on a lower level than the animals. [66] Chrysostom labelled the *Republic* "ridiculous" and "a foe to modesty." [67] Several

---

[63]   De Virg., #14 (PG 48, 544). Anatole Moulard, *Saint Jean Chrysostome: Le Défenseur du Mariage et l'Apôtre de la Virginité* (Paris: Librairie Victor Lecoffre, 1923), p. 48 notes that Chrysostom, like other Greek church fathers, had an exaggerated "spiritual" vision of Eden. Chrysostom must have recognized that there was a difficulty (given his views on the production of children) with the prelapsarian positioning of God's command to "reproduce and multiply," for he interpreted it as a kind of "prophecy" of what would occur only after sin. De Virg., #15 (PG 48, 544). See Grillet, "Introduction générale," *La Virginité*, p. 57, n. 2.

[64]   Hom. 38 Gen., #2 (PG 53, 352); Hom. 50 Gen., #1 (PG 54, 448); Hom. 56 Gen., #3 and #4 (PG 54, 490-1); De Anna 1, #4 (PG 54, 638-9).

[65]   Hom. 49 Gen., #2 (PG 54, 445-6).

[66]   Hom. 4 Acta, #4 (PG 60, 48).

[67]   Hom. 1 Matt., #4 (PG 57, 18-19).

features of Plato's scheme, including physical education for women, received his special attention. The latter proposal Chrysostom found particularly alarming, since girls might exercise naked, exposed to the eyes of men.[68] Although Chrysostom himself frequently used athletic metaphor to describe the spiritual struggles of women — women are said to strip for the contests, descend to the arena for an exhibition of physical prowess, and so forth[69] — he clearly did not intend his words to be taken in a literal sense.

A second objectionable item in Plato's plan was that women would be given military instruction and ride out to battle carrying shields.[70] Chrysostom thought that women's participation in such ventures "unnatural," and linked it in his Fifth Homily on Titus, section 4 (PG 62, 694) with two other practices "against nature": male homosexuality (of which he thought Plato approved[71]) and infanticide. What sort of regulations for women could you expect, Chrysostom asked rhetorically, from a people who allow plays to be produced in which a mother murders her children? And in this same passage, Chrysostom suggested that Plato was catering to women's "lusts" (perhaps their desire for fame and glory?) by allowing them to go to war. Just as Chrysostom described women's spiritual contests through athletic metaphors, so he did through military ones. Women might join the army or put on armor in the combats of the religious life[72] — but not, of course, in the life of the world. Plato's sin, from his point of view, lay in imagining that women both could and should do the same work as men. Such arrangements, said Chrysostom, would serve only to turn everything upside down, throw everything into confusion[73] — a notion reminiscent of Tennyson's lines in *The Princess* (V. 437-441):

> Man for the field and woman for the hearth;
> Man for the sword and for the needle she;

[68] Hom. 1 Matt., #4 (PG 57, 19); Hom. 4 Actà, #4 (PG 60, 48).
[69] Hom. 13 Eph., #3 (PG 62, 98); Ep. 6, #1 (PG 52, 599); Hom. 1 Macc., #2 (PG 50, 619); De S. Droside, #3 (PG 50, 687). See John Sawhill, *The Use of Athletic Metaphors in the Biblical Homilies of St. John Chrysostom* (Princeton: Princeton University Press, 1928), for a complete discussion of the topic.
[70] Hom. 8 Matt., #6 (PG 57, 87).
[71] De S. Babyla, Contra Jul. et Gen., #9 (PG 50, 546). Chrysostom was also worried about pederasty in his own day, as is revealed in Adv. oppog. 3, #8 (PG 47, 360-1). See A. J. Festugière, *Antioch païenne et chrétienne: Libanius, Chrysostome et les Moines de Syrie* (Paris: Éditions E. de Boccard, 1959), pp. 188, 195, 197ff., and 208 for a discussion of the practice — and the literary references to it — in this period.
[72] In S. Barlaam, #4 (PG 50, 681); De SS. Bernice et Prosdoce, #6 (PG 50, 638).
[73] Hom. 4 Acta, #4 (PG 60, 48); Hom. 20 Eph., #1 (PG 62, 136).

> Man with the head, and woman with the heart;
> Man to command, and woman to obey;
> All else confusion.

Women could not or should not, wrote Chrysostom, wield the sword or throw the javelin, but they were entitled to grasp the spindle and weave cloth. [74] Diversity of activities was firmly based, in his opinion, on the supposed difference of male and female "natures."

Lastly, Chrysostom was horrified by Plato's suggestion for a community of women and communal childrearing practices. [75] He called them — as we can now predict — "contrary to nature." [76] That Chrysostom believed Plato was overturning God's law as well as the law of "nature" in this respect is seen in his enlistment of a biblical argument: God said to the first pair, "the *two* shall be one flesh" — not the many, he noted, but only "the *two*." [77] Moreover, Plato was ridiculed for not practicing what he preached regarding the community of women: his new arrangements for marriage did not cause such a disturbance as one might have expected, wrote Chrysostom sarcastically, since no legislator was interested in making his *politeia* an actuality. [78]

The point of Chrysostom's criticisms was not that communal living was evil; to the contrary, he saw many advantages in it, as he indicates by his favorable comments on the sharing of possessions which the book of Acts describes. [79] Rather, it was the position of women in Plato's commonwealth which disturbed him. The woman residing in that *politeia*, Chrysostom apparently feared, was not under the direction of a single man (we can almost hear him puzzling, how can one "body" have many "heads"?) and, worse yet, she was encouraged to develop skills which ran counter to the sex-role distinctions so dear to Chrysostom's heart. Although he advised the richer members of his congregation to give freely of their goods to the less fortunate, he certainly did not envision the sharing of that most personal piece of "property," one's wife. [80] Such behavior was, needless to say, "against nature." [81] For a man to approach another woman than his lawfully prescribed wife was "robbery," "taking

---

[74]   Quales ducendae, #4 (PG 51, 231).
[75]   Hom. 4 Acta, #4 (PG 60, 48); Hom. 2 Joa., #2 (PG 59, 31).
[76]   Hom. 1 Matt., #4 (PG 57, 19); Hom. 5 Tit., #4 (PG 62, 694).
[77]   Hom. 3 Tit., #4 (PG 62, 682).
[78]   Hom. 4 I Cor., #4 (PG 61, 36).
[79]   Hom. 11 Acta, #3 (PG 60, 97).
[80]   Chrysostom found nothing reprehensible about the patriarchs of Genesis lending out their wives or daughters; surely he would have found these acts immoral had they not been performed by biblical characters who were demonstrating their "hospitality" and "generosity." See Hom. 32 Gen., #4-6 (PG 53, 297-301); Hom. 45 Gen., #2 (PG 54, 415-6); Hom. 43 Gen., #4 (PG 54, 400-1).
[81]   Hom. 3 Tit., #4 (PG 62, 682).

more than belongs to us"; to have our woman swept away into a sexual relationship with another would be worse than having our riches plundered. [82] That a "shared" woman would be abhorrent to any man was also suggested by Chrysostom in his comments on the difficulties of remarriage: no one wants a spouse who has been under the authority of or "enjoyed" by another; he wants to be the first and only master (*kyrios*). [83]

The problem with the *Republic*, from Chrysostom's point of view, was that Plato imagined he could erase sexual differentiation in human society. This could not be accomplished in the world here and now, Chrysostom thought, but only in the life to come. Although we already know in the Spirit that the inequalities of the world have been removed (no "bond or free, Greek or barbarian or Scythian, unlearned or learned, male or female," and so forth), [84] "spiritual equality" in no way justified disturbing the status quo or traditional mores. Only in the heavenly realms would "no male and female" really apply. Until that time, "sexual politics" remain in effect.

IV

There were, however, two ways in which Chrysostom thought that Christian women had been able to attain a semblance of equality with men. Martyrdom was the first of the means by which the subjection of women was overturned and parity with males attained. To the female martyrs could be applied Paul's famous words of Galatians 3:28. [85] Although Chrysostom said that these women had lost the distinction of sex, what, apparently, he actually meant was that they had become "male," had acquired such characteristics as "manly spirit" (*andreia*). He gives numerous examples of these "masculine" women. [86] One of them, Domnine, who drowned with her daughters in a river, he even calls a "priest": she baptized her daughters and offered "the spiritual sacrifice" which the firmness of her will, if not the actual consecration to the priesthood, permitted her to do. [87] Such were the masculine prerogatives to which females martyrs might aspire.

---

[82] Hom. 5 I Thess., #2 (PG 62, 424). Engels might well have used this passage as a proof text for his thesis on the "ownership" of women in *The Origins of the Family, Private Property and the State.*

[83] De non it. conj., #5 (PG 48, 617).

[84] Hom. 10 Joa., #2 (PG 59, 75).

[85] In S. Ignat., #1 (PG 50, 587).

[86] De S. Pelagia 2 (PG 50, 585); De S. Droside, #3 (PG 50, 688); De Macc. 1, #3 (PG 50, 621); De SS. Bernice et Prosdoce, #4 (PG 50, 635).

[87] De SS. Bernice et Prosdoce, #6 (PG 50, 638-9).

Once the persecutions ceased in the early Fourth century, martyrdom likewise ended and was replaced with virginity as a means of showing one's extraordinary devotion to God. [88] Chrysostom was aware that martyrdom was no longer a possibility for Christians of his time, [89] but he assured his congregation that by leading ascetic lives, they could imitate those who had gone to their deaths for the faith. [90] Virginity, like martyrdom, gave females an opportunity to rise above what Chrysostom considered the usual limitations of their sex. Although he frequently used the word "virgin" symbolically, [91] I shall here limit my comments to those women who had actually undertaken the celibate life. The profession of the virginal state Chrysostom called a *politeia*, [92] a term which suggests that he might have had in mind Plato's *Republic* as a foil for his own views. He urged the monks who were living with female virgins not to desert the *politeia* they had undertaken (and not to drag their companions along with them in their defection). [93] Likewise, he noted that the virgins astonished the world by demonstrating that in a female nature there could be present an "angelic *politeia*." [94] The true republic of justice — and the change in women's status — was not to be found in Plato's commonwealth but in the Christian ascetic ideal. The exemplar of this life was Jesus, who, Chrysostom commented, although he did not write a book about *his* "state," nonetheless founded one. [95] Plato's *Republic* (in which, Chrysostom wittily remarked, a working man could starve to death before he ever found out what justice was) held a definite second place to the Christian *politeia* which led men to heaven. [96]

Virginity, in Chrysostom's view, offered to all Christians, women as well as men, the opportunity for a life of freedom, the distinguishing mark of the ascetic vocation. Marriage, on the other hand, entailed ser-

[88]   See Herbert Musurillo, "The Problem of Ascetical Fasting in the Greek Patristic Fathers," *Traditio* 12 (1956): 56-9, for a discussion of virginity's replacement of martyrdom in early Christianity. Chrysostom tells us (Hom. 66 Matt., #3, PG 58, 630) that the Antioch church had more than 3000 virgins and widows enrolled on its lists in his time.

[89]   In S. Barlaam, #1 (PG 50, 677).

[90]   In S. Barlaam, #4 (PG 50, 682).

[91]   Chrysostom does not consider the heretical virgins to be true "virgins." (De Virg., #1, PG 48, 533). For him, virginity must involve true faith and such virtues as almsgiving. Even harlots may be called "virgins in Christ" (Hom. de capto Eut., #6, PG 52, 402).

[92]   De Virg., #16 and #21 (PG 48: 545, 548). In the latter passage, the reference to the *politeia* of virginity is found in the context of an exhortation to turn from earthly things and contemplate the sun of righteousness — terminology laden with Platonic overtones.

[93]   Adv. eos, #11 (PG 47, 510-11).

[94]   Quod regulares, #7 (PG 47, 527).

[95]   Adv. Jud. 5, #3 (PG 48, 886).

[96]   Hom. 1 Matt., #5 (PG 57, 19-20).

vitude; he compared it to the situation of fugitive slaves whose legs are bound together with chains. [97] In detail he recounted the commonplaces of Graeco-Roman literature on the miseries which a man would find in marriage: [98] anxieties over wife, children, and slaves, problems with money and in-laws, the sickness and death of loved ones. Marriage, he was sure, was replete with fighting, suspicion, and jealousy. [99] As for the wife, she is exposed to her husband's whims and blows; if it is the "will of the tyrant," he may treat her like a slave. In an amazing departure from his usual male bias, Chrysostom exclaimed, "How many are the ways which men have devised to punish their wives!" [100] Even if the couple were dreadfully mismated, neither husband nor wife had the option of divorce. [101] Divorce was allowed in Old Testament times, Chrysostom conceded, but only because "Moses" feared the bloodshed which might result if a man had to keep a hateful woman in his house; different regulations are in effect since the coming of Christ. [102] And second marriage was an even worse slavery: on top of the woes present in the first, the couple had the problems of stepchildren and guilty or jealous feelings toward the former partner. [103] Anyone who would marry again must be suffering from amnesia regarding the conditions of married life! [104] Chrysostom recalled a traditional proverb to describe the situation of second marriage: "War is sweet to new soldiers" [105] — but not, he was sure, to the seasoned troops. And for the woman, the bondage of marriage must have been doubly severe, for she had a subordinate position to begin with. The difficulties of marriage could only have added to the burden of her womanly servitude.

A woman's escape route — if we may call it that — from the bondage of marriage lay in the profession of celibacy. There the virgin was raised above the curse of Genesis 3:16; she was relieved of the problems of childbearing and of subjection to a husband. [106] In addition, she attained

[97] De Virg., #41 (PG 48, 563).
[98] For Chrysostom's use of pagan *topoi* on the woes of marriage, see Grillet, "Introduction générale," *La Virginité*, p. 31, n. 2; p. 32, n. 1; pp. 36-8.
[99] Ad Theod. lapsum 2, #5 (PG 47, 314); De lib. rep., #4 (PG 51, 223); Explic. Ps. 44 (45), #12 (PG 55, 202); Hom. 81 Matt., #5 (PG 58, 758); Hom. 1 II Tim., #2 and #3 (PG 62, 604-5); De Virg., #37, #44, #46, #52-57 (PG 48: 558, 566-8, 574-9).
[100] De Virg., #40 (PG 48, 563).
[101] De Virg., #41 and #44 (PG 48: 563, 566); Hom. 62 Matt., #2 (PG 58, 597).
[102] De lib. rep., #2 (PG 51, 219-20); De Virg., #41 (PG 48, 563); Hom. 17 Matt., #4 (PG 57, 259).
[103] De non it. conj., #5 (PG 48, 617); De lib. rep., #3 (PG 51, 221).
[104] De non it. conj., #1 and #5 (PG 48: 609, 617).
[105] De non it. conj., #1 (PG 48: 609).
[106] De Virg., #65 (PG 48, 583); Quod regulares, #8 (PG 47, 530).

freedom from the cares and trials of the household. [107] Although virginity offered an easier and surer path to salvation than did marriage, [108] Chrysostom stressed that the rewards for maintaining that status were not just those to be found in the afterlife, but also the ones which could be experienced here and now. [109] The virgin found peace and tranquillity, a contrast to the turmoil of married life, [110] by which Chrysostom perhaps had in mind what he called the "furious frenzy" of sexual intercourse [111] as well as the daily domestic upsets. And the virgin should not be thought of as devoid of a spouse; she is "engaged" (or even "married") to the heavenly Bridegroom, Jesus, and can eagerly anticipate the consummation of her nuptials. [112] But even while she awaits her future bliss, she gains a benefit: freedom from the service required of a married woman. [113] The present advantages of virginity apparently would suffice to make it the preferable state, even if there were no afterlife.

And what elevated status Chrysostom accorded these virgins! In the worldly order, a woman could not hope to equal a man or assume "masculine" functions, but in the spiritual order she can and does. [114] The virgins (and widows) to and for whom Chrysostom wrote were praised for their "manly spirit" (*andreia*), for "playing the man" (*andrizō*). [115] And they had achieved this condition, he is proud to report, not by forcing themselves into the affairs of the world nor by trying to wield authority over men, as did the domineering types of women he so often ridiculed. Olympias, for example, Chrysostom's favorite female friend, provided a model in her discreet behavior; instead of "thrusting herself into the forum" and demanding public attention, she quietly sat in her chamber and waged her spiritual contests there. [116] Women could even surpass men in spiritual combats, since the latter do not depend on youth or strength of body, but only on the vigor of the soul and (amazingly enough) intelligence. [117] In fact, women could equal the an-

---

[107]   Explic. Ps. 44 (45), #12 (PG 55, 202).
[108]   Adv. oppog. 3, #14 (PG 47, 373-4); De Virg., #49 (PG 48, 573).
[109]   De Virg., #49 (PG 48, 573).
[110]   De Virg., #68 (PG 48, 584).
[111]   Hom. 37 I Cor., #6 (PG 61, 320); Adv. oppog. 2, #10 (PG 47, 346).
[112]   De Virg., #1 and #59 (PG 48: 533, 580); Hom. 8 I Tim., #3 (PG 62, 542); Hom. 28 Heb., #7 (PG 63, 201-2).
[113]   Quod regulares, #8 (PG 47, 530).
[114]   Ep. 170 (PG 52, 710); Interp. in Is., 8, #2 (PG 56, 92); Hom. 10 II Tim., #3 (PG 62, 659).
[115]   Ep. 94 (PG 52, 657-8); Ep. 6 (PG 52, 599); Ep. 96 (PG 52, 659); De Virg., #7 (PG 48, 538).
[116]   Ep. 6 (PG 52, 599).
[117]   Ep. 6 (PG 52, 601); Sal. Prisc. et Aq., 1, #3 (PG 51, 191); Hom. 13 Eph., #3 (PG 62, 98).

gels themselves. [118] Since angels, not having bodies, presumably were not plagued with pangs of lust, [119] the virgins, who still must fight bodily desires, perhaps deserve even more credit than the angels for their moral effort. Just as Chrysostom thought that virginity resembled life in Paradise before the Fall, [120] so he considered it an introduction to the angelic realms which we will experience in their fullness after death. [121]

Only in heaven will the virgins be freed from one of the main disabilities which remain with them here on earth: the prohibition against associating with those of the opposite sex. *Why* men and women could not mingle on a friendly basis at the present was somewhat of a mystery for Chrysostom. He was aware that different customs had prevailed in the early church. [122] Then, he said, the "angelic condition" existed in which men and women associated freely, exemplifying Paul's words, "no male and female." [123] Women in that era had much greater liberty than they currently did: they travelled in the service of the faith; [124] they prophesied; [125] they also were called "disciples" (*mathētriai*). [126] Chrysostom even thought the person named in Romans 16:7 was a woman, Junia, rather than a man, Junias, as the text is often translated. He noted that Paul had intended to rank her with the apostles, and remarked, "How great is the *philosophia* of this woman, that she is held to be worthy of the name of apostle." [127] But none of these privileges any longer applied. Chrysostom could suggest only the dissoluteness of present-day life — especially of the women — as a reason. [128] Apparently he did not think to question or blame the conservatism of post-biblical Christianity for the change in freedom allowed women.

In heaven, however, men and women will be friends without the disrupting influence of sexual desire. There our bodies will no longer be a burden to us, [129] femaleness (as well as maleness) will be eliminated, [130] and there will be no marriage. [131] Instead of the sexual inter-

---

[118] Serm. 5 Gen., #3 (PG 54, 602).
[119] De Virg., #10 and #11 (PG 48, 540).
[120] Hom. 68 Matt., #3 (PG 58, 643-4).
[121] De Virg., #11, #27, #29 (PG 48: 540, 551, 591-2).
[122] Chrysostom was also amazed at the freedom which young women had in Old Testament times. Such liberty would not have been possible in his own time, Chrysostom believed. Quales ducendae, #7 (PG 51, 236).
[123] Hom. 3 Acta, #1 (PG 60, 34).
[124] Hom. 31 Rom., #2 (PG 60, 669); Hom. 73 Matt., #4 (PG 58, 677).
[125] Hom. 25 I Cor., #1 (PG 61, 213); Hom. 5 Acta, #2 (PG 60, 52).
[126] Hom. 65 Joa., #2 (PG 59, 362); Hom. 72 Joa., #3 (PG 59, 392).
[127] Hom. 31 Rom., #2 (PG 60, 669-70).
[128] Hom. 73 Matt., #3 and #4 (PG 58, 677); Sal. Prisc. et Aq., 1, #3 (PG 51, 192).
[129] De Virg., #79 (PG 48, 592).
[130] Hom. 6 Col., #4 (PG 62, 342). There is no woman in heaven for the devil to deceive as the weaker one. "For there is no female nor male."
[131] Hom. 18 Gen., #4 (PG 53, 153).

course of our sinful world, there will be a union of souls. [132] "For when physical affections are destroyed and tyrannical desire extinguished," he wrote, "then no hindrance will any longer stand in the way of men and women being together, because all evil suspicion will be cleared away and all who have entered into the kingdom of heaven can lead the *politeia* of the angels and the spiritual powers." [133] Before that time, any attempt to disregard "sexual politics" (as did Plato in the *Republic*) was bound for disaster. The virgin could overcome some of the limitations of her female status here and now — chiefly by avoiding the servitude involved in the role of wife and mother — but sexual distinctions will not be rendered totally inoperative until the future life. No one should imagine that the eschaton had already come; for Chrysostom, our world still lay in bondage to the principalities and powers, however they might be construed.

The Conversion of Women to Ascetic Forms of Christianity

Ross S. Kraemer

Accounts of the conversion of women to ascetic forms of Christianity abound in a collection of texts known as the Apocryphal Acts of the Apostles. Extant in numerous languages, including Greek, Latin, Syriac, Coptic, and Arabic, these Acts often seem to be composite works containing diverse legends associated with the apostles of Jesus. Most scholars doubt that the apocryphal Acts reflect the actual histories of the apostles, or that they relate to the actual conversion experiences of historical women or men: Paul of Tarsus may never have converted Thecla of Iconium; nor Andrew, Maximilla of Patrae; nor Thomas, Mygdonia of India. Nonetheless, these Acts are important sources of information about the postapostolic churches in which they circulated. Analogously, the conversion accounts, in my view, illuminate a significant aspect of women's religion in the Greco-Roman world, namely, the appeal of Christian asceticism, which was particularly strong in the eastern provinces of the Roman Empire.[1]

1. The rise of asceticism in early Christianity apparently dates from the earliest communities (see the so-called undoubted epistles of Paul), but the degree to which it prevailed, either in theory or in practice, varied from community to community, from region to region, and from time to time. On asceticism in the eastern provinces of the Roman Empire, see S. P. Brock, "Early Syrian Asceticism," *Numen* 20 (April 1973): 1–19, and Arthur Voobus, *A History of Asceticism in the Syrian Orient*, Corpus Scriptorum Christianorum Orientalium Subsidia 14 (1958). Asceticism also features prominently in many Gnostic Christian writings, and many, if not most, of the apocryphal Acts of the Apostles are considered to have Gnostic or related provenances.

[*Signs: Journal of Women in Culture and Society* 1980, vol. 6, no. 2]

The problematic nature of these texts, however, makes the endeavor to examine the appeal of ascetic Christianity to women admittedly and consciously speculative. Like much of early Christian literature, both the conversion legends and the collections in which they occur are pseudonymous or anonymous. We do not know whether these legends had their origins in oral or written form, who first circulated them, or who first incorporated them into the various and composite Acts of the Apostles. Frequently, fragments and whole works are lumped under the name Acts of such-and-such-an-apostle, although the relationship between these disparate parts remains unclear. This is especially true of the Acts of Andrew and of John, in contrast to the legends of Thomas which are more tightly woven into single literary entities. Many sections of the Acts appear to have circulated independently at one time or another, such as the Acts of Thecla, which are now embedded within the larger Acts of Paul, and which are usually referred to as the Acts of Paul and Thecla. The story of Paul and Thecla was clearly known to the North African Christian apologist Tertullian by about 200 C.E.,[2] but the dates of the other legends are more difficult to determine. The various apocryphal Acts are attributed by most scholars to the late second and/or early third centuries, whereas the individual legends may date from considerably earlier. Further, since the apocryphal Acts themselves consist of discrete elements thought by many scholars to antedate the composition of the Acts by later author-editors, important questions remain about the audience and the function of both the discrete legends and the various composite Acts. In the absence of explicit dedications and declarations, we may hypothesize that the legends initially arose in Christian circles and functioned both to reinforce the beliefs of the Christian community and to serve as conversion propaganda. Probably, the Acts were intended primarily for Christian audiences, and secondarily as conversion literature for interested non-Christians. In either case, Christians would have viewed such stories as confirmation of their own faith, whether they heard them recounted or read them. Because of the enigmatic nature of these texts,[3] my primary concern is to illuminate the dynamic of conversion depicted in these legends, on the explicitly stated assumption that they accurately describe the patterns of ancient conversions if not the conversions of specific historical persons.

2. Tertullian *De Baptismo* 17.
3. For a more thorough discussion of this complex literature, see the introductions in E. Hennecke, *New Testament Apocrypha,* ed. W. Schneemelcher, 2 vols. (Philadelphia: Westminster Press, 1965) (hereafter cited as Hennecke-Schneemelcher). The majority of Acts may be found in the Greek collection *Acta Apostolorum Apocrypha,* ed. M. Bonnet and R. A. Lipsius (Darmstadt: Wissenschaftliche Buchgesellschaft, 1959). Syriac texts with English translations may be found in W. Wright, *The Apocryphal Acts of the Apostles* (London: William & Margate, 1871). English translations of the Greek texts, with lengthy introductions, may be found in Hennecke-Schneemelcher. See also M. R. James, *Apocryphal New Testament* (Oxford: Clarendon Press, 1924).

All of these conversion stories follow a similar literary pattern. Each relates the conversion of a woman whose husband, fiancé, lord, or father is of relatively high social status in a community which an apostle has recently entered. Persuaded by the apostle's teachings to accept Jesus, the woman adopts a sexually continent way of life, which is the principal feature of her conversion. If already married, she withdraws from her husband; if unmarried, she vows to remain a virgin. A ritual induction of the woman into the Christian community often takes place, although this does not always follow the conversion immediately. Thecla, for instance, baptizes herself a considerable time after she converts to Christian asceticism, and this is also true of Tertia in the Acts of Thomas.[4] The practice of continence does not seem to depend upon formal ritual induction, which thus cannot be considered an integral element of the legend.

The principal male in the woman's life invariably opposes her new-found asceticism,[5] and frequently threatens the woman, the apostle, or both. Such threats are never successful: the woman continues her association with the apostle and her practice of chastity. As a result, both apostle and woman are imprisoned, scourged, or otherwise punished. Frequently, as in the martyrdons of Thomas, Andrew, and Peter, the angered husband is the direct cause of the apostle's death; only rarely does the husband convert.[6] The woman does not denounce asceticism in any of the accounts;[7] rather, she lives chastely outside her husband's home, and in some cases, such as those of Thecla and Charitine, she even joins a band of wandering Christian apostles. Maximilla in the Acts of Andrew continues to live a celibate life within her husband's household, despite his vigorous protestations. Drusiana in the Acts of John, however, lives chastely and harmoniously with her husband, Andronicus, an instance of the "virgin marriage" apparently practiced by some early Christians. But most of the women in these conversion legends do not enter into such chaste partnerships, since chastity is desired only by one partner. Spouses who do convert to an ascetic form of Christianity naturally acquiesce to the chaste marriage, as does, for example, the couple in the wedding episode and Prince Vaisan and his wife in the Acts of Thomas.[8]

4. See the Acts of Paul and Thecla 34; Acts of Thomas 137, 157.
5. Only Charitine's father, in the Acts of Philip, converts with her (Acts of Philip 44).
6. See, e.g., Andronicus in the Acts of John 63, and Misdaeus in the Acts of Thomas 170.
7. However, the tale of Artimilla in the Acts of Paul (Hamburg Papyrus, p. 3) hints at such a possibility when Paul, having baptized Artimilla, sends her back to her husband Hieronymus.
8. See the Acts of Thomas (8–16, 150). How widespread was the custom of "virgin marriage" in early Christian communities is not clear. Two passages in Paul's first letter to the church at Corinth have been interpreted as evidence for very early Christian chaste marriages; 1 Cor. 7:29 advocates that "from now on, let those who have wives live as

In the apocryphal Acts, Christianity is essentially defined as the acceptance of an ascetic way of life. In the Acts of Thomas the basic assumptions of ascetic Christianity and the specific aspects of secular life to be renounced are forcefully articulated:

> Look upon us Lord, since for your sake we have left our homes and our father's goods, and . . . have gladly and willingly become strangers. . . . we have left our own possessions for your sake, that we may obtain you, the possession that cannot be taken away . . . we have left those who belong to us by race, that we may be united with your kindred. . . . we have left our fathers and mothers, and fosterers, that we may behold your Father and be satisfied with his divine nourishment . . . for your sake we have left our bodily consorts and our earthly fruits, that we may share in that abiding and true fellowship and bring forth true fruits.[9]

Similar attitudes are reflected in the beatitudes attributed to Paul in the Acts of Paul: "Blessed are they who have kept the flesh pure, for they shall become a temple of God. Blessed are the continent, for to them will God speak. Blessed are they who have renounced this world, for they shall be well pleasing unto God. Blessed are they who have wives as if they had them not, for they shall inherit God. . . . Blessed are the bodies of the virgins, for they shall be well pleasing to God, and shall not lose the reward of their purity."[10]

The Christianity of the apocryphal Acts demands of its adherents both chastity and severance from family. This had substantial implications, especially for women. Ascetic Christianity, in fact, offered women a new measure of worth which involved a rejection of their traditional sociosexual roles.[11] As do most societies, the larger Greco-

---

though they had none." But it is unclear whether this passage means living together in an asexual relationship, or abandoning the familial household altogether. An enigmatic passage over which there has been much debate, 1 Cor. 7:38, is translated in the Revised Standard Version as "he who marries his betrothed does well, and he who refrains from marriage does better." More important, perhaps, there are significant differences between circumstances of the early churches which Paul addressed and those of the second and third centuries with which this paper is primarily concerned. I agree with Walter Schmithals's judgment that first-century Christian asceticism is rooted in a pragmatic response to the imminent demise of the present world which only later develops into asceticism for the sake of asceticism. Most scholars are in accord that the early evidence for such "virgin marriages" is insubstantial, while the later evidence is more convincing. For an introduction to this debate, see Hans Lietzmann, *An die Korinther, Handbuch zum Neuen Testament 9* (with revisions by W. G. Kümmel) (Tübingen: J. C. B. Mohr, 1949); Hans Conzelmann, *1 Corinthians: A Commentary on the First Epistle to the Corinthians,* trans. James W. Leitch (Philadelphia: Fortress Press, 1975); and Walter Schmithals, *Gnosticism in Corinth,* trans. John E. Steely (Nashville, Tenn.: Abingdon Press, 1971).

    9. Acts of Thomas 61 (translation adapted from Hennecke-Schneemelcher).

    10. Acts of Paul 5–6 (translation from Hennecke-Schneemelcher).

    11. The notion I will pursue in the following pages relies to some extent on a

Roman communities in which ascetic women lived clearly propounded different measures of worth for women than for men. While men were valued by and large for their public achievements in varying realms— hunting or military prowess, financial success, intellectual capability, etc.—women were to derive their worth from the ascribed roles of wife, mother, and household mistress.[12] The texts of the apocryphal Acts provide evidence that women in the Greco-Roman communities from which ascetic Christianity drew its members were defined in terms of traditional sociosexual roles and their relationship to men. In the Acts of Thecla, for instance, the heroine is sentenced to burn to death because she will not marry Thamyris, her fiancé, and because she will not be a bride, not because she has listened to the words of a sorcerer. Paul, on the other hand, is only scourged and exiled.[13] Indeed, Theocleia, Thecla's mother, cries out at her trial, "Burn the lawless one! Burn her that is no bride in the midst of the theatre, that all women who have been taught by this man may be afraid."[14] Thus, to be a woman is to be a wife; she who refuses has committed sacrilege—she is *anomos*.

The predominant definition of women as sexual beings in the conversion legends may also be found in two episodes from the Acts of Peter. In the first,[15] Peter explains that his daughter, who at age ten strongly tempted Ptolemaeus, became paralyzed through a miracle and

---

deprivation-compensation theory of religion. While such a model has many contemporary advocates and critics, they are often particularly anathema to scholars who study antiquity, especially religion in general and Christianity in particular. Criticism of the application of social science theories and models derived from the twentieth-century research to study of early Christianity usually focuses on the internal inconsistencies of deprivation theory, but it often disguises hidden theological agenda. Since deprivation theory may be interpreted to mean that religions express no external ultimate truth because they function to alleviate certain social conditions, scholars with theological interests have an a priori stake in its refutation. In my view, however, a model which sheds light on data should be considered, and data which reveal the inaccuracy of a model should prompt reconsideration, refinement, or rejection of the theory. For excellent discussions and examples of the fruitfulness of such applications, see John G. Gager, *Kingdom and Community: The Social World of Early Christianity* (Englewood Cliffs, N.J.: Prentice-Hall, Inc., 1975), and Gerd Theissen, *Sociology of Earliest Palestinian Christianity*, trans. John Bowden (Philadelphia: Fortress Press, 1978).

12. There is a substantial literature on the roles and status of women in Greco-Roman antiquity. See J. Leipoldt, *Die Frau in der antiken Welt und im Urchrisentum* (Gutersloh: G. Mohn, 1962); Maurice Bardèche, *Histoire des femmes* (Paris: Stock, 1968); Vern Bullough, *The Subordinate Sex: A History of Attitudes toward Women* (Urbana: University of Illinois Press, 1973); Sarah B. Pomeroy, *Goddesses, Wives, Whores and Slaves: Women in Classical Antiquity* (New York: Schocken Books, 1975). For additional references and reviews, see Marilyn B. Arthur, "Review Essay: Classics," *Signs: Journal of Women in Culture and Society* 2, no. 2 (1976): 382–403.

13. Acts of Paul and Thecla 20, 21. Schneemelcher, in Hennecke-Schneemelcher (2:332), attributes this disparity to the fact that the emphasis of the story is Thecla, not Paul, but this seems to me to miss the whole point.

14. Acts of Paul and Thecla 20, translation from Hennecke-Schneemelcher.

15. From a Coptic fragment attributed to a larger Acts of Peter. See Hennecke-Schneemelcher, 2:300–302.

thus ceased to be attractive. Peter argues that it is better for her to be a cripple than to be the subject of further temptation. In the episode entitled "The Gardener's Daughter," an old man asks Peter to pray for his virgin daughter, whereupon she drops dead. The next comments: "O reward worthy and everpleasing to God, to escape the shamelessness of the flesh and to break the pride of the blood."[16] The distressed old man beseeches Peter to resurrect her, which he does, whereupon she is seduced and disappears. The alternatives available to women are here defined as sexuality or death, with death clearly preferable to sexuality. The two stories suggest that these limited alternatives are accepted by both Christians and non-Christians, but that Christian asceticism has reversed the values normally attached to these alternatives.

Even within the ascetic Christian framework of the Acts, the definition of woman in terms of men and marriage persists. In the opening sections of the Acts of Thomas, for example, when Thomas prevents a newlywed couple from consummating their marriage and converts them instead to a spiritual union, the bride speaks of receiving marriage with "the true man," whereas the bridegroom interprets his conversion as receiving knowledge.[17] Indeed, virtually all of the conversion stories contain a motif of erotic substitution. In the Acts of Thecla, the heroine seeks Paul out at every opportunity, but the erotic nature of her attraction is particularly evident in the narration of their encounter in prison: Thecla is discovered with the apostle late at night in his cell, "bound with him, so to speak, in affection."[18] In the Acts of Thomas, Mygdonia explicitly states her preference for Jesus/Thomas to her husband Charisius: "He whom I love is better than you." To which Charisius replies: "Look upon me, for I am [far better and more handsome—Syriac] than that sorcerer . . . you are my family and kinship, and behold he is taking you away from me."[19] Likewise, in the Acts of Paul, Hieronymus is distressed by the rumors that his wife has left him for Paul; and in the Acts of Philip, Nicanora's husband says categorically: "It is better for you to be destroyed by the sword than for me to see you fornicating with such strangers and sorcerers."[20] The repeated presence of the motif of erotic substitution derives in part from the theme of divine marriage. In the Acts of Thomas, for example, Mygdonia says to Charisius: "You are a bridegroom who passes away and is destroyed, but Jesus is a true bridegroom, abiding immortal forever. . . ."[21] However, this erotic motif also suggests that when women are represented as re-

---

16. Pseudo-Titus *De Dispositione Sanctimonii* 83 ff. (in Hennecke-Schneemelcher, 2:298–99).

17. Acts of Thomas 14, 15.

18. Acts of Paul and Thecla 18–19.

19. Acts of Thomas 116, 117; translation adopted from Hennecke-Schneemelcher.

20. The Hamburg Papyrus fragment of the Acts of Paul, p. 4; Acts of Philip 120.

21. Acts of Thomas 4 ff., esp. 6–7, 124 (translation adapted from Hennecke-Schneemelcher).

jecting their traditional sexual roles in the legends of ascetic Christianity, they are nonetheless still defined in terms of men, namely, the male divinity and his agent, the male apostle.[22]

Since the Acts provide ample evidence that women in the Greco-Roman communities in which ascetic Christianity flourished were defined primarily in terms of traditional roles, we may now investigate the appeal of ascetic Christian theology for its female adherents, while recognizing that these texts do not permit us to reconstruct the psychological states of individual women. Here the insights of contemporary anthropological studies of women's religious activities may enable us to grasp the significance of the specific characteristics attributed to women converts. I. M. Lewis, for example, suggested in *Ecstatic Religion* that among Sar and Bori cults in Africa and the Caribbean, women are particularly vulnerable to peripheral spirit possession when their status is in a state of flux—pubescent girls, women on the verge of marriage, newly married women, women whose polygamous husbands are about to take on a new wife, divorced women, and widows. By that token, very young girls and married women raising children and running households are less disposed toward such cultic activities.[23] A high proportion of the Christian women in the Apocryphal conversion legends fall into Lewis's categories. Thecla is a virgin about to be married, Mygdonia in the Acts of Thomas and Xanthippe in the acts which bear her name are newly married women who have no children, and Drusiana in the Acts of John has been married for an indeterminate amount of time and has no children.[24] Only Maximilla in the Acts of Andrew may possibly have borne children during her marriage to Aegeates.[25] Moreover, a number of women in the conversion legends are of inferior sociosexual status. Agrippina, Nicaria, Euphemia, and Doris in the Acts of Peter are all the concubines of Agrippa, and Trophima in the Acts of Andrew is an ex-concubine.[26] It is not surprising that these marginal women who had

22. The erotic triangle also figures prominently in the Greco-Roman romances, a literary form to which the acts are closely related. For various treatments of Greco-Roman romance literature, see Martin Braun, *History and Romance in Greco-Oriental Literature* (Oxford: Basil Blackwell, 1938); T. R. Glover, *Life and Letters in the Fourth Century* (Cambridge: Cambridge University Press, 1901): E. H. Haight, *Essays on the Greek Romances* (New York: Longmans, Green & Co., 1943) and *More Essays on Greek Romances* (New York: Longmans, Green & Co., 1945); B. E. Perry, *The Ancient Romances: A Literary-historical Account of Their Origins,* Sather Classical Lectures 37 (Berkeley: University of California Press, 1967).

23. I. M. Lewis, *Ecstatic Religion* (Harmondsworth, Middlesex: Penguin Books, 1971), pp. 66–69, 191.

24. Acts of Paul and Thecla 7–8; Acts of Thomas 100; Acts of Xanthippe 6. The tale of Drusiana, continent wife of a now-consenting husband, Andronicus, relates the attempt of one Callimachus to fulfill his sexual desire for her, even to the point of raping her entombed corpse. The tale (Acts of John 62–86) makes no mention of any children of the marriage of Andronicus and Drusiana.

25. Acts of Andrew (Vaticanus Gr. 808 4).

26. Vercelli Acts of Peter 33; the Latin *Liber de Miraculos Beati Andreae Apostoli,* compiled by Gregory of Tours in the twelfth century.

no way of gaining prestige in the established social hierarchy would be attracted to cultic activities which offered validating mechanisms and a new measure of worth.

Whether their status is marginal or transitional, all the women in these conversion legends reject traditional female sociosexual roles by rejecting their husbands or fiancés, often leaving their homes and towns and becoming members of the wandering Christian band, if not explicitly teachers themselves.[27] Often, role rejection is expressed as role reversal. Mygdonia, the convert of Thomas, cuts short her hair, as does Thecla, the disciple of Paul.[28] Thecla also dons male clothing when she sets out to follow Paul, as does Charitine in the Acts of Philip.[29]

That the conversion of women to ascetic Christianity constituted a break with the traditional expectations of women is also evident in the sanctions which are taken against them and the labels which are applied to them by their antagonists. The motif of women's madness, for example, occurs to a significant extent in the conversion stories. Thecla's mother several times describes her as mad, or possessed,[30] and in the Acts of Thomas, Charisius emphasizes the insanity of Mygdonia's actions. "Noble lady as she is, whom none of her house ever charged [with impropriety—Syriac] she has fled naked from her chamber and run outside, and I know not where she has gone. And perhaps, maddened by that sorcerer, she has in her frenzy gone to the market-place in search of him. For indeed, nothing seems loveable to her but that man and the things said by him."[31] Later, Mygdonia's friend, Tertia, also suspects her of being mad: "why do you do the deeds of madmen?" she asks.[32] After Mygdonia has won Tertia over to Christianity, both women are described as being possessed. This designation of insanity expresses a judgment, but, as I have emphasized elsewhere, it also serves as a form of social control. Women who defy traditional expectations are ostracized through the label of insanity.[33]

The tale of Trophima in the Acts of Andrew, compiled by Gregory of Tours in the twelfth century, illustrates more clearly the sanctions

27. For example, Acts of Paul and Thecla 23, 26, 40; Acts of John 105.

28. Acts of Thomas 114; Acts of Paul and Thecla 25.

29. Acts of Philip 44; Acts of Paul and Thecla 25.

30. Acts of Paul and Thecla 8–9.

31. Acts of Thomas 99. The element of madness is played down in the Syriac.

32. Acts of Thomas 135. The Syriac text claims that Mygdonia was "like a madwoman because of Judas [Thomas]" (114).

33. For provocative discussions of the social functions of the label of insanity, see Phyllis Chesler, *Women and Madness* (Garden City, N.Y.: Doubleday & Co., 1972); Thomas Szasz, *The Manufacture of Madness* (New York: Harper & Row, 1970); and Thomas Scheff, *Being Mentally Ill: A Sociological Theory* (Chicago: Aldine Publishing Co., 1966). For a study of the function of women's ritual madness in ancient Greece, see R. Kraemer, "Ecstasy and Possession: The Attraction of Women to the Cult of Dionysus," *Harvard Theological Review* 72 (1979): 55–80. See also R. Kraemer, "Ecstasy and Possession: Women of Ancient Greece and the Cult of Dionysus," in *Unspoken Worlds: Women and Religion in Cross-cultural Perspectives*, ed. R. Gross and N. Falk (New York: Harper & Row, 1980), pp. 53–69.

taken against women who reject their traditional roles. For her refusal to have marital relations with her husband, Trophima is suspected of infidelity[34] and condemned to prostitution. Although she escapes through divine intervention, the fact remains that the woman who renounces acceptable forms of sexual behavior in favor of celibacy is doomed to the most degrading form of the very sociosexual identity she has rejected—prostitution. Against such vehement opposition, the language of the ascetic forms of Christianity must have provided a strong set of validating mechanisms, particularly for women. Indeed, the justification of sexual purity preached by the apostle in the Acts of Thomas constitutes a promise of the ultimate rewards for rejecting women's traditional sexual function: "Know this, that if you abandon this filthy intercourse . . . you will not be girt about with cares for life and for children, the end of which is destruction. . . . But if you obey and keep your souls pure unto God, you shall have living children whom these hurts do not touch, and shall be without care, leading an undisturbed life without grief or anxiety, waiting to receive that incorruptible and true marriage, as befitting for you."[35] The notion that women who refrain from bearing children will be rewarded with the gift of divine children[36] contains a deeper message: women who do not fulfill their traditional sociosexual roles can find in ascetic Christianity a new standard of worth by which they are superior to all other sexually bound women.

The conversion stories of the Apocryphal Acts of the Apostles reveal elements of the attraction which ascetic Christianity may have held for certain women in the Greco-Roman world—either women who found the traditional roles of wife and mother inadequate measures of their worth, or women who could not participate in the rewards guaranteed by adherence to those standards—socially marginal women, widows, or barren women. Although the Acts of the Apostles are replete with the conversion accounts of men, the renunciation of sexuality and sociosexual roles, as we have seen, had far greater implications for women than it did for men. Religious systems which legitimize the rejection of the established sociosexual standards, as did ascetic Christianity,

34. This is true of most of the converted women, although the lover is usually believed to be an apostle; in Trophima's case it is her former lover, the now Christian, chaste Lesbius.

35. Acts of Thomas 12.

36. A similar motif appears in the description of the women of a mixed-sex monastic Jewish community outside Alexandria, Egypt, in the first century c.e., called the Therapeutae by Philo Judaeus (*On the Contemplative Life*). Since Philo is the only source for this group, some scholars have suggested that he invented the group as an example of the perfect life; the current scholarly consensus is against this view. For a more detailed discussion of the women of Therapeutae, see R. Kraemer, "Ecstatics and Ascetics: Studies in the Functions of Religious Activities for Women in the Greco-Roman World" (Ph.D. diss., Princeton University, 1976), pp. 203–19.

are likely to attract large numbers of discontented and marginal women and to propound standards of worth and redemption more consonant with their circumstances.

Office of the President
Stockton State College

Misogynism and Virginal Feminism in the Fathers of the Church

ROSEMARY RADFORD RUETHER

The usual image of the Fathers of the Church, especially among those promoting women's liberation, is that of fanatical ascetics and woman haters. Hatred of sex and hatred of women are identified.[1] But this view tends to ignore the high praise of women, in their new role as "virgins," in patristic theology. It also fails to explain the rise of that veneration of Mary that is characteristic of patristic thought in the fourth century A.D. In this chapter I wish to show that this ambivalence between misogynism and the praise of the virginal woman is not accidental. One view is not more "characteristic" than the other. Both stand together as two sides of a dualistic psychology that was the basis of the patristic doctrine of man.

The rise of an alienated experience of bodily reality in late antiquity is one of the puzzles of the history of consciousness which would bear much more study from a worldwide comparative-religions perspective. Contemporary Christians, embarrassed by classical Christian asceticism, are wont to stress the naturalism of the Old Testament and to condemn body-soul dualism as Hellenistic and unbiblical. This procedure fits in with the Protestant quest for an original point of unblemished integrity in the Bible which

150

marks all unpalatable Christian doctrines as due to some later accretion of unbiblical views, usually seen as derived from "Hellenism."[2]

But this thesis is misleading as a historical account of the development of that dualism in antiquity that became the cultural mould within which Christianity was formed. The fact is that every religion in antiquity—Babylonian, Canaanite, Persian, Greek and Jewish—passed from a naturalistic to an otherworldly religious hope in the period from approximately the sixth to the second centuries B.C. Egyptian religion made this transition even earlier, as it changed from the life-affirming religion of the early Kingdom to the death-centered religion of the imperial New Kingdom.[3] Greek religion was transformed from the Apollonian celebration of the body of the Hellenic world to a Platonic flight from the body, after the *polis* lost its freedom and was absorbed into the empire of Alexander the Great. Judaism also was changed from a naturalistic religion of this-worldly hope to one of apocalyptic despair as it lost its national autonomy and passed under the yoke of the Persian, Greek and Roman empires. After the fall of Jerusalem, in 70 A.D., apocalypticism changed into an esoteric subculture of Jewish gnosticism and mysticism.[4] Even the ancient cults of the Earth Mother, with her rain-and-vegetation consort, such as Baalism and its counterparts in the worship of Astarte, Magna Mater and Isis, moved from naturalistic celebrations of the renewal of bodily fecundity to eschatological religions of the salvation of the soul after death. Christianity, born in Jewish apocalypticism and nurtured in the world of Hellenistic syncretism, drew together all the streams of religious consciousness from antiquity, Greek, Jewish and Oriental, but precisely in their *alienated, anticosmic stage of development!*[5]

This alienated experience of reality was expressed in a dualistic doctrine of being. This created a conflict between the biblical view of the goodness of physical creation (derived from the world-affirming religion of earlier Judaism) and the alienated, world-fleeing view of redemption which expressed a pessimism about the world and its possibilities of the later imperial period. This latent conflict in the foundations of Christianity was brought out in the open in the clash between the mainstream Church and left-wing Gnostics in the second century A.D. Gnosticism tried to reconcile the doctrines of creation and redemption by reading an otherworldly doctrine of redemption back into a fallen doctrine of creation. The Gnostics believed that the world was created through an error by an evil Demiurge, while man's original and final home was an otherworldly, spiritual realm far removed from this evil material world. Christianity rejected this solution. Instead it affirmed a unity between the Father of Jesus Christ and the Creator God of the Old Testament and a continuity between Israel and the Church. This unity between creation and redemption was expressed in the appearance of a "cosmological Christology," in which the Christ of the world-to-come was identified with the Word of God, through whom the physical world was made.[6] Yet this affirmation of the unity of the Christ of the end with the Creator of the beginning did not substantially modify Christianity's commitment to an otherworldly, spiritualist view of redemption. So the two doctrines remained (and still remain) in conflict, each modifying the other in strange and incompletely defined ways.

Origen (the Greek theologian of the early third century A.D.) tried to reconcile the two by spiritualizing creation. First there was a heavenly spiritual creation, and then a material creation appeared as a result of the fall of the souls. It was this first creation that was man's true home, to which he returned through redemption.[7] But the Church condemned this view as too much like gnosticism. Nevertheless the orthodox Greek theologians of the fourth century A.D. followed a modified Origenism that saw the original creation and humanity as spiritual and unitary, in contrast to a secondary, more grossly bodily, bisexual form. It was this spiritual creation that was their cosmogonic point of reference for redemption. Origen developed the Pauline doctrine of the "spiritual body" of the resurrection to suggest an original creation that was a "nonbodily sort of body," in which the substance of man was absorbed into his soul in a way that made this original creation "spiritual." In this way he modified the conflict between the Jewish bodily creation and the Greek spiritualist redemption. This allowed Christianity to claim the Jewish doctrine of the resurrection of the body, but with a Platonic spirituality. Second-century Western thinkers, such as Justin, Tertullian and Irenaeus, affirmed more vigorously the original physical creation. But this lent itself to a sensual millenarianism that was offensive to the Eastern tradition.[8] The later Church Fathers compromised by affirming an original bodily creation that wasn't quite sensual and the resurrection of a body that wasn't quite bodily but had been transformed into a "spiritual body." But even this modification of both creation and redemption could only obscure, but could not resolve the contradiction. Despite its body-affirming doctrine of creation, both Greek and Latin Christianity remained committed to a Platonized spirituality and eschatology that defined redemption as the rejection of the body and the flight of the soul from material, sensual nature. The patristic view of woman fell between the two stools of this ambivalence about the goodness of the body and sexuality.

A comparison of the doctrine of creation of the fourth century A.D. Greek Church Father, Gregory of Nyssa, with that of the great Latin Father, Augustine, will illustrate the similarity, but also the difference of emphasis, that remained between the two traditions. The crucial biblical text for the creation of man was Genesis 1:27: "God created man in His own image; in the image of God he created him; male and female He created them." If the Fathers could have had the first part of the text without the final phrase, they would have been happier. Indeed, they often quote only the first part of this text without alluding to the second[9] About the character of the image of God in man they had no doubts. This referred to man's soul or reason. The Hellenistic Jew Philo had already established this interpretation by the first century A.D.[10] The problem came with reconciling this spiritual interpretation of the image of God with the subsequent reference to bisexuality, which they saw as a bodily characteristic. Since God was wholly spiritual and noncorporeal, this appeared to mix contraries and imply either a sexed spirituality or a bodily God. Since it was anathema to think of God as bodily, with male and female characteristics, the two parts of the text must be separated so that the "image" could be defined in a monistic, spiritual way, and bisexuality could refer to something other than the nature of God as reflected in man.

For Greek thought it was axiomatic that spiritual reality was unitary (*monistic*, from which the words "monk" and "monastic" derive). Duality appears only with matter. So God cannot be dual, nor can man's spiritual image be bisexual. This does not mean an "androgynous" view of God and the original humanity, as some recent commentators have thought. The guiding view of the Fathers was not an androgyny that preserved bisexuality on a psychic level, but rather that monism which, alone, is appropriate to spirit.[11] This could be stated by identifying maleness with monism, making femaleness secondary, or else by a nonsexual monism, but not by a true androgyny. Gregory Nyssa chose the latter course, and Augustine the former.

For Gregory Nyssa the image of God is purely spiritual. It reflects the unitary, spiritual nature of the Divine Word, which is, in turn, the image of the transcendent Father. The reference to bisexuality in the second part of the verse does not refer to the image of God in man at all, but to that bodily nature, foreign to God, that was added to man with a view to the Fall.[12] But that spiritual, or "angelic," nature, to which man is restored in redemption, does not preserve this bisexuality, but, like Christ, resurrected man is "neither male nor female" (Gal. 3:28). Thus creation and redemption are coordinated in the monism of the soul, which mirrors its divine Archetype. The virgin or monk (*monos*) is the soul redeemed from the duality of bodiliness to return to that monism of the heavenly world. Thus Nyssa must modify the bisexual character of bodily creation by making it subsequent to an original monistic spiritual creation.

> "In the image of God he created him." There was an end of the creation of that which was made "in the image." Then it makes a resumption of the account of creation, and says "male and female created He them." I presume that everyone knows that this is a departure from the Archetype, for "in Christ," as the apostle says, "there is neither male nor female."[13]

Nyssa takes it for granted that the "image" must be monistic, and bisexuality must refer to something else, namely, to man's bodily nature, which is not made in God's image, but appears only with a view to the fall of soul into carnality, sin and death. Man is a compound of the divine incorporeal nature, to which his soul corresponds, and the irrational, material nature of brutes, toward which his body tends. The two parts of the text refer to this dual nature of man. But only the first part belongs to the divine "image," whereas the second half refers to man's bodily nature, which does not correspond to the divine Archetype.

Nyssa then tries to qualify this identification of the soul with the divine nature and relate it to the dualism of the body, lest he be accused of gnosticism. The nature of the soul is only "like," not identical, with that of God. It is separated from the uncreated divine nature as the mutable from the Immutable. If man, through his spiritual nature, had adhered to the immutable nature of God, through the Divine Word in whose image his soul was made, he would have been immortal. His physical substance would have remained absorbed into his spiritual being in a way that would have rendered him "changeless." But man has a second principle of mutability that reflects his created status. This does not derive from God, but from that "nothingness" from which the world was made. Nyssa does not want to accept the gnostic view of a primordial evil "matter," but he sublimates this idea by taking it back a step farther and calling it "mutability" rather than matter. Matter, created by God, is good, but it has a negative possibility, derived from that nothingness that God overcame in creating the world which expresses itself in "mutability"—that is, a tendency to fall away from being back into nothingness. If man had been obedient to God, his body would have been held by the divine immutability and would have remained undying. But when man turned from God to that mixed reality of the body that tends toward nothingness, his material principle becomes mutable and mortal. It is with a view to this fall into mortality that God created man's bisexuality, so that when man had fallen from immutability to mutability and had become subject to death, he would have a remedy for this in procreation.[14]

Nyssa is not quite sure whether there would have been any marriage in Paradise. Perhaps the original Adam, remaining unfallen, would have been the sole expression of a unitary humanity. Nyssa suggests that there might have been some angelic way of procreating that would have created a multiplicity of souls, just as there is a multiplicity of angels, but without bisexuality or marriage. Origen had solved this problem earlier by making the original spiritual humanity a multiplicity of single souls in the community of the pleroma. Thus, for Nyssa, man's image is spiritual and monistic. Bisexuality pertains to that lower nature which both drags man down to sin and death and provides a remedy in procreation, but redemption is return to the monistic nature of the angels.

In Augustine this same story is told with a somewhat different emphasis, which makes bisexuality more intrinsic to creation, but in a way that makes the "image" itself more androcentric. In other words, Augustine assimilates maleness into monism, and this makes femaleness rather than bisexuality the image of the lower, corporeal nature. For Augustine, man as the image of God was summed up in Adam, the unitary ancestor of humanity. But Adam is compound, containing both male spirit and female corporeality. When Eve is taken from Adam's side, she symbolizes this corporeal side of man, taken from him in order to be his helpmeet. But she is a helpmeet solely for the corporeal task of procreation, for which alone she is indispensable.[15] For any spiritual task another male would be more suitable than a female as a helpmeet.

Inexplicably, Augustine must also affirm that Eve, too, has a rational nature, being likewise a compound of spirit and body. Yet in relation to man she stands for body *vis-à-vis* male spirit.[16] Moreover, Augustine persists in calling this latter her "nature," not only with a view to sin but in the order of nature as well. Augustine defines the male as, alone, the full image of God. Woman, by herself, is not this image, but only when taken together with the male, who is her "head." Augustine justifies this view by fusing the Genesis text with I Corinthians 11:3–12.

> How then did the apostle tell us that the man is the image of God and therefore he is forbidden to cover his head, but that the woman is not so, and therefore she is commanded to cover hers? Unless forsooth according to that which I have said already, when I was treating of the nature of the human mind, that the woman, together with her own husband, is the image of God, so that the whole substance may be one image, but when she is referred to separately in her quality as a helpmeet, which regards the woman alone, then she is not the image of God, but, as regards the man alone, he is the image of God as fully and completely as when the woman too is joined with him in one.[17]

This assimilation of male-female dualism into soul-body dualism in patristic theology conditions basically the definition of woman, both in terms of her subordination to the male in the order of nature and her "carnality" in the disorder of sin. The result of this assimilation is that woman is not really seen as a self-sufficient, whole person with equal honor, as the image of God in her own right, but is seen, ethically, as dangerous to the male. Augustine works this out explicitly, but patristic theology makes use of the same assumptions of woman's subordination to man in the order of nature, and her special "carnality" in the disorder of sin, which imply the same attitudes, however unjustified by the contrary assumption of the equivalence of male and female in the original creation. This definition of femaleness as body decrees a natural subordination of female to male, *as flesh must be subject to spirit in the right ordering of nature.*[18] It also makes her peculiarly the symbol of the Fall and sin, since sin is defined as the disordering of the original justice wherein the bodily principle revolts against its ruling spirit and draws the reason down to its lower dictates.

This double definition of woman, as submissive body in the order of nature and "revolting" body in the disorder of sin, allows the Fathers to slide somewhat inconsistently from the second to the first and attribute woman's inferiority first to sin and then to nature. In Augustine the stress falls decidedly on the side of woman's natural inferiority as body in relation to mind in the right ordering of nature, and thus he is somewhat temperate in his polemics against Eve as the original cause of the Fall. For him, the Fall could only occur, not when the body tempts, but when the male ruling principle agrees to "go along." This, however, does not imply a milder view of sin, only a more contemptuous view of Eve's capacity to cause the Fall "by herself."[19] In other Fathers, such as Tertullian, Eve is made to sound as though she bore the primary responsibility. Tertullian demands an abasement of woman and the covering of her shameful female nature as the consequence of her continuing imaging of this guilty nature of Eve.

> *You* are the Devil's gateway. *You* are the unsealer of that forbidden tree. *You* are the first deserter of the divine Law. *You* are she who persuaded him whom the Devil was not valiant enough to attack. *You* destroyed so easily God's image man. On account of *your* desert, that is death, even the Son of God had to die.[20]

Even the mild Clement of Alexandria, who defends more generously than some of the other Fathers, the spiritual equivalence of woman with man and the dignity of marriage as a relationship, speaks of woman as having to blush for shame "when you think of what nature you are."[21]

This assimilation of woman into bodiliness allows Augustine to explain why woman's subjugation is "natural" within the order of creation, but it makes for some contradiction when it comes time to defend woman's redeemability and her ability, like that of the man, to become "virgin" and return to the monistic incorporeal nature. This conflict does not appear in Nyssa in the same way, because he makes bisexuality, rather than femaleness, the symbol of corporeality, and thus makes woman and man equivalent, both in their spiritual natures and in their sexed bodily natures. But, then, the Greeks had the corresponding conflict of an inexplicable use of language which suggested that woman was subordinate to man in nature and peculiarly identified with "carnality"—a language to which they, too, were addicted.

Augustine attempts to explain this contradiction by distinguishing between what woman is, as a rational spirit (in which she is equivalent to the male), and what she "symbolizes" in her bodily nature, where she stands for the subjection of body to spirit in nature and that debasing carnality that draws the male mind down from its heavenly heights. But he thinks that what she thus symbolizes, in the eye of male perception, is also what she "is" in her female nature! It never occurs to him that defining woman as something other than what she is, and placing her in subjugation in the order of nature *from the perspective of the male visual impression of her as a "body"* is nothing else than an expression, in the male himself, of that disorder of sin, and thus, in no way a stance for the definition of woman's nature! For Augustine, however, this androcentric perspective is never questioned, but presupposed. Yet he, too, must admit that woman has "another" possibility beyond this androcentrically conceived bodiliness. She, too, has a rational nature and can be saved by overcoming the body and living according to the spirit. Augustine cannot deny this since he, along with all the Church Fathers, believes that woman can become "virgin" and live the monistic, angelic life.

There is a parallel tradition in the Church Fathers, however, according to which the doctrine of Eve's role in sin is interpreted as a possibility of her liberation from sexual oppression and male domination under the gospel. This view assumed the equivalence of male and female in creation and interprets woman's subordination as the effects of sin, whereby Eve was cursed to bear children in sorrow and to be under the power of her husband (Gen. 3:16). Virginity, then, is interpreted as the resurrected life of the gospel whereby woman is freed from this twofold curse on Eve of the sorrows of childbearing and male domination. Thus, for example, Cyprian, the great African doctor, says to the virgin: "You do not fear the sorrows of woman or their groans. You have no fear of the birth of children. Nor is your husband your master, but your Master and Head is Christ, in the likeness and in the place of man."[22] This sentiment is voiced by many other ascetic writers, yet, contradictorily, they also speak of this liberation as freeing woman from those "natural" inferiorities of bodily weakness and pettiness, maliciousness and sensuality of mind which are typically feminine, whereas all the virtues that are associated with salvation —chastity, patience, wisdom, temperance, fortitude and justice— are distinctively masculine.[23] Thus Leander of Seville speaks of virginity as freeing woman from the sexual oppression and male domination of the curse of Eve, yet nevertheless speaks of all the weak traits of mind and body, which are contrary to salvation, as feminine *by nature*. The virgin, by contrast, "forgetful of her natural feminine weakness, she lives in manly vigor and has used virtue to give strength to her weak sex, nor has she become a slave to her body, which, by natural law, should have been subservient to a man."[24]

By thus slipping back from what is the consequence of sin to what is natural, and attributing the effects of sin to woman's "nature," the Church Fathers can simultaneously laud virginity as a liberation from sin, and yet, where women are concerned, prevent that from in any way being interpreted as a liberation for a boldness, integrity, or independence unfitting the "nature of a woman." This evidently came up as a very real pastoral problem in the fourth century, when many women were taking literally the Church's ascetic preaching as a mandate for woman's liberation. Thus, for example, we find Augustine writing to a certain self-willed African matron, Ecducia, who had exacted a vow of continence from her husband and had begun to act with that liberty to dispose of her person and property autonomously befitting one whom the converted life had restored to equivalency with the male! Augustine begins the letter by defining the essential subjugation of woman to man as natural law, and decreeing that the woman has no right to dispose of her own body without male permission: "It is a sin to refuse the debt of your body to your husband." Since her husband had once consented, Augustine gives permission for her to continue in the life of continence, but reproves her severely for acting with independence in the disposal of her property and her personal conduct of life, which is incompatible with the nature of a woman, who does not have her own "head" but belongs to her husband, who is her "head."[25]

This slippage between woman's nature as a consequence of sin and the characterizing of these lower traits of mind and body as feminine by nature caused a confusion in patristic thought over the sexual character of the risen body. If woman was essentially body and had sensual and depraved characteristics of mind, then it followed (according to a dualistic view of redemption) that either she was irredeemable or else she was redeemed only by transcending the female nature and being transformed into a male. This is in sharp contrast to the male ascetics, where virginity is seen as restoring men to all those natural traits of nobility of mind and transcendence to the body that are masculine *by nature*. Since it was normal to speak of the virgin who lived the "angelic life" as having transcended her female nature and having become "male" (*vir*),[26] this led to a belief that in the Resurrection there would be only male bodies, all females having been changed into males. Both Augustine and Jerome must inconsistently deny this conclusion, insisting that humanity will rise as "male and female," but in some incomprehensible way that will spiritualize the body so that it is no longer sensual or feels any libido linking the sexes with each other (i.e., having become monistic). And there will be a transformation of the female bodily characteristics so that they are no longer suited to intercourse and childbearing, but are fitted now "to glory rather than to shame."[27]

What all this is supposed to mean is anyone's guess, but it points up clearly the dilemma of patristic anthropology. The Fathers wish to affirm a doctrine of redemption that coheres with the original bisexual creation that God had declared "very good." But since *they* have declared this to be "very bad," and see redemption as the rejection of body, bisexual relations and female "nature," they can only affirm this continuity by peculiarly mutilating these characteristics in their view of both creation and redemption. That woman has a rational mind equivalent to man's is never entirely denied, and indeed is assumed by the view that allows her to lead the monastic life. But since she is somehow made peculiarly the symbol of "body" in relation to the male (i.e., in a male visual perspective), and is associated with all the sensual and depraved characteristics of mind through this peculiar "corporeality," her salvation must be seen not as an affirmation of her nature but a negation of her nature, both physically and mentally, and a transformation into a possibility beyond her natural capacities.

The redeemed woman becomes "unnatural" and "virile" in a way contrary to nature. Such a view not only forces upon the female ascetic a doubled self-subjection of her body and personality but also the duty of that abasement of her "visual image," so that she will in no way appear in the body as a woman before the eyes of the male. It is from this obsession with blotting out the female bodily image that we find that peculiar involvement in the Fathers with questions of female dress, adornment and physical appearance. The woman must be stripped of all adornment. She must wear unshapely dress and a veil that conceals her face and limbs. Finally, she must virtually destroy her physical appearance so that she becomes unsightly.[28] This induces a literal schizophrenia in the relation of the male to the woman; he is exhorted to love her as redeemable "soul," but in a way that totally despises her in all her bodily functions as a woman and identifies all depraved psychic characteristics with femininity. Thus, in Augustine's words:

> A good Christian is found in one and the same woman to love the creature of God whom he desires to be transformed and renewed, but to hate in her the corruptible and mortal conjugal connection, sexual intercourse and all that pertains to her as a wife.[29]

Augustine goes on to compare the relation of the Christian husband to his wife as comparable to the mandate to "love our enemies."

In contrast to Nyssa, Augustine defended the bisexual character of the original creation, defining woman as the original material principle in relation to spirit. What was lacking in original creation was not bisexuality but sexual libido—that is, instead of making the original creation nonsexual, he makes it nonsensual. This view leads to Augustine's belief that in Paradise man would have "used" woman in a completely "unfeeling" way, just as he moves his hand or his foot dispassionately and in a way that is totally under control of the rational will. Specifically, the male would have been innocent of that "hideous" erection of his sexual organ and that rush of sensual feeling that defies rational control in his response to the visual image of woman. With the same rationality and dispassion that a farmer sows his seed in the furrow of a field, the man would have sowed his seed in the woman.[30] Procreation, indeed, is the only purpose for the existence of a female as distinct from a male body. In Augustine's view, then, rightly ordered sex is properly such as to be depersonalized, unfeeling and totally instrumental. It relates to the female solely as a body to be used for procreation—that is, literally a "baby-making machine." When, however, man loses this original justice and succumbs to the body, then sinful carnality, signifying the revolt of the bodily against the intellectual principle, enters in. Then man loses control of his own bodily members and finds his sexual organ responding with an irrational "will of its own" to the female bodily presence, the *sole purpose of which is sensual pleasure*. Thus in the sinful relation woman is likewise totally depersonalized, but now in a masturbatory rather than in an instrumental way. At no time, for Augustine, do bodily relations appear as a vehicle for personal relationships.

Augustine believes that the seat of this disordered affection due to sin is the male penis, whose spontaneous tumescence, in response to sensual stimuli and independent of consciousness, is the literal embodiment of that "law in the members that wars against the law of the minds."[31] Augustine's horrified description of the male erection and its key role in his doctrine of sin and the transmission of original sin usually brings embarrassed laughter from historians of doctrine, if they have the temerity to refer to this view in explicit terms at all. It is usually supposed to reflect some personal sexual hang-up of Augustine's resulting from obsessions caused by his illicit sexual experiences, and thus not to reflect on these doctrines themselves.[32] A personal obsession it may well have been, but one that reflected a collective obsession of Augustine's religious culture. Such a pointing to the erection of the penis as the essence of sin was a bit graphic, but nevertheless a perfectly consistent expression of that view of man and redemption that we have been discussing. Thus there is no way to criticize this particular conclusion in Augustine's thought without finally entering into a fundamental reconstruction of this entire system of theological anthropology of which it was an expression.

But if the male erection was the essence of sin, woman, as its source, became peculiarly the cause, object and extension of it. This, as we have noted, results in an essentially depersonalized view of the relationship to woman. She becomes literally an extension of the male body, to be used either in a masturbatory way for "carnal pleasure," or, in a right ordering of the male body in relation to its "head," in an instrumental way as a mechanism under male control for impregnation and incubation of the fetus. In neither case does she appear as a true "other" or "thou" to which the male relates as a person. Such a depersonalization of woman must be seen as a necessary consequence of the assimilation of the male-female relationship into the soul-body relationship, which implies a subject-object relationship between man and woman. The soul-body or subject-object relationship between the self and the "other," as visually perceived object, essentially abolishes the "other" as a "thou" or a person to be related to with a mutuality due to the meeting of person with person in and through the body. The very soul-body dualism of the Fathers blotted out the possibility of such a personal relationship through the body, and made the relationship of man to woman essentially a subject-object relationship, in which the woman as "sex object" was to be either wrongly abused for carnal pleasure or "rightly used" in a dispassionate and objective (even clinical!) way as a material means or "machine" for the achievement of a further objective, that is, the building up of the implanted male seed into a child.

This depersonalized view of sexual relations gives three basic images of the possibilities of woman in the Church Fathers: woman as whore, woman as wife, and woman as virgin. As whore, woman is wholly the image of that "revolting carnality" that entices the rational mind down from its heavenly seat to "wallow" in the flesh. Here woman is depicted as the painted strumpet, strutting forth with all her natural and artificial allures, the very incarnation of that "fleshly" principle in revolt against its "head" which subverts all right ordering between mind and sense. As wife, woman is also essentially body, but now the image of that totally submissive body, obedient to her "head," which serves the male without a murmur even under harsh and unjust treatment. Such a woman has no personal rights over her own body, but must surrender her body to her husband on command, receiving from such use no personal pleasure, but allowing herself to be used solely as an instrument of procreation.[33] This definition of the wife allowed Augustine even to rationalize patriarchal polygamy, since this was done out of no lust on the part of the biblical worthies, nor did their wives derive any sensual gratification therefrom, but they gave themselves to this excessive "marrying and giving in marriage" only in obedience to God's accelerated command to "increase and multiply" in order to make up that whole of the people of Israel from whom Christ was to be born.[34] But under the dispensation of the Resurrection there is now a third possibility for woman—as virgin. Here alone woman rises to spirituality, personhood and equality with the male, but only at the expense of crushing out of her being all vestiges of her bodily and her female "nature."

However, since man no longer exists in Paradise, where a right ordering of spirit to body in marriage is possible, totally sinless procreation is no longer available. Here again we see the dominance of an antibodily view of redemption over a bodily view of creation in the Fathers. The converted life is not interpreted as giving a new possibility of integrity within marriage or "Christian marriage," but rather it is seen simply as rejection of body. To marry at all is seen as choosing the lower course, not really living in the resurrected order, and hence being under that dispensation of sin which makes sexual relations intrinsically debasing to the mind. Marriage, then, is seen as intrinsically inferior to virginity. It is not debased entirely, since it has the honor due to its instrumental purpose of procreation. But the sex act is only forgiven and not redeemed thereby, and so marriage is seen as bringing forth only the thirtyfold of virtue, in contrast to the sixtyfold of widowhood

and the one hundredfold of virginity.[35] Only continence corresponds authentically to the redeemed life. Many would allow no
second marriage, while those who allow it see it justified only as a
remedy for concupiscence, bringing forth no virtue at all.[36] The
married, moreover, are exhorted to be totally continent except
when about the intentional work of procreation, and even better,
to abjure procreation for a vow of total continence.[37]

The marital act is seen as intrinsically debasing to a woman,
and she is consoled for her loss of "integrity" only by dedicating
her daughters to virginity and thus regaining in them what she has
lost in herself.[38] If she must sink to the lowest position short of
outright evil and become a "mere wife," she is exhorted to be
totally meek and to submit herself, mind and body, totally to her
husband, who is her "head" and has complete proprietary rights
over her body, even to the point of physical abuse or death. The
husband is exhorted, of course, to love his wife, but to love her
"as he would his own body." But this is because it demeans his
own dignity as the "head" to do otherwise, and not because the
wife has an intrinsic dignity as a person or rights over her own
body.[39] Such a theory of the married woman in Christianity not
only did not lift up the position of woman beyond what it had
been in antiquity but even fell below those legal rights to personal
and economic autonomy which the married woman had been
winning in late antique society. Thus the frequent claim that
Christianity elevated the position of woman must be denied. It
actually lowered the position of woman compared to more enlightened legislation in later Roman society as far as the *married
woman* was concerned, and elevated woman only in her new "unnatural" and antifemale role as "virgin."

However, even the total submissiveness of the wife in the
marital relationship does not succeed in restoring the marital act
to that sinless instrumentality of Paradise, according to Augustine.
In the disorder of the bodily nature due to the Fall, however much
the couple intends to perform the act in a totally dispassionate and
instrumental way, the disorder of the bodily members inevitably
produces an involuntary "side-effect" of "filthy" carnal pleasure.
This is forgiven in the couple themselves if it is totally involuntary,
unintentional and despised, their only conscious intent being procreation.[40] However, this cannot remedy the fact that the act, al-

though good in its intent and end, is now inherently sinful in its means. This results in a corruption of its object as well, in the form of a child who is born "tainted" by original sin.[41] Moreover, if the couple intends to enjoy carnal pleasure as well, although not impeding procreation, the act becomes venially sinful, although forgiven under that secondary apostolic concession as a remedy for illicit fornication—namely, because "it is better to marry than to burn." But the Fathers endlessly stress the fact that this "remedy for concupiscence" is only a concession to weakness, and never a good in itself. As Jerome, with his strict logic would put it, "If it is good not to touch a woman, then it is bad to touch a woman" always and in every case.[42] Finally, if the couple intends only carnal pleasure and impedes procreation (and this would include all methods making use of the natural infertility of the woman's body during menstruation, pregnancy, lactation or menopause), then the act is wholly sinful and equivalent to fornication.[43]

Sex is thereby conceived of as narrowly as possible, as either impersonally instrumental or carnally masturbatory, with no role left for the expression of a personal love relationship as a legitimate purpose of sex. Of Augustine's oft-quoted three purposes of marriage—procreation, remedy for concupiscence and "symbol of unity"[44]—only the third falls within a possible definition as a personal relationship. Recent Catholic authors have tried to build such a view out of this "third purpose" of marriage, but Augustine himself never developed this idea of "symbol" as meaning that the sex relationship had as a legitimate purpose the expression of personal love. Rather, the idea remained vague and underdeveloped in his thought as an abstract symbol of the unity between God and the soul, or Christ and the Church. This lack of any development of the sex relationship as a personal love relationship, then, committed patristic thought to a puritan-prurient ambivalence toward sex as either "dirty" or objectively instrumental. Woman in both cases is "used" as a sexual object, not loved through the body as a person.

This same puritan-prurient ambivalence, needless to say, still continues to condition post-Christian society today, even as it revolts against the puritan side of the ambivalence to embrace the prurient instead. However, this new "sexual liberation," as much as the older sexual puritanism, does not liberate but confirms woman as the object of sexual oppression, for in this case, too, woman appears essentially as "body" rather than as a person. Moreover, it is common for the Fathers to regard the sexual act as so inherently "polluting" that even the married who have recently indulged in it are advised not to approach the church or the sacraments. For Jerome and others it is axiomatic that one cannot pray if one is living in carnal union. Either temporary or permanent vows of continence are the prerequisite for prayer, and so the priest, who must pray constantly, should be wholly continent.[45]

With such a view, it is no wonder that the Fathers regard the sexual act, even in marriage, with a constantly anxious eye and exhibit an inordinate compulsion to persuade couples to have as little of it as possible. They hope for that dispassionate sex used solely for procreation, but obsessively imagine to themselves those "inordinate and excessive embraces" in which the couples are doubtlessly indulging themselves under cover of the decency of marriage.[46] They expect the slightest encouragement to pleasure for its own sake to lead on endlessly to riotous, all-consuming rut. In their excessive repressiveness toward sensual libido of any kind (this includes all pleasurable experiences of the body, with sex as only the "worst" of these), they magnify its power to gigantic proportions and image it as a "beast in the belly," which, given an inch, will immediately take a mile. Only the ever-vigilant and total effort to keep this beast chained down to the slightest twitching of its tail will suffice to contain its fierce, mind-consuming energy.[47] Modern Freudian psychology can well explain why such a mechanism of repression was bound to be self-defeating and always to produce its own opposite in obsession with sexual fantasies. Unable to contain this result, asceticism dealt with it in two ways: first, by a pruriency that exercised a perverted sexual libido through constant excoriations of sensuality in ascetic literature; second, by a sublimation of sexual libido that rejected it on the level of physical experience, but allowed it to flourish on the level of fantasy elevated to represent the ecstatic nuptials of the bridal soul with Christ. That spiritualizing of the Song of Songs, to represent the marriage of the virgin soul with Christ, allowed the ascetic imagination to dwell in the most pictorial detail upon the sensations of the sexual act while fantasizing this as a spiritual relationship. Thus Leander of Seville, in a treatise on the training of nuns, speaks of the virgin's mystical communion with Christ as "lying on the chaste couch with the bridegroom, while he encircles your head with his left hand and fondles you with his right."[48]

Even though Augustine's definition of original sin, as transmitted through an inherently sinful character of sexual libido, only brought to definitional form the emotional prejudices of the Church Fathers generally, this view was shocking to many in its apparent debasement of the goodness of marriage and the blessings of progeny, so contrary to the Old Testament view. Jerome and Augustine endlessly defend themselves against the charge of Manichaeanism by arguing that marriage is honorable because of its *good end* in procreation, even though the *means* are debasing. Children remain a good end, even though intrinsically *tainted* by these debased means, so that, without spiritual rebirth, they are not children of God and are doomed to damnation. Moreover, in these latter days God's command to increase and multiply has been rescinded. There is no more need for children, even though they are still "allowed."

It is obvious that such a defense of the goodness of marriage and children, after all these qualifications, became, in the popular mind, indistinguishable from outright condemnation. To the charge that Christians wished to bring the human race to an end in one generation Jerome replies testily that, continence being such a heroic path, possible for only a few, there is no danger of such a result. Both he and Augustine agree, moreover, that the Old Testament blessing on fecundity has now been rescinded by God.[49] This command to increase and multiply was given only to the Jews, the type of the "carnal" people (an interesting correlation here between patristic misogynism and anti-Semitism), to create the physical people of God from whom the Messiah was to be born in his bodily nature. Indeed, God, in this earlier dispensation, even allowed polygamy in order to hurry up the process, although Augustine argues against polyandry on these some grounds, since one man can impregnate many women, but one woman cannot be impregnated simultaneously by many men. Polyandry is also ruled out on the basis of the nature of the man-woman relationship, since "nature allows multiplicity in subjugations, but demands singularity in dominations"; as many members can be subject to one head, and many slaves to one master, but not *vice versa*.[50]

Here we see how intrinsic to Augustine was that assimilation of the man-woman relationship into the subject-object relationship—one of domination and subjugation.

However, now that Christ has been born from Israel and has brought about the reborn life of the Resurrection, the need for physical progeny is fast coming to an end. The pagans, indeed, create sufficient offspring to provide the raw material for spiritual rebirth, and so it would be well for Christians to abjure the first entirely, in order to concentrate all their attention on the second, which is their proper task. Such a strange divorce of physical nurture from spiritual birth in Augustine was doubtless a cause of that almost complete lack of any genuine model of Christian marriage as itself a "school of the soul," such as might have been expected by the New Testament modeling of the Church upon the family. The charge that this view would bring the human race to an end does not discomfit Augustine at all. He declares that there have already been enough souls to fill heaven, and if only all men would follow the Christian example and refrain from the obsolete command to increase and multiply, and ·rise to the angelic life where there is no more "marrying and giving in marriage," the end of the world would be hastened and the time of blessedness, when the physical cosmos would be transformed into the spiritual New Creation, would dawn all the sooner.[51] Such views in the Fathers show clearly not only a continuation of early Christian apocalypticism but also its linkage with a *fin de siècle* mentality in late antiquity at the time of the fall of civilization.

Viewing virginity as the shortest route to heaven, not only for man but for the cosmos, it is not surprising that the Fathers were assiduous in their urgings of the superiority of virginity to marriage, and dedicated both treatises and personal letters to the task of persuading Christians to renounce marriage for continence. Jerome was the most indefatigable champion of this particular task. One has only to read through his collected letters to be astonished at the number of these addressed to women and which have as their main purpose the dissuasion of marriage and the exhortation to continence. During his years in Rome as secretary to Pope Damasus, Jerome was intimate with the highest Roman aristocratic circles and became the counselor of a coterie of women from these families who cultivated the ascetic life in the privacy of their mansions. Scarcely was a mother or daughter bereft of her husband but Jerome had pen in hand to spell out the horrors of marriage, the disgust of childbearing, and the glories of the new continence of widowhood that was now within their grasp. They had lost, to be sure, the first glory of virginity, but the second glory of widowhood was now open to them.[52] (Jerome, like Augustine, was incontinent in his youth.)[53] If a mother decides to dedicate her daughter to virginity, Jerome is prepared to prescribe an entire course of education for the newborn girl.[54] He will be her *paedagogus*, as Aristotle was for Alexander. The child must be kept secluded and never allowed to stir from her mother's side, so that all independence becomes foreign to her mind. She must not go to the baths with eunuch servants (as was customary), because these men, although they have lost the power for the act, still retain the lewd desire. Nor should she be allowed to bathe with married women, for the pregnant bodies of women are utterly disgusting and will arouse in the girl thoughts about the potential of her own body injurious to her vocation. After she grows older she should shun the company of married women altogether and should forswear all bathing, for she should blush for shame at the very idea of seeing her own unclothed body. She should be trained in vigils and fasts, and by "cold chastity" put out the flames of lust. Any food or drink that will arouse the natural bodily heats should be avoided. Squalid dress and neglect of hygiene will spoil her natural good looks and keep her from becoming an object of desire. For Jerome a "clean body signifies a dirty mind." The girl should not busy herself with secular learning or cultivated ways, but should cling only to the scriptures and make the writings of the Church Fathers her only literature. Banqueting, the bustle of the streets, the sight of fashionably dressed women or curled and perfumed fops, the social rounds of high Roman society—all this is anathema. Finally, Jerome despairs of the child's receiving this proper upbringing among the myriad temptations of the great city and urges the young mother to send the infant to him and her grandmother Paula, so she can be trained in the "angelic life," which, "while in the body lives as though it were without flesh" in a suitable environment.

Jerome is quick to transmit the gospel of virginity and abhorrence of marriage not only to his intimates but also to recently widowed women with whom he has only a hearsay acquaintance. His vivid descriptions of the lusts of the eye and the burnings of inner bodily cravings are lavished with as much intimate detail in letters to women whom he has never met as in those to women for whom he has been a personal counselor.[55] Therefore, it is a mistake for the reader to suppose that this detail indicates either such intimate relations with the women thus addressed or frustrated personal sexual desires toward them. The frustration is generic rather than personal, and the detailed prurient language comes forth on any and all occasions as the rhetorical *topoi* of the overheated ascetic imagination. Thus to the wealthy, recently widowed Roman aristocrat Salvina, whom Jerome had never met and who has in no way communicated with him, he addresses this unbidden advice:

> Never let pheasants be seen on your table . . . nor fancy that you eschew meat diet when you reject . . . the savory flesh of other quadrupeds. It is not the number of feet but the delicacy of flavor that makes the difference [i.e., fowl are also to be prohibited]. . . . Let those who feed on flesh serve the flesh, whose bodies boil with desire, who are tied to their husbands and who set their hearts on having offspring. Let those whose wombs are burdened cram their stomachs with flesh. But you have buried every indulgence in your husband's tomb . . . Let paleness and squalor be henceforth your jewels. Do not pamper your youthful limbs with bed of down or kindle your young blood with hot baths . . . Take no well curled steward to walk with you, no effeminate actor, no devilish singer of poisoned sweetness, no spruce and well shorn youth . . . Keep with you bands of widows and virgins . . . Let the divine Scriptures be always in your hands and give yourself frequently to prayer that such shafts of evil thoughts as ever assail the young may find thereby a shield to repel them.[56]

To a young ascetic woman in Gaul, living in spiritual marriage with a priest, who has quarreled with her mother but whom Jerome has no reason to suspect of other wrongdoing, he addresses a letter filled with vivid descriptions of her mincing gait, her pretended ascetic dress, carefully ripped to display the white flesh beneath; her shawl, which she allows to slip and quickly replaces to reveal her curving neck; the enticements of the table and youthful gallants, which she pretends to avoid but actually seeks out; her sexual fantasies and probable fornications with the priest, whom she pretends to have only as spiritual counselor. All this is pure fantasy, since Jerome has never met the woman![57]

Descriptions such as these, which fill Jerome's letters, leave the reader with a dilemma as to how to understand such ascetic enthusiasm that compels such remarkable pruriency toward women, known and unknown alike. This most probably should be taken as the by-product of violent libidinal repression that generates its own opposite in vivid sensual fantasizing under the guise of antisensual polemics. In this his views and psychology do not differ essentially from those of other Church Fathers, although he was more skilled than most in their rhetorical expression. But Jerome may also be seen as having found a somewhat better outlet for this frustration than some others, for he sublimated the repression of physical relations with women into a sincere and deep spiritual companionship with several women friends (unlike Augustine, whose rejection of physical concourse with women was sublimated only into an odd love-hate relationship with his mother, and who saw his conversion as the discarding of any relationships with other women, expressing otherwise only contempt for the possibilities of women as spiritual companions of men). Jerome, however, cultivated a close spiritual friendship with a group of ascetic women whom he regarded genuinely as his companions in the pursuit of the higher life. Although many were quick to accuse him of less honorable designs (and he was ready to return the compliment toward other monks intimate with women), there is no doubt that his love for these women was both authentic and yet platonic, especially toward Paula, who joined him as his companion to build the monastic life in Palestine. As Jerome leaves Rome for Jerusalem, with Paula soon to follow, he writes of this to Ascella, another intimate of the ascetic circle:

> It often happened that I found myself surrounded with virgins, and to some of these I expounded the divine books as best I could. Our studies brought about constant intercourse; this soon ripened into intimacy, and this, in turn, produced mutual confidence. If they have ever seen anything in my conduct unbecoming a Christian, let them say so! . . . No; my sex was my one

crime, and even on this score I am not assailed save when there is talk of Paula coming to Jerusalem . . . Of all the ladies in Rome, but one had power to subdue me and that one was Paula. She mourned and she fasted. She was squalid with dirt; her eyes were dim with weeping. . . . The Psalms were her only songs; the gospel her whole speech; continence her one indulgence; fasting the staple of her life. The only woman who took my fancy was one whom I had not so much as seen at table. But when I began to revere, respect and venerate her as her conspicuous chastity deserved, all my former virtues forsook me on the spot [his reputation as such in Rome]. . . . I write this in haste, dear Lady Ascella, as I go on board, overwhelmed with grief and tears. Yet I thank God that I am counted worthy of the world's hatred. . . . Salute Paula and Eustochium, who, whatever the world may think, are always mine in Christ. Salute Albina, your mother and Marcella, your sister; Marcellina also and the holy Felicitas; and say to them all: "We must all stand before the judgement seat of Christ" and there shall be revealed the principle by which each has lived. And now, illustrious model of chastity and virginity, remember me, I beseech you, in your prayers, and by your intercessions calm the waves of the sea.[58]

Jerome is generous to the point of extravagance in his praise of these ascetic women. His encomium on Paula, written to her daughter Eustochium after her death, gives us a sketch of Jerome's ideal of the spiritual woman as both ascetic and "mother of virgins," in the double sense of training her own daughters in this ideal of life and becoming the prioress of a community of virgins, next to Jerome's community of monks (for whose physical support she provided her fortune).[59] For Jerome these women are not merely disciples, but they, especially Paula, are in the fullest sense spiritual comrades in the ascetic battle, whom he is happy to regard as peers and even his teachers.

Women in Jerome appear in three roles, the strumpet, the wife and the virgin, but the image of the wife has almost disappeared between the two contraries, the strumpet and the virgin. Marriage he regards as inherently polluting, and childbearing disgusting. He turns warm toward infants only when he can imagine them, not as the verminous offspring of defiling sex, but as candidates for virginity. He can see no reason for anyone to marry except lust or covetousness. To the widow Furis he writes: "Confess the shameful truth. No woman marries to avoid cohabiting with a husband. At least if passion is not your motive [for wanting to remarry], it is mere madness to play the harlot just to increase your wealth."[60] Toward the desire for progeny he expresses a similar asperity. Once having experienced disgusting intercourse, the heaving stomach, the vomits of pregnancy, any woman who would wish to try this again is like a dog that returns to its vomit.

> Do you fear the extinction of the line of Camillus, if you do not present your father with some little fellow to crawl upon his breast and slobber on his neck? . . . Your father will be sorry, but Christ will be glad . . . Let your father do what he likes with what is his own. You are not his to whom you have been born, but His to whom you have been born again.[60]

If the wife is not on her way to continence in widowhood, she is on her way down to harlotry. The image of the "good wife," even in the sense of the submissive wife, is largely absent from Jerome, who paints the wife under the rubric of the nagging, whining bitch of Greek satiric misogynism.[61]

Jerome waxes warm only when describing the virgin and her contrary, the strumpet. The image of the "sensual woman" haunted his imagination even in the midst of his most violent ascetic rigors. To Eustochium he describes his period of severest asceticism in the desert thus:

> Although in my fear of hell I had consigned myself to this prison where I had no companions but scorpions and wild beasts, I often found myself amid bevies of girls. My face was pale and my frame chilled with fasting, yet my mind was burning with desire and the fires of lust kept bubbling up before me when my flesh was as good as dead.[62]

In his violent excoriations of sensuality Jerome can conjure up the most vivid word pictures of all the typologies of the sensual life. First of all, there is the wanton woman herself, with painted face, artificial allurements of ornament and coiffure, her dress carefully draped to reveal her figure, her flashing eyes and coquettish airs. But around her are all the other types of fleshly society; the arrogant matron surrounded with a troop of eunuchs; the effeminate curled and perfumed fop; and also the types of depraved pseudo-religiosity—the false virgin who plays the wanton beneath her dark dress of feigned modesty; the avaricious priest who haunts the homes of wealthy widows; the lusty monk who, under the pretense of spiritual counsel, pushes his way into the very bedrooms of high-born women.[63] In Jerome the acid of Christian asceticism has sharpened the pen of that tradition of Roman satire that was always ready to depict depraved lust and hidden vice in purple prose.[64]

But once women have set their feet firmly on the path of continence, Jerome is filled with warm affection for them. All of his rhetorical skill in depicting the temptations of the flesh and the hidden devices of the mind, by which sensuality breaks out in new forms, is brought to bear upon their spiritual counseling. Jerome turns an ever-anxious eye upon the temptations that beset their spiritual combat, but he is also warm in praise of their virtues. Not only do his ascetic sisters learn Greek and Hebrew more quickly than he, but they speak these languages, which he himself has struggled so hard to master, fluently and without accent. Their exegetical skills match his own, and when he departs for Jerusalem, Marcella takes his place as the leading scripture authority in Rome, to whom laity, priests and bishops turn for explanations of difficult passages.[65] Jerome, however, never allows it to be suggested that even such abilities cancel out the apostle's prohibition against women teaching in the Church. They exercise their learning only with the modesty and concealment befitting a woman.[66]

Their ascetic prowess also matches or surpasses his own. If he has given much to the poor, Paula has given all and has exhausted her fortune in almsgiving and support of the monks. If he has fasted to the point of paleness, she has fasted to the point of death. Indeed, in his encomium on Paula, Jerome paints himself in the role of the moderate, ever fearful for her health and financial security, while she, with far greater faith and commitment, throws all restraint to the winds and puts his pusillanimity to shame.[67] In other words, in those very areas in which Jerome most prized his own accomplishments he is willing to depict his spiritual sisters as his peers and even his teachers.

Not least does he praise these women for their "unnatural-

ness." The virgin woman is seen as rising to a "virility" that con-
quers the fickle mind and feeble flesh intrinsic to woman. The
angelic life demands the male to rise above his body, but it demands that woman rise above her "nature," crushing out from herself all that pertains to her "femaleness." To Demetrias, an aristocratic lady who has chosen virginity, Jerome writes a letter of praise
in which he says:

> You must act against nature or rather above nature if you are to
> forswear your natural functions, to cut off your own root, to cull
> no fruit but that of virginity, to abjure the marriage bed, to shun
> intercourse with men and, while in the body, to live as though out
> of it.[68]

Moreover, this unnaturalness can include defying the wills of their
fathers, abandoning the responsibilities of their households—the
supervision of wealth, estates and servants which was the economic
sphere of the Roman matron—and even turning their backs on
their children to seek the "higher life." In his encomium on Paula,
Jerome describes admiringly how she left behind her house, children, servants and property in Rome, to the great outcry of worldly
society. As her ship departs from the dock her infant son, Toxotius,
stretches forth his hands and her older daughter, Rufina, sobs
silently on the pier, but, "overcoming her love for her children with
her love for God," and turning her eyes heavenward, she sails out
to sea, with never a backward glance, into the glorious virginal
horizon to join Jerome in monastic rigors in the East.[69] Jerome
even regards an occasional outburst of grief on the death of parents
or children as backsliding into that "lower female nature" that the
woman must crush from her being in order to rise to the angelic
life—understandable, but nevertheless to be reproved.[70]

Jerome's view of marriage and virginity differs in emphasis
from that found in Greek Fathers such as Gregory of Nyssa. The
Greeks are likely to stress more the transience of the goods of
marriage than the defiling character of sex. This fits in with Nyssa's
stress on mutability rather than sexuality as the essence of the
lower nature. Nyssa, in his treatise on virginity, inveighs against
marriage, not by making sex dirty, but by speaking sadly of the
mutability of all worldly loves. Sentimentally he depicts the hand-

some young husband who dies, the beloved child who goes to an
early grave. These things are not made to sound depraved, but are
merely seen as passing goods. Those who fix their affections on
these finite relationships are doomed to tragedy and loss. Better,
then, not to place one's heart on passing goods but to look to
heavenly things that do not pass away.[71]

Nyssa has a much more positive outlook on married life than
do Augustine and Jerome; he was probably himself married and
lived in a positive context of Christian homelife in his own family
and those of his friends, such as Gregory Nazianzus. Both of these
Greek writers tend to view the forum and the marketplace, the
entanglements of economic and political life, as much more symbols of "worldliness" than sex; they speak positively of the married
household as the place where the woman particularly can practice
the "philosophical life" without denying her role as wife or
mother.[72] For Gregory Nyssa "virginity" comes close to being a
metaphor for an inner attitude of detachment and spiritual up-
lifting of the mind, rather than being fixed upon the question of
lack of sexual union. He can readily imagine the married woman
living this "virgin" life in the semiseclusion of the Greek household, without denying her marital and maternal duties, but rather
discharging these simply and without overmuch absorption while
giving her full affection to the life of vigils, fasting and prayer.
In this he had the examples of such notable women of his own
family and acquaintance as his own mother and sister and the
mother and sister of Gregory of Nazianzus.[73]

Nyssa, indeed, even believes that the person who can combine
both the lower and the higher goods in a right ordering in this
fashion has the first rank of virtue, whereas only he who is weak of
will, and for whom the presence of these lower things will lead to a
disordered affection for them, should be advised to shun marriage
for celibacy. Celibacy thus becomes second in rank to the ideal
state, which would combine the active and the contemplative life
in a right harmony. Nevertheless Nyssa believes that such a combination is so difficult that it is in practice impossible for most
people. Therefore, those who wish to live the life of detachment
and contemplation usually must purchase it by headlong flight
from the body, the woman and the world.[74]

One finds in other Greek writers, of course, the more contemptuous view of marriage and the wife, the horror of sex and sensuality found in the Latins. But, in general, the shift of emphasis from sex to mutability as the source of danger causes less of the obsession with sex as the chief symbol of sin in the Greek ascetic writers of this period, who keep some sense of the Platonic ideal of life as a harmony of goods. In the Greeks, too, we find the portrait of the ascetic woman and encomiums of praise on the new Christian spiritual woman, but unlike Jerome's, these women are their own married sisters and mothers, rather than women who must be wrenched from their context in the home in order to rise to the "angelic life." The Greeks, moreover, generally sided with Pelagius and Julian in their suspicion of Augustine's view of original sin, and found his excessive emphasis on the sinfulness of even marital sexuality and the transmission of sin thereby unpalatable.

In this twilight period of antiquity, we see, then, the image of the virginal woman appearing as a new cultural ideal, raising up the possibility of woman as capable of the highest spiritual development, which could lead to the *summum bonum* of communion with the divine, intellectual nature of the Divine itself. Such heights had previously been reserved for men in antiquity, although the twilight of Neoplatonism also boasted a woman sage, Hypatia. Many streams of imagery flowed together to make up the portrait of this "spiritual woman." The Song of Songs, which had been adapted as a Hebrew marriage hymn from the Ba'alistic cult of fecundity, was spiritualized by Origen and made into an allegory of the nuptials of the soul with the Logos, or the Church with Christ.[75] The soul, although masculine in relation to the body, was depicted as feminine in relation to the divine Logos. This feminine character of the soul lent itself to a sublimated erotic imagery that described the lovemaking of the Virgin Psyche with Christ. Another feminine image was derived from that of Israel as Bride of Yahweh in the Covenant. The Church inherited this image in its eschatological form as the Bride of Christ in the Resurrection (Rev. 21:2 and 9). The Church can also be depicted in the colors of the Sibyl, or muse—that wise old woman who is as old as creation, and who guides the soul on its spiritual path. Here the Church is the mother of reborn souls and the "wise counselor" who instructs the seer in the Shepherd of Hermes. Finally, there is the image of Sophia, who, like Athena, springs from the head of Zeus. She is the Wisdom of God, the daughter of Yahweh, who sits at his right hand and is the mediatrix of all redeeming knowledge (Sir. 14:20–15:8; Wis. 8:2 ff. *et passim*).

All these traditions of feminine spiritual imagery were gathered together into Mariology, which began to emerge in the fourth century A.D. This new praise of Mary, as the epitome of all these images of spiritual womanhood, soon succeeded in restoring to Mary the ancient titles of Queen of Heaven and Mother of God of the ancient Mediterranean Earth Goddess, crowning her with the moon and the stars of Isis, the turret crown of Magna Mater, placing her enthroned with the divine child on her lap in an ancient image derived from the iconography of Isis and Horus, rededicating ancient temples of these Earth goddesses to Mary,[76] and finally escorting her to the very Throne of God to take her seat beside the Jewish Ancient of Days and his son Messiah, who had once ruled the heavens in exclusive patriarchal splendor. The doctrine of Mary's assumption waited for official declaration until the peculiarities of twentieth-century ultramontane Roman Catholicism, but it had already emerged in popular piety in Egypt by the early fifth century A.D. and from there, spread rapidly north and west.[77] Virginal woman was thus bound for heaven, and her male ascetic devotees would stop at nothing short of this prize for her. But they paid the price of despising all real physical women, sex and fecundity, and wholly etherealizing women into incorporeal phantasms in order to provide love objects for the sublimated libido and guard against turning back to any physical expression of love with the dangerous daughters of Eve.

Perhaps the task of Christians today, as they take stock of this tradition and its defects, is not merely to vilify its inhumanity but rather to cherish the hard-won fruits of transcendence and spiritual personhood, won at such a terrible price of the natural affections of men and the natural humanity of women. Without discarding these achievements, we must rather find out how to pour them back into a full-bodied Hebrew sense of creation and incarnation, as male and female, but who can now be fully personalized autonomous selves and also persons in relation to each other, not against the body, but in and through the body.

NOTES

1. William Phipps, *Was Jesus Married?* (New York: Harper & Row, 1970), pp. 142–163.
2. Ibid., pp. 120–124. This view was popularized by the great Church Historian, A. Harnack, writing at the turn of the century.
3. Franz Cumont, *Oriental Religions in Roman Paganism* (New York: Dover, 1956); see also S. Dill, *Roman Society from Nero to Marcus Aurelius* (New York: Meridian Books, 1956), pp. 547–626.
4. G. Scholem, *Major Trends in Jewish Mysticism* (Jerusalem: Schocken Books, 1941), chap. 1 and *passim*.
5. I have worked out this thesis in detail in an unpublished study of the origins of Christology, entitled *Messiah of Israel and the Cosmic Christ.*
6. The Synoptics are innocent of cosmological Christology. It probably appeared first in Hellenistic Jewish synagogues familiar with Philonic Logos speculation by the second decade after the death of Jesus, being taken from this source by Paul in Col. 1:12–20. It appears also in Eph. 1:20–23, Heb. 1:2–4 and John 1:1–13.
7. Origen, *De Principiis* 2, 8, 1.
8. Justin Martyr, *Dial.* 80 ff.; Tertullian, *Adv. Marcion.* 3, 24; *De Spec.* 30; Irenaeus, *Adv. Haer.* 5, 32, 1.
9. For example, Athanasius' *De Incarnatione* and Origen's *De Principiis* develop an anthropology built on the doctrine of the "image" without any mention of bisexuality.
10. Philo, *Leg. All.* I, 31–32; *De Conf.* 62–63; also see *De Migr. Abr.* 174.
11. M. N. Maxey, "Beyond Eve and Mary," *Dialog.* X (Spring 1971), 112 ff.
12. Gregory Nyssa, *De Opif. Hom.* 16.
13. Ibid., 16.7.
14. Ibid., 16.14; 17.1.
15. Augustine, *De Grat. Ch. et de Pecc. Orig.* II, 40.; *De Genesi ad Lit.* 9.5.
16. Augustine, *Confessiones* 13.32; *De Opere Monach.* 40.
17. Augustine, *De Trinitate* 7.7, 10.
18. Augustine, *De Contin.* I.23; Augustine parallels the supra- and subordinations of Christ and the Church; man and woman and the soul and the body. On the ambivalence between an equivalent and a subordinate view of women in the Fathers, especially Augustine, see Kari Elizabeth Børresen, *Subordination et Équivalence; Nature et rôle de la femme d'après Augustin et Thomas d'Aquin* (Oslo: Universitets-forlaget, 1968).

19. Augustine, *De Civitate Dei* 14, 11; *De Genesi ad Lit.* 11, 42.
20. Tertullian, *De Cultu Fem.* 1, 1.
21. Clem. Alex., *Paedagogus* 1, 4; 3, 1–2; *Stromata* 2, 23; 3; 4, 8 and 19; cf. *Paedagogus* 2, 2.
22. Cyprian, *De habitu Virg.* 22; Jerome, *Ep.* 130, 8.
23. Ambrose, *De Cain et Abel* 1, 4; see also Jerome, *Ep.* 130, 17.
24. Leander of Seville, *De Instit. Virg.*, preface.
25. Augustine, *Ep.* 262, to Ecducia.
26. Leander of Seville, *De Instit. Virg.*, preface; also Jerome, *Comm. in Epist. ad Ephes.* 3.5; and *Adv. Helvid.* 22.
27. Augustine, *De Civitate Dei* 22.17; Jerome, *Ep.* 108, 23, to Paula.
28. Tertullian, *De Cultu Fem.* 2, 2.
29. Augustine, *De Sermone Dom. in Monte*, 41.
30. Augustine, *De Civitate Dei* 14, 26; *Contra Iulian.* 3, 13, 27; *De Grat. Chr. et de Pecc. Orig.* 2, 40.
31. *De Civitate Dei*, 14, 24; *De Grat. Chr. et de Pecc. Orig.* 2, 41; *De Nupt. et Concup.* I, 6–7, 21, 33.
32. D. S. Bailey, *The Man-Woman Relation in Christian Thought* (London: Longmans, Green, 1959), pp. 55–58.
33. See Augustine's description of his mother as the perfectly submissive wife even under unjust treatment (*Confessions* 9); also see John Chrysostom, *Epist. ad Eph.*, hom. 13; hom. 22; hom. 26, 8.
34. Augustine, *De Nupt. et Concup.* 9–10; *De Bono Viduit.* 10.
35. Mark 4:20; Cyprian, *De Habitu. Virg.* 21; Athanasius, *Ep.* 48.2; Tertullian, *De Exhort. Cast.* 1; *Adv. Marcion.* 5, 15; Jerome, *Eps.* 22, 15; 48, 3; 66, 2; 120, 1, 9; *Adv. Jov.* 1, 3; Augustine, *De Sancta Virg.* 45; Ambrose, *De Virg.* 1, 60.
36. Hermas, *Mand.* 4, 4; Tertullian, *Ad. Uxor.* 1, 7; *De Exhort Cast.* Cyril of Jerusalem, *Cat.* 4, 26; Minucius Felix, *Oct.* 31; John Chrysostom, *In Epist. ad Tim.* 7, 4; *In Epist. ad Tit.* 2, 1; Ambrose, *De Offic.* 2, 27; *De Vid.* 12, 89, 58; Augustine, *De Bono Viduit.* 6; *De Bono Conj.* 21; Epiphanius, *Haer.* 59, 6; Gregory Nazianzus, *Orat.* 37, 8; Basil, *Ep.* 99, 50; Jerome, *Eps.* 48, 8; 79, 10; 123, 9; *Ad. Jov.* 1, 15, 16.
37. Leo I, *Epist.* 14, 5; 167, 2; Augustine, *Adv. Iulian.* 5, 16; *Eps.* 188, 1 and 220; *De Bono Conj.* 3; *De Sermone Dom. in Monte.* 1, 14; *De Consensu. Evang.* 2, 2; *C. Faust. Manich.* 23, 8; *De Nupt. et Concup.* 1, 12.
38. Augustine, *De Bono Conj.* 3, 15; *De Bono Viduit.* 8, and 11; Jerome, *Ep.* 107, 13, to Laeta.
39. John Chrysostom, *Epist. ad Eph.* hom. 26, 8; Augustine, *De Conj. Adult.* 2, 15.
40. Augustine, *De Grat. Chr. et de Pecc. Orig.* 2, 38, 42; *De Nupt. et Concup.* I, 8–9, 19, 25–26; *De Bono Conj.* 10; *Duas Epist. Pelag.* 1, 27, 30.
41. Augustine, *De Pecc. Merit. et Remiss.* 1, 29; *De Grat. Chr. et de*

Pecc. Orig. 1, 27; 2, 41–44; *De Nupt. et Concup.* 1, 13, 22; *Adv. Iulian.* 3, 7; 5, 14.

42. Jerome, *Ep.* 48, 14; Augustine, *De Nupt. et Concup.* 1, 16; *De Bono. Conj.* 6, 11.

43. Augustine, *De Nupt. et Concup.* 1, 17; *De Bono Conj.* 10, 11; *De Conj. Adult.* 2, 12.

44. Augustine, *De Grat. Chr. et de Pecc. Orig.* 2, 39; *De Nupt. et Concup.* 1, 19; *De Bono Conj.* 17; *De Genesi ad Lit.* 9, 7.

45. Ambrose, *De Poenit.* 2, 10; *De Elias* 7, 9; *De Offic.* 1, 50; Pseud-Clement, *Hom.* 11, 28, 30; *Recog.* 6, 10, 11; Augustine, *De Fid. et Op.* 6; Tertullian, *De Exhort. Cast.* 11; Jerome, *Eps.* 22, 22; 48, 15; *Adv. Helvid.* 22; *Adv. Jov.* 1, 7, 34.

46. Jerome. *Hom.* 80; Methodius, *Conviv.* 9, 4; Augustine, *De Bono Conj.* 11.

47. Jerome, *Eps.* 22, 11; 123, 9; 54, 9.

48. Leander of Seville, *De Instit. Virg.*; Jerome, *Eps.* 22, 6; 19, 25; 53, 7–9; 48, 10; 123, 13.

49. Jerome, *Adv. Jov.* 1, 36; Augustine, *De Nupt. et Concup.* 1, 14–15; *De Bono Conj.* 13; *De Bono Viduit.* 8, 11; *De Sancta Virg.* 9, 9, 16.

50. Augustine, *De Bono Conj.* 17–20; *De Nupt. et Concup.* 1, 9–10.

51. Augustine, *De Bono Conj.* 10; *De Bono Viduit.* 9–11, 23–28; Jerome, *Eps.* 123, 17; *Adv. Jov.* 1, 16, 29; *Adv. Helvid.* 22.

52. Jerome, *Eps.* 38, to Marcella; 54, to Furia; 79, to Salvinia; 123, to Ageruchia; 74, to Rufinus. A third of Jerome's letters and many of his longest letters are to women.

53. *Ep.* 48, 20.

54. *Ep.* 107, to Laeta.

55. *Ep.* 79, to Salvina.

56. *Ep.* 79, 7–9.

57. *Ep.* 117.

58. *Ep.* 45, 2–7.

59. *Ep.* 108.

60. *Ep.* 54, 4.

61. *Adv. Jov.* 1, 41–47, quoting Theophrastus.

62. *Ep.* 22, 7.

63. Jerome, *Eps.* 13, 24–29; 22, 16; 52, 5; 54, 7, 13; 107, 8; 108, 15; 117, 6, 7; 125, 16; 127, 3.

64. S. Dill, *Roman Society in the Last Century of the Western Empire* (New York: Meridian Books, 1958), pp. 125–136.

65. *Eps.* 127, to Marcella; 39, on Blesilla.

66. *Ep.* 127, 7.

67. *Ep.* 108, on Paula to Eustochium.

68. *Ep.* 130, 10.

69. *Ep.* 108, 6.

70. *Ep.* 39, 6.

71. Gregory Nyssa, *De Virg.* 2.
72. Gregory Nyssa, *De Virg.* 8; Gregory Nazianzus, *Orat.* 8, 8, on Gorgonia.
73. Gregory Nyssa, *Dial. de Anima et Resurrect.*, to Macrina; Gregory Nazianzus, *Orat.* 8, on Gorgonia; *Orat.* 7, on Caesarius; *Orat.* 43, on Basil (the brother of Gregory Nyssa).
74. Gregory Nyssa, *De Virg.* 8.
75. Origen, *Comm. on the Canticle of Canticles*; Jerome, *Adv. Jov.* 1, 30.
76. See text and notes in G. Miegge, *The Virgin Mary* (Philadelphia: Westminster Press, 1955).
77. Ibid., pp. 83–106.

The Journal of Religious History
Vol. 15, No. 1, June 1988

JANE SIMPSON

Women and Asceticism in the Fourth Century: A Question of Interpretation

Much feminist scholarship over the last two decades has been concerned with the attempt to rediscover our foremothers. The achievements of twentieth-century feminism are being viewed increasingly against the background of earlier feminist campaigns in the nineteenth century[1]. Far from being abstract theorists, nineteenth-century feminists reacted strongly against particular circumstances and engaged with determination in the struggle against the injustices and limitations imposed upon their freedom. Most felt a conflict between being both feminist and feminine, but all attacked the image of woman as passive and inactive except in matters concerning the home. While much of the recent feminist historiography is clearly revisionist in its attempt to rectify the invisibility of most women in the past, it also serves the purpose of bringing a sense of identification and of overcoming a sense of isolation for women of today. It is in this sense that women of the past may be considered our foremothers.

Writers of church history have also been active in feminist reclaiming of the past. The preoccupation of most patristic scholarship with the Church Fathers has been challenged by a number of writers who affirm women's leadership roles in the early church with terms such as 'Desert Mothers',[2] and 'Mothers of the Church'.[3] Just as feminism involves a way of looking at and thinking of life for all women, feminist revisionist church historians have introduced new ways of looking at the past. These have provided women in the church today with a new set of inspiring women apostles, prophets, teachers, ascetics, and mystics. Indeed, women ascetics of the fourth century have even been described in terms of their 'Virginal Feminism'.[4] Revisionists, in particular Rosemary Ruether and Elizabeth Clark, have done much to improve understanding of the theological setting

1. See Margaret Forster, *Significant Sisters: The Grassroots of Active Feminism, 1838-1939*, Harmondsworth 1984.
2. Leonard Swidler, *Biblical Affirmations of Woman*, Philadelphia 1979, p. 340.
3. Rosemary Ruether, 'Mothers of the Church: Ascetic Women in the Late Patristic Age', in *Women of Spirit: Female Leadership in the Jewish and Christian Traditions*, Rosemary Ruether and Eleanor McLaughlin (eds), New York 1974, pp. 71-98.
4. Rosemary Ruether, 'Misogynism and Virginal Feminism in the Fathers of the Church', in *Religion and Sexism; Images of Woman in the Jewish and Christian Traditions*, Ruether (ed.), New York 1974, pp. 150-83.

Jane Simpson is Ross Fellow of Knox College, Dunedin, New Zealand.

of the asceticism of the fourth century.[5] Their focus results in part from a rising women's consciousness, and in part from rejection of present ecclesiastical norms, many of which continue to exclude women from leadership positions in various denominations.[6]

This article argues that certain major distortions have occurred, however, in the image portrayed of women ascetics by Ruether and Clark. Their interpretations, while rectifying to some extent the neglect of 'Church Mothers', have undervalued the very real emancipation from societal norms that asceticism brought for those women who chose its rigours. The revisionists, attempting to see these women as feminist sisters, have failed to appraise sympathetically the contribution of women ascetics in their own terms. An analysis of certain crucial phrases suggests that they have judged celibate fourth-century 'pre-pill feminists' according to the standards of conventional sexual expression of the post-pill liberty of the 1960s and 1970s sexual revolution. Furthermore, because the revisionists have concentrated their investigative efforts in the area of theological and philosophical explanation, they have necessarily excluded adequate consideration of the relevant political, economic, sociological, and religious contexts of fourth-century asceticism. This emphasis on the misogynism of the Church Fathers, to the exclusion of a systematic study of contextuality, has created a portrayal of fourth-century ascetics as victims of male theology, who were de-sexed with the tools of theological argument. Their conclusions that these women were 'perceived as hovering in the limbo of liminality' of asexuality,[7] were subject to an attempt to be 'biologically neutralized'[8] and chose a path of accomplishment that was 'anti-sexual',[9] are examined in the light of passages by male ascetics which are read positively.

The main purpose of this article, therefore, is to demonstrate that women's self-perception did not necessarily conform to the image of woman portrayed in the writings of male ascetics. First, the asceticism of the fourth century is seen as the fruition of a long development of ascetic ideals from earlier times. Second, women's pioneering role in the shift from the encratite isolation of asceticism to the communally based monasticism of the third and fourth centuries is emphasized. The nature of early monasticism is discussed briefly, and the spirituality of third-century asceticism and monasticism seen in terms of wholeness, rather than of dualism. Third, the possible 'feminist' motivations women had towards adopting asceticism in the fourth century are identified, and then viewed alongside the complex motivational factors which drew both men and women towards asceticism in the midst of the rapidly changing political, economic, sociological, and religious dimensions of that time. Fourth, an

5. See Elizabeth A. Clark, 'Sexual Politics in the Writings of John Chrysostom', *Anglican Theological Review*, January 1977, pp. 3-20, and *Jerome, Chrysostom and Friends: Essays and Translations* (Studies in Women and Religion), New York 1979.
6. See Ruether, 'Entering the Sanctuary: The Struggle for Priesthood in Contemporary Episcopalian and Roman Catholic Experience', II, 'The Roman Catholic Story', in *Women of Spirit*, Ruether and McLaughlin (eds), pp. 373-83.
7. Clark, Jerome, Chrysostom and Friends, p. 59.
8. *Jerome, Chrysostom and Friends*, p. 58.
9. *Women of Spirit*, Ruether and McLaughlin (eds), p. 93.

analysis of key phrases used by Ruether and Clark shows the reasons for their devaluing the achievements of fourth-century women ascetics; namely, they have judged them from their own context of the continued exclusion of women from ordained ministry in many a contemporary denomination. A brief case study of the not inconsiderable teaching ministry of Marcella in Rome shows that a positive interpretation is possible. Fifth, the pioneering role played by women ascetics in adapting eastern ideals of asceticism for later transplantation to the west is discussed. Sixth, the revisionists are shown to have downgraded celibate feminism, because they appear to have taken as normative post-pill views of sexuality, defined chiefly in terms of genital expression. The use by both Clark and Ruether of overarching typologies distorts the image of woman portrayed. Last, their work is placed in the larger contemporary academic and social context and certain conclusions drawn.

Only after persecution ceased in the fourth century could the ascetic tendencies, which first emerged in Egypt, Palestine, and Caesarea, be systematized and institutionalized. The general character of asceticism, even as late as the 380s, remained essentially oriental. Asceticism had its roots in Jewish desert spirituality[10] and found expression in certain ascetic tendencies in the gospels[11] and in the Pauline epistles. The term asceticism itself comes from the comparison of the Christian life to the training of an athlete.[12] Paul, the ardent Hellenistic Jew, practised self-discipline and compared the Christian life to the restraint in all things exercised by every athlete.[13] Although Paul conceived of himself as mastering his body in a cosmic contest between Christ and the believer on one side and Satan and the flesh on the other,[14] it does not follow that the Pauline duality of the 'flesh' and the 'Spirit' is at all comparable to Greek and Manichean dualism.[15] The majority of the Essenes shunned marriage.[16] Marcion demanded absolute continence within marriage, and Marcionite communities in Syria admitted to their congregation as full members only celibates and continent married persons.[17] Montanism, which arose in Asia Minor from c. 157, was noted not only for its fanaticism, but also for

10. See H. Strathmann, 'Askese I (nichtchristlich)', *Reallexikon für Antike und Christentum, Sachwörterbuch zur Auseinandersetzung des Christentums mit der Antiken Welt*, Theodor Klauser (ed.), Vol. 1, 1950, pp. 750-1.
11. Mark viii.34-6, Luke iii.11, ix.23-5, xiv.26; cf. Matthew ix.15, xi.17; Mark ii.20; Luke v.35; vii.34.
12. The Greek for exercise, *askēsis*.
13. I Corinthians ix.24-7.
14. II Corinthians xii.7-10.
15. While Mervin Monroe Deems views Paul's asceticism within the context of late Judaic and Greco-Roman ideology (regarding the world as demonic) and of the dualism of Orphism, Neo-Pythagoreanism and Neo-Platonism (the body a drag upon the soul), Louis Bouyer has argued that Paul is not concerned with the 'specifically Greek dichotomy between the soul and the body', but is faithful to the realism of Jewish thought in thinking of 'man as a whole'. See Deems, 'The Sources of Christian Asceticism' in *Environmental Factors in Christian History*, John Thomas McNeill, Matthew Spinka, and Harold R. Willoughby (eds), New York 1970, pp. 150-2, and Bouyer, *A History of Christian Spirituality*, Vol. 1, *The Spirituality of the New Testament and the Fathers*, London 1968, pp. 79-80.
16. Strathmann, 'Askese I', p. 752.
17. Hippolytus, *Elenchus*, X.19, col. 343; Irenaeus, *Adv. Haereses*, I.28.1, p. 259; Tertullian, *Adv. Marcionem*, IV.11.

its call to the encratism of a strictly disciplined Christian life.[18] The Montanists did not repudiate marriage, but neither did they encourage it. Second marriage was prohibited and designated as adultery.[19] Tertullian, who lived at the end of the second century and the beginning of the third, was Montanism's most famous convert. He did not condemn marriage, although he once said that marriage is the essence of fornication.[20] Consistent with his views on second marriage, he asked his wife to remain celibate if he should die before her.[21] The Montanists encouraged virginity within marriage, and many made themselves eunuchs voluntarily and by mutual consent. In this early period Christian apocalypticism was strong and every persecution reinforced the negative approach of the Christian to the world.[22] Origen, who led a strict ascetic life of fastings, voluntary poverty, and vigils, best demonstrates the continuity from martyrdom to asceticism.[23] The studied moderation of the asceticism of Clement of Alexandria is in sharp contrast to the extremism of that of the Montanists and Origen. Clement drew on both scripture and tradition to promote a disciplined life for Christians. Teachers and pupils of the Christian philosophic school in Alexandria, over which Clement and then Origen presided, upheld in their own lives the very discipline which they advocated for all true 'Gnostics'. This community bore little resemblance, however, to the communal asceticism pioneered on Egyptian soil in the middle of the third century.

The creativity of women's leadership in the first attempts at communally based asceticism in the West in the fourth century was anticipated to some extent by the pioneering role played by women ascetics in the East in the previous century. Monasticism appeared in Syria and Egypt at about the same time, but independently from each other. The bulk of writing on the historical developments from solitary asceticism to communally based monasticism focuses on the contribution of the 'Desert Fathers'. First, a man described by many as the founder of Christian monasticism, Anthony of Egypt (c. 251-c. 356), could find no communities for ascetic men when he renounced the world. Yet he was able to place his sister in a 'house of virgins'.[24] When she had advanced in years in this ascetic lifestyle, she

18. On the two competing dates for the origin of Montanism, AD 156-7 (Epiphanius), and AD 172 (Eusebius), see Robert M. Grant, *Augustus to Constantine: The Thrust of the Christian Movement into the Roman World*, New York 1970, pp. 130-1. I am indebted to Colin Brown, Reader in Religious Studies, University of Canterbury, for this reference.
19. Tertullian 'De monogamia', William P. Le Saint (trans.), *Ancient Christian Writers*, vol. 13, London 1951, p. 93. The hope for reunion after death is used to argue against a second marriage, interpreted as adultery. [*Ancient Christian Writers* is cited subsequently as *ACW*.]
20. 'De exhortatione castitatis' 9, in *The Ante-Nicene Fathers*, Alexander Roberts and James Donaldson (eds), Edinburgh 1864-72, Vol. 4, p. 55; 'De anima' 27, *Ante-Nicene Fathers*, Vol. 4, p. 207.
21. *Ante-Nicene Fathers*, Vol. 4, p. 10.
22. See W. H. C. Frend, *Martyrdom and Persecution in the Early Church: A Study of a Conflict from the Maccabees to Donatus*, Oxford 1965.
23. Origen, *Exhort. ad Mart.*, XVIII.
24. Athanasius, 'Vita Antonii' 3, *ACW*, Vol. 10, p. 20. According to Robert T. Meyer, women religious at this time (c. 271) generally continued to live with their families, meeting together for common exercises. This is the first instance of *parthenoi* in the Christian sense of 'a house or group of virgins', or possibly a place or home for religious, *that is*, a convent, p. 107.

became the superioress of a group of virgins.[25] 'Desert mothers' therefore saw the possibilities for the sharing of ascetic ideals on a communal basis while their Christian brothers were living a hermit or anchorite existence. Second, according to Margaret Smith, communities of women could come into existence earlier than those of men in Egypt, where 'the legal position of women had always been on an equality with that of men, and wives enjoyed the same rights as their husbands and where women were therefore more free to devote themselves at their own choice to the religious life'.[26] Ruether fails to cite this work in support of her interpretations of the protofeminism of women ascetics.[27] Third, many ascetics continued to live in the world in their own homes. Jean LaPorte has argued against the dominant 'escape from the world' thesis of asceticism, and has claimed that this form of virginal life was more important in the early church than convent monasticism.[28] From the time of Cyprian and of Methodius in the middle of the third century to the time of Chrysostom and Gregory the Great in the fifth and sixth centuries and later, thousands and thousands of virgins in all churches in the East and the West lived in their own homes without being subjected to a superior and a rule, under the general supervision of the bishop.[29] Despite the usual emphasis on Desert Fathers, it is clear that it can be argued that women in the East pioneered ascetic communities, sometimes in their own homes, long before the 'rules' of institutionalized monasticism were formulated by males using a military camp model.

Gradually the solitary asceticism of Anthony developed into the communally organized institutionalized monasticism of his younger contemporary Pachomius (290-346). As has been seen, women were the pioneers of the communal approach, although Pachomius, a former soldier, was the first to formulate the 'rule' which monasteries would follow. This final stage in the development from pure anchoritism or mitigated anchoritism to cenobitism grew out of the recognition of the need for an abbot. In the Pachomian ideal communal living was a preparation for solitary asceticism, and was considered inferior to encratite isolation. The Pachomian Rule stipulated the type of training required in the community life and drew on the military model of the camp.[30] Pachomius

25.   Athanasuis, 'Vita Antonii' 54, *ACW*, p. 66.
26.   Margaret Smith, *Studies of Early Mysticism in the Near and Middle East*, Amsterdam 1973, pp. 35-6, citing J. Amélineau, *Les Moines Egyptiens*, Paris 1889, p. 7.
27.   Ruether, *Women of Spirit*, pp. 73-4, 94, suggests tentatively that Macrina (c. 327-79), sister of Basil the Great and Gregory of Nyssa, 'perhaps should be credited with being the immediate source of the plan of life that came to be called the "Basilian rule" ', citing Gregory's *The Life of St Macrina*, in *Ascetical Works: Fathers of the Church*, Vol. 58, Washington 1967, p. 167.
28.   Jean LaPorte, *The Role of Women in Early Christianity: Studies in Women and Religion*, Vol. 7, New York 1982, pp. 70-1. See chapter 'Women in Contemplative Life', pp. 53-107.
29.   LaPorte, *Women in Early Christianity*, pp. 70-1.
30.   Derwas Chitty lists as the similarities between the general plan of the monastery and the military camps Pachomius would have known as a soldier: the coenobium which had an enclosing wall, the gate-house, guest-house, assembly hall, refectory with kitchen, bakehouse, hospital, and a number of houses comparable to the barrack-blocks in a legionary camp which held between twenty and forty monks each. See Derwas J. Chitty, *The Desert a City: An Introduction to the Study of Egyptian and Palestinian Monasticism under the Christian Empire*, Oxford 1966, p. 22.

divided his houses according to trade: weavers, tailors, makers of matting, shoemakers, bakers, cultivators, carpenters, and other trades. Compared with the number of cenobites, hermits were few. Pachomius, the founder of cenobitic monasticism proper, built a convent for his sister Mary opposite his own monastery on the bank of the Nile. There are, however, cases known of women living as hermits.[31] Mary became a leader in her own right, establishing a nunnery there and becoming its abbess.[32] Among other ascetic women was the desert mother Amma Talis. She spent eighty years in asceticism by the time she ruled over a women's monastery, one of twelve established in the city of Antinoë before the close of the century. One of her nuns, a certain Taor, was very beautiful, but her modesty and chastity were her protection, according to Palladius.[33] The popularity of asceticism among women in the East was attested to by Palladius, who reported finding 20,000 virgins and 10,000 monks in the city of Oxyrhynchus alone.[34] The male military model for institutionalized monasticism was to have certain implications for later monasticism. Pachomius was only the first among many male monastic pioneers to come out of a military background. In the work of Pachomius, Martin of Tours, Francis of Assisi, and Ignatius of Loyola, the singlemindedness of a soldier in the service of a particular cause was evident. However such singlemindedness was also to create certain blindspots, seen perhaps most clearly in the involvement of the Dominicans in the Inquisition.

In the light of the dualistic arguments used in particular by Ruether, it is necessary to emphasize that the spirituality of third-century asceticism and monasticism could perhaps best be described in terms of wholeness, rather than of dualism. For Anthony, asceticism was not an end in itself. His retirement into the desert for twenty years of complete anchoritism, in an effort to confront deliberately the power of the spirit of evil, also provided the basis of a liberation of the self. Only through such means could the ascetic be awakened to 'a consciousness of self which will be truly human and Christian'.[35] Anthony did not emerge from the desert as an emaciated 'shell', or as one showing signs of physical neglect. Rather, he was seen as one spiritually pure, neither shrunken with regret nor swollen with pleasure.[36] Etherealization, the devaluing of corporeality, or a wholly spiritual asceticism was not the ideal. Indeed, Louis Bouyer has warned post-Enlightenment observers of the inappropriateness of reading back such conclusions from the position of a 'false spiritualism, vaguely Cartesian'.[37] Viewing the human being as inseparably soul and body, ascetics had no contempt either for the creation or for the body. Taken

31. LaPorte, p. 80.
32. Smith, *Studies in Early Mysticism*, p. 36. No reference given.
33. Palladius, *Hist. Laus.*, lix, *ACW*, Vol. 34, p. 140.
34. Palladius, *Paradise of the Fathers*, i.337, E. A. Budge (trans.), New York 1905, p. 337-8. These 'rounded figures' may have been 'rounded up'. On the accuracy of Palladius, see P. Peeters, 'Une vie copte de St Jean De Lycopolis', *Analecta Bollandiana*, Vol. 54, 1936, pp. 359-83, and W. Telfer, 'The Trustworthiness of Palladius', *Journal of Theological Studies*, Vol. 38, 1937, pp. 379-83.
35. Bouyer, *The Spirituality of the New Testament*, p. 308.
36. 'Vita Antonii' 14; col. 864C.
37. Bouyer, p. 319.

that the term *monachos* (monk) could well be a rendering of a Syrian technical term meaning 'sole or single', it would seem that the principal aim at first of ascetic monasticism was to 'attain an inner unity, the opposite of sexual duality, even going so far as a union with "the only begotten Son" of God'.[38] Although spectacular austerities appeared in Syria in the third century, the mainstream of monastic asceticism was characterized by a 'materiality'. The practice of charity was a safeguard against ascetic escapism in the form of fantasizing, and the very materiality of monastic asceticism was 'an integral part of that "reasonable" character which these ancient masters never ceased to emphasize'.[39] The third-century concern with inner unity was gradually displaced in the fourth century by an increasing emphasis on virginity and celibacy. However, the extraordinary popularity of Athanasius' *Life of Anthony* in the second half of the fourth century ensured that Anthony's heroism and spirituality remained a model of ascetism. It was also at this time that monasticism gained the potential to be transformed into a school of learned spirituality, primarily through the influence of Basil the Great (*c.* 330-79) and Eustathius of Sebaste (*c.* 300-*c.* 377). Bouyer interprets this in terms of decline from 'an essentially popular and evangelical movement' to a monasticism which was to become 'wholly permeated with the heritage of Alexandria and, above all, of Origen'.[40] In any consideration of third- and fourth-century asceticism and monasticism, the writings of intellectuals must be treated with some caution. Gribomont's warning that the writings of 'intellectuals, who were experienced in understanding doctrinal nuances and were carried away by the words and prestige of the philosophers, are seldom reliable guides, for the ascetic movement drew its following mainly from among the ordinary people',[41] could well be taken into account in evaluating the practice of asceticism by women, who likewise cannot be judged through their own writings.

Properly organized monasteries in the West came only in the early years of the fifth century. The revisionists Elizabeth Clark and Rosemary Ruether have analysed acccording to a feminist interpretation male ascetics' writings, some of which described the first ascetic communities of women in Rome, Bethlehem, and Jerusalem. Once the specifically 'feminist' motivations women may have had towards asceticism in the fourth century have been identified, they can be viewed within the larger context of complex motivational factors, arising from the changing political, economic, sociological, and religious dimensions of the fourth-century world.

---

38.   Jean Gribomont, 'Monasticism and Asceticism', Marie Miklashevsky (trans.), in *Christian Spirituality: Origins to the Twelfth Century*, Vol. 16 of *World Spirituality: An Encyclopedic History of the Religious Quest*, Bernard McGinn and John Meyendorff (eds), London 1986, p. 90.
39.   Gribomont, 'Monasticism and Asceticism', p. 90.
40.   Gribomont, p. 330; cf. Deems, who sees in the last quarter of the third century the completion of the popular basis for fourth-century asceticism, primarily through the syncretistic Greco-Roman world, the renaissance of the mysteries, the extension of the popular Neo-Pythagoreanism and Neo-Platonism, and the discipline of the body for the good of the soul or for union with deity. Deems, p. 165.
41.   Gribomont, p. 92.

In her article 'Sexual Politics in the Writings of John Chrysostom', Elizabeth Clark has used Kate Millett's theory of 'sexual politics' to explain the perceived imbalance of power between men and women in the fourth and fifth centuries.[42] 'Patriarchy' is accordingly blamed with coopting the Christian God and aligning this male-perceived deity with the immutabilities of 'nature' in order to preserve the structures of a society based essentially on distinctions of sex. Clark defends the use of this theory against claims of anachronism, in the light of Chrysostom's use of the term *politeia* to designate the celibate state. Born in Antioch of rich and noble parents, Chrysostom (*c*. 347-407) lived under the Pachomian rule for about eight years, before being made deacon in 381. Most of his homilies were written from 386-98, after which he became Patriarch of Constantinople. It is through a consideration of these works that Clark argues that Chrysostom believed that 'female subjection' could be partially overcome through 'the women's profession of celibacy, whether in virginity or widowhood'.[43] Clark does not describe women thus liberated as 'feminists', or credit them with 'virginal feminism'. Her feminist position is clearly expressed, however, in the claim that Chrysostom would employ 'theological rationalizations for his conservative views' in 'one of the more interesting—and deadly—manifestations of the workings of "sexual politics" '.[44] This alleged 'deadliness' is not subsequently demonstrated. She argues that, as far as Chrysostom was concerned, for those not willing to 'espouse the heroic life of abstinence it was "patriarchy as usual" '.[45] If any among the 3,000 virgins and widows enrolled in the Antioch church[46] doubted the nobility of their ascetic lifestyle they could have received encouragement from Chrysostom. He believed that ascetics and those leading continent sacrificial lives could imitate those who had given their lives for the faith in martyrdom,[47] no longer a possibility since the State recognition of Christianity after 312. Because Chrysostom once likened marriage to two fugitive slaves whose legs are bound together with chains,[48] Clark proceeds to depict a 'woman's escape route' from the bondage of marriage in the profession of celibacy.[49]

While Clark does not claim to portray accurately the women ascetics of the fourth century, her preoccupation with Chrysostom's more misogynist passages results in the creation of woman in the image of male prejudice. Women have accordingly been subject to a dubious form of twentieth-century reductionism in the attempt to illustrate 'the contemporary feminist thesis that sexual domination has supplied western culture with "its most fundamental concept of power" and that the genius of patriarchy lay in aligning the Christian God with the preservation of

42. Clark, 'Sexual Politics', p. 3. See Kate Millett, *Sexual Politics*, New York 1970.
43. 'Sexual Politics', p. 4.
44. 'Sexual Politics', p. 4.
45. 'Sexual Politics', p. 4.
46. Chrysostom, 'Homiliae in Matthaeum' 66.3, *Patrologiae Cursus Completus . . . Series Graeca*, ed. J. P. Migne, Vol. 58, col. 630. [*Patrologiae . . . Graeca* is cited subsequently as *PG*].
47. Chrysostom, 'S. Babylam' 1, *PG*, Vol. 50, cols 533-76.
48. Chrysostom, 'De Virg.' 41, *PG*, Vol. 48, col. 563.
49. 'Sexual Politics', p. 17.

the status quo'.[50] Any possible 'feminist' motivation for fourth-century women to become ascetics is seen to be a direct consequence of male misogynism. The claim that virginity gave females an opportunity to rise above Chrysostom's perception of 'the usual limitations of their sex'[51] encourages the conclusion that the popularity of asceticism among women at this time settles the matter. No evidence is presented of societal factors to question the elevation of misogynism to be the key interpretative principle in Clark's schema. Male perception of woman is thus mistaken for women ascetics' self-perception.

'Feminist' motivations of fourth-century women for adopting the ascetic life are identified more clearly by Rosemary Ruether in 'Mothers of the Church: Ascetic Women in the Late Patristic Age'.[52] She also provides a narrative description of the lives of Paula, Melania the Elder, Melania Junior, and other women ascetics. Ruether seeks to reinterpret the ascetic movement, not usually seen as a liberating influence for women, as something that 'paradoxically suggested that women might now be liberated from their definition' by the traditional roles of marriage and motherhood. In support of this she describes Christ as the founder of the new virginal humanity, at least according to the perception of later male writers.[53] The decision of some women to seek the ascetic life, even when their families objected strongly on the grounds of losing a marriageable daughter, is trivialized by reference to the 'patriarchal clan'.[54] The church is viewed in a monolithic sense in its alleged support for women who made such decisions and of its offering the new alternative embraced by many women. Ruether claims that male writers justified sweeping disobedience to 'the established order of family and state' by dubbing great ascetic women 'new Theclas'.[55] Acknowledging the relativity of what is liberating for different persons, Ruether sees the most important factor of the liberating choice as 'the sense of taking charge of one's own life; of rejecting a state of being governed and defined by others' and of having the 'sense of moving from being an object to becoming a subject'.[56] She wishes to argue accordingly that asceticism in the fourth century was experienced by women as a liberating choice: first, because it allowed women to 'throw

50. *Jerome, Chrysostom, and Friends*, p. 3.
51. 'Sexual Politics', p. 16, and *Jerome*, p. 16.
52. In *Women of Spirit*, Ruether and McLaughlin (eds), pp. 72-98.
53. 'Mothers of the Church', p. 72.
54. 'Mothers of the Church', p. 72.
55. 'Mothers of the Church, pp. 74-5. The life of Thecla, the legendary disciple of Paul, is recorded in the *Apocryphal Acts of Paul and Thecla, c.* 170. She is said to have turned her back on the demands of home and sacrificed her fiancé to follow Paul, leading a life of adventure and self-sacrifice, and at the end of her life still teaching and healing all who came to her. Both Reuther and feminist biblical theologian, Virginia Ramey Mollenkott, take Thecla as historical. Neither attempts to account for the origin of the Thecla legend, or to separate fact from legend. See Mollenkott, *The Divine Feminine: The Biblical Imagery of God as Female*, New York 1984, for feminist reinterpretation of Thecla, in which her masculine behaviour is seen to reflect the masculinizing results of centuries of patriarchy when religious women were told to model themselves on an exclusively male deity. Contemporary Christian feminists who do not wish to masculinize themselves are encouraged to consider as appropriate the Psalmist's image of Yahweh as role-model for her [sic] female slaves, p. 63.
56. 'Mothers of the Church', p. 73.

off the traditional female roles'; second, because it 'offered female-directed communities where they could pursue the highest self-development as autonomous persons'; and third, because it offered security.[57]

Ruether's description of various women ascetics intersects at no point with her earlier work which attempted to explain the ambivalence of both virginal feminism and misogynism in the fathers of the church according to a dualistic psychology, alleged to be the basis of the patristic doctrine of the human person.[58] The feminist interpretative framework fails to affect the narrative description, but Ruether concludes that asceticism drew women in the fourth century due to: its possibilities which 'departed dramatically from their traditional role definitions under patriarchy', its enabling of women to 'successfully combat demands for unwelcome marriage alliances', its opportunities to turn to 'intense study, self-development and independent life in female-run communities', and lastly, its assurance of 'absolute equality with men on the plane of their spiritual kingdom'.[59] None of her consideration of the lives of women ascetics as recorded by men sways her from the almost monocausal feminist explanation offered at the beginning. Here, these feminist motivating factors were listed, with the conclusion that: 'As a result, throngs of women were attracted to asceticism at this time, especially as the old Roman way of life was disintegrating'.[60] Other motivations for women to take up the ascetic life, in particular the high-born Roman women associated with Jerome from 382, can now be discussed.

The fourth century brought considerable changes to the political and economic realms in which Christians lived. The last four decades of the previous century, following the first Empire-wide persecution in 250, brought the Church into a climate of sustained growth in numbers, wealth, and property. Christianity emerged from the Decian persecution with renewed strength, and increasingly became an attractive option to the upper classes, as against the pagan religions of the day. The asceticism that took root in this period of relative tolerance was only to take particular shape after the conversion of Constantine in 312, due in no small measure to the nominalism which characterized the church in the post-persecution context. Coming just nine years after the Great Persecution under Galerius and Diocletian, the conversion of the Emperor was a revolution of immense proportions in the life of the Church and radically changed the political and economic realms in which Christians lived. The Edict of Milan in 313 recognized the legal status of churches, and within a matter of decades Christianity became respectable and fashionable in high society, which was itself in a state of flux. Rapid upward social mobility was possible in the Christianized Roman Empire. According to Eusebius, Constantine showed direct favour to Christians of low degree, lavishly bestowing codicils of equestrian rank , and even senatorial dignity, on those following the new State religion.[61] While the powerful Roman families making up

57. 'Mothers of the Church', p. 73.
58. Ruether 'Misogynism and Virginal Feminism in the Fathers of the Church'.
59. 'Mothers of the Church', p. 93.
60. 'Mothers of the Church', p. 73.
61. Eusebius, *Vita Const.* iv. 54; cf. 37-39.

the old senatorial order remained faithful to their traditional religion down to the end of the fourth century, Constantine was able to build up a Christian aristocracy sympathetic to his religious position.[62] The presence of Christians in the army, before persecution ceased, attests to the nominalism of the church, even before imperial patronage was gained.[63] It is within this context of the emergence of a predominantly Christian society that the appeal of asceticism for fourth-century women and men must be viewed. Retreat from that society became more and more common.

The dangers facing the church in the post-persecution context were not those of survival, but of worldliness, a lowering of moral standards, and the misuse of power. Total withdrawal from the world, following the Jewish and Christian traditions of desert spirituality, had already emerged in the East in the late third century with hermits and anchorites. Voluntary exile from worldly engagement was seen as a solution by those caught in the onset of the economic disintegration of the Empire. The continuities between martyrdom and asceticism were also apparent in the fourth century, when ascetic withdrawal became a form of 'voluntary persecution'. The spirit of the pre-Constantine days was captured in the call to idealism, self-renewal and joyful service. The non-orthodox sects which still survived in the mid-fourth century remained true to their former ascetic practices.[64] The drift into respectable Christianity and the nominalism of the church, now not only hellenized and at peace but more importantly imperially patronized, provided the necessary impetus for many fourth century Christians to leave conventional Christianized society. They withdrew to the desert in pursuit of perfection outside the community which had failed to mirror their own ideals. The sense of laxity was heightened as the church became more lenient in its treatment of the lapsed. Christians increasingly expressed their disapproval by retreating from active involvement into the spiritual silences of the ascetic in the desert. In this political and economic context, it is understandable that really serious Christians not infrequently judged it necessary to break with the world, abandoning material possessions, career and marriage, so as to be completely free to serve one master, Christ. This many women did, either at their baptism or when they had experienced a deeper commitment to Christ. The conversions of the Roman matrons who formed deep friendships with Jerome were from the world, rather than from paganism.[65] Whether ascetics played a political role, as claimed by Rosemary Ruether, is open to question.[66]

Some of the sociological factors that contributed to the rise of asceticism among women have already been alluded to, in particular affluence and

62.   A. H. M. Jones, 'The Social Background of the Struggle Between Paganism and Christianity', in *The Conflict Between Paganism and Christianity in the Fourth Century*, Arnaldo Momigliano (ed.), Oxford 1963, especially pp. 26-36.
63.   Jones, 'Struggle Between Paganism and Christianity', p. 24.
64.   W. H. C. Frend, *The Rise of Christianity*, London 1984, pp. 567-8.
65.   Peter Brown, *Religion and Society in the Age of Saint Augustine*, London 1972, p. 173.
66.   Ruether says: 'In a Christianized Roman Empire that believed that the ascetics were at least as important to its defense and favour as were armies and statesmen, they exercised a public and even a political role', *Women of Spirit*, p. 93, citing Peter Brown's article, 'The Rise and Function of the Holy Man in Late Antiquity', *Journal of Roman Studies*, Vol. 61, 1971, pp. 88ff. But Brown's passage does not support Ruether's claim.

nominalism in a predominantly Christian society. What were the social constraints that seemed to place such severe restrictions on women in the fourth century, as against their male counterparts? Such constraints must have made the possibility of leading an ascetic lifestyle all the more attractive. Marriage was the most important societal norm challenged by these new heroines of the faith. This need not necessarily be interpreted according to a feminist framework, as Peter Brown has shown.[67] The ideal of virginity had social implications both for men and for women in the early church. Virginity meant lifelong abstinence from sexual intercourse, and the precise physical state of virginity 'was upheld as the state to which all human beings—men quite as much as women—had every right to aspire'.[68] While the virginity of a young woman was guarded by her family until marriage, continence of men involved the 'irrevocable renunciation of all future sexual relations', sometimes following youthful sexual activity, widowerhood, or a vow of continence within marriage. In Roman society, bethrothal, marriages, and divorces among the upper class were seldom arranged for sentimental reasons. Although men usually arranged these events for the political and financial profit of the families involved, some women had been able to choose their own husbands.[69] Peter Brown interprets the social significance of the ideal of virginity in the fourth century in terms, first, of the demonstration that 'the body itself was held to be no longer permeable to the demands that society made upon it'; second, of the creation of the yardstick of 'the ideal structures of a truly "human" society' formed by purely voluntary joinings, in contrast to the present structures of human society; third, of the attraction of a form of 'mediation' between the divine and the human; and fourth, of the assertion of the right of the individual to seek for himself or herself different forms of solidarity consonant with the high destiny of free persons.[70] It was in these terms that the virgin body was profoundly asocial, not belonging to society as naturally defined.

The decision, then, of wealthy, high-born Roman women and heiresses like Marcella and Melania (and their younger followers) to lead celibate ascetic lives would have been extremely perplexing to both men and women in society at large. There were already some means for women to control their own fertility, other than through abstinence, although these were by no means absolutely reliable.[71] The Roman ascetic widows gave up the sole responsibility they bore for the management of their own homes once they left these for life in communities jointly supervised with male ascetics.[72] The greater educational opportunities made possibly by freedom from family responsibilities no doubt compensated for such loss. Ruether's assimilation of societal factors into general feminist factors seems plausible

67. See P. Brown, 'The Notion of Virginity in the Early Church', in *Christian Spirituality*, pp. 427-43.
68. Brown, 'The Notion of Virginity', p. 427.
69. Sarah B. Pomeroy, *Goddesses, Whores, Wives, and Slaves: Women in Classical Antiquity*, New York 1975, pp. 155-7.
70. Brown, pp. 429, 430, 432-4, 436.
71. See Pomeroy, *Goddesses, Whores, Wives and Slaves*, pp. 166-8.
72. Pomeroy, p. 169; cf. Ruether, *Women of Spirit*, p. 93.

only because of her almost exclusive emphasis on the negative aspects of Roman society.[73]

Key phrases used by Clark and Ruether indicate that the true context within which they have analysed fourth century women ascetics is not that of the fourth century. Rather the implicit contexts of their work are, first, that of the continued exclusion of women from ordained ministry of many a contemporary denomination (Ruether); and second, a post-pill view of sexuality which devalues and downgrades celibate feminism (Clark and Ruether). These contexts need to be made explicit, in order to judge the accuracy of their perception of women ascetics.

Ruether's emphasis on 'rights' reflects the activist dimension of her Christian feminism within church structures which many are trying to change in the United States of America and elsewhere. Her language is clearly intended to prick the consciences of those who think otherwise. The male magisterium is blamed for the non-survival of the letters written to Jerome by Marcella, Paula, Melania, the younger Paula, and the younger Melania: 'This exclusion of even the holiest and most learned women from the public magisterium seems to have prevented work from their own hands from being included in the corpus of the Church's tradition'.[74] The explanation offered for 'not a line' surviving from their pens, 'seems to derive from the official Church's view that women, no matter how holy, cannot qualify as teachers of the Church'.[75] The influence is depicted as being exercised 'behind a façade of male direction'. A certain philosophical naïveté is betrayed by Ruether in her conclusion that: 'We are forced to reconstruct their lives and personalities through the uncertain mirror of their male admirers (or detractors)'.[76] Interpretation, critical evaluation, and the rule of evidence would still apply even if the letters of these women had survived. Following this a number of ascetic women are portrayed as being courageous and independent. Yet Ruether can curiously round off her narrative by portraying them in terms of tragedy. Their alleged tragedy is that in choosing an 'antisexual' path of accomplishment, and in 'accepting in good faith the ideals held out to them by the Church, they were nevertheless denied their *rightful* place in the Church's tradition'.[77] The very real achievements of women ascetics, in their own terms, can be appreciated to a greater extent once this implicit context of Ruether's interpretation is made explicit. The exclusion of women from official positions of leadership from the third century could then be seen as a vital religious factor in the rise of asceticism among women in the fourth century.

Even after the middle of the second century, women had an active role in church leadership. This included public roles as prophets and teachers, as well as the less controversial functions of widow and deaconess.[78] But

73.   The question for Ruether seems to be one of 'rights': *Women of Spirit*, p. 93; cf. the positive portrayal of opportunities for Roman women who had access to both money and power by Pomeroy, p. 189.
74.   *Women of Spirit*, p. 76.
75.   *Women of Spirit*, p. 75.
76.   *Women of Spirit*, p. 76.
77.   *Women of Spirit*, pp. 93-4, (my emphasis).
78.   Elisabeth Schüssler Fiorenza, *In Memory of Her: A Feminist Theological Reconstruction of Christian Origins* London 1983, pp. 300-4.

the third century church order, *Didascalia Apostolorum*, maintained that women were not appointed by Jesus to teach. Female leadership became circumscribed and restricted to the office of deaconess in the *Apostolic Constitutions* of the fourth century.[79] She was largely expected to minister to other women, and was certainly not considered part of the clergy until the end of the fourth century.[80] At about this same time, Chrysostom provided one possible theological justification of this state of affairs of the retrogression in women's official ministry for any ambitious women ascetics in the fourth century. He affirmed that women had leadership roles not as a right, but as a privilege in the primitive Christian communities. Women could only travel in the service of the gospel when the 'angelic condition' existed[81] and to prophesy or be called disciples or apostles was now ruled out.[82] The ministry of women in the early Church could not be seen as a precedent, and women were now excluded from any public teaching role because of the dissoluteness of life in Chrysostom's age. He perceived women playing no small part in the moral downturn, being preoccupied with the womanly concerns of how to make themselves seductive with splendid clothing and to decorate their faces with pigments and dyes, thus causing their husbands ever-increasing expense.[83] Although women were away from their own homes in the early church, they did this without detriment to their own reputations, but 'now even in their own bedrooms they do not escape suspicion'.[84] The following discussion of Marcella's not inconsiderable teaching ministry in Rome shows that women worked creatively within the restrictions of their day. An interpretation altogether different from that of Ruether can be gained even from Jerome's writings.

There were no deaconesses in the West in the fourth and fifth centuries. I would wish to argue that it was the women ascetics in Rome who fulfilled this teaching role in some part. The Roman ladies who turned their mansions into retreat houses exercised a private teaching ministry in their own homes. The most telling record of the scholarly pursuits of the Roman monastic circle is found in sixteen letters from Jerome to Marcella. None of her queries survives. Marcella was the first Roman lady of rank to accept asceticism, and her monastic circle came into existence following the popularisation of ascetic ideals from the East by Athanasius. Athanasius, the focal point of Arian attack in the fourth century, was forced into exile and went to Rome from 339 to 342, bringing with him models of asceticism from Egypt. Jerome reported that:

79.   The Constitutions say: 'We do not permit our women to teach in the Church, but only to pray and hear those that teach', and they limit the liturgical ministry of the deaconess to the functions of keeping the doors and assisting the 'presbyters in the baptism of women for reasons of decency.' See *Apostolic Constitutions*, III, 6: 1-2. See also George H. Tavard, *Woman in Christian Tradition*, London 1973, pp. 94-5.
80.   At the time of the New Testament women were deacons just as men were. By the late fourth century the women deacons were called deaconesses, coming after deacons in status. From the fourth century on, references to deaconesses multiplied in the East, except in Egypt, where no traces of them appear. See Roger Gryson, *The Ministry of Women in the Early Church*, Minnesota 1976, pp. 109-10.
81.   Hom. 3 Acta 1 *PG*, Vol. 60, 34.
82.   Hom. 73 Matt. 3-4, *PG*, Vol. 58, 677; Sal. Prisc. et Aq. 1, 3 *PG*, Vol. 51, 192.
83.   Sal. Prisc. et Aq. 1, 3 *PG*, Vol. 51, 192.
84.   Hom. 73 Matt. 4, *PG*, Vol. 58, 677.

it was from some priests from Alexandria, and from Pope Athanasius, and subsequently from Peter, who, to escape the persecution of the Arian heretics, had all fled for refuge to Rome as the safest haven in which they could find communion — it was from these that Marcella heard of the life of the blessed Anthony.[85]

Marcella read Athanasius' *Life of Anthony*, and her admiration of the virgins, widows, and monks of Egypt deepened when she met Bishop Peter of Alexandria. He had been forced to flee to Rome for religious reasons and was an exile there from 373 to 378. Soon after the death of her husband, Marcella gathered around her a whole group of noblewomen and girls, who met for scripture study at her home on the Aventine and shared her ascetic ideals. Thus she became the founder of the Roman ascetic circle. Open-minded and intellectually curious, Marcella was a demanding philologist and fluent Hebraist. Well schooled by Jerome, she found an independence in a new teaching role after his departure from Rome in 385. Although exercised in the privacy of her home, this teaching ministry reached public prominence. Marcella's accomplishments as a leader behind the scenes gain their full significance in the light of a particularly fierce misogynistic outburst by Jerome, in which he attacked women who exercised a leadership role through their teaching:

> What do these wretched women want! . . . Simon Magus founded a heretical sect with the help of the harlot Helena. Nicholas of Antioch, that contriver of everything filthy, directed women's groups. Marcion sent ahead of him to Rome a woman to infatuate the people for him. Apelles had Philomena as a companion for his teaching. Montanus, the proclaimer of the spirit of impurity, first used Prisca and Maximilla, noble and rich women, to seduce many communities by gold, and then polluted them with heresy . . . Even now the mystery of sinfulness takes effect and the two-timing sex trips everyone up.[86]

But in his tribute to Marcella, Jerome testifies that 'in case of a dispute arising as to the testimony of Scripture on any subject, recourse was had to her to settle it'.[87] Priests overcame the ecclesiastical prejudices of their day, and questioned her concerning doubtful and obscure points. Marcella was not one to parrot Jerome's replies. She made them her own, but diplomatically attributed her ideas to her former instructor, so as not to 'inflict a wrong upon the male sex', at least in Jerome's perception.[88] This does not reflect a loss of nerve or low self-esteem, and in no way diminishes Marcella's very real achievements in overcoming prejudice in a male-only

85.   Ep. cxxvii. 5, in *Nicene and Post-Nicene Fathers*, 2nd series, Schaff and Wace (eds), Oxford 1890-1900, Vol. 6, pp. 254-5. J. N. D. Kelly questions whether it was Athanasius himself who personally fired her interest in the Desert Fathers. He says this is unlikely as she would have only been a girl of ten or twelve at the time, and in any case subsequently married. However, regardless of these biographical considerations, it is clear that Athanasius' popularization of ascetic ideals had filtered through to Marcella by the time she turned down an attractive offer of remarriage and dedicated herself to chaste widowhood along ascetic lines. See Kelly, *Jerome: His Life, Writings, and Controversies*, London 1975, p. 185. [*Nicene and Post-Nicene Fathers* is cited subsequently as *NPF*.]
86.   Ep. cxxxii. 4, *NPF*, 2nd series, Vol. 6, p. 254; *Patrologiae Cursus Completus . . . Series Latina*, Vol. 22, 1152ff. [*Patrologia . . . Latina* is cited subsequently as *PL*.]
87.   Ex. cxxvii. 7, *NPF*, 2nd series, Vol. 6, p. 255.
88.   Ep. cxxvii. 7.

domain. In this remarkable way, asceticism gave women a certain independence and recognition in the church of their day, and won back some of the ground previously lost, or taken from them. Jerome assessed the impact of the handful of high-born Roman women of Marcella's circle in terms of changing the popular attitude toward asceticism from one of hostility to one of praise:

> I had the joy of seeing Rome transformed into another Jerusalem. Monastic establishments for virgins became numerous, and of hermits there were countless numbers. In fact so many were the servants of God that monasticism which had been a term of reproach became subsequently one of honour.[89]

Some sixty years earlier, in the middle of the fourth century, 'no high born lady at Rome had made profession of the monastic life, or had ventured — so strange and ignominious and degrading did it then seem — publicly to call herself a nun'.[90]

Far from being passive conformers to misogynist male theology, women ascetics from the Roman circle pioneered monastic communities that were to play an important role in the adaptation of eastern monastic experience for later transplantation to the west. Properly organised monasteries in the west came only in the early years of the fifth century. When Jerome lived in Rome from 382 to 385 there were no communities for male ascetics. Women from Marcella's circle provided the communal model here. This was starting to be rectified in 387, when Augustine reported seeing several communal lodging houses, both of men and of women, following the ascetic lifestyle. Jerome conducted an ascetic campaign in Rome with the approval of Pope Damasus from 383 to 384. Marcella practised a moderate asceticism and did not withdraw from the world altogether. But Jerome advised a young ascetic, Eustochium, not to leave her room, keep only the company of virgins, and give herself completely to prayer and Bible study. The rigorous mortifications willingly accepted by her sister Blaesilla earned Jerome the charge of fanaticism from many moderate Christians. Her death, the suspicions felt towards the new asceticism by Pope Siricius in 385, and an inquiry by the authorities of the Roman church all contributed to Jerome's departure in August 385 for the East. With Paula, a member of the Roman monastic circle, he planned to form a permanent monastic community on Oriental soil. Paula played an indispensable role in the establishment of a men's monastery and triple monastery for women in Bethlehem. Only through the sale of her vast estates in Italy could Jerome exercise leadership in a monastery subsequently built. J. N. D. Kelly notes that these monasteries in Bethlehem, and monasteries established by Melania the Elder and Rufinus in Jerusalem became 'living illustrations of how the forms of community living developed in the east could be moulded to western habits and temperaments'.[91] They were indeed pioneers, and the thousands of pilgrims from the West took home positive reports of their disciplined ascetic communities. Rufinus returned to Italy

89. Ep. cxxvii. 8, *NPF*, 2nd series, Vol. 6, p. 256.
90. Ep. cxxvii. 5, *NPF*, 2nd series, Vol. 6, p. 254.
91. Kelly, *Jerome*, pp. 139-40.

in 397, and Jerome continued to provide advice for fledgling communities in the west. Unfortunately, Kelly gives sole credit for this creativity to *male* leadership, when he concludes: 'Many factors played their part, but these foundations of Rufinus and Jerome, Latin outposts of eastern soil which had absorbed and adapted eastern experience, were prominent in showing the way'.[92] No specific mention is made in this passage of Paula, who ruled a triple monastery for women and a guest house for passing travellers until her death in 404. Eustochium then inherited the leadership of a monastery housing fifty virgins. Some monasteries of women may have emerged independently in Gaul as early as the fourth century.[93] Without the wealth, sacrifice and perseverance of these women leaders the West would have lacked adequate models for the monasticism of later centuries. Critically important influences on the shaping of western monasticism were to be John Cassian's *Institutes* (425-30), the work in Gaul of Martin of Tours, and the Rule of Benedict (*c.* 540).[94]

Far more serious than Ruether's downplaying of the achievements of women ascetics is the revisionists' portrayal of women ascetics as being de-sexed by the tools of theological argument. Clark's thesis of 'sexual divestment' follows necessarily from her attempt to interpret women's asceticism according to the twentieth century anthropological concept of liminality, especially as expounded by Victor Turner.[95] Ruether's interpretation is based on the questionable thesis that male-female dualism was assimilated into soul-body dualism in patristic theology. Curiously, neither considers the explanation offered by early feminist church historian Mary Daly, that projection mechanisms were involved in the misogynistic attitude of the Church Fathers.[96] Woman is left created primarily in the image of male prejudice.

Clark's image of fourth-century woman ascetics derives its authority from the success with which her colligatory concept of women's sexual divestment integrates details into the larger interpretative scheme.[97] Her interpretation is flawed to the extent that she does not critically evaluate the image portrayed by misogynistic writings against other evidence. In her initial statements, Clark is careful to emphasize that the transformation of women occurs from a male perspective. She argues that if true friendship is possible only among equals, 'the women must (from the men's viewpoint) be transformed into equals who share their interests'. However, a possible

92.   Kelly, p. 140; he does, however, link the houses of Rufinus and Melania the Elder on the Mount of Olives with the contribution Jerome's monasteries made to the emergence of monastic institutions in the west, p. 139.
93.   Sulpicius Severus, Dialogues II. 11-12, and Ep. 2.
94.   See Philip Rousseau, *Ascetics, Authority, and the Church in the Age of Jerome and Cassian*, Oxford 1978, especially pp. 152-60 and 169-88.
95.   Victor Turner, *The Ritual Process: Structure and Anti-structure*, Chicago 1969, especially pp. 102-7.
96.   For her argument that compensation for misogynism in the honouring of Mary served unconsciously as a means to relieve any possible guilt feelings about injustice to the other sex that came about through their transferral to 'the other' of their own guilt feelings over sexuality and hyper-susceptibility to sexual stimulation, see Mary Daly, *The Church and the Second Sex* ('With a new feminist postchristian introduction by the author'), New York 1975, pp. 64-7.
97.   See W. H. Walsh, 'Colligatory Concepts in History', in *Studies in the Nature and Teaching of History*, W. H. Burston and D. Thompson (eds), London 1967, pp. 72, 78.

differentiation between this transformation, and women's self-image, is not subsequently made. Her acknowledgement that 'partially informed guesses' about women ascetics' personalities and interests are possible only, seems to have served as a major detraction to further questioning.[98] Certain 'conceptual transformations' of the status of Paula, Marcella, and others is alleged to have taken place, which allowed Jerome and Chrysostom to accept them on an equal footing. Women were 'in transition' towards a 'transcendence of femaleness'.[99] An uncritical acceptance of Victor Turner's concept of liminality results in a remarkable piece of reductionism. Not only is monasticism a 'chronic liminality', but the women ascetic friends of Jerome and Chrysostom were 'liminars par excellence'.[100] Clark's claim that women ascetics had 'renounced their very gender identity' leads on swiftly to her theme of sexual divestment of women, in which renunciation of 'sexual identity' as well as sexual relations is stressed.[101] Advice positively insensitive to human feeling follows the attempt by Jerome and Chrysostom to 'turn them into something other than female'. This is amplified by the over-zealous desire to divest women of husbands, children, money, and property, in effect to 'reduce them to the poverty and humility characteristic of the liminal state'.[102] Women's and men's decision to accept voluntary celibacy within marriage is regarded as a successful outcome of the attempts to turn spouses into brothers and sisters, with 'sexuality and family relations' being removed accordingly. With these removed, all that remains 'is the need for the women to transcend their femaleness'.[103] Clark's claim that the most preferable thing would be 'the women's transformation into "men" ' rests on the assumption that patristic thought likened the man to the soul and the woman to the body.[104] Neither the passage cited, nor alleged to be cited in support of Clark's claim that Jerome 'likens the woman to the body and the man to the soul', could sustain such an interpretation.

The distortions in Clark's portrayal of the ascetic women follow from her acceptance of genital sexual expression between heterosexuals as normative and as constituting 'sexual relations'. Olympias is removed 'even further from the realm of sexual functioning: rumor has it, he reports, that although she had been married for over a year and a half, she remained a virgin'.[105] The attempted reduction of the appearance of femininity, as socially defined at that time, is mistaken by Clark for an attempted reduction of 'the sexuality of their female friends.' By decrying the use of feminine clothing, jewellery, and make-up, were not Jerome and Chrysostom rather trying to reduce the *appearance* of female sexuality? Clark then audaciously claims that Jerome's concern that spiritually minded women renounce cosmetics and silk dresses 'points to his attempt

98.   *Jerome, Chrysostom, and Friends*, p. 46.
99.   *Jerome, Chrysostom and Friends*, p. 48.
100. *Jerome, Chrysostom and Friends*, p. 49.
101. *Jerome, Chrysostom and Friends*, pp. 49-50.
102. *Jerome, Chrysostom and Friends*, pp. 50-52.
103. *Jerome, Chrysostom and Friends*, p. 55.
104. Jerome, 'Epistola and Ephesios' III (Eph. 5: 25ff.), *PL*, Vol. 26, 565ff. The passage appears to be wrongly cited in Clark, fn. 168, p. 93.
105. *Jerome, Chrysostom, and Friends*, p. 57.

to neutralize their femininity, as that was socially defined, as well as their biological femaleness'.[106] One is left perplexed as to how such female biological neutralization could have taken place, in the days before hormone treatments, sex-change operations, and genetic manipulation! Clark's claim that Jerome was concerned that Blaesilla not use her *cingulus* to cut herself in two, so as to accentuate the femaleness of her form,[107] could hardly be taken as evidence for biological neutralization. Here again, it was the *appearance* of femininity which was of concern. Suddenly in Clark's conclusion to this section on liminality, the attempt by males to portray women in certain ways is transformed into women's self-image. One of Clark's reasons why friendships between the early male and female ascetics flourished was that: 'the women, divested of family and sexual relations, indeed of sexuality itself, were perceived as hovering in the limbo of liminality in transition to a higher-than-female state'.[108] Perhaps scholars today would consider these 'celibate females', who 'provide us with near-perfect examples of a new being in the making, complete with all the ambivalence we might expect would attend such a venture', as androgynous.[109] No attempt to correct this image through a consideration of women's self-perception is made.

Any de-sexing of women and the exaltation of virginity above the married state had been the subject of official inquiry by the mid-fourth century church. Masculinising tendencies in asceticism were firmly checked by the Council of Gangra in Paphlagonia (340). Eustathius of Sebaste, whose efforts from 330 to 340 led to the first appearance of organised asceticism in Armenia, had taught that the distinction of sex was to be done away with as far as possible. Marriage was condemned and family ties were to be ignored. The women who had left their husbands due to Eustathius' persuasion had been cutting their hair short and had adopted male dress to minimize the appearance of femininity.[110] This council, however, forbade virgins to exalt themselves above the married, condemned any who lived unmarried for any reason other than the beauty and holiness of virginity, and anathematized those who condemned marriage as inconsistent with salvation.[111] Margaret Smith notes that the very fact of the condemnation proves that the celibate life was in practice held to be the highest type of religious life, and that it had been widely adopted by women.[112]

Like Clark, Ruether is wont to resort to overarching typologies to account for male attitudes towards women and the friendships built with women ascetics despite such prejudices. Ruether's analysis creates an inevitable distortion of the image of women ascetics, but in a different way. Her chapter 'Virginal Feminism in the Fathers of the Church' is peppered with a misleading use of the term 'bisexuality', when the intended

106. *Jerome, Chrysostom and Friends*, p. 58.
107. *Jerome, Chrysostom and Friends*, p. 58.
108. *Jerome, Chrysostom and Friends*, p. 59.
109. *Jerome, Chrysostom and Friends*, p. 59.
110. Forbidden in canons XIII and XVII, *NPF*, 2nd series, Vol. 14, pp. 97-99.
111. Canons IX and X, *NPF*, 2nd series, Vol. 14, pp. 95-6.
112. Smith, p. 43.

meanings seem to be human sexuality in general, or male sexuality in the male person and female sexuality in the female person. Crucial to her analysis is the assumption that the patristics thought in dualistic terms of soul and body, an assumption which cannot be entirely sustained in the consideration of ascetic spirituality. A selective reading of Augustine leads her to conclude that: 'Augustine assimilates maleness into monism, and this makes femaleness rather than bisexuality the image of the lower corporeal nature'.[113] No support from patristic sources is given for this statement.[114] It is incongruous that Ruether should still attempt to portray fourth-century women as moving from being an object to becoming a subject,[115] when five years earlier she had argued that 'a depersonalization of woman must be seen as a necessary consequence of the assimilation of the male-female relationship into the soul-body relationship, which implies a subject-object relationship between man and woman'.[116] Furthermore, she claims that for Augustine: 'man as the image of God was summed up in Adam, the unitary ancestor of humanity. But Adam is compound, containing both male spirit and female corporeality.'[117] Augustine was unlike some Greek fathers, in his refusal to see the sexual division of humanity as a result of the fall.[118] His literal Commentary on Genesis makes it clear that he insisted that the image resides in the interior person *(homo interior)*. Thus, Bernard McGinn has argued that 'it is clear that Augustine did not conceive of the image of God in a sex-specific sense as if the male alone bore the true image of God.'[119] The consequence of the alleged 'assimilation of male-female dualism into soul-body dualism in patristic theology' is that 'woman is not really seen as a self-sufficient, whole person with equal honour, as the image of God in her own right, but is seen, ethically, as dangerous to the male'.[120] The question of the difference between this male perception of woman and women's self-perception is not raised by Ruether. However, the most glaring example of Ruether's misreading of patristic authors comes in her identification of qualities considered by Ambrose and Jerome to be 'typically feminine' and 'distinctively masculine'. Ruether claims that many other ascetic writers spoke of the liberation of women from the sorrows of childbearing and male domination through the ascetic lifestyle, while 'contradictorily' also speaking of:

113. Ruether, *Religion and Sexism*, p. 156.
114. The only reference in this specific paragraph is to Augustine, 'De Grat. Ch. et de Pecc. Orig.' II, 40, *PL*, Vol. 44, 405; and 'De Genesi ad Lit.' 9.5, *PL*, Vol. 34, 396. No evidence of soul-body dualism, or of the reinterpretation of male-female dualism as soul-body dualism, is evident in these passages.
115. *Women of Spirit*, p. 73.
116. *Religion and Sexism*, p. 163.
117. *Religion and Sexism*, p. 163.
118. Augustine, *City of God*, 14.21.
119. Bernard McGinn, 'The Human Person as Image of God', II, 'Western Christianity', in *Christian Spirituality*, McGinn andd Meyendorff (eds), p. 318. See the *Literal Commentary on Genesis* 3.22.34. McGinn differentiates between Augustine's insistence in his essential teaching on the equality of men and women as partakers in the *imago Dei*, and the symbolic value he gave to the genders which 'shared the limitations of his culture', p. 319.
120. *Religion and Sexism*, pp. 156-7.

this liberation as freeing women from those 'natural' inferiorities of bodily weakness and pettiness, maliciousness and sensuality of mind which are typically feminine, whereas all the virtues that are associated with salvation—chastity, patience, wisdom, temperance, fortitude and justice—are distinctively masculine.[121]

This is a clear misreading of the passages cited, since Ambrose is comparing not male and female, but two types of women, the first hateful and the second believing, the one sweet, loving, and accommodating, and the other bitter and harsh, whose seductive gestures and wandering eyes ensare young precious souls.[122] In his letter to Demetrias, Jerome is critical of both male and female anchorites for elevating themselves through sharp criticism of those not bound by the solitary life.[123] He blames both sexes, but specifically identifies women, 'whose fickle and vacillating minds, if left to their own devices, soon degenerate'. This is immediately qualified by his observation that anchorites of both sexes have, by excessive fasting, 'so impaired their faculties that they do not know what to do or where to turn, when to speak or when to be silent'. No distinctively masculine qualities are identified in either passage. Such misinterpretation is a mistaken basis for her argument that ascetic women in the fourth century chose a path of accomplishment that was antisexual.[124] However, it is her implicit assumption that the sexual values of the twentieth century are normative that leads to her patronizing conclusion that, in choosing this 'antisexual' path, 'they were no more than enthusiastic participants in the Zeitgeist of their age'.[125] Ruether's vocabulary of sexuality must be examined, then, in order to judge the validity of her view of fourth-century ascetic attitudes towards sexuality.

Ruether rejects the commonly held view that Augustine's concern at the unruliness of male sexuality resulted from 'obsessions caused by his illicit sexual experiences'.[126] She interprets any personal obsession as one that reflected the 'collective obsession' of Augustine's religious culture and the theological anthropology of the time. Ruether draws on a Freudian interpretation of ascetic views towards sexuality to describe it in terms of its repression and sublimation. A mechanism of repression was 'bound to be self-defeating' and liable to produce always 'its own opposite in obsession with sexual fantasies'.[127] Her conclusion is that:

Unable to contain this result, asceticism dealt with it in two ways: first, by a pruriency that exercised a perverted sexual libido through constant excoriations of sexuality in ascetic literature; second, by a sublimation of sexual libido that rejected it on the level of physical experience, but allowed it to flourish on the level of fantasy elevated to represent the ecstatic nuptials of the bridal soul with Christ.[128]

121.   *Religion and Sexism*, p. 159, citing Ambrose, 'De Cain et Abel' 1, 4; and Jerome Ep. 130, 17.
122.   Ambrose 'De Cain et Abel', Lib. I, iv, *PL*, Vol. 14, 339-342.
123.   Ep. cxxx, 17 *NPF*, 2nd series, Vol. 6, p. 270.
124.   *Women of Spirit*, p. 93.
125.   *Women of Spirit*, pp. 93-4.
126.   *Religion and Sexism*, pp. 162-3.
127.   *Religion and Sexism*, p. 167.
128.   *Religion and Sexism*, p. 167.

Jerome's outpourings to a woman, whom he has never met, is taken as evidence of a 'generic' rather than a personal frustration of sexual desires towards women.[129] Lastly, Ruether accounts for the warm friendships Jerome had towards ascetic women in the fourth century in terms of sublimation. Unlike Augustine, he 'sublimated the repression of physical relations with women into a sincere and deep spiritual companionship with several women friends'.[130]

In Ruether's interpretative structure, then, the Platonic distinction between body and soul is viewed as one that could be transformed into a patriarchal patristic ordering of male as spirit, and therefore superior to female, who is corporeal. The elevation of mind over matter, and the search for the good, is portrayed as the subject of a patriarchal plot by the church fathers. The fundamental gap in humanity between the ideal and the reality may have been used in patriarchal ways in certain passages by the church fathers. Rather than a reinterpreted soul-body dualism being the source of such alleged assimilation in Ruether's framework, it would seem that her identification of the female with the corporeal might well be drawn from the more contemporary emphasis on the 'earth mother' of ecologically aware citizens of the world. Many of the ascetic writers, faced with the powers of the untamed flesh, drew 'all too heavily on the old Platonic dichotomy of self and body'.[131] Yet within the church there were writers such as Evagrius and John Cassian in the fourth century and Dorotheus of Gaza and John Climacus in the sixth who, according to Peter Brown, realized that a different image of the body implied a 'subtly different approach to the moral struggle'. The struggle was directed away from the dismissal of the body towards 'its intimate santification: hence an attention to the precise ebb and flow of sexual feelings in the body', viewed as 'merciful reminders of the deeper tensions of the soul, made manifest by God's patient kindness in the mysterious recesses of the body'.[132] We have no direct evidence from fourth-century ascetic women to demonstrate that they did not perceive of their sexuality in this integrated way, rather than in the genital ways accepted by society as a whole. On the other hand, if women ascetics in the fourth century were indoctrinated with the misogynist views of Jerome and Chrysostom, they would indeed have seen themselves as dangerous to the male, lacking self-sufficiency or completeness, not having been created in the image of God in their own right.[133] Few writings of women survive to make such an assessment, but the courageous independence shown by some exceptional women ascetics reveals that at least some women had minds of their own. One woman's writings that have survived, those of Egeria, reveal an independence, sense of courage, and deep humanity.[134]

---

129. *Religion and Sexism*, p. 171.
130. *Religion and Sexism*, p. 172.
131. Brown, p. 435.
132. Brown, pp. 435-6.
133. Chrysostom, 'Sermo 2 in Genesim' 2, *PG*, Vol. 54, 589.
134. While not strictly speaking an ascetic, Egeria, in her diary of her pilgrimage in the early fifth century, describes four journeys into difficult terrain seldom visited by the average pilgrim. Patricia Wilson-Kastner argues that Egeria and her community in Spain were the ancestors of the communities of canonesses in the Middle Ages, whose stories have not yet

In the 1970s Elizabeth Clark and Rosemary Ruether were among the ground-breakers of a new branch of patristic scholarship, feminist revisionist scholarship. To their names must be added those of Mary Daly, Elisabeth Schüssler Fiorenza, Elaine Pagels and others too numerous to mention. They have raised many questions which still need to be pursued diligently. The works already discussed in relation to women and asceticism in the fourth century have joined others as textbooks for new university courses on women in religion.[135] While scholarship is starting to enter a post-revisionist phase in terms of re-evaluation of the earlier feminists' claims regarding the first three centuries,[136] little attention has been given to the fourth century. Yet the overarching typologies of the feminist revisionist pioneers must be challenged, particularly when they result in an injustice to the women in the past. Feminist scholarship which creates such distortions is hardly worthy of the name feminist. Yet all historians must work from their own contemporary context; the more acutely aware the historian is of her context, the less likely distortions are to occur. It is understandable that twentieth-century observers, living in the aftermath of the sexual revolution, should gloss over the magnitude of the change from the use of monasticism as a term of abuse to its use as a term of honour. The difference created by the availability of relatively easy and reliable contraception must be acknowledged. This has enabled women to control their own fertility in ways other than through the abstinence of previous centuries. These new possibilities have played no small part in redefining traditional male/female roles. In a context where non-celibate feminism is the norm, celibate feminism must not be downgraded through lack of sympathetic understanding. Few in our world would see celibacy as a liberating choice for women in these sexually more enlightened times. Sympathetic understanding of the motives of fourth-century women ascetics is difficult to achieve, and much misogynism must be endured in any attempt at historical reconstruction. The danger, as always, is to read back into the 'voiceless' the preoccupations of those who recorded their accomplishments. If critical re-evaluation of the revisionists' claims regarding fourth-century women ascetics were to receive the same attention that the first three centuries have started to receive, then the churches today could well have a creative contribution to make to a western society extolling for the first time in several decades the value of monogamy, abstinence, celibacy, and an integrated vision of human sexuality.

---

been adequately written, in *A Lost Tradition*, New York 1981. See also *Egeria: Diary of a Pilgrimage*, George E. Gingras (trans.), New York 1970; and John Wilkinson, *Egeria's Travels*, London 1971.

135. See also Karen Armstrong, *The Gospel According to Woman; Christianity's Creation of the Sex War in the West*, London 1986; *Women and Religion; A Feminist Sourcebook of Christian Thought*, Elizabeth Clark and Herbert Richardson (eds), New York 1977; and Rosemary Radforth Ruether, *Womanguides: Readings Towards a Feminist Theology*, Boston 1985.

136. See Susanne Heine, *Women and Early Christianity: Are the Feminist Scholars Right?*, London 1987.

Christianization in the Fourth Century:
The Example of Roman Women

ANNE YARBROUGH

At the beginning of the fourth century the Roman aristocracy was, for the most part, pagan in its religious attitude.[1] By the end of that century the aristocracy had undergone what Peter Brown has described as a "sea change": its pagan values had become redefined within the context of Christianity.[2] This "drift into respectable Christianity" was the result of the process of socialization in the households of the Roman senatorial class over several generations. Brown suggests that the fourth-century Christianization of the aristocracy was the achievement of those upper-class Roman women who, by continuing to practice their Christian religion in the households of their pagan husbands, established the syncretistic milieu which would influence the religious attitudes of the next generation. But the apparent calm of Brown's anonymous culture-bearers is disturbed by a small group of women whose religious extremism delineates them sharply from their peers. Rejecting wholly the society into which they were born, they fled the cloying Roman atmosphere for the harsh air of the desert. The "respectable Christianity" that Rome was adopting offered them no satisfaction.

This paper will attempt to modify Brown's somewhat benign and impressionistic sketch of Christian aristocratic Roman women in the fourth century. It will consider the cluster of ascetic women who stand out in sharp relief against that background. It will analyze the social bonds that held these women together; then it will deal with the relationship between members of the group and their own immediate families. Having treated her immediate environment, the paper will describe a composite ascetic woman by considering the necessary elements of her asceticism. Finally, it will consider the effect of the group on its society.

For clarity the paper includes two stemmata. The first shows the familial relationships among most of the women who will be discussed.[3] The second is a spiritual stemma indicating schematically the web of influences among the women and their relationships to some major figures of the fourth-century church. They are as follows:

1. For Roman aristocratic paganism in the course of the fourth century see A.H.M. Jones, "The Social Background of the Struggle between Paganism and Christianity," in *The Conflict Between Paganism and Chrstianity in the Fourth Century*," ed. A. Momigliano (Oxford: Clarendon Press, 1963), pp. 17-37; H. Bloch, "The Pagan Revival in the West at the End of the Fourth Century," ibid., pp. 193-217; J.A. McGeachy, "Quintus Aurelius Symmachus and the Senatorial Aristocracy of the West" (Ph. D. diss.: University of Chicago, 1942); F. Paschoud, *Roma Aeterna: Etudes sur le patriotisme Romain dans l'occident Latin a l'epoque des grands invasions* (Rome: Institut Suisse de Rome, 1967).
2. P.R.L. Brown, "Aspects of the Christianization of the Roman Aristocracy," *Journal of Roman Studies* 51 (1961): 4.
3. The first stemma is taken from A. Chastagnol, "Le senateur Volusien et la conversion d'une famille de l'aristocratic Romaine au bas-empire." *Revue des Etudes Anciennes* 58 (1956): 249 for the Caeionii: from F. X. Murphy, "Melania the Elder: A Biographical Note," *Traditio* 5 (1947): 63 for Melania the Elder and her antecedents (but accepting Chastagnol over Murphy for her descendents); and from *Select Letters of St. Jerome,* tr. F. A. Wright (New York: G. P. Putnam's Sons, 1933), Appendix 1, p. 482 for Paula and her family.

Ms. Yarbrough is assistant professor of history in Catawba College, Salisbury North Carolina.

319

STEMMA OF THE CAEIONII FAMILY

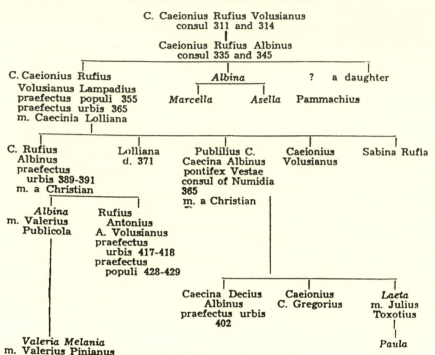

C. Caeionius Rufius Volusianus
consul 311 and 314

Caeionius Rufius Albinus
consul 335 and 345

C. Caeionius Rufius   *Albina*   ?   a daughter
Volusianus Lampadius
praefectus populi 355   *Marcella*   *Asella*   Pammachius
praefectus urbis 365
m. Caecinia Lolliana

C. Rufius   Lolliana   Publilius C.   Caeionius   Sabina Rufia
Albinus   d. 371   Caecina Albinus   Volusianus
praefectus   pontifex Vestae
  urbis 389-391   consul of Numidia
m. a Christian   365
                      m. a Christian

Albina   Rufius
m. Valerius   Antonius
  Publicola   A. Volusianus
           praefectus
           urbis 417-418
           praefectus
           populi 428-429

Caecina Decius   Caeionius   *Laeta*
Albinus   C. Gregorius   m. Julius
praefectus urbis   Toxotius
    402

Valeria Melania   *Paula*
m. Valerius Pinianus

PARTIAL STEMMA OF MELANIA THE ELDER

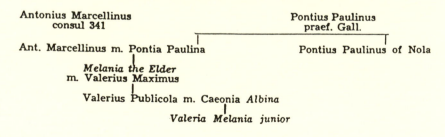

Antonius Marcellinus   Pontius Paulinus
   consul 341   praef. Gall.

Ant. Marcellinus m. Pontia Paulina   Pontius Paulinus of Nola

Melania the Elder
m. Valerius Maximus

Valerius Publicola m. Caeonia *Albina*

Valeria Melania junior

PARTIAL STEMMA OF PAULA

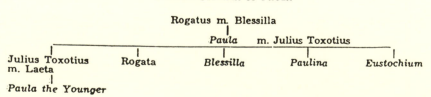

Rogatus m. Blessilla

Paula   m. Julius Toxotius

Julius Toxotius   Rogata   *Blessilla*   *Paulina*   *Eustochium*
m. Laeta

Paula the Younger

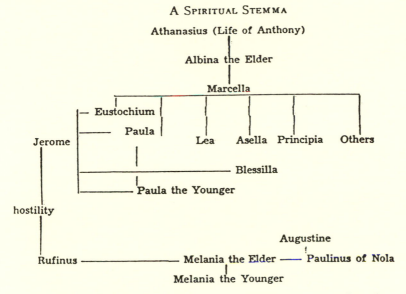

A Spiritual Stemma

Because of the close familial and spiritual ties it is possible first of all to present a group portrait of about a dozen women who span four generations from the first quarter of the fourth century to the early years of the fifth. It will soon become evident that the composite is mostly the work of Jerome.[4] A study of these women reveals much of Jerome himself. It is his concept of asceticism, for example, that is illustrated in his letters to and about Paula, Eustochium, Marcella, and others. His picture of Melania the Elder ("cuius nomen nigredinis perfidiae tenebras") must be corrected by other, more positive sources.[5] But then, Jerome is uniquely qualified to describe them to us, since he had a hand in forming and directing their asceticism. He affects our understanding of them today to the same extent that he affected their lives.

Once the portrait is drawn, there remains the task of sketching the relationship of the group to society in general. If the testimony of Jerome and Ambrose is to be accepted, these women represented the crest of a small but significant wave of asceticism in the West.[6] Their asceticism was other worldly and eschatological in tenor. It suggests that there existed among the aristocracy some unexplored sense of an approaching catastrophe. For most, of course, the end did not arrive at all: Sir Samuel Dill's provincial aristocrats continued to pursue the cultural ideals of Rome, and urban aristocrats in fifth-century Rome believed that Roman principles were alive and well in Christian garb. But in considering a "while Rome slept" theory of the decline and fall,[7] it is well to remember that

4. See E. P. Bourke, "St. Jerome as a Spiritual Director," in *A Monument to St. Jerome*, ed. F. X. Murphy (New York: Sheed and Ward, 1952), pp. 145ff.; *Select Letters*, Appendix, pp. 483-497; F. Cavallera, *Saint Jerome: sa vie et son oeuvre* (Paris, 1922), pp. 75-92.
5. Jerome *Epistulae* 133; see also Cavallera, pp. 193-286; F. X. Murphy, *Rufinus of Aquileia. His Life and Works* (Washington, D.C.: Catholic University of America Press, 1945), pp. 31-55, 155-157; idem., "Melania the Elder," pp. 59-77.
6. In addition to those, see D. Gordini, "Origine e sviluppo del monachesimo a Roma," *Gregorianum* 37 (1956): 220-260.
7. An example can be found in P.R.L. Brown, *The World of Late Antiquity, A.D. 150-750* (New York: Harcourt Brace, 1971), p. 118.

Christian asceticism both evoked and answered in its aristocratic converts a sense
of dissatisfaction, excitement and a longing for escape. There was an uneasiness
in Rome in the late fourth century. Though those aristocrats who slid into
Brown's "respectable Christianity" were not noticeably affected by it, the uneasiness is reflected in these ascetic women.

THE SOCIAL BACKGROUND AND MILIEU OF THE ASCETIC WOMEN

Through their husbands and fathers this group of ascetic women shared a
position in the "inner aristocracy" of the senatorial order.[8] Since the reforms of
Diocletian and Constantine, the senatorial order had no longer been a rigidly strati-
fied hierarchy solely dependent on hereditary position. A "nobility of service" had
been infused into the nobility of blood. The infusion of new men was due to the
power struggle between emperor and senate, a struggle which was perceived as a
contest between Christianity and paganism.[9] By opening up new channels of mobility, by introducing into the senate both the achieving members of the lower
social strata and men of good, but provincial, families, the emperor attempted to
mitigate the opposition of a hitherto monolithic institution. The "nobility of service" was a vehicle for the Christianization of the senatorial order. The "inner
aristocracy" consisted both of the old nobility of blood and the most successful
members of the "nobility of service." In either case membership in this most elite
circle could be recognized by the possession of the consulship or of the urban
prefecture.[10]

The number of their relatives who held the offices of consul or urban prefect
indicates that the ascetic women belonged to the families of the "inner aristocracy."[11]
The father of Albina the Elder held the consulship both in 335 and in 345;[12] her
grandfather was consul in 311 and in 314.[13] Her nephew, the father of Albina the
Younger and the grandfather of Melania the Younger, was urban prefect from
389 to 391.[14] The brother of Albina the Younger was Volusianus, who held,
among other offices, the office of urban prefect from 417 to 418[15] Melania the
Elder was the daughter of a consul; her grandfathers were consul in 341 and
prefect of Gaul;[16] her husband was urban prefect from 361 to 363.[17]

8. See A.H.M. Jones, *The Later Roman Empire* (Norman, Oklahoma: University of Oklahoma Press, 1964), 1:523-563 for an analysis of the structure of the senatorial aristocracy.
   He notes (p. 529) that the legal rank of an aristocratic woman depended on the rank of
   her husband or father. S. Mazzarino, *The End of the Ancient World* (New York: Alfred
   Knopf, 1966), pp. 131-132, also considers this point.
9. M. K. Hopkins, "Elite Mobility in the Roman Empire," *Past and Present* 32 (1965):
   12-26, complements Jones' description of the senatorial order, but suggests that social
   mobility could be recognized before the reforms of the emperors. Aside from imperial
   machinations, he believes that a second reason for social mobility was the aristocratic
   ethos itself, which stressed achievement as well as hereditary status, and therefore required that the aristocracy remain open to men of skill. In his "Social Mobility in the
   Later Roman Empire: The Evidence of Ausonius," *Classical Quarterly* 11 (1961): 246-
   247, he offers an example of his theory.
10. Jones, *Later Roman Empire*, p. 550.
11. Secondary sources considering their relations' social positions are: Chastagnol, pp. 241-
    253 for the Caeionii; Murphy, "Melania the Elder," pp. 61-62. Gibbon, *Decline and
    Fall of the Roman Empire*, chap. 31, gives some consideration to the nobilty of Paula's
    family.
12. Chastagnol, p. 246; Seeck, ed. of Symmachus, p. 175; *Vita S. Melania*, ed. Rampolla, p.
    148.
13. Chastagnol, p. 246.
14. Ibid., p. 247.
15. Ibid., pp. 244-245.
16. Murphy, "Melania the Elder," pp. 61-62, cites Palladius and Jerome on this question
17. Ibid., p. 64.

It is probable that the membership of these women's families in the "inner aristocracy" was by virtue of their position in the old nobility of blood rather than in the new nobility of service. At least three of their male relatives were members of Symmachus' reactionary pagan circle.[18] In addition, Jerome and Paulinus of Nola described these women in terms of their ancient lineages.[19] Such claims of a long and exalted lineage may have been tenuous, but they did reflect a social reality. The members of that nucleus of families which made these claims "regarded themselves and were accepted as aristocrats of the bluest blood."[20] A summary of familial ties suggests that these women belonged to the elite of the senatorial order through lineage rather than through achievement only. But in the attempt to reconstruct their social background certain *lacunae* appear at crucial points, and force a slight qualification of this conclusion.

The brother of Albina the Elder, who was urban prefect in 365, was married to a priestess of Isis.[21] They had four sons and two daughters, none of whom is known to have been Christian. Two of the sons—both portrayed in Macrobius' *Saturnalia*—married Christian women whose names and families are unknown. Their marriages produced, respectively, Albina the Younger, who married the son of Melania the Elder and whose daughter was Melania the Younger; and Laeta, who married the son of Paula and whose daughter was Paula the Younger. The identity of the mothers of Albina the Younger and Laeta is crucial in attempting to determine the social background of these aristocratic households. The fact that they are unnamed suggests that they were members either of the rising social strata of "new men," who were frequently Christian, or that they were, like the mother of Melania the Elder, members of the provincial aristocracy. The presence of both groups in the senatorial order of the late fourth century makes either of these possibilities likely. The social background of the ascetic women is not yet completely understood. While they were all members of the "inner aristocracy," it is possible that some of them were also the daughters or granddaughters of marriages that were mixed socially as well as religiously.

The social environment of Roman aristocratic women in this period has been memorably described both by Ammianus Marcellinus[22] and by Jerome, especially in his letter on virginity addressed to Eustochium.[23] They describe a society of idle and wealthy women living in a ghetto peopled by children, servants, and sycophants. The frustrated productivity of these aristocratic women sought outlets in what has been described as the "competitive salon culture."[24] They seem

18. Chastagnol, p. 247.
19. Jerome *Epistulae* (*Corpus Scriptorum Ecclesiasticorum Latinorum* [hereafter *CSEL*], editum consilio et impenois Academiae Litterarum Caesarae Vindohonensis, v. 55), *Ep.* 108, 1.5-8, describes Paula as: "Nobilis genere, sed multo nobilior sanctitate . . . . Gracchorum stirps, suboles Scipionus, Pauli heres, cuius vocabulum trahit." Ibid., *Ep.* 127: "Neque vero Marcellam tuam, immo meam et, ut verius loquar, nostram, omninmque sanctorum et proprie Romanae urbis inclitum decus, institutis rhetorum praedicabo, ut exponam illustrem familiam, alti sanguinis decus et stemmata per consules et praefectos practorio decurrentia." Ibid., *Ep.* 77, 2.9-15, on Fabiola: "ordine rhetorum praetermisso tota de conversionis ac paenitentiae incunabulis adsumenda. Alius forsitan scholae memor Quintum Maximum, 'Unus qui nobis cunctando restitutit rem,' et totam Fabriorum gentem proferret in medium, diceret pugnas, describeret proelia et per tantae nobilitatis gradus Fabiam venisse iactaret." Paulinus of Nola *Epistulae* (*CSEL*, v. 29), *Ep.* 29, 6.4-6, says of Melania the Elder: "quae consulibus avis nobilis nobiliorem se contemtu corporeae nobilitatis dedit."
20. Jones, "The Social Background," p. 29.
21. Chastagnol, p. 251.
22. *The Roman History of Ammianus Marcellinus*, 14.6.
23. Jer. *Ep.* 22.
24. Hopkins, "Elite Mobility," p. 25.

to have filled up their days by constantly vying among themselves for social prestige. "[The widows'] houses are full of flatterers, full of guests. The very clergy, whose teaching and authority ought to inspire respect, kiss these ladies on the forehead, and then stretch out their hand—you would think, if you did not know, that they were giving a benediction—to receive the fee for their visit. The women meanwhile seeing that priests need their help, are lifted up with pride."[25] This feminine society mirrored the complexity of the male senatorial order, and its own complexity appears to have been long-established. The mother of the emperor Elagabalus (218-222) had established a "little senate of ladies"[26] whose purpose was to determine the proper relations among the women of the Roman aristocracy. The spirit of this unique institution appears to have descended upon the women of the mid-fourth century. The group of ascetic women whom we are considering must be defined against the background of the "competitive salon culture."

Conversion to Asceticism: Familial Opposition

The present group of ascetic women had more in common than social status. Of those for whom evidence is available, it is clear that they came from families where Christianity was already an influence. But in spite of the presence of Christian influence, there is a pattern of familial opposition to their conversion to asceticism. Familial opposition sheds some light on the aristocratic family of the fourth century: two of the primary duties of children to their families, it seems, were the transmission of familial wealth to the next generation and the continuation of the lineage itself. Conversions to asceticism were inimical to the fulfillment of these responsibilities. At least for these two reasons, the typical conversion to the ascetic life was accomplished in spite of the strenuous objections of the family.

Among the women of the two earlier generations, the question of Christian influence within the family cannot always be answered. It is unknown whether the mother of Albina the Elder was a Christian or whether there was any Christian in her family. It is also unknown whether Paula's parents, Rogatus and Blessilla, were Christians. Albina's own daughters did grow up as Christians, however, and Melania the Elder was the daughter of a Christian mother.[27] In the third generation of ascetic women Paula's daughters had grown up as Christians. In the fourth generation Melania the Younger and Paula the Younger were both the daughters and granddaughters of Christian women. Nevertheless, opposition to the proposed conversion occurred in five out of seven instances. Albina the Elder wanted her daughter Marcella to remarry when her first husband died after only seven months of marriage. An old but wealthy and aristocratic man promised to will her his fortune if she would marry him, and "her mother Albina was excessively anxious to secure so illustrious a protector for the widowed household."[28]

Marcella's sister, Asella, though she had been dedicated by her parents to virginity, encountered familial opposition in her determination to pursue that life:

> When her resolution was still fresh she took her gold necklace . . . and sold it without her parents' knowledge. Then putting on a dark dress such as her

25. Jer. *Ep.* 22.16; Eng. tr. in *Select Letters*, p. 85.
26. Mazzarino, p. 131.
27. For the relationship between Melania the Elder and Paulinus of Nola, see Murphy, "Melania the Elder," p. 62.
28. Jer. *Ep.* 127.2; Eng. tr. in *Select Letters*, p. 441.

mother had never been willing that she should wear, she concluded her pious enterprise by consecrating herself forthwith to the Lord. She thus showed her relatives that they need hope to wring no further concessions from one who, by her very dress, had condemned the world.[29]

Paula was not only a Christian, but herself a convert to asceticism. But Jerome's letter to her on the death of her daughter Blessilla indicates that she had been opposed to Blessilla's conversion to asceticism after the death of her husband: "When you were carried fainting out of the funeral procession, whispers such as these were audible in the crowd: 'Is not this what we have often said? She weeps for her daughter, killed with fasting. She wanted her to marry again, that she might have grandchildren.' "[30] In the same letter Jerome speaks for Blessilla, describing her happiness after death. He concludes, "Many other things does she say which I pass over here; she prays also to God for you. For me, too, I feel sure, she makes intercession, and asks God to pardon my sins in return for the warnings and advice that I bestowed on her, when to assure her salvation I braved the ill-will of her family."[31]

On the other hand, Paula actively supported the ascetic tendencies of her daughter Eustochium. When she sailed for Jerusalem, leaving the rest of her family behind, "she concentrated herself quietly upon Eustochium alone, the partner alike of her vows and of her voyage."[32] Her opposition to conversion seems to have been similar to Albina's: each opposed the conversion of the last remaining daughter, both of whom they had previously married off. Marcella was Albina's only daughter aside from the already dedicated Asella. One of Paula's other three daughters, Rogata, had died, and her daughter Paulina lived chastely with her Christian husband. Aside from the son Toxotius, then, Blessilla was the only child who might have conceived the next generation. Albina's opposition to Marcella's conversion was not couched in terms of Marcella's duty to provide grandchildren, but it was based on Albina's view of Marcella's duty to her family. Both of these mothers seem to have realized that at least one daughter should take upon herself the familial responsibilities that converts to asceticism denied.

The decision of Melania the Elder to embrace the ascetic life was made after the death of her husband and two of her three young children. Paulinus of Nola wrote, "Many were her skirmishes down to the very elements in this warfare against the vengeful dragon. . . . For the whole force of her noble relatives, armed to restrain her, attempted to change her proposal and to obstruct her passage."[33] The conversion of Melania the Elder's granddaughter and namesake, more than any other conversion, indicates the familial responsibilities which bound the child to the parent and which were rejected by the ascetic. Melania was an only child, though she may have had a brother who died in childhood.[34] Her father, Valerius Publicola, had been the only surviving son of Melania the Elder. Her mother, Albina the Younger, had had one brother, Volusianus, who did not marry. Melania was therefore the last member of these branches of two aristocratic fami-

29. Jer. *Ep.* 24.3; Eng. tr. in *Nicene and Post-Nicene Fathers*, 2d ser., 6:43.
30. Jer. *Ep.* 39.6; Eng. tr. in ibid., 6:53.
31. Jer. *Ep.* 39.7; Eng. tr. in ibid., 6:54.
32. Jer. *Ep.* 108.5; Eng. tr. in ibid., p. 312.
33. Paulinus of Nola *Ep.* 29.10 (*CSEL*, v. 29): "Multa illi et in ipsius huius militae rudimentis adversus draconem invidum fuero certamina . . . sed tota nobilium propinquorum potentia ad retinendum armata propositum inpedire et eunti obstare conatus est": Eng. tr. in Murphy, "Melania the Elder," p. 65.
34. Gerontius, *Vie de sainte Mélanie*, tr. D. Gorce, Sources chretiennes, 90, Introduction, pp. 33-34.

lies. She was anxious to embrace the life of her grandmother;[35] but her parents expected her to produce children to whom the wealth of the family would be transmitted and in whom the lineage would continue.[36] After her marriage she produced first a daughter, who was dedicated to God as a virgin at the time of her birth. Subsequently she gave birth to a son, on whose shoulders the continuation of the line would presumably fall. Both children died in infancy; after their deaths, Melania prevailed upon her husband to live chastely with her. They both began to sell all their property so that they might undertake the ascetic life. Their action met with fierce opposition from Melania's parents, who attempted to bring legal action against the two on the grounds that they were still minors. Melania's brother-in-law, Severus, also attempted to block the sale of his brother's portion of family wealth. The situation eventually elicited the intervention of Serena, wife of Stilicho and sister of the emperor Honorius. The support of Honorious for their cause finally discouraged the opposition which had been brewing among the entire Roman aristocracy.[37]

The *Vita S. Melaniae* in particular suggests the opposition that the conversion to asceticism could arouse in the aristocracy as a whole. The reason for such opposition could lie in the fact that by dispersing a significant amount of aristocratic wealth Melania irrevocably diminished the wealth of the next aristocratic generation. Hopkins points out that the only socially approved means of obtaining wealth were through inheritance, dowry, and the rewards of government office.[38] Since office was usually held for only a few years, inheritance and dowry were the two real possibilities of income. The total amount of Roman aristocratic wealth, therefore, had no way of ever increasing significantly; it could be exchanged among families through marriage but there was no external source of income that would make the aristocracy richer. It could only become poorer. Melania's action was a scandal because it threatened the financial basis not only of her own family, but of her entire class.

Aside from the inheritance of property, the continuation of the family itself may have been an issue in the conversion of Melania the Younger as it was in the conversion of Blessilla. In this connection Chastagnol suggests, "Il semble que les pères de famille ont tenu à maintenir la tradition pour leur principal héritier et que, faisant 'la part du feu,' ils ont abondonné leurs autres enfants à l'influence de leurs épouses."[39]

Chastagnol's stemma corroborates his conclusion. In families where the mother was Christian and the father pagan, the oldest son seems to have been designated the inheritor of family tradition and responsibilities. Julius Toxotius, the only son of Paula and her husband, remained a pagan until he was converted by his Christian wife.[40] Laeta herself, the daughter of a mixed marriage, had two brothers; the older, urban prefect in 402, was certainly considered the inheritor of the pagan tradition. He was portrayed as a character in the *Saturnalia*

---

35. Gerontius does not mention Melania the Elder, but Palladius, *The Lausiac History*, tr. R. T. Meyer (London: Longmans Green and Co., 1965), says that Melania the Elder returned home from Jerusalem in 399 in order to instruct her granddaughter in the ascetic life.
36. *Vita Melaniae junioris*, ed. Rampolla, p. 21 and n. 17, pp. 176-180.
37. Gerontius, *Vie de sainte Melanie*, pp. 130-157.
38. Hopkins, "Elite Mobility," p. 20.
39. Chastagnol, p. 251.
40. Jer. (*CSEL*, v. 55) *Ep.* 107.1: Laeta's father, a pagan, will be converted by the religion of his daughter's household: "Despuat licet et irrideat epistulam meam et me vel stultum vel insanum clamitet, hoc et gener eius faciebat, antequam crederet."

along with his father and his uncle. Albina the Younger was also the daughter of a mixed marriage. Her brother Volusianus remained a pagan up to the time of his death, when he was converted.

To push Chastagnol's suggestion one step further, not only was a male child designated as the inheritor of the male, pagan aspect of family tradition, but it was considered undesirable for more than one daughter to be dedicated to the ascetic life. The examples of Blessilla and Melania the Younger indicate that there was a desire for at least one daughter to marry and have children. Chastagnol's pattern of male inheritance of the pagan tradition seems to have been mirrored by a female inheritance of the Christian tradition. Paula and Albina the Younger must have expected that their granddaughters would be Christian. The Christian mother, then, had a reason of her own for wishing to have only one ascetic daughter.

The Nature of the Ascetic Life

The most dramatic form of asceticism, and the type most frequently associated with the women of fourth-century Rome because of Jerome's descriptions of it, was the flight to the desert. But there was a second type of asceticism in fourth-century Rome which was more congruent with the aristocratic tradition of the philosophic life.

Jerome mentions Marcella, Asella and Lea as maintaining the ascetic life in Rome.[41] Marcella and Lea founded religious monasteries in the city, where they gave themselves over to fasting and prayer, living simply and charitably. Marcella had introduced a new kind of religious life into Rome: "At that time no great lady knew anything of the monastic life, nor ventured to call herself a nun. The thing itself was strange and the name was commonly accounted ignominious and degrading."[42] But Marcella, who had learned from Athanasius about the life of Anthony, and about the monasteries founded by Pachomius, "and of the discipline laid down there for virgins and widows," took up the monastic life in Rome. Her example was followed by other aristocratic women, among whom were Paula and her daughter Eustochium. Marcella, as the center of what was probably an informal group of practicing ascetics, moved her household to a farm near Rome, "the country being chosen because of its loneliness."[43] She lived there with the other women who had joined her company until her death soon after the sack of Rome in 410.

The life of retirement away from Rome was a traditional alternative for the aristocracy. Peter Brown describes its development in the late fourth century:

> The tradition of *otium* had taken on a new lease of life. It had become more complex, and, often, far more earnest. On their great estates in Sicily, the last pagan senators continued to re-edit manuscripts of the classics. . . . Many had come to think that this essentially private life might be organized as a community. . . . Indeed, some of the first monasteries in the West were these "lay monasteries" of sensitive pagans and Christians.[44]

Augustine looked upon his retirement to Cassiciacum in the autumn of 386 as a *Christianae vitae otium*. Marcella's retirement away from Rome was part of the same tradition. The ascetic life chosen by these women was influenced more by the Western tradition of the philosophical life than by the Eastern tradition of a

41. Jer. *Ep.* 23, 24, 127.
42. Jer. *Ep.* 127.5; Eng. tr. in *Select Letters*, p. 449.
43. Ibid.
44. P.R.L. Brown, *Augustine of Hippo: A Biography* (London: Faber, 1967), p. 115.

flight to the desert. Like Augustine, Marcella adapted a convention of the pagan
aristocratic life to her own Christian use.

But it is desert asceticism which comes to mind in connection with Jerome
and his spiritual daughters. The Eastern ascetic life was embraced by Paula,
Eustochium, and Paula the Younger; by Melania the Elder and by Melania the
Younger. Their asceticism was dominated by one concern: to preserve a singular
attachment to God. In order to achieve this goal they practiced detachment from
the world through physical deprivation, poverty of spirit and a life of virginity or
chastity. At the same time that they struggled to flee the world they strengthened
their attachment to God by the study of scripture and by their passion for the historical, concrete elements of the Christian tradition. Like their other achievements,
the ascetics' scorn for their bodies was dramatic. Jerome describes Paula's practice
of the ascetic life: "As often too as she was troubled by bodily weakness (brought
on by incredible abstinence and by redoubled fastings), she would be heard to
say: 'I keep under my body and bring it into subjection; lest that by any means,
when I have preached to others, I myself should be cast-away.' "[45] When Melania
the Elder returned to Italy for a short visit after twenty-five years in Jerusalem,
she was met by her children and grandchildren. Their short trip from Naples to
Nola was described by Paulinus: "She sat on a tiny thin horse, worth less than
any ass; and they attended her on the journey, their trappings emphasizing the
extraordinary contrast. . . . Be sure that there is such divine strength in that
weak woman that she finds refreshment in fasting, repose in prayer, bread in the
Word, clothing in rags."[46]

Physical poverty was akin to poverty of the spirit, since both were seen as
means of preserving detachment from the world. In his letter on the life of Paula,
Jerome describes her great humility:

> Humility is the first of Christian graces and hers was so pronounced that one
> who had never seen her, and who on account of her celebrity had desired to
> see her, would have believed that he saw not her but the lowest of maids. When
> she was surrounded by companies of virgins she was always the least remark-
> able in dress, in speech, in gesture, and in gait.[47]

Subjection of the body and of the spirit were both important elements in the concept of chastity. The preservation of chasity, more than anything else, was considered by Jerome as the essence of worldly detachment. His letter to Eustochium
on virginity compares the life of the virgin to the life of the married woman:
"The unmarried woman cares for the things of the Lord, that she may be holy
both in the body and in spirit; but she that is married cares for the things of the
world, how she may please her husband."[48] The condition of virginity influences
every aspect of a woman's behavior; she is modest in all things, she rejects the
society of married women and avoids any situation that might compromise her
status.[49]

Through physical and spiritual poverty and through the life of chastity the
ascetic woman sought to put aside worldly concerns so that she might concentrate
all her attention on God. The women of Jerome's circle sought God through
study of scripture and through pilgrimages. In his letter to Eustochium on Paula

45. Jer. *Ep.* 108.1; Eng. tr. in *Nicene and Post Nicene Fathers*, 6:196. See also *Ep.* 108.21,
    108.19, 108.15.
46. Paul. of Nola *Ep.* 29.12.
47. Jer. *Ep.* 108.15; Eng. tr. in *Nicene and Post-Nicene Fathers*, 6:202.
48. Jer. *Ep.* 22.21; Eng. tr. in *Select Letters*, p. 101. See also *Ep.* 22.22.
49. Jer. *Ep.* 22.

Jerome describes how Paula and Eustochium read the Old and New Testaments under his guidance: "Whenever I stuck fast and honestly confessed myself at fault (Paula) would by no means rest content but would force me by fresh questions to point out to her which of many different solutions seemed to me the most probable."[50] Though Jerome himself had learned Hebrew with great difficulty, "Paula, on making up her mind that she too would learn it, succeeded so well that she could chant the psalms in Hebrew and could speak the language without a trace of the pronunciation peculiar to Latin. The same accomplishments can be seen to this day in her daughter Eustochium." At least two of the ascetic women were involved in the theological controversies of the time: Marcella was instrumental in having Origenists condemned in Rome,[51] and Melania the Elder, the friend of Rufinus, was excoriated by Jerome for her alignment with Origenism. Melania the Elder also had a reputation for serious study. Palladius writes that

> being very learned and loving literature, she turned night into day perusing every writing of the ancient commentators, including three million (lines) of Origen and two hundred fifty thousand of Gregory, Stephen, Pierus, Basil and other standard writers. Nor did she read them once only and casually, but she laboriously went through each book seven or eight times.[52]

Their intellectual pursuits were a means of understanding the tenets of the church; but they also sought understanding in a more concrete way. The accounts of the travels and adventures of Paula and Eustochium, and of Melania the Elder, are filled with descriptions of people, places and objects which were touched by sanctity. Though they deprived their bodies of material comforts, they delighted their souls with pilgrimages. They wanted to see everything with their own eyes and experience everything for themselves. Of Paula in Jerusalem Jerome wrote,

> In visiting the holy places so great was the passion and enthusiasm she exhibited for each, that she could never have torn herself away from one had she not been eager to visit the rest. Before the cross she threw herself down in adoration as though she beheld the Lord hanging upon it: and when she entered the tomb which was the scene of the Resurrection she kissed the stone which the angel had rolled away from the door of the sepulchre. Indeed so ardent was her faith that she even licked with her mouth the very spot on which the Lord's body had lain, like one athirst for the river which he has longed for.[53]

When Melania the Elder arrived in Alexandria she sold what was left of her possessions

> and then went to the mount of Nitria where she met the following fathers and their companions: Pambo, Arsisius, Serapion the Great, Paphnutius of Scete, Isidore the confessor, bishop of Hermopolis, and Dioscorus. And she sojourned with them half a year, travelling about in the desert and visiting all the saints.[54]

Their travel was perhaps, a kind of souvenir-hunting, but it was imbued with a passion for the historical, concrete elements of the Christian tradition. It was of a piece with their intellectual curiosity. This ascetic life offered mortification of the flesh indeed, but it also offered something more. It must have seemed an adventure of the highest kind, to throw over everything that was tedious and boring

50. Jer. *Ep.* 108.26; Eng. tr. in *Nicene and Post-Nicene Fathers*, 6:209-210.
51. Jer. *Ep.* 127. See also n. 5, and see the *Dictionnaire de Theologie Catholique* v. onzieme, pt. 2 (1932), cols. 1563-1570 for the condemnation of Origen at Rome.
52. Palladius, *The Lausiac History* 59 (C. Butler, *The Greek Text* . . . [Cambridge, 1904], p. 149); Eng. tr. in Murphy, "Melania the Elder," p. 71.
53. Jer. *Ep.* 108.9; Eng. tr. in *Nicene and Post Nicene Fathers*, 6:198-199.
54. Pallad. *Lausiac Hist.* 46 (Butler, p. 135); Eng. tr. in Murphy, "Melania the Elder," p. 68.

in Rome and to strike out for a life of freedom and the company of saints and wild
monks in the desert.

THE EFFECTS OF ASCETICISM ON THE FOURTH-CENTURY ROMAN ARISTOCRACY: THE RISE OF ASCETICISM

The fourth century witnessed both a rise in ascetic practices among the Roman aristocracy and a decline in the birth rate of the aristocracy. Though late
fourth-century sources suggest that Christian asceticism was one of the causes of
decreasing population,[55] it is more likely that the increase in asceticism and the
decrease in population were two phenomena that occurred simultaneously and in
response to the same social conditions. The growing independence of aristocratic
women and the great expense of initiating children into adulthood have been seen
as two of the causes of population decrease. The practice of asceticism grew in
popularity as it became an increasingly acceptable way for women to exercise their
independence, and because it provided one answer to the financial burdens of child
raising. Though familial opposition to ascetic conversion suggested that the dis-
sipation of family wealth and the failure of the line were to be avoided, asceticism
appears to have had two positive functions.

The growing independence of aristocratic women can be traced as far back
as the beginning of the third century, when "the little senate of ladies" endeavored
to insure that aristocratic women who married outside the senatorial order would
not lose the social rank of their fathers. At the same time, Pope Callistus made a
similar ruling for the benefit of Christian aristocratic women who married non-
aristocratic Christians. Aristocratic women were beginning to exercise more control over the choice of their husbands than they had done before.[56] But although
they more often claimed for themselves the choice of whom they should marry,
until the fourth century aristocratic women nearly always married. It was only in
the course of that century that unmarried aristocratic women began to appear.[57]

Aristocratic women in the Roman Empire married early. Literary and epigraphic evidence[58] indicates that 42.03 percent of pagan women were first married
between the ages of ten and fourteen. Since mortality was high and divorce law
lenient, there was a good chance that one or other of the marriage partners would
participate in a second marriage. Laws from the time of Augustus limited the
period between marriages to two years for widows and eighteen months for divorced women. The unmarried woman was an anomaly in aristocratic society.[59]
The Christian Constantine abolished laws limiting the period between marriages,

65. See, for example, Ambrose *De Virginitate* 11. 24. 35-38. Ambrose's response, that the
   population was increasing in the East where asceticism flourished most, has been echoed
   by A.H.M. Jones, "The Social Background to the Struggle Between Paganism and
   Christianity," p. 17. However, M. K. Hopkins, in "The Age of Roman Girls at Marriage," *Population Studies* 18 (1965): 309-327, has presented epigraphic indications
   that Christian aristocratic women of the fourth century tended to marry later than their
   pagan peers. Such a practice would possibly have a bearing on the birth rates of Christians.
56. Mazzarino, pp. 131-133. This is Mazzarino's thesis in his segment on women in late Rome,
   in which he undertakes to refute Seeck's theory that a declining birth rate could be
   blamed on arranged matches.
57. Hopkins, "Elite Mobility," p. 25.
58. Hopkins, "The Age of Roman Girls at Marriage," p. 320.
59. J.P.V.D. Balsdon, *Roman Women: Their History and Habits* (London: Bodley Head,
   1962), which is a book generally irrelevant to our inquiry since it does not deal with the
   late period, mentions that the law promulgated under Augustus in A.D. 9, *lex Papia
   Poppaea*, placed these limits on the period between marriages.

as well as the laws penalizing celibacy.[60] Asceticism in Rome was noticeably present for the first time during the fourth century. As evidence of its appearance we have Jerome's descriptions of an ascetic "fad" among the aristocratic women of Rome; we have Ambrose's account of the institutionalization of virginity within the church; and we have an indication that a parallel institutionalization of widowhood was attempting to take root in the West. These indications, impressionistic as they are, suggest that asceticism was increasing in the West and, therefore, that it had a function to fulfill in the society.

In his letter to Eustochium on virginity, Jerome makes several references to a fashionable asceticism which seems to have penetrated the "competitive salon culture" of Rome. He says to Eustochium,

> Some women indeed actually disfigure themselves, so as to make it obvious that they have been fasting. As soon as they catch sight of anyone they drop their eyes and begin sobbing, covering up the face, all but a glimpse of one eye, which they just keep free to watch the effect they make. They wear a black dress and a girdle of sackcloth; their feet and hands are unwashed: their stomach alone—because it cannot be seen—is busy churning food.[61]

Again he says, "Cast from you like the plague those idle and inquisitive virgins and widows who go about to married women's houses and surpass the very parasites in a play by their unblushing effrontery."

Ambrose's campaign on behalf of virginity was successful enough to bring about an order of virgins in the church in Milan.[62] Virgins were often dedicated to God by their parents at birth, as was the case with Asella, and with Paula the Younger. Under Ambrose, these children who had been devoted to God took public vows of virginity in a ceremony of consecration when they reached puberty.[63] After their consecration they continued to live with their parents, but were under the special care of the bishop.[64] They sat together in a special screened-off area of the church. Ambrose prescribed for them a life of a seclusion, devotion and abstinence.[65] They became a recognized part of church life.

Jerome's treatment of Blessilla and Marcella, in particular, suggests that his dealings with the Western women may have been influenced by the Eastern concept of Christian widowhood. In the East, the early Christian order of widows had by the third century begun to work actively among the women members of the congregation. In the same century this group began to share some of the functions of the made order of deacons. The third-century order of deaconesses, then, drew from both the diaconate and the order of widows in establishing itself as a third entity. Deaconesses did not appear in the West before the fifth century.[66] The Eastern order of widows, expanding as it did into the order of deaconesses, seems to have provided widows with a more viable place in the life of the church than was offered them in the West. In this respect, as he did in so many others, Jerome may have been acting as a conductor of Eastern innovations to the West.

60. Ibid., p. 222.
61. Jer. Ep. 22.27; Eng. tr. in Select Letters, pp. 117 and 123.
62. Amb. De Virginibus 1.57, 59. But see ibid., 1. 57, 58, for his problems with overcoming parental opposition in Milan. For a general treatment of Ambrose in this connection see W. J. Dooley, Marriage According to Saint Ambrose (Washington, D.C.: Catholic University of America Press, 1945); F. H. Dudden, The Life and Times of St. Ambrose (Oxford: Clarendon Press, 1935), especially pp. 133-159.
63. Ambrose, Exhortatio Virginitatis 17; idem. De Lapsu Virginis, 19-20.
64. Ibid. 28, 29.
65. Idem. De Virginitate 15; Ep. 5.6; Exhort. Virginatis; De Virginibus.
66. J. G. Davies, ''Deacons, Deaconesses and the Minor Orders in the Patristic Period,'' Journal of Ecclesiastical History 14 (1963): 1-15.

The rise of asceticism provided the aristocratic woman with an increasingly acceptable alternative to marriage. She might either remain a virgin or, after the death of her husband, remain a widow. The dedication of a virgin by her parents is a practice that should be considered in more detail. While it was necessary to have enough children to insure the continuation of the line, the great expense of initiating children into adulthood could be ruinous to a family with too many children for its resources to bear.[67] It was necessary to provide each daughter with a sufficient dowry and each son with a respectable celebration of quaestorian and praetorian games.[68] Dedication to virginity may have been a way of providing for surplus daughters without straining the resources of the family. Sons could then be launched into the senatorial order in a fitting way, and other daughters could be given a dowry adequate enough to insure for them an appropriate marriage.

Parents lacked control both in limiting and in sustaining their families. On the one hand, there was little notion of contraception;[69] on the other hand, the high mortality rate often rendered futile their attempts to insure the continuation of the line. The practice of dedication of daughters to virginity may have returned to the parents some element of control over the number of children whose entry into adulthood could be adequately financed by the family.

The Effects of Asceticism on the Fourth-century Roman Aristocracy: The Christianization of the Household and the Failure of Asceticism

Jerome's ascetic response to the concept of marriage has been mentioned.[70] But there is another side to his attitude toward marriage; it is perhaps summed up in his words, "I praise marriage, because it produces virgins for me."[71] Less flippantly, he quotes Paul: "The woman that hath an husband that believeth not, and if he be pleased to dwell with her, let her not leave him. For the unbelieving husband is sanctified by the believing wife, and the unbelieving wife is sanctified by the believing husband; else were your children unclean, but now they are holy."[72] In this same letter to Laeta on the education of her daughter, Paula the Younger, Jerome describes two purposes of the marriage of a Christian: the conversion of the other members of the household to Christianity, and the education of a new Christian generation. The final end of the Christianization of the household for Jerome is the production of Christian ascetics.

In his letter to Laeta Jerome suggests that one result of her Christian household will be the conversion of her father, a *pontifex Vestae*, to Christianity:

Who would have believed that the granddaughter of the Roman pontiff Albinus would be born in answer to a mother's vows; that the grandfather would stand by and rejoice while the baby's yet stammering tongue cried "Alleluia;" and that even the old man would nurse in his arms one of Christ's own virgins? We

---

67. M. K. Hopkins discusses this problem of a "balancing act" in his "Elite Mobility in the Roman Empire," pp. 24-26. By the mid-fourth century, three children was considered the upper limit or the unattainable ideal for aristocratic families, due to the high rate of infant mortality. The survival of too many children, however, would be as disastrous to the family fortune as the survival of none.
68. Hopkins, ibid., p. 25, cites Olympiodorus, frag. 44 (*Fragmenta historicorum Graecorum*, vol. 4) on the expense of raising children into adulthood. See also McGeachy, pp. 101-110, for a description of the provision made by Symmachus for his son's games.
69. As is shown in M. K. Hopkins, "Contraception in the Roman Empire," *Comparative Studies in Society and History* 8 (1965-66): 124-151.
70. See above p. 158.
71. Jer. *Ep.* 22.20.
72. Jer. *Ep.* 107:1 (1 Cor. 7:13); Eng. tr. in *Select Letters*, p. 339.

did well to expect this happy issue. The one unbeliever is sanctified by a saintly household of believers.[73]

There are, in fact, two instances of conversions by Christian women of their pagan male relatives. Jerome alludes to one in his letter to Laeta. Her husband, Toxotius, was a pagan when he married Laeta, in spite of the fact that his mother, Paula, and all his sisters were Christians. He was apparently converted after his marriage. Volusianus was the pagan son of a pagan father and Christian mother; his sister, Albina the Younger, was Christian, and it was his Christian niece, Melania the Younger, who converted him to Christianity as he lay on his death bed.[74] It was not entirely fanciful for Jerome to suggest that Laeta's father, one of the inner circle of staunch pagans, might be converted by the Christianity of his household.

But the primary point of Jerome's letter was to outline the ideal education of a Christian girl. Paula was to be raised in a strictly Christian environment.[75] Her maid and all the women servants around her were to be of sedate and unworldly character. From her earliest years she was to be encouraged in learning in the guise of games.[76] She was also to be instructed from the very beginning about her paternal grandmother and aunt, Paula and Eustochium: "Let her crave their company and threaten you that she will leave you for them."[77] As Paula grew older, she was to be dressed as simply as possible, without the aid of cosmetics or jewelry.[78] She was never to be separated from the watchful eyes of her mother.[79] She should eat simple dishes and with restraint; she should take a little wine only for her health.[80] She should be deaf to all musical instruments.[81]

Jerome devotes a large proportion of the letter to the problem of Paula's education. She was to memorize portions of the scripture daily in Greek and Latin. He sets down the order in which she was to study them, beginning with the Psalter and ending with the Song of Songs, "for if she were to read it at the beginning, she might be harmed by not perceiving that it was the song of a spiritual bridal expressed in fleshly language."[82] She was to read Cyprian, Athanasius, Hilary, and those others who "maintain in their books a steady love of the faith.[83] Anything else should be read only from a critical point of view. The culmination of Jerome's long letter to Laeta is a charge: "Do not take up a burden which you cannot bear."[84] In order to raise Paula as a true ascetic it would be best to send her to her grandmother Paula and her aunt Eustochium. There, far away from the influences of Rome, she will be taught in such a way that she will be a credit to the church. What Jerome described in his letter to Laeta and what he repeated in his letter to the baby Pacatula,[85] is a careful and deliberate socialization of the child by the household. For Jerome, the success of the Christian household is measured by the asceticism of its children. Since the children are not raised according to the values and expectations of the larger society, which might

73. Ibid.; Eng. tr. in *Select Letters*, pp. 339-341.
74. Gerontius, *Vita S. Melania*, ed. Rampolla, pp. 53-55.
75. Jer. *Ep.* 107.4.
76. Ibid. 107.4.
77. Ibid. 107.4; Eng. tr. in *Select Letters*, p. 351.
78. Ibid. 107.5.
79. Ibid. 107.11.
80. Ibid. 107.8.
81. Ibid.
82. Ibid. 107.12; Eng. tr. in *Select Letters*, p. 365.
83. Ibid. 107.12.
84. Ibid. 107.13.
85. Jer. *Ep.* 128.

be pagan or nominally Christian or syncretic, the values which they receive through their socialization within the household must be particularly strong. The best household environment, Jerome suggests, would be the one that most closely approximated the environment of Jerusalem.

A similar situation existed in the Puritan household of pre-revolutionary England.[86] A Puritan writing at the time said that it was important for catechizing to be carried on at home "because houses are the nurseries of the Church."[87] The household became "spiritualized"; its purpose was to fill the ranks of the faithful. The distinction between seventeenth-century asceticism and fourth-century asceticism is important, however, because it contains the answer to the failure of Jerome's dream. In seventeenth-century England Puritan asceticism acted positively to bring the actual world into consonance with its own vision of the good society. In the words of Max Weber it was an "inner-worldly asceticism." "Active asceticism operates within the world; rationally active asceticism, in mastering the world, seeks to tame what is creatural and wicked through work in a worldly 'vocation.' "[88]

In contrast to inner-worldly asceticism Weber posits an other-worldly asceticism, or "asceticist flight from the world." "If active asceticism confines itself to keeping down and to overcoming creatural wickedness in the actor's own nature . . . it then enhances the concentration on the firmly established God-willed and active redemptory accomplishments to the point of avoiding any action in the orders of the world."[89] Puritan asceticism effected a revolution within the household which produced a new generation of inner-worldly ascetics. The asceticism of the fourth century was other-worldly rather than inner-worldly: the goal of fourth-century asceticism was not the mastery of the world but the mastery of self. Jerome's dream of a society of Christian households busily producing future ascetics was doomed to fail. Most prosaically, his Christian families would soon die out if they were to produce only ascetics. But secondly, the typical response of the larger society to asceticism is opposition. If the asceticism is of the inner-worldly type, it will attempt to overcome that opposition, as in the case of Puritan England. But if the asceticism is other-worldly, it will make no attempt to deal with the response of the larger society, and so will have little or no positive impact on the society.

Fourth-century ascetics quite literally fled from Roman society. The result was that, with the influence of asceticism minimized by distance both physical and psychological, the way was open for a syncretic working-out of the pagan and Christian cultures.[90] Though the commitment to the ascetic life may have been rejected by the larger society as counter-productive, Christianity itself was seen in an increasingly positive light. We see indications of a new syncretism in the families of the ascetic women. Albinus, the pagan grandfather of Melania the Younger, a character in the *Saturnalia* and a friend of Symmachus, corresponded

86. See Christopher Hill, *Society and Puritanism in Pre-Revolutionary England* (New York: Schocken Books, 1964), pp. 443-481, "The Spiritualization of the Household."
87. Thomas Cartwright, cited in ibid., p. 455.
88. H. H. Gerth and C. Wright Mills, eds., *From Max Weber: Essays in Sociology* (New York: Oxford University Press, 1970), p. 325.
89. Ibid., p. 326.
90. See Brown, "Aspects of the Christianization." But see also R. Meiggs, *Roman Ostia* (Oxford: Clarendon Press, 1960), p. 401: "It is at least a tenable hypothesis that a large section of the upper classes (in Ostia) remained pagan for much of the fourth century and that Christianity flourished mainly among the poor."

with Ambrose on points of doctrine.[91] His son, Volusianus, who remained a pagan up to his death-bed conversion, corresponded with Augustine on questions of the Christian faith.[92] The proximity of paganism and Christianity within the families of the late Roman aristocracy was probably the single most potent factor in the gradual substitution of Christianity for paganism as the religion of the senatorial order.

It has been suggested, first by fourth- and fifth-century contemporaries,[93] then by Gibbon,[94] and more recently by A.H.M. Jones,[95] that Christianity contributed to the weakening of the Roman Empire by positing an alternative ethos to that of *Roma aeterna*. Paulinus of Nola, the friend and relative of Melania the Elder, bears out this suggestion in a letter which expresses his sentiments on Roman society: "We ought not to put loyalties or fatherland or distinctions or riches before God, for scripture says: 'The fashion of this world passeth away.' And those who love this world will also perish with it."[96] The present group of ascetic women also corroborate the notion of a Christian asceticism alien to the traditional aristocratic ethos. They provided Jerome, the chief architect of fourth-century asceticism, with the examples he used to inspire and prod more hesitant disciples. They were an important weapon in his propaganda war against the Roman aristocracy.

The gradual Christianization of the Roman aristocracy in the fourth and fifth centuries has been laid at the feet of the women of the aristocracy; but the "drift into respectable Christianity" was accomplished in spite of the presence of one group of women whose Christianity was most certainly not respectable. Like Paulinus of Nola, they would not effect a transformation of their society because of their certainty that only in fleeing that society would they arrive at the End they so fervently desired.

91. Chastagnol, pp. 247-248, argues for this identification.
92. Augustine *Epistolae* 135, 136.
93. See Augustine *The City of God* 1:35.
94. Gibbon, *Decline and Fall*, chap. 31.
95. A.H.M. Jones, *The Decline of the Ancient World* (New York: Holt, Rinehart and Winston, Inc., 1966), p. 369.
96. Paul. of Nola *Ep.* 25.2; Eng. tr. in *Letters*, tr. P. G. Walsh (Westminster, Maryland: Newman Press, 1966).

Acknowledgments

Benko, Stephen. "Second Century References to the Mother of Jesus." *Religion in Life* 26 (1956–7): 98–109. Reprinted with the permission of Abingdon Press. Courtesy of Yale University Divinity Library.

Ramsay, W.M. "The Worship of the Virgin Mary at Ephesus." In his *Pauline and Other Studies in Early Christian History* (London: Hodder and Stoughton, 1908): 125–60. Courtesy of Yale University Seeley G. Mudd Library.

Milburn, R.L.P. "Appendix: The Historical Background of the Doctrine of the Assumption." In his *Early Christian Interpretations of History* (London: Adam and Charles Black, 1954): 161–92. Courtesy of Yale University Divinity Library.

Frend, William H.C. "Blandina and Perpetua: Two Early Christian Heroines." In *Les Martyrs de Lyon (177): Lyon 20–23 Septembre 1977* (Paris: Éditions du Centre National de la Recherche Scientifique): 167–77. Reprinted with the permission of Éditions du Centre National de la Recherche Scientifique. Courtesy of Yale University Sterling Memorial Library.

Cardman, Francine. "Acts of the Women Martyrs." *Anglican Theological Review* 70 (1988): 144–50. Reprinted with the permission of the *Anglican Theological Review*, Richard E. Wentz, Editor-in-Chief. Courtesy of the *Anglican Theological Review*.

Klawiter, Frederick C. "The Role of Martyrdom and Persecution in Developing the Priestly Authority of Women in Early Christianity: A Case Study of Montanism." *Church History* 49 (1980): 251–61. Reprinted with the permission of the American Society of Church History. Courtesy of Yale University Seeley G. Mudd Library.

Coyle, J. Kevin. "The Fathers on Women and Women's Ordination."
    Église et Théologie 9 (1978): 51–101. Reprinted with the permission
    of St. Paul University. Courtesy of *Église et Théologie*.

Corrington, Gail Paterson. "The 'Divine Woman'? Propaganda and the
    Power of Celibacy in the New Testament Apocrypha: A Reconsid-
    eration." *Anglican Theological Review* 70 (1988): 207–20. Reprinted
    with the permission of the *Anglican Theological Review*, Richard E.
    Wentz, Editor-in-Chief. Courtesy of the *Anglican Theological Re-
    view*.

Goehring, James E. "Libertine or Liberated: Women in the So-called
    Libertine Gnostic Communities." In Karen L. King, ed., *Images of
    the Feminine in Gnosticism* (Philadelphia: Fortress Press, Inc., 1988):
    329–44. Reprinted with the permission of Augsburg Fortress Press.
    Copyright 1988 The Institute of Antiquity and Christianity. Cour-
    tesy of Augsburg Fortress Press.

Church, F. Forrester. "Sex and Salvation in Tertullian." *Harvard Theo-
    logical Review* 68 (1975): 83–101. Copyright 1975 by the President
    and Fellows of Harvard College. Reprinted by permission. Courtesy
    of the *Harvard Theological Review*.

McNamara, Jo Ann. "Sexual Equality and the Cult of Virginity in Early
    Christian Thought." *Feminist Studies* 3 (1976): 145–58. Reprinted
    with the permission of the publisher, FEMINIST STUDIES, Inc., c/o
    Women's Studies Program, University of Maryland, College Park,
    MD 20742. Courtesy of Yale University Sterling Memorial Library.

Clark, Elizabeth A. "Sexual Politics in the Writings of John Chrysostom."
    Anglican Theological Review 59 (1977): 3–20. Reprinted with the
    permission of the *Anglican Theological Review*, Richard E. Wentz,
    Editor-in-Chief. Courtesy of Yale University Divinity Library.

Kraemer, Ross S. "The Conversion of Women to Ascetic Forms of
    Christianity." *Signs* 6 (1980): 298–307. Reprinted with the permis-
    sion of the University of Chicago Press, publisher. Courtesy of Yale
    University Sterling Memorial Library.

Ruether, Rosemary Radford. "Misogynism and Virginal Feminism in
    the Fathers of the Church." In Rosemary Radford Ruether, ed.,

Religion and Sexism: Images of Woman in the Jewish and Christian Traditions (New York: Simon and Schuster). Reprinted with the permission of Simon & Schuster. Courtesy of Yale University Cross Campus Library.

Simpson, Jane. "Women and Asceticism in the Fourth Century: A Question of Interpretation." *Journal of Religious History* 15 (1988): 38–60. Reprinted with the permission of the Association for the Journal of Religious History. Courtesy of the *Journal of Religious History*.

Yarbrough, Anne. "Christianization in the Fourth Century: The Example of Roman Women." *Church History* 45 (1976): 149–65. Reprinted with the permission of the American Society of Church History. Courtesy of Yale University Seeley G. Mudd Library.